Memoir 11

A MANUAL OF PHONOLOGY

By
CHARLES F. HOCKETT

This volume was originally published as Memoir 11 of Indiana University Publications in Anthropology and Linguistics, October 1955.
It is reprinted by the University of Chicago Press, June 1974.

PREFACE

This manual was begun during the Spring Semester of 1952–3, while I was on Sabbatical Leave from Cornell University, and also the recipient of a grant from The Rockefeller Foundation, administered through the University. I wish to express my gratitude to both of those institutions, whose assistance made it possible for me to spend my time in research and writing rather than in directly remunerative activities.

When first planned, what appears here was to be but the initial section of a treatise designed to cover all phases of linguistics. The size of the present volume will convince the reader, I am sure, that my original notion was hardly feasible. I hope that in due time other portions of the treatise as originally conceived may appear, but the expression of this hope must not be construed as a guarantee.

My debt to my colleagues, both at Cornell and elsewhere, is of course enormous. The bibliographical references will indicate some small portion of this debt. It would be impossible to single out, for mention here, all the individuals who have been of more direct assistance; were I to attempt such a thing, I would be bound to commit unforgivable errors of omission. However, there are several acknowledgments which must be overtly made.

First: to Gordon H. Fairbanks, who has read the entire manuscript in (almost) final form. I have not always accepted his suggestions, and the book is doubtless the worse for that fact; but it is certainly the better for those which I have accepted, and no blame must attach to him for errors which remain.

Second: to Roman Jakobson, who has been, over the years, a source of inspiration which I value highly. I am particularly anxious to be emphatic about my debt to him because, in several places in the body of the book, I have been forced to express sharp disagreement with, or criticism of, some of his most fondly held views. Unfortunately, the spirit of scientific investigation leaves no place for a softening of criticism for friendship's sake, nor for any worship of the Idols of the Marketplace.

Third: to Martin Joos, who read an earlier draft of §5 with extreme care, and was (by request) remorseless in his criticism. He has also scrutinized §5 as it now appears, and allows me to state that he is in complete agreement with the points of view and the interpretations of fact which the reader will find in that section; wherever there is disagreement between what is said there and Joos's earlier statements in his Acoustic Phonetics (1948), the more recent statements represent his current view, as well as my own. This sort of help verges on collaboration, and I should have been happy to acknowledge the fact by having Joos's name appear on the title page as co-author of §5; but he has preferred merely this prefatorial credit.

Fourth: to Carl F. Voegelin, editor of the series in which this work appears, to Thomas A. Sebeok, the business manager, and to Mrs. Elsie F. Dosch, their very competent editorial assistant—for accepting the work, for raising most of the necessary funds for publication, and for their great care in guaranteeing that the typography and format should be of maximum help to the reader.

Fifth: to Indiana University for defraying the cost of the text of this book, and to the Hull Memorial Publication Fund of Cornell University for defraying the cost of illustrations.

This volume is dedicated to the Grand Old Man of American linguistics, George Melville Bolling, in sincere appreciation of his clear guidance when the writer was first discovering what Bloomfield has called the "strangeness, beauty, and import of human speech."

CHARLES F. HOCKETT

Cornell University
26 January 1955

TABLE OF CONTENTS

0. *Purpose and Plan.* As its title implies, this manual is intended as a survey of the methods so far developed, and of the results so far attained, in the field of phonology. The title fails to indicate certain restrictions on the intended coverage. First, we shall not be concerned with the phonologic aspect of linguistic change: the coverage is *synchronic.* Second, we shall not be concerned with variations of phonologic pattern from individual to individual, or from group to group, within a speech community, but with coherent linguistic systems viewed as undifferentiated into dialects or idiolects: the coverage is not merely synchronic, but *descriptive.* What we take as a "coherent linguistic system" will in one case be an idiolect; in another case, the common core of a number of idiolects; in yet another, the overall pattern of a number. The logic of common core and overall pattern is dealt with briefly in §03 below.

Despite the presence of some discursive sections, this book is intended to be consulted, not to be read—certainly not to be read as a unit. The discussion is therefore not broken up into chapters, in the ordinary pedagogic way. Instead, the entire text is sectioned by brief descriptive headings preceded by section numbers in decimal notation: §23 is the third subdivision of §2, §232 the second subdivision of §23, and so on. A cross-reference ending in zero, such as §10, refers to that part of §1 which precedes §11, though the actual section numbers never end in zero. The index is also a glossary of technical and semi-technical terms. Notes are few, mainly by way of scholarly credit, and are placed at the end (cross-referenced by section number) rather than being run as footnotes.

01. *Special Features.* Our approach to phonologic pattern is marked by two special features which must be described here.

The first is that we attempt to develop a typology—a taxonomic frame of reference in terms of which different phonologic systems can be classified and compared. This is by no means a new aim in phonologic study. Trubetzkoy, Jakobson, and others of the so-called "Prague group" did a great deal of typologic classification: Trubetzkoy's Grundzüge is, among other things, a suggested typologic framework. Some American linguists have felt not only that Trubetzkoy failed, but that failure in such an attempt is inevitable—the goal is a false one. I do not agree with either part of this view. Trubetzkoy's frame of reference was not sufficiently complex, but it was a worthwhile first approximation, some parts of which cannot yet be improved on. More recently, and it would seem quite independently, Voegelin has proposed the value of a general (even if arbitrary) typology for archiving purposes. The typology developed in §2 of the present manual is not supposed to be arbitrary, and it is considerably more complex than either Trubetzkoy's or Voegelin's; but I am sure that it falls far short of what we must eventually develop.

We are in an incomparably better position for typologic work now than we were in the thirties. We have reasonably reliable and reasonably homogeneous reports on a much larger number of languages than we did twenty years ago, or even ten; unfortunately, some of the reports which were unquestioningly used in earlier years must now be regarded as not wholly trustworthy. A number of

1

factors have contributed to this widening of our empiric base, but one above all others deserves mention here: the far-flung field research of missionaries trained by the Summer Institute of Linguistics. Their brief factual reports are perhaps rarely exciting, but show on the average a high reliability; furthermore, since much the same methodologic approach is involved in most of them, one quickly learns to interpret them. Also worthy of special mention is the vital archival role of the International Journal of American Linguistics since 1944.

The other special feature is closely related to the first: we have sought a consistent and complete working-out of an immediate constituent approach on the phonologic level. This, also, is not a new aim. Bloomfield's terminology of "simple primary phonemes," "compound primary phonemes," and "secondary phonemes" is a hint in the direction of a hierarchic approach. The insistence of Hjelmslev on a kind of parallelism ("isomorphism," though not in the usual mathematical sense) between the level of expression and the level of content opens the way for an extension to phonology (expression) of the immediate-constituent approach which has long held a prominent place in grammatic study (study of content); Kurylowicz has recently developed this theme. Last—but by no means least—a few years ago Pike and Pike prepared and published an IC analysis of Mazateco phonology. Their article seems almost to have been worked out with tongue in cheek, as a sort of offhand experiment; but in my opinion it is one of the really germinal contributions to linguistics in the last few decades. When more fully elaborated, the IC approach in phonology proves to be of key importance in the development of a phonologic taxonomy; we shall see in §2 how this is.

Although it hardly constitutes a "special feature" of this manual, it would be well to state explicitly that our view will be empiric: I accept Bloomfield's assertion that "the only useful generalizations about language are inductive generalizations," and hence affiliate with the "god's-truth" school of thought rather than with the "hocus-pocus" school. A mere acceptance of this approach does not in itself guarantee success, and the manual is certainly full of mistakes of every sort. One result of an empiric approach that will be regretted by some is that it inevitably involves a recognition of areas of indeterminacy. Empiricism forces the overt formulation of criteria for making classificatory decisions, and always, it would seem, the criteria fail in some instances. The hocus-pocus approach does not encounter this difficulty in quite the same way, since it allows greater freedom in making ad hoc decisions arbitrarily.

Arbitrariness can manifest itself at various different levels of abstraction. Trubetzkoy's typical manipulation of the data on a single language is not arbitrary, since he operated with a fairly well formulated set of principles, which specified in advance, for example, the conditions under which a segment would be regarded as a single phoneme and those under which it would be interpreted as a cluster. Yet these general principles can in turn be regarded as arbitrary, at least in that various other equally self-consistent operating principles can be formulated. This particular kind of arbitrariness is comparable to our free choice between feet and meters in measuring lengths, except for one detail: conversion from feet to meters, or vice versa, is easy and mechanical. The non-arbitrary phenomenon of length, which one measures in terms of this or that arbitrarily selected unit, is an entirely relative matter between different objects the lengths of which can be measured. The danger which we encounter in letting ourselves become too firmly attached to any one arbitrary unit (feet; Trubetzkoy's principles; Bloch's postulates) is that we will fail to realize the extent to which our generalizations are dependent on the frame of reference. Some of the Praguian generalizations turn out to be of this sort: they are not invariant under selection of different analytic criteria. Certainly we should like for our generalizations to be as free of this as possible; I hope that the approach developed in this manual will represent a step in the right direction.

02. *Phonology and Language Design.* There is currently no general agreement on the precise relationship of the phonologic pattern of a language to the rest of the linguistic system. Certain investigators, among them Pike, believe that in order to understand a phonologic system it is necessary not only to know certain things about the accompanying grammatic system, but to make active use of the latter knowledge as criteria for phonologic decisions. Others disagree. But the issue is not clear: in actual fact, we are probably in covert disagreement as to what our overt disagreements are about. Rather than dwell in detail on this and kindred differences of opinion, I shall simply describe my own current view.

021. *A Theory of Speech Communication.* As a first step in describing this view, we present in this section a mechanical and mathematical model of a human being regarded as a talking animal. The model developed here goes beyond any previous ones, particularly in that meaning is taken into account in a potentially precise way.

It will be well to indicate at the outset the limitation of our aims. Humans share a great many categories of behavior with other animals: learning, goal-seeking activity, some measurable degree of "intelligence," trial-and-error patterns in solving problems, probably (though it is hard to demonstrate for sure) implicit trial-and-error followed by explicit successful action, and the like. It is no part of our purpose to try to account for features of behavior shared by speaking and non-speaking species; this is the business of biology or of biophysics. Furthermore, if there are distinctively human modes of behavior not dependent for their development and continued existence on human language, these also fall outside the scope of our interest. For our purposes, then, a human being is an animal, partly like and partly unlike other animals, but unique among all animals in the possession of speech; our mathematico-mechanical model is intended to account only for this single uniqueness.

It may also be well to say something here, in advance of our detailed discussion, as to the nature of a mathematico-mechanical model. We shall be presenting a picture which looks vaguely like the block-diagrams ("control-flow charts") used by electrical engineers, and shall be assigning various names to the units portrayed in the diagrams; but we shall also be speaking as though these units were to be found somewhere inside a human being—say in his central nervous system. Now, in the present state of knowledge of neurophysiology, there is no guarantee that the units which we posit do exist inside a human skin—nor, for that matter, is it currently possible to prove that they do not. This implies that our mode of discussion is not physiologic. Rather, it is a type of "as if" mode, which can be explicated in the following two ways: (1) humans, as users of language, operate *as if* they contained apparatus functionally comparable to that we are to describe; (2) an engineer, given not just the rough specifications presented below but also a vast amount of detailed statistical information of the kind we could work out if we had to, could build something from hardware which would speak, and understand speech, as humans do. Indeed, given such a device, and the solution to the problem of neuron-to-wire linkage, one could produce a talking dog. Let me add at once that I am entirely serious.

Whether or not a mechanical model for a phenomenon constitutes an explanation of the phenomenon depends, not on the model, but on the temperament of the investigator. An explanation is something which satisfies one until one has looked deeper; then one asks for an explanation of the explanation. Certainly even those of us with the greatest fondness for mechanical models must avoid the error of argument from analogy. Mechanical devices have been constructed which will "learn" to run a maze, overtly in much the same way that a rat will. We know the structure of the mechanical "rat," and can thus describe quite precisely the correlation between its structure and its behavior. But to infer from this, and from the overt similarity of behavior of the mechanical rat and the live one, that the structure of the latter is in some sense comparable to that of the former, is to argue from analogy. The experimentum crucis is wanting: dissection of the live rat, demonstrating that its structure is indeed as the analogy suggests —or revealing that, after all, it is not. The analogy tells us, in the last analysis, nothing more than what should be looked for when physiologic techniques have evolved far enough. The model proves only that an entity need not *necessarily* be endowed with a non-material mind or soul in order to learn mazes as rats learn them.

0211. *The Control-Flow Chart.* Most of the materials we shall need for our exposition are displayed in Figure 1, which shows, in highly schematic fashion, two speakers of a single language, one of whom is in the process of speaking to the other. In a time-honored tradition, we have labelled the two Jill and Jack. When Jill transmits a message in linguistic form to Jack, the sequence of events and the route followed by the message are, according to our theory, as follows:

(1) Jill's *Grammatic Headquarters* (= "G.H.Q.") emits a discrete flow of *morphemes*. This flow constitutes the input to the transducer, within Jill, labelled "Phoneme Source."

(2) Jill's Phoneme Source, operating in conformity with a certain code, transduces the discrete flow of morphemes which is its input into a *discrete flow of phonemes* which is its output. The code involved is the *morphophonemics* of the language spoken by Jill and Jack.

(3) The output from Jill's Phoneme Source constitutes the input to Jill's Speech Transmitter. This transducer is in part directly observable from the outside (Jill's mouth, nose, throat, and so forth—the so-called "speech tract"), and we have therefore drawn the box which represents it in such a way that it

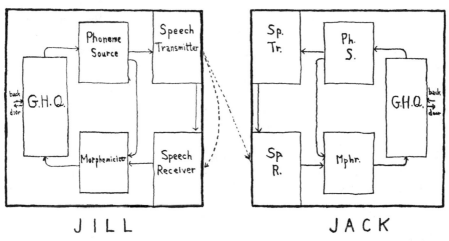

Fɪɢ. 1

shares parts of its boundary with the larger box which represents all of Jill. But the region of Jill which performs the transduction about to be described must also include portions just as inaccessible to direct observation as are her Phoneme Source or G.H.Q. The Speech Transmitter converts the discrete flow of phonemes which comes to it into a *continuous speech signal*—a continuous train of sound waves. The code by which the Speech Transmitter performs this transduction is the *phonetic system* of the language.

(4) The speech signal reaches Jack's Speech Receiver, wherein it is retransduced into a discrete flow of phonemes; the latter constitutes the output of a Speech Receiver. The code by which the Speech Receiver operates is thus necessarily the same as that by which a Speech Transmitter functions, except that the Speech Receiver applies the code hind-end to.

(5) The output of Jack's Speech Receiver constitutes the input to his Morphemicizer. This transducer converts the discrete flow of phonemes back into a discrete flow of morphemes, which is its output. In performing this transduction, the Morphemicizer operates according to the morphophonemics of the language (also the code by which the Phoneme Source operates), but, once again, applies it in reverse.

(6) The resulting discrete flow of morphemes is fed back into Jack's G.H.Q.

In the above we have used the terms "morpheme" and "phoneme" advisedly, though without implying that the unit signals emitted by a G.H.Q. or a Morphemicizer (morphemes) or by a Phoneme Source or Speech Receiver (phonemes) can be identified in any simple one-to-one fashion with the similarly labelled units which a linguistic analyst uncovers and describes in the course of his work with a language. Within our theory, the *aim* of the linguist, in working on a single idiolect, would be to determine just the units of internal flow to which we have assigned these two terms; but the accuracy of his analytic conclusions can only be tested indirectly, so that various types of discrepancy no doubt remain.

Possibly it would be better if we used, in the present context, the terms "grammatic units" and "phonologic units," since this at least would avoid the identification of the units of internal flow with the sorts of morphemes and phonemes established by any one brand of grammatic or phonologic analysis. But, for the sake of conciseness, we will use the one-word terms.

As so far discussed, our representation could be interpreted as an enlargement and modification of Bloomfield's much simpler diagram:

$$S \rightarrow r \ldots \ldots \ldots s \rightarrow R.$$

Here "S" represents a stimulus on Jill; the arrow stands for obscure inner activity of some sort within her, and "r" for her overt speech response to the stimulus. The row of dots represents sound waves passing through the air from Jill's mouth to Jack's ears (quite like our dotted arrow, in Figure 1). "s" represents the speech stimulus on Jack; the second arrow represents obscure inner activity in him; and "R" represents his non-speech response. According to Bloomfield, that represented by "S," by "R," and by the arrows stands outside the strict sphere of interest of linguistics, which is concerned only with the segment "r . . . . s".

Our more complex diagram contains no analog for Bloomfield's "S" and "R," for a reason which has already been stated: humans are not essentially different from other animals in possessing sense-organs and muscles. We might, however, say that Bloomfield's "S" and "R" are provided for by the indicated "back doors" to Jill's and Jack's G.H.Q.'s: it is through these back doors (as we shall see later) that the impulses pass which account for the partial correlation between what people say or hear said, and what they do. Our diagram pretends to push back the boundary between what concerns a linguist and what does not, by stealing some things from what Bloomfield represents with his arrows and drawing boxes to represent them: everything covered by the five boxes we draw within Jill and within Jack might be regarded as correlating with Bloomfield's "r" and "s."

0212. *Feedback and Monitoring.* However, our representation provides for certain features not covered by Bloomfield either in his diagram or in his discussion: *feedback* and *monitoring.* The Figure shows a second dotted arrow outside of Jill and Jack, passing from Jill's Speech Transmitter back to her own Speech Receiver. This is included for the obvious reason that Jill hears herself as she speaks. Also, a solid arrow is drawn from Jill's Transmitter, close to her outer boundary, directly to her Receiver: Jill also feels the motions of her articulatory organs as she speaks. There is in addition a solid arrow leading from her Phoneme Source directly to her Morphemicizer, but this feedback route is more purely hypothetic.

There is evidence to show that the first two sorts of feedback, respectively *auditory* and *kinesthetic*, are of great importance in the act of speaking: a speaker constantly observes his output, and monitors it by these types of feedback just as the monitor in a radio station listens to what is being sent out over the air and makes minor adjustments in it as necessary. Joos describes a pair of "experiments" which can test, separately, the importance of the two types of feedback named above. To test auditory feedback, one goes slightly deaf. A partially deaf person often speaks rather mumblingly; or, if he manages to speak clearly (without a hearing aid), he makes more than the usual use of kinesthetic feedback for monitoring purposes. To test kinesthetic feedback, one imbibes a certain amount of ethyl alcohol. Anyone who has done so reports that in order to make one's speech sound right, it is necessary to articulate more slowly than usual and to monitor one's speech by listening to it more carefully that usual. A sufficiently drunken person does not do this, and the resulting slurred effect is familiar to us all.

We may conclude, from such evidence, that under normal conditions one constantly monitors one's speech via both types of feedback. Jill's Speech Receiver is not quiescent as she speaks, but is functioning just as are her Speech Transmitter and her deeper units. Similarly, we may suspect that Jack's Speech Transmitter is not completely quiescent just because at the moment he is broadcasting nothing. As he listens to Jill, his Speech Receiver is able to decode the signal partly because the incoming signal is constantly compared with the articulatory motions which Jack himself would have to make in order to produce an acoustically comparable signal. There is only less direct evidence for this assumption, but we can at least point out that in learning a foreign language one has considerable difficulty hearing correctly until one can also pronounce correctly.

In our theory of the functioning of G.H.Q., developed below, we shall incorporate feedback as one of the key mechanisms.

0213. *G.H.Q. as a Source.* The functioning of G.H.Q. is complex, since it serves both as a source of a discrete flow of morphemes, the destination of such flows, and also, via its "back door," as the unit within which is brought about some degree of correlation between what people say and hear and what they do. We shall describe one part of this functioning at a time, beginning here with the temporary assumption that G.H.Q. does nothing at all except emit morphemes.

A unit regarded as purely a source of a discrete flow of signals can be mathematically characterized in a complete fashion on the basis of the statistics of the signal-flows which it emits; the technique for doing this was developed by Claude Shannon. We imagine that G.H.Q. can be in any number of a very large number of different *states*. At a given moment it is necessarily in one or another of these states. Associated with each state is an array of probabilities for the emission of the various morphemes of the language: a certain relative probability that the morpheme *and* will next be emitted, a certain relative probability that the morpheme *tackle* will next be emitted, and so on. When some morpheme is actually emitted, G.H.Q. shifts to a new state. Which state the new one is depends, *in a determinate way* (not just probabilistically) on both the preceding state and on what morpheme has actually been emitted. There are vastly more states than morphemes, since a given morpheme may bring about not only a transition from state A to state C, but also that from B to C, or from D to E, and so on—noting, as already asserted, that a specific combination of preceding state (say A) and actually emitted morpheme (say *tackle*) results always in the same next state (say C).

Given complete information on G.H.Q. states and transition-probabilities, a complete mathematical specification of G.H.Q. as a source can be formulated in the shape of a square matrix, with n rows and n columns, where n is the total number of states: the entry p_{ij}, in the ith row and the jth column, is the probability that when G.H.Q. is in the ith state it will next pass to the jth. The sum of all the probabilities in a row is necessarily unity. To this mathematical specification we need only add an indication of what morpheme is emitted in connection with each state-transition.

A tiny example is not hard to construct, though it does not show everything that needs to be shown, and will thus have to be supplemented. Figure 2 gives the matrix for an almost infinitesimally small G.H.Q.; the "morphemes" emitted by this G.H.Q. are English words and phrases, plus one sentence-final intonation (denoted by /./ in the Figure). Arbitrary symbols would do just as well mathematically, but it is more satisfying to make the results look like English. Once set into motion, this miniature G.H.Q. will emit, over and over again, one and another of the following eight English sentences:

(1) *Jones takes the ball.*   (5) *Smith takes the ball.*
(2) *Jones takes him out.*   (6) *Smith takes him out.*
(3) *Jones passes the ball.*   (7) *Smith passes the ball.*
(4) *Jones passes the ball to Smith.*   (8) *Smith passes the ball to Jones.*

	S_0	S_1	S_2	S_3	S_4	S_5	S_6	S_7	S_8	S_9	S_{10}
S_0	.00	.50 *Jones*	.50 *Smith*	.00	.00	.00	.00	.00	.00	.00	.00
S_1	.00	.00	.00	.60 *takes*	.40 *passes*	.00	.00	.00	.00	.00	.00
S_2	.00	.00	.00	.80 *takes*	.00	.20 *passes*	.00	.00	.00	.00	.00
S_3	.00	.00	.00	.00	.00	.00	.90 *the ball*	.10 *him out*	.00	.00	.00
S_4	.00	.00	.00	.00	.00	.00	.00	.00	1.00 *the ball*	.00	.00
S_5	.00	.00	.00	.00	.00	.00	.00	.00	.00	1.00 *the ball*	.00
S_6	1.00 /./	.00	.00	.00	.00	.00	.00	.00	.00	.00	.00
S_7	1.00 /./	.00	.00	.00	.00	.00	.00	.00	.00	.00	.00
S_8	.40 /./	.00	.00	.00	.00	.00	.00	.00	.00	.00	.60 *to Smith*
S_9	.60 /./	.00	.00	.00	.00	.00	.00	.00	.00	.00	.40 *to Jones*
S_{10}	1.00 /./	00	.00	00	00	.00	00	.00	.00	.00	.00

Fig. 2

With the indicated transition probabilities, the relative frequency of each sentence in the long run (and thus the probability that, starting from state S_0, a given sentence will next ensue) is as follows: (1) .27, (2) .03, (3) .08, (4) .12, (5) .36, (6) .04, (7) .06, (8) .04. Naturally these eight figures add up to unity, since it is certain (or at least has probability unity), whenever the G.H.Q. is in state S_0, that one or another of the eight sentences will be emitted before the unit returns again to state S_0.

Another important measurement is that of the *fluency* or *entropy* of each of the states: that is, the uncertainty, for each state, as to what the next state will be. To measure this we make use of the function $I(p)$, the *informational component* of the probability p, where p is any of the transition probabilities. The function $I(p)$ is defined as

$$I(p) = -p \log_2 p \qquad \text{for } 0 < p < 1$$
$$= 0 \qquad \text{for } p = 0 \text{ or } p = 1,$$

and is expressed in binits. The fluency of a G.H.Q. state is the sum of $I(p)$ for all the transition probabilities from that state to any other state; that is, in terms of Figure 2, the sum of $I(p)$ for all the probabilities in a single row of the matrix. Computation shows the following values:

for S_0: 1.0000
S_1: .9709
S_2: .7219
S_3: .4690
S_4, S_5, S_6, S_7, S_{10}: 0.0000
S_8, S_9: .9709.

It is to be noted that the state of greatest indeterminacy is that, so to speak, "between sentences." True enough, we so selected the probability figures as to make this hold good. The decision to do this was based, however, on realistic considerations: when we listen to someone speak, we can often guess pretty accurately how he will finish a sentence when he has gotten far enough into it, but are far more uncertain in such guessing if we try it at the beginning of a sentence. Of course this statement is an oversimplification—but so is our miniature G.H.Q.

The average entropy per state of the model G.H.Q. of Figure 2 is .4640 binits. If the G.H.Q. emits "morphemes" at the rate of n per second, then the entropy is $.4640n$ binits per second, or shannons; if n is, say, 6 (which is about the rate at which a person produces morphemes in speaking English), the entropy is 2.7840 shannons. The actual entropy of English (and maybe of any real language) has only been estimated by indirect methods, but comes out several times larger— say 5 or 6 shannons in normal rapid speech.

Our sample can be made more realistic if we pretend that the non-zero probabilities in Figure 2 are all slightly smaller than there listed, and that some of the zero figures are slightly greater than zero. We can suppose, for example, that the G.H.Q. might pass, rarely, from S_0 to S_3, emitting (we shall say) the "morpheme" *takes*, and then going on (with highest probability) to produce such a quasi-sentence as *takes him out /./*; or, again, that the transition from S_4 to S_0 might occasionally occur, to result in a fragment like *Jones passes* (without the sentence-closing /./, but nevertheless returning to state S_0). With or without such modifications, it is important to note that, although any morpheme-sequence which can *occur* can also *recur*, it is also possible for a particular morpheme-sequence to be emitted *for the first time*. The *first occurrence* of a morpheme-sequence is suspiciously similar to what in everyday parlance we call "originality" or "innovation."

By making an enormous count of relative frequencies of occurrence of all the morphemes and many morpheme-sequences in actual English, followed by an enormous amount of computation, and by writing very small entries on an enormous sheet of paper, the entire grammatical structure of the language could be portrayed in just the style of Figure 2. No one is going to do this, but it is important for us to consider (1) the assumptions which would be involved if we did do it; and (2) the further assumptions which are involved in the sort of grammatic analysis we do indulge in.

(1) For this, our assumptions are necessarily as follows:

(a) The number of states does not change with passage of time. This is certainly contrary to fact, since a child learns a language, and even an old person may learn new morphemes. One is forced to assume in the first instance that a linguistic system is *static*.

(b) The transition probabilities do not change with passage of time. Mathematically, this means that the system is a *stationary Markoff process*. This, also, is a contrary-to-fact assumption, just within the framework of our theory, as will be shown below.

(c) *Any state may recur*, and has a greater-than-zero probability of recurring in a finite amount of time. Mathematically, this means that the system is *ergodic* in the weak or Wienerian sense. Linguistically, it is the assumption always made, at least tacitly, that the actual occurrence of a particular string of morphemes does not change the system in such a way as to reduce to zero the probability that the same string will occur again. This assumption renders analysis descriptive and synchronic; we know that it is false to fact, and when we abolish the assumption we are working historically.

(2) In our actual grammatical analyses, we take a further and (from the practical point of view) crucial step: we replace zero probability, and all extremely low probabilities, by *impossible*, and all higher probabilities by *possible*. (Perhaps we keep some vestige of the continuous grading of probabilities when we remark, of certain arrangements of morphemes, that they are "grammatically possible but not very likely.") This greatly reduces the complexity of our description. In Figure 2 it is necessary to distinguish between S_4 and S_5 for just one reason: we wish to eliminate entirely the possibility that the G.H.Q. will emit the utterances *Smith passes the ball to Smith* and *Jones passes the ball to Jones*, because these utterances, within our small pseudo-system, are semantically improbable. But in ordinary description we should, in effect, identify S_4 and S_5, and exclude the likelihood of the two utterances just cited by appealing to the common sense of the reader of our description.

In effect, then, ordinary grammatic analysis handles morphemes in batches, classing together those the occurrences of which have *approximately* the same effect in switching G.H.Q. from one state to another. By the same token, G.H.Q. states cease to be that, and become something like form-classes.

0214. *G.H.Q. as a Destination.* There is another key difference between conventional grammatic analysis and the view of grammatic pattern required within our theory: the former focusses attention largely on morphemes; our theory focusses attention on the "inter-morpheme" states of G.H.Q., and morphemes take very much of a back seat. But to show in just what way this works, we must enlarge our description of G.H.Q. and show how it functions as a destination for morpheme-flows.

When G.H.Q. emits a morpheme, a feedback report comes to the same G.H.Q. telling what morpheme has been emitted. Figure 1 shows three feedback routes for this, but it is perfectly conceivable that there is another—one leading out of G.H.Q. and back thereto without passing through any other unit. We assume that *it is the feedback report of what morpheme has been emitted which serves to "trigger" G.H.Q. into its next state.*

By assuming this, we can account for the behavior of a G.H.Q. as a destination. A morpheme arriving at Jack's G.H.Q. has exactly the same triggering effect thereon whether it comes, ultimately, from Jill's G.H.Q. or, via feedback, from Jack's own G.H.Q.

Thus when Jill speaks to Jack, the effect of her speech is to lead Jack's G.H.Q. into a series of states and state-transitions paralleling more or less closely those through which her own G.H.Q. passes as she speaks. Jack "understands" Jill— that is, communication is effected—if this parallelism is close enough. The morphemes which leave Jill's G.H.Q. and which, after a double coding and decoding, finally arrive at Jack's, are merely triggers by virtue of which the migration through successive states of Jill's G.H.Q. can "induce", as it were, a similar migration of Jack's. *This we take to be the essential nature of speech communication.*

We can think of an individual's G.H.Q. as continually clacking from one state to another, throughout the individual's life from the development of speech in early childhood until death. A vast amount of this state-migration leads only to an emitted morpheme flow which is turned back in, via feedback, without "breaking through" to the surface so that someone else may hear: we account, thus, for "thinking in words." From time to time the morpheme flow breaks through and is perceived by others; from time to time, a morpheme flow emitted by someone else's G.H.Q. arrives and takes control (complete or partial) of the state-migration of the first individual's G.H.Q.

0215. *The Semantic Link.* There remains one essential factor to consider: goings-on through the "back door" of G.H.Q.

It is fashionable to say that a human being, as he speaks, "encodes experience into linguistic form." This is more cute than true. It is apt to suggest that a human being, as a speaker, works—though at a more complex level—essentially like a speedometer, a sphygmomanometer, or a Geiger counter. A speedometer, for example, has a single "sense organ" through which it constantly "experiences" a rate of motion, and this "experience" is continuously encoded into the position of a pointer on a dial. The position of the pointer is a message, and the message is *about* something—it has *meaning*.

Now it is of course true that some of our speech is about something in this same narrow sense—we report, let us say, on what is happening to us at the moment of reporting. But this is by no means the only way in which speaking takes place. Suppose one sees a cat. One may immediately say *There's a cat*—like the speedometer giving its report. But one may not. One may say nothing at all about the cat (even to oneself, "thinking in words"). And it is possible to talk about cats when there are none around. A sports announcer can give a running account of the football game he is actually watching—like the speedometer; but an author can write a story about things that have never happened and probably never will.

This points up also the second major defect in Bloomfield's simple stimulus-response diagram: no matter how complex the obscure internal activity subsumed by his arrows may be, the inclusion of his "S" and "R" still seems to imply that what one says is necessarily immediately and deterministically related to the individual's field of stimulation of the moment. The link between G.H.Q. and the other, non-speech, goings-on in and around a person must for accuracy be viewed as probabilistic.

The probabilistic linkage can be provided for at the back door to G.H.Q., without venturing into the welter of complexity in an individual outside his speech units (a complexity which is beyond our concern because it is much like that in any non-speaking animal). We need only say that any internal or external stimulus of an appropriate kind—say the sight of a cat—works through G.H.Q.'s backdoor to *increase* all those transition-probabilities for transitions which are accompanied by the emission of the morpheme *cat* (and those associated with certain other morphemes, like *pussy, meow, animal, feline*, etc.). Such an increase by no means *guarantees* that any of the transitions in question will actually occur: G.H.Q. may at the moment be wandering through a series of states where the probability of emission of *cat* is so low that the slight increase is not apt to have any result. But at least it implies that, *other things being equal*, one is more apt to say *cat* when a cat is in evidence than otherwise.

We must also provide for impulses passing through the back door of G.H.Q. in the opposite direction. If someone says *Look at that cat*, the incoming morphemes direct our G.H.Q. through a certain series of states, and those states have a probabilistic (not deterministic) effect on what we do in a non-speech "practical") way: we may—but do not necessarily—look for a cat. Quite similarly, if the state-to-state migration of our G.H.Q. leads to the emission of the morpheme *cat*, that morpheme, fed back into G.H.Q., may lead us to look around for a cat, even if we have not uttered the word aloud. It is along these lines that presumably the entire matter of the impact of linguistic patterns on behavior (as discussed, for example, by Whorf) can be provided for.

0216. *Summary.* Suppose that we went through the laborious process of gathering the statistics and making the computations whereby the grammatical pattern of English could be described with an n^2 matrix. It would then be possible for engineers to build a G.H.Q. of hardware—though a truncated G.H.Q., without any back-door connections. (The problem of designing the ancillary speech units—Phoneme Source, Speech Transmitter, Speech Receiver, and Morphemicizer—might prove technically much more refractory; but for our purposes these could be replaced by some other sort of input and output channels —say keyboard.) This hardware G.H.Q. would speak and "understand" English. It would emit understandable utterances, and from time to time (depending on the statistics of its construction) would emit sequences of morphemes which had never occurred before, either in its own life-history or in the English-speaking world. That is, it would *coin* utterances—which, linguistically, is a necessary condition for creative or innovating activity. The condition is not sufficient: it is also necessary for the new utterance to be of some use to someone, and one may suspect that many of the coinages of the mechanical G.H.Q. would be classed as nonsense. Of course, so far as the mechanical G.H.Q. was concerned, neither repeats nor coinages would be *about* anything, since we have not equipped the device with a back door: our machine would be the archetype of the would-be purely a priori philosopher.

If, next, we were able to build our mechanical G.H.Q. into a larger device which had receptors and effectors something along the line of those found in all animals, linking these with each other and, through a back door, into the G.H.Q., we would have an even closer analog to a human being. This enlarged device would run a greater chance of saying things that had not been said before and that were worth hearing.

But it would still have one crucial limitation as compared with humans: it would have, as long as it operated, only the number of G.H.Q. states which were originally built into it. This can't be the case with humans. As infants we have no G.H.Q. states at all—perhaps no G.H.Q. When we learn to speak we acquire at first a very simple G.H.Q., which then becomes increasingly complex, and need not cease to be restructured from time to time until the death of the organism. Our model does not provide for any such "growth" under the impact of experience (change of transition-probabilities is perhaps also "growth," but would seem to be of a different sort). But mechanisms of a much less complex order have been designed to "learn" new responses; the problem is certainly intricate, but not necessarily insurmountable.

The model also does not provide for certain obvious facts about speech, because they are not exclusive to speech or to humans. What determines whether a flow of mòrphemes is coded into overt speech or remains inside? One could depict a switch somewhere in the diagram of Figure 1; the problem is not where the switch is, but what turns it off and on. But we can also "at will" think of walking or actually walk, think of slapping someone or actually slap him, and so on: the problem of the mechanism for such decisions is real, but not necessarily linguistic. Related to this is implicit trial-and-error: it is introspectively obvious that we often "plan" what we are going to say aloud before saying it. In creating a poem, one works with a retained pattern of stress and pitch distribution, and performs trial-and-error until a morpheme-sequence comes out which fits; in proving a theorem, one works with an understood pattern to which a statement must conform in order to count as a proof, and works by trial-and-error until a morpheme-sequence is produced which does conform. Where are these "patterns" retained? Where do we store the acceptable morpheme-sequence when it has been produced? Again, if we memorize a verse or a bon mot, where is the memorized morpheme-sequence stored? But these questions can be paralleled by questions which are not about language at all. Where (and how) does a dancer "store" the sequence of innervations which, when "read off" from storage, will put his body through the desired sequence of motions? Where (and how) does a lion "store" his knowledge of how to stalk a gazelle? It is wrong to ask questions of this kind, however important they may be, purely in a speech context.

It is evident that a key feature of our model of a human being as a speaking animal is that it evokes the mathematically manipulable notion of probability in place of the mentalist's free will, mind, soul, or ectoplasm. However, it does this *only insofar as man's linguistic behavior* is concerned. It should be recognized that even if the experimentum crucis had been performed, showing that the mechanism of human language is as here described, one would still not have proved the non-existence of the mentalist's non-physical entities. In the light of the extent to which language seems to be responsible for many of the differences between humans and non-humans, it would only become somewhat more likely that souls, if they exist, are shared by men with other animals, rather than being the exclusive prerogative of homo sapiens.

022. *The Design of a Language.* The discussion of the preceding section (§021) supplies the frame of reference in which we can describe the design of a language and the position of phonologic pattern within it.

A language is a complex system of *habits*, involving five interrelated subsystems. Three of the subsystems are *central*, the other two *peripheral*.

The three central subsystems are:

(1) the *grammatic* system: a stock of morphemes, and the arrangements in which they occur relative to each other;

(2) the *phonologic* system: a stock of phonemes (or phonologic units) and the arrangements in which they occur relative to each other;

(3) the *morphophonemic* system, which ties together the grammatic and phonologic systems.

Some investigators prefer to regard the proper sphere of linguistics as including only the three central subsystems which we have just listed. I agree, to the point of labelling them "central," but beyond that it seems largely a matter of taste in defining terms; we shall not so restrict the coverage of the word "linguistics."

The two peripheral subsystems are:

(4) the *semantic* system: this associates various morphemes or sequences of morphemes with certain things or situations, or kinds of things or situations, in the world around us;

(5) the *phonetic* system: this is the code which governs the slurring of a discrete flow of phonemes into sound waves and the recovery of the former from the latter.

The semantic system resides in the probabilistic ties through G.H.Q.'s back door.

The grammatic system is the economy of the signals emitted by G.H.Q. The special assumptions which we make, for practical reasons, in ordinary grammatic analysis have already been mentioned (§0213).

The morphophonemic system is the code according to which the Phoneme Source operates, converting its input (a flow of morphemes) into its output (a flow of phonologic units); the same code governs the inverse operation of the Morphemicizer.

The phonologic system is the economy of the signals emitted by the Phoneme Source. This has available only a certain stock of signals, and can emit them only in certain arrangements to the exclusion of others. Whatever may be the input to the Phoneme Source, it can emit signals only within the economy of the phonologic system by which it operates.

The phonetic system is the code according to which the Speech Transmitter converts its input (a flow of phonologic units) into sound waves; the same code governs the inverse operation of the Speech Receiver.

We must discuss some of the differences between this conceptualization of language design and certain more traditional views.

There is a traditional view which sees phonologic and grammatic units as differing primarily as to size-level, so that the whole design of language involves but a single hierarchy: a morpheme consists of one or more phonemes; a word consists of one or more morphemes; a phrase of one or more words; and so on. The present view is radically different. Morphemes are not *composed* of phonemes at all. Morphemes are indivisible units. A given morpheme is *represented by* a certain more or less compact arrangement of phonologic material, or, indeed, sometimes by one such arrangement and sometimes by another. If we call any such representation a *morph*, then it becomes correct to say that a morph has a phonologic structure—that it consists of an arrangement of phonemes.

An analogy may help. In telegraphy, two short voltage pulses represent the letter I. The letter does not *consist of* two short voltage pulses—a letter is an indivisible unit in a writing system. But the *representation* of the letter in telegraphy has a structure in terms of smaller recurrent units—the representation consists of two dots. Similarly, the English morpheme {boy} does not consist of phonologic material. It is *represented* phonologically by a morph /boy/, which indeed consists of an arrangement of smaller phonologic units.

Under this view, then, morphophonemics becomes not the way in which different morphs, in different environments, "belong to" one and the same morpheme, in the sense that elements belong to a class, but rather the complicated code governing the phonologic representation of morphemes and morpheme sequences.

In quite the same way, of course, we cannot say that a phoneme or other phonologic unit is physically present in the speech signal: what is present therein, susceptible of direct observation, is a *representation* of the phoneme.

Neither morphemes nor phonologic units, then, are susceptible to direct observation. Both must be deduced from what is directly observable: the behavior of humans, be it speech or otherwise. Within our frame of reference, we are free to use any sort of evidence which can be obtained. Normally we use actual samples of speech, plus observations of accompanying behavior or descriptions by an informant of the "meanings" of utterances, to build our portrayal of both the grammatic and the phonologic systems, and use whatever we have learned about either of the latter, however we can, to help us find out more about the other. In this heuristic sense, there can be no objection to the use of grammatic information for the elaboration of our understanding of the phonologic system, any more than there is to the reverse. The logical validity of the procedure depends only on how we conceptualize the results. If we have found words, as grammatic units, and automatically decide that there is a phonologic mark of some sort—an open juncture, let us say—between each two successive words in a phrase, then we are misusing our evidence. But if on the basis of grammatic words we merely decide that we must *look* for a more or less regular marker of word boundary on the phonologic level, we are proceeding soundly. The frame of reference which has been elaborated above should help to prevent misuse of evidence.

The technique of descriptive study of a language becomes, in this conceptualization, very closely akin to cryptanalysis. The cryptanalyst has one or more messages in some secret system, plus, in the most favorable (and rarest) case, information as to the meanings of the messages: by comparing the two, he works out the code. The linguist observes speech and other behavior, and by comparing the two works out the complicated three-step code which correlates them.

Our frame of reference meshes well with Hjelmslev's terminology of expression and content (at least as I understand that terminology: Hjelmslev's actual intentions may be something else). Morphemes are units of content: analysis of the content "plane" is grammatic analysis. Phonemes and other phonologic units are units of expression. Content should not be confused with "meaning," which has to do with the way in which experience is encoded into arrangements of morphemes. Nor should expression be confused with "sound," the latter term referring rather to the physically measurable sound waves which constitute the speech signal. It is also either a mistake, or a difference in terminology, to think of morphemes as elements on the expression "plane": if this is merely a difference in terminology, then it involves a use of the term "morpheme" for our "morph." Hjelmslev also distinguishes between "form" and "substance": the latter term has to do with what we have called the phonetic and semantic subsystems of a language, while the former has to do with phonology and grammar. Finally, Hjelmslev distinguishes between "pattern" and "usage." With somewhat less certainty, I find it convenient to identify the latter with *behavior*, the former with *habits* (§4). Only behavior can be observed: habits must be inferred. The methodology of linguistic analysis is the methodology of making such inferences; for phonology, it will concern us in §3.

The term "tactics," which I was using in this frame of reference until recently, will not appear in this manual. Its coverage was that now assigned to the term "grammar," while the latter term was used to subsume both tactics and morphophonemics. But the word "tactics" has unfortunate overtones, and there seems no real need for a generic term to cover just "tactics" and morphophonemics; consequently, the terminologic adjustment can be made.

023. *The Boundaries of Language; By-Systems.* The preceding two subsections (§§021–2) leave one problem untouched. Granting that linguistic messages become overtly observable in the form of a speech signal, we must nevertheless recognize that not all observable sound-producing behavior of a human is to be classed as speech. Some instances are so obvious as to preclude discussion: coughing, laughing, hiccuping and the like. But then just where is the boundary between sound-producing behavior which counts as speech and that which does not?

Perhaps no hard-and-fast line can be drawn, but there are two criteria which seem useful: *discreteness of contrast* and *duality of pattern.*

By discreteness of contrast we mean that no phonologically relevant contrasts are of the continuous-scale type. In a language where voicing and voicelessness are phonologically functional, a given bit of speech is either voiced or voiceless— not, structurally, half-voiced or three-quarters voiced. The opposite situation is found, for example, in the dynamic scale for Western music: there is no theoretic limit to the fine shades of contrast of volume which may be used by an expert composer or performer. The embedding medium of linguistic messages also shows a continuous scale of dynamics, organized to some extent in any given culture: one may speak softly, or more loudly, or more loudly still, or anywhere in between, with no theoretic limit to the fineness of gradation. But we distinguish between this (applying to relatively long stretches of speech) and the sharper contrasts of prominence between different smaller pieces within an utterance which, in some languages, function as an accentual system (§23). In general, then, if we find continuous-scale contrasts in the vicinity of what we are sure is language, we exclude them from language (though not from culture).

By duality of pattern we refer to the fact that linguistic signals have both a phonologic and a grammatic (morphemic) structure. Few other communicative systems—of the sort which are close enough to language that we might not know where to draw the boundary between them and language proper—have such a duality of pattern. If music is a communicative system (and this is not clearly the case), then we find ourselves unable to sort out any analog for pho- nologic units *and* for grammatic units—music has the sort of unitary structure, with units of all sorts differing only as to size-level, which, as we pointed out in §022, has been assumed by some to be the case for language, but which we have rejected.

A combination of these two criteria serves, at least in a practical way, to con- struct a working boundary to what we shall call "linguistic behavior"; this does not necessarily imply that the term "language" *must* be restricted in this way for efficient use. Yet even these combined criteria leave certain marginal cases untouched. These marginal cases can be referred to collectively as linguistic *by-systems*: they derive from a language, and are closely related to it, yet are not perhaps to be classed as language in the primary sense.

One example is Mazateco whistle-talk. Mazateco has a complicated tone-accent system; in whistle-talk, one whistles the melodic contours of an utterance, retaining all the relevant features of stress, pitch, and rhythm, but leaving out (necessarily) vowel color contrasts and all the consonantism. This whistle-talk is used for quite complicated messages; it is more powerful than one might at first imagine. African drum signals are reputedly derived from the tonal contours of utterances in certain African languages in a more or less similar way, but one suspects that there has been greater conventionalization.

Another example, widespread if not universal, is whispering. A whispered utterance mocks the phonologic structure of the same utterance spoken in the normal way, but almost always omits certain contrasts which are functional in normal speech. The details depend on the language. But by classing whispering as a by-system, one can describe the whispering habits associated with any one language, and then not complicate one's phonologic analysis of the language as one might have to if whispered utterances were thrown into the same analytic hopper as ordinary speech.

A final example, also widespread, is singing words. English, as sung, is intonationless, because the melodic contours of the music claim the machinery used in ordinary speech for intonation. Certain styles of Chinese singing are toneless in just the same way.

That such by-systems are in general easy for a speaker of a language to learn, and that messages transmitted in them rather than in ordinary speech are usually intelligible, are facts tied up with the redundancy of the speech signal, a point on which we shall touch in §§5 and 6. For the bulk of our discussion we regard by-systems as not properly a part of the object of our analysis.

03. *Common Core and Overall Pattern.* Our diagrammatic portrayal of Jill and Jack (Figure 1) assumes that they can understand each other: this in turn implies that there is no great discrepancy between Jill's idiolect (including its semantics, grammar, morphophonemics, phonology, and phonetics) and Jack's. In actual experience, we find some pairs of idiolects so close that we are hard put to it to discriminate between them at all, whereas other pairs are radically different. Close similarity implies mutual intelligibility, but a fair degree of difference need not imply mutual unintelligibility. People manage to understand each other even though they signal by different codes.

A detailed discussion of the implications of this fact lies outside the scope of this manual, but brief mention is necessary. People whose idiolects are virtually identical often understand each other despite the presence of a good deal of external *noise*—that is, sound of various sorts from various sources which strikes the ears of a hearer along with the speech signal from a speaker. Such external (or *channel*) noise sometimes renders communication difficult or impossible, but often it does not. When it does not, it is because the speech signal actually contains (as it leaves the speaker) a great deal more evidence as to what message the speaker is transmitting than the minimum which the hearer must receive in order to reconstruct the message accurately. Channel noise distorts and destroys some of that evidence, but does not seriously impair communication so long as a sufficient percentage remains undistorted.

Divergence between the codes of two people who communicate with each other via speech can be regarded as another sort of noise: *code noise*. The reason why people can understand each other despite code noise is exactly the same as the reason why channel noise, up to a point, does not destroy communication. The speech signal which leaves one person contains, in terms of his own total code, a great deal more evidence as to what message he is transmitting than the minimum which he himself would have to receive to understand the message. Some of this evidence is irrelevant for a particular hearer, but if a sufficient percentage of it falls within the identical portions of the two codes, the hearer will still understand.

The effect of the two sorts of noise on communication is entirely the same. If, for a certain two idiolects, there is virtually no code noise, then communication is possible despite a relatively great amount of channel noise. If, for another pair of idiolects, there is on the average a larger amount of code noise, then communication is possible only in the presence of relatively less channel noise. All of us have had experiences which show this. I can follow almost any sort of English even in a noisy cafeteria. At one time, I was able to follow Mexican Spanish quite well providing I could *hear* it well enough, but was completely lost under conditions approximating the noisy cafeteria.

Effective communication in the face of divergence of idiolects is due to two factors. One is that the set of idiolects involved share certain features: the whole set of shared features we shall call the *common core* of the set of idiolects. Barring channel noise, speech in any one of the idiolects is understandable to speakers of all the others so long as it remains within the common core, while any momentary resort to the features peculiar to the speaker's idiolect and not shared

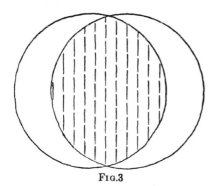

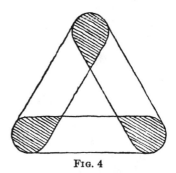

Fig.3   FIG. 4

FIG. 3. TWO IDIOLECTS WITH A COMMON CORE

Each circle represents an idiolect; the vertically hatched area represents their common core.

FIG. 4. THREE MUTUALLY INTELLIGIBLE IDIOLECTS WITH NO COMMON CORE

Each of the elongated lozenges represents an idiolect. Each two share a common core, represented by an area with vertical hatching, but the three taken together share nothing. (There is, of course, no "scale" to the diagram: all that counts is regions, boundaries, and intersections. Speaking mathematically, this and the other similar diagrams are topologic, not metric.)

by the others constitutes code noise. Even in the most homogeneous speech community, there are some individual idiosyncrasies, and it happens from time to time that someone says something that others do not understand.

In Figure 3 we show, in a very simple way, two idiolects which have a common core. Theoretically, a set of three idiolects might be mutually intelligible to some degree, without implying that the three, as a whole set, had any common core at all. We show in Figure 4 how this is possible: idiolects A and B have a common core; idiolects B and C also do; and idiolects A and C; but A, B, and C, taken together, have none. If speech is produced in idiolect A, the speakers of B and C may both understand, but on the basis of different portions of the whole

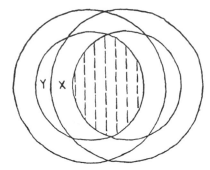

FIG. 5. TWO IDIOLECTS WITH A COMMON CORE, SHOWING THE DISTINCTION BETWEEN
PRODUCTIVE AND RECEPTIVE CONTROL

The left-hand circles represent A's idiolect: the smaller circle for his sphere of productive control, the larger for his sphere of receptive control. The right-hand circles similarly represent B's idiolect. The hatched area is their common core; i.e., their shared spheres of productive control. If something A says falls in region X, it is still perfectly understandable to B, though B would not have said it; if something A says falls in region Y, it constitutes code noise for B.

signal. In practice, however, this sort of situation hardly seems to be discoverable. More typical is the situation in which hundreds, thousands, or even millions of different idiolects share a discernible common core, which can be observed approximately (via statistical sampling) and described subject to some degree of indeterminacy.

But the common core of two idiolects is not the only factor responsible for mutual intelligibility despite divergence. A given speaker may constrain his own speech, largely or wholly, to the bounds of his own code, and yet be trained to understand speech which falls well outside. In Figure 5 we elaborate the representation of Figure 3 to show this. For each speaker, the inner circle marks the bounds of his own (productive) idiolect, while the outer circle marks the bounds of what he is trained to understand. Speech from A may thus fall outside the productive idiolect of B without automatically constituting code noise: it constitutes code noise only if it falls outside the larger circle for B.

Furthermore, we know that the boundaries of a given individual's productive and receptive control are highly labile. A private uses the word *sir* oftener than a

commissioned officer, but the latter knows the word just as well as the former:
if a private is commissioned, his productive system is slightly changed. Language-
learning never ceases. What stands outside an individual's sphere of receptive
control today may be within it tomorrow; what stands outside his productive
idiolect today may be within it tomorrow. In these terms, it makes sense to
speak of an *overall pattern* for any set of idiolects which are in direct or indirect
contact with each other and which contain a common core. The overall pattern
includes everything that is in the repertory of any one idiolect, productively or
receptively. It includes, typically if not by definition, more than any one idiolect,
while any one idiolect includes, typically if not by definition, more than the
common core. In Figure 6 we show three idiolects, their common core, and their
overall pattern, to make more graphic the statements just given.

It is possible for two people to communicate without their idiolects sharing
any common core at all. Imagine a Frenchman who understands, but cannot
speak, German, and a German, who likewise has receptive but not productive
control of French. The situation is depicted in Figure 7: the circles representing
the (productive) idiolects do not intersect, but the larger circles representing the
boundaries of receptive control do. In such a case (or any rough approximation
to it) we do not speak of an overall pattern. It makes practical sense to talk of
an overall pattern only when there is also a clear common core.

Linguistic description can be based on observation of a single idiolect, or on

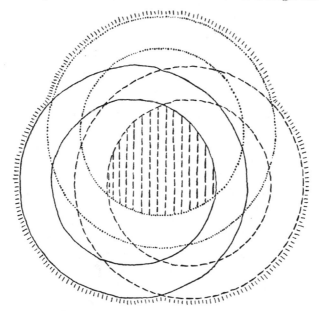

FIG. 6. THREE IDIOLECTS WITH COMMON CORE AND OVERALL PATTERN

Here we use solid-line circles for one idiolect, dashed-line circles for the second, and
dotted-line circles for the third. The vertically hatched area is the common core of the
three; everything within the outermost boundaries (marked with parallel ticks) belongs
to the overall pattern.

that of two or more idiolects; in the latter case under conditions which we would describe conventionally by saying that the idiolects all belong to the same language, or even to the same dialect. If description is based on observations of two or more idiolects, then we are free to follow either a common core approach or an overall pattern approach—both make sense, and neither is necessarily any more "valid" than the other. Often enough, an investigator does not consciously and intentionally chose between these two lines of interpretation; in the case of a small speech community with an obviously high degree of homogeneity, this usually does not matter. In the present manual we shall not be concerned with the ultimate ramifications of the idiolect, common core, and overall pattern frame of reference. We shall be concerned only with the analysis and classification of phonological systems *as systems*, whether they be idiolectal, or common

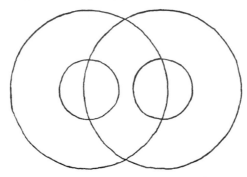

FIG. 7. MUTUAL INTELLIGIBILITY WITH NO COMMON CORE

The idiolects of A and B share no common core, and there is therefore no overall pattern; yet each can understand the other at least some of the time.

core, or overall pattern. In the few cases where we know which sort of system is being reported, we shall state the fact, but we regard it as of secondary importance.

This type of abstraction of a system, from the actual network of speakers and speaker-relationships in which it is in one or another way manifested, is what produces, as I see it, a purely *descriptive* (or "structural") approach, as over against one which is purely *synchronic* but more than purely descriptive. In other words, descriptive study is a phase of synchronic study, but the latter is more inclusive than the former.

04. *Outline.* The sector of language design which is of concern to us in the present manual can be delimited in the diagram of Figure 1: everything between Jill's Phoneme Source and Morphemicizer and Jack's Phoneme Source and Morphemicizer, exclusive of the named units. However, our discussion cannot devote equal portions to all the features included within these limits.

As a preliminary task, we must describe in detail the structure of the observable parts of the Speech Transmitter—that is, the organs of speech (§1). The technical jargon of phonologic description is largely articulatory, so that this survey is essential. It is worthy of note that the terminology ordinarily used in phonologic description is not *completely* articulatory. Some terms make reference, at least in the first instance, to acoustic features of the sort that can be measured quite accurately enough for linguistic purposes by the trained human ear: for example, "high" and "low" with reference to pitch. It is also quite probable that some often-used terms are understood among specialists only because their meanings have been demonstrated by actual example. These are what Pike calls "imitation-label" terms: one illustrates a variety of speech-sound, trains one's audience to identify and imitate it, and then gives it a label. We shall see in due course (§4) that the somewhat hodge-podge nature of our initial descriptive terminology does not—or at least need not—impair the accuracy of our work for most of the purposes which we seek. Indeed, in 1851 Böhtlingk published an excellent description of the phonology of Yakut, quite as reliable for linguistic purposes as many recent reports, in which the "imitation-label" technique is the only one used: he describes Yakut sounds in terms of the sounds of French, English, German, and Russian which are presumably familiar to his readers through direct experience. It has only been by a slow process that a more general, and largely articulatory, frame of reference has become available, and in large measure this frame of reference, however useful, is meaningful for any individual only to the extent to which he has received face-to-face instruction in general phonetics. Thus, the "imitation-label" procedure is by no means a last resort in case of desperation: rather, in a sense it is the fundamental procedure, to which any others are ultimately reducible.

In §2 we shall turn to our main task: the elaboration of an empirically-based typology of phonologic systems and subsystems, involving a thoroughgoing immediate-constituent approach. In this we will spend little time on methodologic quibbles, though some minor points of a methodologic sort will have to be touched on. Then §3 will be devoted completely to the problem of methodology. In §4 we discuss the problem of structure, pattern, and abstraction; in §5, acoustic phonetics, and in §6, functional load and analytic norms.

1. *The Organs of Speech and their Functions; Phonetic Notation.* An utterance in any language involves a series of motions in certain portions of the body: "The lungs, together with the diaphragm and the other muscles that control them, the larynx, the vocal cords, the arytenoid cartilages, the pharyngeal musculature, the faucal pillars, the velum, the uvula, the buccal walls, the lower jaw, the tongue, the teeth, and the lips." Collectively we call these, by a sort of metonymy, the *organs of speech*, or refer to the whole region as the *speech tract*.

The upper portion of the speech tract is shown diagrammatically in Figure 8; omitted are the lungs and the bronchial tubes below the larynx. The figure shows a vertical cross-section along the plane of symmetry of the body (sagittal section).

This is often the only figure supplied in discussions of phonetics—and will be here, because of the cost of printing plates. Heffner gives a bit more, but the best way to acquire a real acquaintance with the anatomy of the speech tract (short of dissecting a cadaver) is to consult good anatomy textbooks. Extremely useful illustrations are to be found in Gray (Figures 360, 3, 5; 375; 393-4; 850-3,

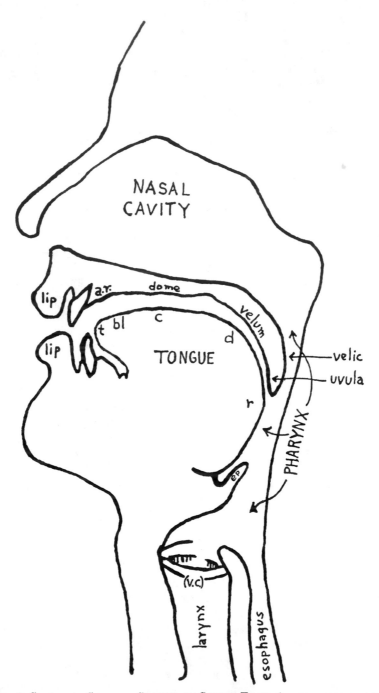

Fig. 8. Schematic Sagittal Section of Speech Tract (upper portion only)

Abbreviations: a.r. = alveolar ridge; t = tip; bl = blade; c = center; d = dorsum; r = root; ep = epiglottis; v.c. = vocal cords (parenthesized because they are not visible; the figure shows only the entrance to the larynx).

856; 944–55; 989–93; 1006–7, 9; 1017–18, 20–23) and in Sobotta (Figures 348–51, 373–4; 381; 387–91; 457–60; 471–83; all in volume 2).

Nevertheless, for most purposes a sagittal section serves quite well. There is an interesting reason for this. Almost all known articulatory motions manifest the same sort of rough bilateral symmetry which characterizes the human body. There is no case on record in which a raising of the left side of the tongue, let us say, takes place independently of and in contrast to a raising of the right side of the tongue. The nearest thing to an exception is that in some languages the front and one side of the tongue may be pressed against the roof of the mouth while the other side is held far enough away that air can pass through. However, in such cases it seems not to matter on which side one leaves the opening: some speakers leave the passage on the left side, some on the right, and doubtless some vary.

It is not hard to see why articulatory motions should show bilateral symmetry. We must remember—not only here but throughout our discussion of the speech tract—that in their function as "organs of speech" these portions of the body necessarily produce sound. A difference of articulatory motion which cannot be heard by others cannot be linguistically relevant. It is, of course, surprising in some cases to discover what very slight differences can indeed be relevant, but this does not alter the principle. Now the very fact of the approximate bilateral symmetry of the speech tract implies that articulatory motions which differ only as to "left-sided" versus "right-sided" will be practically impossible to discriminate. One might equally well expect the tone of a flute to change as one turns the main tube into various alignments with the mouthpiece. It does not, which leaves the player free to adjust the alignment so as to fit the mouthpiece optimally to his embouchure and, at the same time, to render the keys optimally manipulable by his fingers.

Apart from bilateral symmetry, the speech tract as a sound-producing mechanism is a highly irregular and peculiarly-shaped region, as compared, at least, with some apparatus that one might construct of buzzers and metal or glass resonance cavities. This would lead us to expect that any phonologic system would be a highly irregular matter. Yet every known system manifests some variety of partial symmetry or balance; we shall see in the sequel how this comes about.

We shall now work through the speech tract, from "south" (the lungs) to "north" (the lips), specifying the varieties of motion and position of which each movable part is capable, insofar as these motions and positions are known to be relevant in some language. As we proceed, we shall supply a rough notation for phonetic transcription, placing the symbols, as is customary, between square brackets. At the outset, certain terms, particularly "vowel" and "consonant," will be used in very loose senses, and should be so accepted, even though later on some of them will be assigned more precise technical meanings.

11. *The Lungs.* In their relaxed state, when one is not speaking, the lungs are of course not quiescent: they are drawing air inwards through the nose or mouth or both, or releasing (or actively pushing) air out by the same routes. In almost

all speech, the lungs are actively pushing, more or less forcibly, whether at a given moment the air can pass out unimpeded or, at the opposite extreme, is completely cut off by some closure in throat, or in mouth and nose. Since this is the normal situation, no special mention is ordinarily made of it (in this manual or elsewhere).

The relative force with which the lungs push, on the other hand, is often of importance. This is governed by a rather complex musculature, including the diaphragm and the exterior and interior intercostals. No one knows nearly as much as should be known about the articulatory functions of these muscles: the attention of most linguists has been focussed on the region from the glottis northwards, and all too often the lungs have been dismissed with the casual remark that they can do nothing but push and pull. One theory, by no means proved, holds that (at least in English) successive pulses of the diaphragm correlate with larger rhythmic units, while the more rapid successive pulses of the intercostals correlate with the rhythmic units we ordinarily call syllables. Be this so or not, casual dismissal of the sub-glottal region is out of order; we set aside more detailed discussion here only because the facts are still unknown.

In a few recorded instances, speech takes place during the intake of air. The various different functions of the larynx (§12) are more difficult to control during inhalation than during exhalation (at least for speakers of Western languages, and probably for everyone); in particular, voicing sounds a bit rough or "hoarse," and pitch differences are reduced and modified. Occasional speech during intake occurs even in English, under various abnormal circumstances. Less sporadic is the habit of some speakers of English of producing an assenting "grunt," something like *yeah*, with inflowing air. Even this, however, is in some sense marginal. But in Maidu there are reported to be two consonants, otherwise much like *b* and *d*, which occur only before a vowel, and which, together with the vowel, are pronounced with inflowing air. This occurs in the middle of a word or sentence the rest of which is pronounced with outflowing air, and can in no sense be regarded as marginal.

The business of breathing has to be carried on whether one is speaking or not. This sets a rough outer limit to the length of the segment of speech which can occur without pause, both to get more oxygen to the system and to get more air into the lungs with which to speak. The term "breathgroup" has sometimes been used, either for actual stretches of speech between successive inhalations, or, more usually, for the kinds of stretches of speech which it is not normal to interrupt for inhalation, and which are often separated by some slight pause even if no breath is taken. The correlation between actual interruptions for inhalation and any kind of phonologically relevant longer stretch (of a number of successive syllables) is at best rather rough, and one can suspect that other criteria for such segmentation are of more fundamental importance. This matter will come up again in §210.

12. *The Larynx.* The organs of importance in the larynx or glottis are the vocal cords, which are capable of a rather wide variety of functions. In their quiescent, non-speaking, state, the vocal cords are relaxed and relatively far apart, leaving a

passage so wide that air can pass through, in either direction, quite noiselessly. (A sore throat, or other pathologic or unusual condition, can of course render ordinary breathing "noisy" by impeding the passage of air just at this point; linguistically, the least "noisy" passage of air in such a case counts as functionally "noiseless.") Articulations further north in the speech tract which are accompanied by this relaxed position of the vocal cords (and usually by exhalation from the lungs) are called *voiceless*. At the beginning of an English word such as *heap, hand, hose*, there is a brief moment of such voicelessness, with the lips and tongue in approximately the position for the vowel which is to come next. Such a brief phase can be symbolized by [h]; or, when there is any special reason for it, by a symbol for a vocoid (roughly, a "vowel": see §151) accompanied by some diacritic to represent the voicelessness. Thus the beginning of the English word *he* might be represented as [hi . . .] or, using capitalization as the diacritic for voicelessness, as [Ii . . .]. The latter notation is awkward, but does have one great merit: it circumvents the common tendency to think of [h] as a "spirant" (§1522). The articulatory phenomenon which we are here dealing with is *not* a spirant; the best term for it is simply "aitch."

At the opposite extreme, the vocal cords can be drawn tightly together so that no air can pass by. This is variously called a *glottal catch*, a *glottal stop*, an *aleph* or a *hamzah:* symbol [ʔ]. We shall use the first of the four terms listed. There is a perfectly valid definition of "stop" by which [ʔ] counts as one, but it is more convenient to restrict the term in a way which excludes [ʔ] (§1521). In English, we often begin an emphatic exclamation such as *ouch!* with a glottal catch (though phonologically we usually say that it begins with a vowel). In many languages glottal catches occur much more frequently than in English, and in a greater variety of environments in utterances.

The vocal cords can be stretched taut, with little space between them, but held flexibly enough that the passing airstream forces itself through, and, in so doing, sets the cords into vibration, rapidly opening and closing in turn. This vibration of the vocal cords is *voice*, and articulations further north which are accompanied by voice are called *voiced*. In an English word like *heap*, the brief initial voiceless phase is followed by a much longer voiced phase, which ends only with the consonantal closure of the lips at the end of the word (the *p*). We do not use a separate letter-sized symbol for voicing; instead, pairs of symbols are in general available for articulations further north in the speech tract, one of them for voiceless, and one of them for voiced. Thus [p] and [b] represent the same articulatory motions and positions in mouth and nose, but the former implies that the vocal cords are quiescent, the latter that they are in vibration. In some cases there is only one symbol readily available, perhaps implying voicelessness, perhaps implying voice, and a diacritic of some sort can be added to indicate the other.

By varying the tension on the vocal cords during voicing, and the force of the passing stream of air, one can vary the *pitch* and the *volume* of the voicing. Different individuals have pitch-ranges of from one to three octaves. There is no simple meâsure for the range of volume variation, which is any case is not as great at the extremes of pitch as in the middle of the pitch range. A misunderstanding often found among beginners in phonetics is the assumption that the vocal tract produces no *sound* save when the vocal cords are in vibration. This is of course quite false; there are momentary phases in utterances in many languages during which nothing at all is audible, but these are not coterminous with the phases between successive periods of voicing. What voicing does is to supply a musical note, the *glottal tone*, extremely rich in harmonics, which can then be modified as to overtone structure and as to distribution of energy at various frequencies by the conformation of the speech tract north of the glottis. When this musical note is not involved, there are still, most of the time, cavity-friction and friction at various local points, rich enough to carry most of the differences which are carried during voicing.

Various notations are used for the indication of pitch and volume differences; there is no need to present them until they are required in our typologic survey (§2).

The vocal cords can be drawn close together, and held taut, so that the passing air stream is set into local turbulence, and this turbulence can be accompanied by slight voicing (*murmur, voiced glottal spirant*) or not (*voiceless glottal spirant, whisper*). Words like *heap, hand, hose* are pronounced by some people with an initial voiceless glottal spirant rather than simply with voiceless vowel.

The term "whisper" is also used to cover another mechanism: the vocal cords are closed together, but the arytenoid cartilages behind them are spread apart so as to afford a triangular passageway for air. The acoustic effect is much the same as that of voiceless glottal spirant. In what is ordinarily called whispering, the distinction between the initial *h* and the following vowel of a word like *heap* is apparently maintained in either of two exactly opposite ways: one may begin with pure voicelessness, and tense the vocal cords so as to produce the vowel with glottal spirantization, or one may do the reverse. The former is probably more typical, since it is during the normally voiced stretches that whispering sometimes breaks into slight (murmur-type) voicing. A medial *h*, as in *ahoy* (spoken aloud, not whispered) is often pronounced as a glottal murmur: so-called "voiced *h*."

In our survey of articulatory motions further north in the speech tract we shall see some further ways in which the various glottal functions described above can be combined with motions elsewhere.

13. *The Pharynx.* As in the glottis, a complete closure can be made in the pharyngeal region, by drawing the root of the tongue back against the back wall of the pharynx. Such a *pharyngeal catch* occurs in Arabic dialects, but usually (if not always) only as one alternative pronunciation of a consonant which is more typically pronounced in a different way: as a *voiced pharyngeal spirant*. A pharyngeal spirant involves, not complete closure in this region, but sufficient constriction to set the passing airstream into local turbulence; it can be voiced or voiceless. The usual symbol for a voiceless pharyngeal spirant is [ḥ], and for a voiced one, [ʕ].

A narrowing of the pharyngeal passage may not produce any local friction;

instead, it may simply modify the coloring of a sound in which one or another oral articulation participates. In Arabic, many consonants, involving oral articulations, come in pairs, one with pharyngeal constriction (the so-called *emphatics*) and one without. A diacritic, say a dot under the letter, suffices to indicate pharyngealization. Nootka has both a voiceless pharyngeal spirant [ḥ] and a glottal catch pronounced with pharyngeal constriction, [ʔ̣]; these pair off, structurally, much as do the ordinary [h] and [ʔ] of the same language.

14. *The Velic.* The term "velic," as can be seen in Figure 8, refers to the upper and rear surface of the velum, which constitutes part of the bounding surface of the nasal cavity, at the boundary between the latter and the throat. This is the only structure in the nasal cavity which is capable of significant sound-producing or sound-modifying motion, and its motions are strictly limited. At one extreme, the velic can be closed against the back wall of the pharynx; this cuts off the nasal cavity from the rest of the speech tract, so that any air passing in or out must go through the mouth, and so that the nasal cavity functions as an *unconnected* rather than as a *connected* resonance chamber. At the other extreme, the velic can be pulled well away from the back wall, so that passage of air between throat and nasal cavity is unimpeded. The size of the aperture can naturally vary, and in some languages it is necessary to specify at least one degree of aperture between the two extremes.

A cold in the nose can fill the rear portion of the nasal cavity with phlegm, impairing the contrast between articulation with closed and with open velic; this, as everyone knows, makes *m*'s and *n*'s sound much like *b*'s and *d*'s. Colloquially we are apt to say that the voice of a person with a bad cold sounds "nasal," but this sense of the term "nasal" is almost the opposite of its sense as a technical term. Technically an articulation with open velic is called *nasal*, and one with closed velic is called *nonnasal* or *oral*. If there is an intermediate degree of aperture, one speaks of *slight* versus *strong* nasalization, or the like.

For some articulations the contrast of velic position is irrelevant. A glottal catch, for example, cannot be "nasalized," since while the passage of air is cut off completely at the glottis the open or closed position of the velic is quite inaudible.

In describing speech sounds, nonnasal articulation is usually assumed, the presence of nasality being specified when necessary. In notation, many symbols imply by definition the absence or the presence of nasality: thus [p t k b d g] imply nonnasal articulation, while [m n ŋ] imply presence of nasalization. Where basic symbols imply nonnasal articulation and there are no special paired symbols for the corresponding nasal articulation, a diacritic is used: thus oral [a] but nasal [ą] or [ã].

15. *The Oral Cavity.* It is within the oral cavity that the greatest variety of articulatory motion occurs. It is convenient to divide the whole range of articulatory motions in the mouth roughly into two classes: those which most typically are involved in the production of *vocoids*, and those often involved in the production of *contoids*. As indicated by the wording, the distinction between

a vocoid and a contoid cannot be made completely in terms of what goes on in the mouth. The two terms are acoustic or impressionistic rather than strictly articulatory: a vocoid is a sound in which resonances of one sort or another seem to be of primary importance, whereas contoids are sounds involving clearly audible turbulence in the airstream at one point or another in the vocal tract, or else complete shutting-off of that airstream. Thus in the English word *fat* the vowel in the middle is a vocoid, whereas the *f* and the *t* are contoids.

Two illustrations will show why the contrast cannot be made completely in terms of the functioning of parts of the oral cavity. A *b* and an *m* (*bat, mat*) are made with precisely the same motions of mouth parts, yet the first is a contoid, the second either a vocoid or else on the boundary between contoid and vocoid. The difference is brought about, of course, by the different functioning of the velic. More striking is the following example: hold the tongue in the proper position for a prolonged buzzing *z-z-z-z*, and produce such a prolonged buzz. This sound is a contoid. Now without moving any part of the speech tract north of the lungs, a diminution of pressure from the lungs can eliminate the "buzz" of this prolonged *z-z-z-z*, whereupon the result sounds like an obscure vowel— a vocoid.

Such examples demonstrate that the vocoid-contoid distinction must be taken with a grain of salt, but do not destroy its usefulness as a rough basis for classifying oral articulations.

151. *Vocoid Articulations.* Most vocoids in most languages can be described in terms of three factors: *lip position, tongue-height,* and *tongue frontness or backness* (there is, unfortunately, no convenient short term for the designation of the last of these three factors).

Lip position is specified along the scale *rounded-unrounded* or *rounded-spread.* If we compare the articulation of the words *he* and *who*, we find the lips relaxed and (relatively) spread for the former, but somewhat rounded for the latter; for many speakers of English, the rounding for *who* increases during the pronunciation of the word. The maximum difference in degree of lip-rounding in English is not very great; in some languages it is much more prominent.

If we compare the vowels of *bit, bet,* and *bat,* we find that the lower jaw is held progressively further away from the upper jaw, and that the front part of the tongue, at least, is progressively further away from the region of the upper teeth and alveolar ridge, moving downwards in the mouth. The different positions of the lower jaw and of the tongue are related, and in a sense only the latter counts. For what counts, in differentiating such sounds, is the shape of the oral cavity as a resonance chamber; this shape can be modified by different degrees of aperture between the front of the tongue and the roof of the mouth, and the wider or narrower opening of the jaws is merely part of the mechanism by which this degree of aperture is controlled. A similar kind of difference appears if we compare *sue, sew,* and *saw,* though it is not so clear in this case that it is the *front* part of the tongue that is held in positions to give varying degrees of aperture. But, in both cases, the scale of contrasts involved is that of tongue-height, from *high* (through varying intermediate heights, *mid*) to *low.*

The third scale of contrasts is harder to describe in accurate articulatory terms. If we compare *he* and *who*, setting aside the difference of lip-position which has already been noted, we find (at least for many speakers of English) that in *he* the whole upper surface of the tongue, from dorsum to blade, is close to the roof of the mouth, whereas in *who* only the dorsum is high, the remainder of the tongue curving downwards and away from the roof of the mouth. In both *he* and *who* we have high vocoids; where the front of the tongue, as well as the back, is high we speak of a *front* vocoid, but where the back is high and the front is not we speak of a *back* vocoid. Intermediate between front and back are (varying degrees of) *central*; it should be noticed that the adjective "mid" is arbitrarily assigned to intermediate positions on the height scale, while "central" is, equally arbitrarily, assigned to the front-back scale. A high central vowel occurs in the speech of many Americans in the adverb *just* (as in *I was just going*; not in the the adjective with the same spelling, as in *a just man*). The back and central portions of the tongue are fairly high for this vowel, but the tip is held somewhat further down.

This description serves for the front-back scale in the case of various high vocoids, and perhaps for mid vocoids, but is not so certain for the low ones. It is customary to speak of the vocoids of *back*, *bock*, *saw*, all low, as respectively front, central, and back, and these assignments are perfectly usable, even if it happens that in this case we are using an imitation-label procedure (§04) rather than accurate reference to articulation. In the writer's own pronunciation, the vocoid of *buck* has the tongue tip down, behind the lower teeth, and the central portion of the tongue pushed somewhat upwards and to the front; in *bock* this upwards and frontwards bunching is less, and in *law* there is a concavity instead of a convexity. Other speakers may achieve acoustically equivalent results with other tongue positions— this, indeed, is possible, though less drastically so, for the other varieties of vocoid which have been discussed so far. However this may be, the terminology which has been presented is that ordinarily used, and for linguistic purposes it serves quite well.

In addition to the three scales of contrast which have been described so far, one often hears of a distinction between *tense* and *lax*. It is easy to demonstrate this difference in English: hold the fingers on the bundle of muscles which is to be found above and in front of the glottis, within the framework of the lower jaw, and say *bit, beat, bit, beat*. For *beat*, one can feel a bunching and tension in the bundle of muscles which is lacking, or at least much less pronounced, for *bit*. The same difference can be detected with *could* and *cooed*; for some speakers it can be detected with *bet* and *bate*, but for many or most it is harder to feel in this case. There is some problem as to just what is accomplished, in the oral resonance chamber and thus in the speech signal, by this tension. Presumably the tension brings about a slightly different contour of the upper surface of the tongue, thus changing the shape of the resonance chamber. In English, other factors also differentiate the voiced vocoid parts of *bit* and *beat*, *could* and *cooed*, *bet* and *bate*, and it seems probable that the lax-tense distinction is secondary rather than primary. The writer has found no reliable report of a language in which the distinction plays a primary phonological role, though this has been suspected to be the case for certain languages of West Africa.

There are not many purposes for which one needs on hand a great variety of symbols for the notation of vocoids (differentiated in the ways so far described); those engaged in some specific enterprise, such as dialect geography, where a well-defined and elaborate set of symbols is needed, will devise one. Most of these symbologies make identical or highly similar use of certain letters, and some of this we can indicate here. [i e ɛ æ] normally represent front vocoids, without lip rounding, from high to relatively low. [u o ɔ] normally represent back vocoids, with lip rounding, from high to low. [a] represents a low vocoid, sometimes fairly far front (in contrast to [ɑ] representing a central or back variety), but often central. Small cap [ɪ] and [ʊ], or else the Greek letters [ɩ] and [ʋ], are often used in addition to [i] and [u] if some sort of contrast has to be indicated within, respectively, the high front unrounded and the high back rounded region: usually in such a case the modified (or Greek) letters represent slightly lower or laxer varieties than the ordinary letters. Mid and high central vocoids without rounding can be represented by front-vocoid symbols plus a diacritic, either a superposed dot or, in the case of "i", a bar: [ɨ]. With rounding, the back-rounded symbols can be used with similar diacritics. There are also available a couple of special letters, [ʌ] and [ə], the former for a central or back mid unrounded vocoid, the latter for a mid or high central unrounded vocoid. Two dots ("umlaut") over a back-vocoid symbol represent a front rounded vocoid, e.g. [ü ö]; two dots over a front-vocoid symbol represent a back unrounded vocoid. For convenience of reference, these symbols, and a few others, are presented in Figures 9 and 10, the former for unrounded vocoids, the latter for rounded ones. Some of the symbols appear in two or more of the boxes in these figures, because the purpose of the figures is to show the ranges of value often currently assigned to the symbols, rather than to supply a unique symbol for each position. As soon as an analyst has discovered, even in part, how the vocoid system of a particular language works structurally, he will normally simplify his notation, choosing, wherever possible, "simpler" letter-shapes rather than more complex or alien ones, though with some care to supply mnemonism in terms of traditional associations.

		front	central	back
high:	higher	i	ɨ ə	ï ɯ
	lower	i ɪ ɩ	ɨ ɨ ə	ï ɯ ï ɣ
mid:	higher	e	ė ə ʌ	ë ʌ ɣ
	lower	e ɛ	ė ɛ̇ ə ʌ	ë ë ʌ
low:	higher	æ ɛ	ʌ	ʌ
	lower	æ a	a ɑ	a ɑ

FIG. 9. UNROUNDED VOCOIDS

		front	central	back
high:	higher	ü	u̇ ʉ	u
	lower	ü̆ ʊ̈	u̇ ʉ ʊ̇	u ʊ ʋ
mid:	higher	ö ɸ	ȯ	o
	lower	ö ɸ ɔ̈ œ	ȯ ɔ̇	o ɔ
low:		ɔ̈ œ	ɔ̇ ɑ	ɔ ɑ ɒ

FIG. 10. ROUNDED VOCOIDS

1511. *Modifications.* There are not many further purely oral factors which can participate in the differentiation of vocoids. One which can and sometimes does is *retroflexion*: the curling back of the tip of the tongue, towards the dome of the roof of the mouth. Many speakers of American English (not in eastern New England or certain other regions of the East and South) pronounce a word like *bird* with a mid central or mid high slightly rounded retroflex vocoid. In Badaga, all vocoids come in threes, differing fundamentally in the presence of no retroflexion, slight retroflexion, or strong retroflexion. An acoustic effect quite indistinguishable from the retroflex vocoid of *bird* is achieved by some speakers of English not actually by a curling-back of the tongue tip, but by a peculiar contour of the central part of the tongue, the tip being held down behind the lower teeth. We can define the term "retroflexion" to subsume the result, whether achieved in the one way or in the other.

Symbols which connote retroflexion include [ɚ], for a mid-central vocoid with retroflexion, and [r] or an inverted [ɹ]; the last is apt to be used in the rare case that a language has also a trill (§153) for which the [r] is being used. Where there are more extensive contrasts between retroflexed and nonretroflexed, one makes use of some diacritic not otherwise needed.

Various non-oral factors can distinguish vocoids produced with identical positions of the mouth parts. A vocoid is most frequently voiced, and the ordinary vocoid symbols imply concomitant voicing unless there is special indication to the contrary. But vocoids also occur voiceless, or whispered, or pronounced with glottal murmur—not, of course, with glottal closure, although sometimes a vocoid is produced with intermittent closure of the glottis too slow to be called a glottal murmur. As we mentioned in §12, the *h* at the beginning of a word like *he* is for most speakers pronounced without glottal (or other) obstruction of any kind: that is, as a voiceless vocoid, not as a spirant. If we wish to use the symbol [h] for this, writing say [hi . . .] (*he*), [ha . . .] (*hot*), [ho . . .] (*hope*), then "h" must be defined as representing a whole family of voiceless vocoids: before any given voiced vocoid, it represents a voiceless vocoid of the same oral properties.

Vocoids can also be modified by pharyngeal constriction. As this involves pulling back the root of the tongue, the position of the upper surface of the tongue is likely to be somewhat different from what it is with the root of the tongue not retracted, and the difference in orally-produced coloring may be more prominent than anything added directly by the pharyngeal constriction. In Arabic, for example, a vocoid more or less of the [æ] type occurs after nonpharyngealized consonants, and one more or less of the [a] type after pharyngealized consonants; functionally, the two are the "same," the difference residing in the consonants, yet in some instances it may be the orally-imposed vowel coloring which serves as the main acoustic signal to the hearer, to identify the preceding consonant as nonpharyngeal or as pharyngeal.

Nasalized vocoids are of course very common; the mechanism has already been described (§14).

152. *Typically Contoid Articulations.* To describe these, we distinguish between different *articulators*, along the lower margin of the oral cavity, and between different *points of articulation*, along the upper margin; and we distinguish between *closure*, in which an articulator closes against a point of articulation so tightly that no air can pass, and *spirantization*, in which there is a constriction which sets the passing air-stream into local turbulence. If an oral closure is accompanied by velic closure, then we speak of a *stop*: this is the only sense in which this term will be used (cf. §§12, 13).

The articulators which it is convenient to differentiate include dorsum, center, blade of tongue (the frontmost upper surface), tip of tongue, and the lower lip. Sometimes it is necessary to specify whether "blade" includes or excludes tip; there is no convenient shorthand expression for the distinction.

The points of articulation are the velum (sometimes requiring subdivision into front and back), the dome, the alveolar ridge, the backs of the upper teeth approximately at the edge of the gum, the edges of the upper teeth, and the upper lip; occasionally the last two function together.

A combination of articulator and point of articulation constitutes a *position of articulation*; these are labelled by a compound descriptive term, the first part referring to the articulator, the second to the point of articulation: *dorso-velar, front* and *back dorso-velar, centro-domal, lamino-domal, lamino-alveolar, apico-domal, apico-alveolar, apico-dental, apico-interdental, apico-labial, labio-dental,* and (*labio-labial* =) *bilabial*. The term "lamino-alveolar" may have to be supplemented by the specification that the tip is, or is not, included in the articulator; in either case, the reference to the alveolar ridge does nothing more than to specify that it is included in the area touched or approached by the blade, since a laminal articulation cannot involve merely a point or a thin transverse line along the roof of the mouth as its "point" of articulation. When the lower lip meets both the upper lip and the upper teeth, the situation requires lengthier description.

Other combinations of articulator and point of articulation, not covered in the preceding paragraph, are impossible (apico-velar), improbable (labio-alveolar), or simply so far unreported (lower teeth and upper lip). However, it should be marked clearly that the listed positions of articulation are simply a small set of points of reference. Some selection of them almost always suffices for the description of the relevant contrasts in any one language, but articulations in two different languages, both conveniently describable as, say, apico-alveolar, may differ slightly in their most typical conformation and in the resulting acoustic characteristics.

1521. *Stops.* Stops can be made at all the positions of articulation listed above, and in one or another language all of these positions for stop-closure are known to occur. In English we have dorso-velar [k] and [g], respectively voiceless and voiced: these two are sometimes front (*key, geese*), and sometimes back (*cool, goose*), but the difference is accompanied by difference of environment and is not in itself distinctive. We also have typically apico-alveolar [t] and [d], and bilabial [p] and [b]. Lamino-alveolar stop closure occurs in English at the beginning of *check, jack,* but stop closure in this position in English is never followed immediately by a vocoid articulation or by silence, as are the others.

Various symbols are available for the indication of stops, voiceless and voiced (or otherwise modified), in other positions of articulation. In the present monograph a dot will be placed under "p" and "b" to indicate labio-dental stops, under "t" and "d" to indicate apico-domal stops, and under "k" and "g" to indicate back dorso-velar closure when there is a significant contrast with a more front dorso-velar position; as an exception to this, "q" will be used instead of "k" with a dot. A small crescent ($_{\smile}$) above or below "k" and "g" will indicate centro-domal; under "t" and "d" the same diacritic will indicate apico-interdental when this contrasts with apico-dental or apico-alveolar. A superscript "y" after "t" and "d" will indicate lamino-alveolar. Where other distinctions have to be made, simple symbols will be chosen, supplemented by description.

Oral closures are subject to various accompaniments at velic and in pharynx and glottis. If the velic is open, the resulting total articulation is not a stop, but a *nasal continuant* (a vocoid): starting with [m n ŋ] for bilabial, apico-dental or apico-alveolar, and dorso-velar, the diacritics already described serve to distinguish other positions of articulation as necessary. Pharyngealization (§13) has already been mentioned, as have voicing contrasts. Another variety of articulation occurs in *glottalized stops.* To produce a glottalized stop, the glottis and the velic are closed and some oral stop closure is made; the muscles of throat and mouth then squeeze the air contained in this completely closed chamber, causing pressure at all three closures. Typically the oral stop closure is released first, the compressed air bursting past the releasing closure, and then the glottis is opened. But various timings are possible, and various degrees of pressure before the release. The notation for a glottalized stop is the symbol for a voiceless stop with an apostrophe either over it or immediately to the right; we use the latter (e.g., [p']), as easier to print.

Two other "styles of delivery," as it were, of stops can be described. In the case of a voiced stop, it is possible approximately to reverse the muscular motion involved in glottalization, so that even though some air is passing north through the vibrating vocal cords, the chamber above them contains air which is being rarified rather than compressed. A release of the oral closure is then followed by a slight inward rush of air, giving a sort of popping sound. Such voiced stops are called *injectives*; our diacritic will be that mentioned above for glottalized stops, since the letter so marked will in this case always be that for a voiced stop.

With a dorso-velar closure, a closure further forward in the mouth can be made and the air in the chamber thus established can either be compressed or rarefied; the latter variety of articulation, with the more frontward closure released first, is attested in speech. Such sounds are *clicks*. We use clicks in English in one or two interjections (*tsk-tsk!*) and in signals to horses, but they do not occur in ordinary speech. But in a number of languages of South Africa and a couple in East Africa they do. A click may be voiced or voiceless—and even nasalized, since the status of the velic does not affect the possibility of the necessary oral articulations.

Different from clicks are *coarticulated* stops: usually a simultaneous dorso-velar and bilabial closure. In coarticulated stops there is no compression or rarefaction of the air between the two stop closures, but simply the approximately simultaneous closing and opening at the two positions. These, also, are apparently most widespread in Africa, but in this case perhaps mainly in West Africa.

1522. *Spirants*. Spirants can also be produced at all the positions of articulation which have been described above. For dorso-velar spirants the customary symbols are [x] and [γ], respectively voiceless and voiced; for bilabial spirants [φ] and [β], for labiodental spirants [f] and [v]. The diacritics described earlier for more subtle indication of position of stops can be used with these symbols also, except that the common "f" and "v" obviate any need for them in the labial range.

But for the front part of the tongue further distinctions have to be made, not applicable in the case of stops. In English both *s* (*sick*) and *th* (*thick*) are (normally) apico-alveolar, but the former is a *rill* spirant, the latter a *slit* spirant. In a rill spirant, the front edge of the tongue closes against the upper teeth or the gum on both sides, leaving only a tiny opening through which the airstream can pass. In a slit spirant, instead of this tiny opening there is a transverse slit. The difference is comparable to that between water coming out of a hose and water pouring through a horizontally wide but vertically narrow sluice-gate. For rill spirants we have symbols [s] and [z], to which the positional diacritics presented for stops can be added; for slit spirants the basic symbols are [θ] and [ð], to which the same diacritics can be added.

It is also possible to make a lamino-alveolar rill spirant; many speakers of English do this for their *s*, holding the tip of the tongue down behind the lower teeth, and the acoustic effect can be quite indistinguishable from that of an apico-alveolar [s]. Other lamino-alveolar spirants are not slit spirants but involve close approximation of a whole area, from side to side and from front to back, of the blade of the tongue, to a comparable area behind the upper teeth and perhaps including the backs of the teeth. In contrast to rill and slit spirants, these may be called *surface* spirants. Our English *sh* (*she*) and *zh* (*vision*) are of this type; the symbols which will be used in this monograph are [š] and [ž]. In British English, lamino-domal spirants usually occur where in the United States we use a lamino-alveolar position; the symbols would be [ṣ] and [ẓ], with the underposed dot for the retracted point of articulation.

There is one more variety of articulation which occurs perhaps most typically in spirants, though not in the languages most familiar to us: *lateral* articulation. An apico-alveolar lateral spirant, for example, is in a sense the reverse of an apico-alveolar rill spirant: in the latter the sides of the tongue close off the air, the tip being so held as to leave a small passageway, while in the former the tip is closed against the alveolar ridge and the sides are held close enough to the sides of the upper teeth to cause turbulence in the passing air, but not close enough to cut off the air altogether. The symbol for a voiceless lateral spirant is [ɬ], and for a voiced lateral spirant [l]; but the latter is also used for a nonspirantal lateral (a variety of vocoid), so that one has to specify in words, or use a diacritic, to distinguish the two.

Spirants are subject to most of the modifications involving action outside the mouth which we have mentioned for stops. Nasal spirants seem to be very rare: perhaps it is difficult, when the outflowing stream of air meets no obstruction at the velic and can go through the nose, to obtain enough pressure behind an oral spirantal closure to produce audible turbulence. Apart from this, pharyngealization, voicing contrasts, and glottalization, are all quite feasible for spirants. Glottalized spirants seem to be as rare as are nasal spirants, but one can find no comparable articulatory rationalization.

Figure 11 displays the basic symbols for the stops, spirants, and nasals with which we have dealt in this section (§152).

	bila-bial	labio-dental	apico-labial	apico-inter-dental	apico-dental, apico-alveolar	apico-domal	lamino-alveolar	lamino-domal	centro-domal, fronted dorso-velar	dorso-velar	back dorso-velar
Stops vls	p	ᵱ		ṭ	t	ṭ	tʸ	tʸ	ḵ	k	q ḵ
vd	b	ḅ		ḍ	d	ḍ	dʸ	dʸ	ĝ	g	ɡ
Nasals vd	m	ɱ ŋ̆		ṇ	n	ṇ	nʸ ɲ ñ	ṇʸ	ŋ̂	ŋ	ŋ̣
Spirants vls	φ	f	RILL:	ṣ̆	s	ṣ	š	š̮	χ ç	x	x χ
vd	β	v		z̮	z	ẓ	ž	ž̮	γ̂	γ	γ
SLIT: vls				θ̮	θ	θ·					
vd				ð̮	ð	ð̣					
LATERAL: vls				ɬ̮	ɬ	ɬ					
vd				l̮	l	l	ʎ lʸ	ɭ lʸ			

FIG. 11. STOPS, VOICED NASALS, AND SPIRANTS

The symbols for voiced laterals are also used for laterals of the vocoid (non-spirantal) type. There are no generally accepted symbols for apico-labials. In §2 we shall use the apical symbols with the small curve placed beneath them (as, in this table, for apico-interdentals), since there will be no ambiguity.

153. *The Vocoid-Contoid Borderline.* We have already pointed out that the boundary between vocoid and contoid is not sharp (§15). One can start with a clearly contoid voiced spirant, and, by either relaxing the air pressure slightly or by relaxing the tension with which the articulator is held against the point of articulation, eliminate any local turbulence in the air and have left only a vocoid of particular coloring. In many cases the precise degree of tension or pressure is irrelevant in a language, and one finds a sound-type which occurs with varying degrees of local turbulence but always with noticeable coloring of the vocoid type. The Arabic voiced pharyngeal spirant is a sound-type of this kind: in fact, only rarely does one hear the friction of the airstream passing through the contracted pharynx.

For spirants a distinction is sometimes made between *fricative* and (relatively) *frictionless*, and for some languages this is of importance. The former term implies a greater amount, the latter term a lesser, of local friction. Labiodental spirants typically have more friction than bilabial ones; apical rill spirants usually have more than slit spirants; a similar contrast can be made in the range of dorsovelars.

Although voiceless laterals are usually spirantal, many more nonspirantal— that is, vocoid—voiced laterals are reported in various languages than voiced laterals of the contoid type. Our English *l* is vocoid rather than contoid. For vocoid laterals several distinctions are worth noting. Dorso-velar laterals occur— closure in the center, but open passageway on both sides; some speakers of English use this instead of an apical closure. Where the closure is apical, the point of articulation can be dental or alveolar or domal ([ḷ]), and in any case the position in which the remainder of the tongue is held can be relevant. Some languages contrast an apico-dental or apico-alveolar lateral of the vocoid type with an apico-domal one. Other languages contrast an apico-dental or apico-laminal lateral with a lamino-alveolar one ([ʎ] or [ĺ] or [lʸ]). Still other languages contrast two apico-dental or apico-alveolar laterals, one made with the middle portion of the tongue held down away from the roof of the mouth, the other made with the middle portion of the tongue held up close to the roof of the mouth, giving a kind of "i"-color to the lateral. This last scale of difference is often referred to as *dark* versus *clear*. British English has a clearer lateral at the beginning of a word like *little* and a darker one at the end; the difference in most American English is far less noticeable.

Vocoids produced with tongue retroflexion, like the American English [r], can be rendered spirantal (and contoid-like) by either increasing the tension in the tongue or the pressure of the airstream; Mandarin has a type of [r] which differs from the American English [r] largely in this way. Contoids made with apico-domal or lamino-domal position of articulation involve tongue retroflexion, and so the particular retroflex coloring which we associate with the English [r] accompanies them even when they are clearly contoids rather than vocoids.

Finally, there is a variety of articulation, *trilling*, which it seems quite impossible to classify as contoid or as vocoid save completely in terms of the environing articulations, in its occurrences in actual forms in specific languages. Most common is the apical trill: the tip is held in a semirelaxed state, perhaps near the teeth, perhaps near the alveolar ridge, and perhaps retroflexed, in such a way that the outflowing airstream causes it to flutter rapidly back and forth, first touching and then moving away from some point of articulation. Trills differ in length; the shortest trill, with only one flutter, is usually called a *tap* or a *scrape* depending on the contour of motion. For most Americans the *t* of *matter* or *automobile* is a voiced tap or scrape, not lasting long enough to qualify as what we would ordinarily call a stop. Trills may be voiced or voiceless, or otherwise modified by events outside of the mouth, but only rarely are such accompanying events in contrast.

The "Bronx cheer" is often a bilabial trill; this must be distinguished from bilabial *voicing*, made by pressing the lips tightly together and squeezing air through so that the lips vibrate rapidly and produce a sound of definite pitch. Neither of these bilabial articulations, however, is reported as an ordinary event in the process of speaking any language. *Uvular* trills are well attested, for example in many varieties of French, German, and Danish. If the uvula is held just too tensely, then instead of a trill one gets a spirant, but in many cases a language has a single sound-unit which is sometimes one and sometimes the other, perhaps depending on environment. No other types of trills are known to occur in a language, though phonetic virtuosos can produce several.

16. *Timing and Coordination.* We have now completed our topographic survey of the speech tract, and yet some vitally important matters have not been mentioned. These concern not the more or less clearly isolable and individually describable functionings of the different parts of the speech tract, but the timing and coordination with which various motions of different parts take place in the process of speech. Speaking is a temporal process, a succession of articulatory events in time, and any static survey of the speech tract misses many significant contrasts which appear only by virtue of the arrangement of events in time.

161. *Length.* The simplest timing contrast is that of *length*. In many languages, two utterances may be composed of exactly the same key articulatory motions, yet be distinctively different because some articulatory position is held for a longer time in one than in the other. The distinction may be made for a vocoid or for a contoid: in Italian, *fato* has a relatively long [a] and a short [t], whereas *fatto* has a shorter [a] and a longer [t]. The symbol is [·] or [:] after the letter for the longer variety: [fa·to] and [fa:to].

162. *Transition and Release.* Somewhat different is the relative timing of two articulations or changes of articulatory function in two different parts of the speech tract. In English, utterances like *big, dig, get* begin with voiced stops, but the voicing begins quite weakly and increases during the holding of the stop closure; in French, utterances like *belle, digne, gare* begin with stops which are strongly voiced from the outset. In French, *pas, tasse, cul* begin with voiceless stops, and voicing begins almost exactly as the stop closure is released; in English, *pass, touch, catch* begin also with voiceless stops, but the onset of voicing for the vowels which follow is delayed for a perceptible length of time after the

release of the stop closure, and a brief phase of voicelessness, sometimes involving some local turbulence of the air at the point of articulation of the stop, is clearly audible. For this type of stop with audible voiceless release there is a descriptive term: they are *aspirated* stops; the French voiceless stops are *unaspirated*. The common symbol for aspiration is an inverted comma: [p'].

Exactly the same factor of relative timing makes the difference between *mince* and *mints* for some speakers of English, particularly along the American east coast (for many the two words are alike). For the [n] of either word, the tip of the tongue closes against the alveolar ridge, and the velic is opened—the latter often within the preceding vowel, if indeed it has not remained open from the beginning of the word. Subsequently the velic is closed, voicing is stopped, and the tongue is moved to the apico-alveolar rill position. If the velic is closed precisely as the other two changes take place, one has *mince*; if the velic is closed as voicing stops, but tongue motion is delayed a bit, then one has *mints*.

163. *Timing of Chest Pulse.* In a great many languages (perhaps in all) the pressure of air from the lungs is not constant, but occurs in a series of pulses. The timing of these pulses relative to other articulatory motions can be very important. It may be that one of the main differences between *an aim* and *a name* (for those who say them differently even in moderately rapid normal speech) is this particular timing factor: the pulse begins after the *n* in the first, but with it for the second.

164. *Affricates.* The recognition of one variety of articulation, the kind involved in *affricates*, seems to turn largely on matters of timing, though the articulatory details are by no means clear. In (*i*)*t sh*(*ouldn't*), one has a sequence of apico-alveolar voiceless stop, usually not audibly released, followed by lamino-alveolar voiceless spirant; the beginning of the latter is accompanied by beginning of a chest pulse. In a rapidly spoken (*I'm going to hi*)*t y*(*ou*), the last word usually begins with a voiceless lamino-alveolar spirant, rather than with a *y*; this, with the preceding *t*, which may often be assimilated to lamino-alveolar position, still constitute two clearly successive articulations, even when the chest pulse for the last syllable is very slight. But in (*pi*)*tch*(*er*) one does not have what can in any sense be identified with these two versions of stop-spirant sequence; one has a unitary articulatory motion which begins with a complete stop closure, very short, in lamino-alveolar position, and passes immediately into spirantal closure in the same position, also held for a very short time. Such a close-knit stop-spirant sequence sharing a position of articulation is an affricate.

An efficient phonetic notation needs separate symbols for affricates, since they occur so very commonly. The alphabet of the IPA has never supplied them, which is an interesting reflection of the history of the IPA: their original semi-phonemicized work was done under the very large influence of French, in which affricates do not occur as unit phonemes, and of German, in which the same is probably true though many affricates occur phonetically; the presence of distinct affricates in English did not carry enough weight to tip the scales of general IPA theory. If the IPA movement had taken place in the Caucasus, or in aboriginal northwestern North America, the story would have been otherwise. A uniform source of unit symbols for affricates is to modify a spirant symbol with some constant diacritic, say a "hat" (ᴧ). This is useful in the case of an affricate for which no other symbol is available; for example, apico-interdental or apical-dental affricates with slit-spirantal offglide are very rare, but do occur, and there are no better symbols than those just described. But for apico-dental or apico-alveolar with rill-spirantal offglide the symbols [c] and [ȝ] are available; these with an underposed dot serve for apico-domal. Lamino-alveolar affricates are most often written as [č] and [ǯ], to which, once again, an underposed dot can be added for lamino-domal. Affricates with lateral release can be represented by [ƛ] and [λ].

Affricates not involving some part of the front of the tongue as articulator are much rarer, but the "cap" diacritic is always available if a symbol is needed.

Affricates seem to be subject to all the modifications by pharyngeal and glottal functions which are found for stops: paired symbols are available to indicate voiceless and voiced, and the diacritics used for stops can be used for other modifications.

165. *Glide and Peak Vocoid.* Differences of timing are also fundamentally (though perhaps not exclusively) involved in the distinction between *glide vocoids* and *peak vocoids*. In *bird*, as pronounced in the Middle West, one has a retroflex peak vocoid, a vocoid preceded and followed by articulations that last less long and which produce less clearly audible acoustic effects. But in *red* the same retroflex vocoid is pronounced quite quickly, and with the chest pulse only half-strong, followed by a non-retroflex vocoid which lasts longer and for which the chest pulse has gained full strength; the initial [r] in this case, then, is a glide vocoid. The same difference applies to the lateral vocoid in the second syllable of *battle* and that initial in *let*, or to the high front vocoid in *bit* and the *y* of *yet*. One can prolong the *y* of *yet* and obtain what sounds like *ee-et* or *ee-yet*, or prolong the *r* of *red* and get what sounds like *rr-red* or *rr-ed*. (This is a rather artificial phonetic experiment, of course, but well worth performing in articulatory analysis.) In *parade* some speakers have a clear nonretroflex vocoid before the glide vocoid [r], whereas others have simply a peak vocoid [r], contrasting with the glide vocoid [r] in, say, *pray*. Much the same contrast appears in *are* (with glide vocoid [r] after the *a*) versus a conceivable *ah-er* 'one who says "ah" all the time'.

The development of phonetic understanding and notation has been such that some of our symbols for vocoids imply glide vocoid unless specially marked, whereas others imply peak vocoid unless the contrary is indicated. "r", "l", and symbols for nasal vocoids like "m", "n", "ŋ", all in the first instance imply glide vocoids (verging on contoids, as was indicated in §150); to indicate a peak vocoid, some diacritic may have to be added. Common for this is a small circle under the letter. Vowel letters like "i", "a", or "u" imply peak vocoid unless specially marked: a small curve, concave downwards, under the letter, is often used (e.g., [i̯]). But for what might be indicated with [i̯], [u̯], and [ü̯], special letters are available: [y w ɥ].

Outside of the United States the letter "j" is far more widespread than "y" for the high front unrounded glide vocoid, and "y" is used for a high front rounded peak vocoid (instead of the symbol [ü]). The writer tends to prefer the latter usage, but in this monograph we shall follow the more prevalent current American practice.

166. *Timing in Longer Stretches.* The above paragraphs cover the most important ways in which the factor of timing and coordination makes differences between short stretches of otherwise highly similar articulatory movements. Over longer stretches, the same factor also plays a part, but by and large in less subtle ways, easier to describe. One example will suffice here. In answer to the question *Have you been to the store?* one might say *Yes, and I bought a cake.* In answer to the question *Is there any soap?* one might say *Yes, I just bought a cake.* The terminal portions of these two utterances, from *bought* on, do not sound alike. In the first, the pitch is of moderate height through *bought a*, then jumps upwards at the beginning of *cake* and falls during the word *cake* to quite low. In the second, the pitch is high at the beginning of *bought* and falls to quite low during the whole sequence *bought a cake*, more rapidly during *bought* and then a bit more slowly. In the first, *cake* begins with a slightly stronger chest pulse than *bought*; in the second, this is reversed. As can be seen, much the same articulatory motions are involved, even to the changing rates of vibration of the vocal cords and the strength of the successive chest pulses; but the precise sequence in time of these last two factors makes an essential difference between the two fragments. It is a little more difficult, but perfectly possible, to illustrate whole utterances which differ in just such ways.

The matter of the overall rhythmic effect of longer stretches of articulation cannot be overlooked, and yet it is exceedingly difficult to cover in the sort of essentially timeless topographic survey with which we have been primarily concerned. Rhythmic differences result from different temporal sequences of chest pulses of varying strengths, from varying speeds of articulatory motion, from varying arrangements of vocoids and contoids in sequence, from varying pitch-arrangements, and so on. The two examples contrasted in the preceding paragraph differ in rhythm, resulting from the factors there specified. Languages differ very greatly in their characteristic rhythms, a matter of some importance when it comes to the problem of establishing a taxonomy of phonologic systems (§2). For example, it has been pointed out that while English and Spanish both have distinctive contrasts of stress, in English there is an essentially *stress-timed* rhythm, whereas in Spanish one has a *syllable-timed* rhythm. This means that in English higher stresses in an utterance are normally separated by about equal lengths of time, no matter how many syllables with lower stresses may intervene: *Find a board for me* and *Interpret this poetry for me* each have three higher stresses, and the interval of time between *find* and *board* in the first is not much shorter than the interval between *-ter-* and *po-* in the second. In Spanish, on the other hand, an utterance of ten syllables takes approximately twice as long to say as one of five syllables, regardless of the number and location of higher stresses in either.

2. *A Typology of Phonologic Systems.* When a particular language is subjected to phonologic analysis, we find in due time a stock, not only finite but fairly

small, of *ultimate phonologic constituents*, each one a "target area" of articulatory motion, such that any utterance in the language, short or long, consists of some arrangement of elements selected from the stock. In English (and in a great many languages, though not in all) momentary closure of the lips is one ultimate phonologic constituent: in the sentence *Pay the man, Bill*, this particular element occurs three times, once at the beginning and twice medially, variously environed by other elements. The stock of ultimate phonologic constituents, and the arrangements in which they occur relative to each other in utterances, constitute the phonologic pattern of the language. As we pass from one language to another, both the stock of elements and the occurrent arrangements vary, in many different ways. Articulatory motions which are not in the stock of a particular language may nevertheless occur sporadically; they represent, so to speak, "bad aim" at a "target area" and are normally compensated for by the hearer without conscious effort.

Ultimate phonologic constituents do not occur in an utterance as the individual bricks occur in a row of bricks. Rather, they occur in clusterings, these occur in still larger clusterings, and so on, up to the level of the whole utterance. That is, the phonologic structure of an utterance shows a *hierarchic* organization, involving units of various relative size-levels: the units at any size-level save the smallest consist of arrangements of units of the next smaller size-level. In theory, the patterns involved in such hierarchic structures can be described in either of two ways: beginning at the lowest level (the ultimate phonologic constituents) and working up the scale, or beginning at the highest level and working down. Either choice entails certain difficulties, but we shall choose the second procedure, since it seems to afford a rather better basis for an effective comparison of different phonologic systems.

In the following we shall have occasion constantly to cite forms or parts of forms from various languages, in a notation which in each case is supposed to show only the phonologically relevant factors. Following current custom, we shall in general enclose such notations between slant lines (/. . ./). The symbols used in this way are for the most part those introduced in §1; any others are described as they occur. We cannot call this notation "phonemic," at least for the present; the term "phoneme" will not be officially introduced until §242. However, the distinction between the sort of notation indicated by slant lines and that indicated by square brackets is roughly the distinction customarily shown in this way in current linguistic work. In centered tables, slant lines will be omitted.

21. *Pause and Macrosegment.* When we decide to proceed, in our survey, from large to small rather than vice versa, we force on ourselves at the very outset the problem of determining how far upwards the hierarchic pattern goes. How long, in other words, can a speech-event be and still count as a phonologic unity of some sort? Since the vast bulk of linguistic investigation so far has been concerned primarily with relatively short stretches of speech, we cannot be sure that we shall find the definitive answer to this question. That is, we cannot be certain that the larger unit which we shall take as point of departure for our

large-to-small survey is actually the largest unit of phonologic relevance. All that we can do is to make a tentative guess—the alternative is to abandon the survey altogether.

If a single individual proceeds from silence to speech, speaks for a relatively short time (say a second or so), and relapses into silence, we can be reasonably sure that he has produced some sort of phonologic unity. If the duration of the speaking is considerably greater, then very often it includes perfectly clear articulatory *pauses*. In a good many of the languages which have been investigated in sufficient detail, that which occurs between successive pauses (or between the beginning of the utterance and the first pause, or between the last pause and the end of the utterance) has very much the kind of internal organization which is to be found in a whole very short utterance with no internal pauses. We therefore define such a stretch of speech to be a *macrosegment*, and say that an utterance in such a language consists of a sequence of one or more macrosegments. We shall assume that something much like this is the case in every language.

In English, a macrosegment is known to consist of two immediate constituents. One of them is an *intonation*; for the other there is no good term, and we will call it simply a *remainder*. There are a relatively small number of different intonations (certainly less than a hundred, though the precise number is not known), but a very large number indeed of different remainders—for all intents and purposes the number is transfinite. In a moment we shall deal with English intonations in greater detail, showing their internal hierarchic organization. The characteristic features which mark the end of an English intonation supplement pause as a mark of the boundary between successive macrosegments, and may very well in some instances replace it; the structural unity of the macrosegment is none the less well marked—perhaps even better—and the validity of the term is reinforced rather than weakened.

It is not known whether all languages have this same binary structure for macrosegments. Many reports on different languages pass over the matter of intonation in complete silence. A few specifically state that there are no intonational differences which can be subsumed within the description of the linguistic system, even though there are ups and downs of pitch (or of volume) which seem to be semi-organized culturally, at least to show some correlation with speaker's mood. Since detailed and effective intonational analysis is relatively recent, statements of the kind are not to be trusted; more thorough work with such languages may reveal full-fledged, if simple, intonational systems. If, indeed, there are languages in which no distinctive intonational differences are to be found, then this affords us a typologic criterion.

Not all utterances in a language conform neatly to the macrosegment-pause-intonation-remainder scheme. Almost always one is forced to recognize that some utterings are broken off before they reach a normal boundary between macrosegments. If a man is shot, or has to sneeze or hiccup, in the middle of a sentence, it is easy enough to regard the linguistically relevant event as having been cut off by an intrusive agent, and to discard the particular event as irrele-

vant for linguistic analysis. But in the normal process of speaking, such interruptions, or medial hesitations, occur with no obvious intrusive agent, and these
events cannot be regarded as unpatterned. There are even *hesitation-forms*,
varieties of speech-sound made while "pausing to think," which differ greatly
from language to language. These matters are not marginal in any statistical
sense: they occur very frequently, though more in the speech of some individuals
than in that of others. If we seem to disregard these for our analytic purposes, it is
because they are more easily described in terms of uninterrupted speaking as a
frame of reference.

If we were proceeding in accordance with what some investigators would call a
"completely objective" approach, then we would not be able to set broken fragments aside, since we should have no "objective" way to determine whether a
given bit of speech was a broken fragment or was "complete." But there seems
to be nothing to recommend this degree of so-called "objectivity": in the end,
it can at most supply us with exceedingly complex means of obtaining results
which can more quickly—and just as accurately—be obtained by taking into
consideration a certain amount of the behavior of people other than their speech
behavior in the narrow sense. When we listen to a language we do not know, we
often cannot distinguish between fragment and complete utterance; but if we
know the language, we can, and if we do not, someone who does know the
language can usually tell us. Actors often have to try to deliver lines which involve fragments, and one of the most difficult things in the realistic recitation of
the lines of a play is to make fragments sound the way they naturally do. As a
speaker of the language, the actor has all the drive towards utterance-"closure"
that any native speaker does, and the intonational and other mechanisms which
produce such "closure" are very hard to avoid when trying to deliver any pre-set
utterance or part of an utterance.

211. *English Intonation.* English intonations are built out of seven ultimate
phonologic constituents, which occur only in certain arrangements relative to
each other and relative to the remainder of the macrosegment. There are three
pitch levels (for short: PLs); three *terminal contours* (TCs); and one feature of the
all-or-none type which we shall simply call "extra height." (The number of PLs
is usually put at four rather than three, but the topmost of the usually-enumer-
ated four functions in a different way; we provide for it with our "extra height.")
The PLs are of course relative, not absolute in terms of cycles per second: a
man's voice produces the three in a lower register than a woman's, and the same
individual speaks now in one "key," now in another, with varying intervals
between the PLs.

We shall represent the three PLs with superscript numbers, from $/^1/$ for the
lowest through $/^3/$ for the highest. One of the TCs is neutral, involving simply
articulatory pause (which can be extremely short), without any rise or fall in
pitch; this one we shall write with a vertical line $/|/$—which, because of the sym-
bols we choose for the other two PLs, can be taken as an arrow shaft without
any point. A second involves normally a lowering of pitch from the last PL in
the macrosegment, accompanied by a relaxation of force of articulation—a

sort of "dying-away" effect. This one we shall represent by an arrow pointing downwards: /↓/. The third involves a rise of pitch from the last PL; the amount of rise varies a good deal without contrast, and is accompanied, not by relaxation in force of articulation, but either by relatively steady force or, perhaps, by a slight increase. Our symbol is an arrow pointing upwards: /↑/.

The above are illustrated by such examples as the following (where we transcribe only the PLs and TCs, using conventional orthography otherwise):

(normal colorless statement:) $^2It's$ $three$ $o'^{31}clock↓$

(question:) ^2Is it $three$ $o'^{33}clock↑$

(a quiet call:) $^{32}John|$ or $^{32}John↑$

(concessive, but with objections to be added:)

    $^{31}Yes↑$

(quiet approval of a question indicated by gestures rather than by words:)

    $|^{31}Yeah|$ $^3It's$ an ^{22}ash $tray↑$

The parenthesized comments are not intended primarily as descriptions of the meanings of the intonations; rather, it is intended that by following the clues afforded by the comments, and also trying to follow the intonational marking, the English-speaking reader can stand a good chance of correctly identifying the intonations which the transcriptions are supposed to represent.

It will be noticed that in each of the transcribed macrosegments two PLs are written together somewhere in the stretch. This is a purely graphic convention, and must be interpreted as follows: (1) The syllable where the two PL numbers appear is the *center* of the intonation; this syllable is at least slightly more prominent than anything before or after it. (2) The first of the two PL numbers which are written together at the center represents the PL on which that particular syllable begins. (3) The second of the two numbers represents the *reference* PL for the *end* of the macrosegment. This PL may be actually reached at the end of the macrosegment, or it may be reached slightly before the end, the remaining changing contour of pitch depending on the TC which is written at the end of the macrosegment. It is therefore necessary to discuss conjointly the last PL of the macrosegment (that is, the second of the two written together at the center) and the TC:

In the combinations /2↓/ and /3↓/, the pitch of the voice reaches the indicated PL and dies out on that level.

In the combination /1↓/, the pitch of the voice reaches the indicated PL (usually, but not always, having fallen down to it from a different PL at the center), and continues falling even lower, together with a dying-away of force of articulation.

In the combinations /1|/, /2|/, and /3|/, the pitch of the voice reaches the indicated PL and is cut off abruptly, without any dying-away.

In the combinations /1↑/, /2↑/, and /3↑/, the pitch of the voice reaches the indicated PL and then rises, the amount of rise apparently being non-distinctive.

Our notational conventions, as just in part explained, largely imply the arrangements in which the constituent intonational features (PLs and TCs) are to be found in English intonations. In a macrosegment there are two, three, or four positions for distinctive occurrence of a PL, never fewer and never more. There is always one at (or, phonetically, near) the end of the macrosegment, and there is always a TC at the end. There is always another PL at the center. There is always a PL at the beginning of the macrosegment, but this may coincide with the center, in which case we have a two-PL intonation. If the center and the beginning are distinct, we may have a three-PL intonation; or, as the last possibility, one PL may occur somewhere between the beginning and the center, giving a four-PL intonation.

The following examples show the same intonation and the same remainder, but with the center variously placed:

²I want to go ³¹there↓
²I want to ³¹go there↓
²I ³¹want to go there↓

The following is the same insofar as it can be, but as the center is at the beginning there are only two PLs:

³¹I want to go there↓

The following examples contrast a three-PL and a four-PL intonation, on the same remainder and with the center fixed:

²I've been here five ³¹minutes↓
²I've been here ³five ³¹minutes↓

Such a fourth PL (second from the beginning, in terms of linear order) is necessarily different than the PL at the beginning of the macrosegment; the syllable on which it occurs is somewhat more prominent than those before and after it, save, of course, for the syllable at the center. The PL at the beginning of a macrosegment, when it is not also the center, implies no extra prominence of the remainder at that point.

In addition to the limitation on sequence which requires that the first and second PLs of a four-PL intonation must be different, there is another limitation of importance: the last PL of the macrosegment is never higher than the one at the center. This does not mean that the pitch of the voice cannot rise between the center and the end, but when it does, the rise is interpreted as /↑/, not as a higher PL at the end. Thus in the notation of

²Is it three o'³³clock↑

the first of the two /³/'s written at the center defines the pitch at that point, while the second, together with the /↑/ at the end, mean: "pitch rises from the center to the end, reaching a point *higher than* /³/." The /↑/ means "higher than," and the second /³/ specifies "higher than what." Thus in /33↑/ there is steady rise from the center to the end; in /32↑/ there is a dip from /3/ to /2/ and then a rise; in /31↑/ and /21↑/ there is a dip down to /1/ and then a rise.

Taking these systematic limitations of sequence into consideration, we should expect eighteen different two-PL intonations (/11 21 31 22 32 33/, each with any of the three TCs); fifty-four different three-PL intonations; and 108 different four-PL intonations (the first two PLs being limited to /12 13 21 23 31 32/). Not all of these actually occur. Most, or perhaps all, of the two-PL combinations are attested, but some of the theoretically possible three-PL combinations, and a good many of the four-PL combinations, are lacking. The gaps, however, seem to reveal no possibility of further simplification.

The best way to get at the "extra height" phenomenon is to imagine, for a moment, that there are four PLs instead of three: the fourth, symbolized by /⁴/, is higher than the other three. None of the intonations which we have so far displayed or subsumed is affected by this tentative assumption, but we are able to provide for a certain number of occurrent intonations which the scheme, as so far described, cannot cover. We find, for example, such pairs as the following:

> ²*It's three o'*³¹*clock*↓ :
> ²*It's three o'*⁴¹*clock*↓ ;
> ²*Is it* ³³*three o'clock*↑ :
> ²*Is it* ⁴⁴*three o'clock*↑ ;
> ³²*John*| :
> ⁴²*John*| ;
> ³¹*Yes*↑ :
> ⁴¹*Yes*↑ ;
> ²*Are you* ³³*going*↑ ³*said* ³³*John*↑ :
> ²*Are you* ⁴⁴*going*↑ ⁴*said* ⁴⁴*John*↑ .

The second of each of these pairs differs from the first only in having /4/ wherever (and only where) the first has /3/. Furthermore, the first of each pair has /3/ at the center. If we consider intonations which have /2/ or /1/ at the center, we find no contrasts between intonations without /4/ and intonations with /4/. That is, we find a /3 21↓/, but no contrasting /4 21↓/.

This distribution renders it inefficient to treat /4/ simply as another PL. Instead, we set up a feature of "extra height," which we shall symbolize by /ᴧ/ directly before the PL-sign at the center of the intonation. This feature either occurs, or does not occur, in a macrosegment. All intonations with /3/ at the center may occur either with or without this extra feature; intonations with /2/ or /1/ at the center do not show it. The phonetic effect of /ᴧ/ is to raise any and all /3/'s in the macrosegment from [3] to [4]. Thus we can write:

> ²*It's three o'*³¹*clock*↓ :
> ²*It's three o'*ᴧ³¹*clock*↓ ;
> ²*Is it* ³³*three o'clock*↑ :
> ²*Is it* ᴧ³³*three o'clock*↑ ;

and so on. Since there are (theoretically) nine different two-PL intonations with /3/ at the center, twenty-seven three-PL intonations of this sort, and fifty-four four-PL intonations, these are the outside limits on the number of different intonations involving /ᴧ/; actually, fewer than this occur, but it does seem that every occurrent intonation with /3/ at the center is attested with /ᴧ/ as well as without it.

In the above we have dealt with English intonations directly in terms of the ultimate phonologic constituents of which they are composed. It is necessary now for us to show their hierarchic organization or IC (= "immediate constituent") structure.

This can be done very briefly. Let us consider the most complex sort of intonation, with four PLs, the /ʌ/ feature, and a terminal contour. Our first IC cut separates /ʌ/ from the rest, since every intonation with /ʌ/ is matched by a simpler one without it: /ʌ/ is "satellite" and the rest is "nucleus." The second IC cut separates the first two PLs from the one at the center, the one at the end, and the TC: every intonation has the latter apparatus, but only some intonations have the former. Therefore the first two PLs are "satellite" and the rest is "nucleus." The satellite in turn consists of the macrosegment-initial PL as "nucleus" (since it always occurs if the center is not at the beginning of the macrosegment) and the other PL as "satellite." The final two PLs and the TC, lastly, must be taken as standing in a three-part "coordinate" construction, since every intonation involves all three. Thus, the intonation of

$$^2Is\ it\ ^3three\ o'ʌ^{33}clock↑$$

is /2 3 ʌ33↑/; this is satellite /ʌ/ and nucleus /2 3 33↑/; this is satellite /2 3/ (consisting of nucleus /2/ and satellite /3/) and nucleus /33↑/; and the latter is a coordinate construction of the three ultimate constituents /3/, /3/, and /↑/. The IC structure of any simpler intonation is clearly implied by the above description of that of the most complex intonation.

212. *Other Intonational Systems.* Sierra Popoluca has an intonational system which at first appears remarkably—one might even say suspiciously—similar to that of English. Thus the system involves four PLs and three TCs, plus one "terminal feature" which is of the all-or-none type of English /ʌ/. However, the precise nature of these features and the arrangements in which they occur differ strikingly from the English system. Each macrosegment ends, by definition, with one or another of the three TCs, and this may either be accompanied or not by the "terminal feature." Apart from this, intonations fall into two sets: one-PL intonations and two-PL intonations. A one-PL intonation accompanies a remainder in which there is only one occurrence of the phoneme of stress, and the PL occurs distinctively on the syllable which bears that stress. A two-PL intonation accompanies a remainder in which there are two or more occurrences of stress: the first PL occurs on the first stressed syllable, and the second PL occurs on the last. In two-PL intonations, any of the four PLs may occur in the first position and any of the four in the second. The TCs are directions of glide of pitch from the last PL in the macrosegment to the end: one is an upwards glide, one a downwards glide, and one a suspension of the same pitch level. The "terminal feature" consists of a dying-away effect, often accompanied by whispering, but this may appear with any of the TCs, rather than (as in English) only as an integral part of one of the TCs. Certain types of macrosegment-terminal vowel-and-consonant phenomena preclude the appearance of the "terminal feature," which is thus limited just as is /ʌ/ in English, but in a very different way.

Preliminary investigation seems to show that many or most of the languages of Europe have intonational systems more or less like that of English. Many of the languages of northern Europe (French, German, and northern Slavic) seem to have three PLs and a feature comparable to English /^/—or, it may be, simply four PLs. Many of the languages of southern Europe, on the other hand (Romance except for French; Greek, Turkish, southern Slavic) seem to have systems with just two PLs plus something like English /^/—or else, it may be, three PLs and no /^/.

Very little is known of Fox intonation, but it is clear that there is at least a two-way contrast of TCs (or something more or less like TCs). One, the more frequent, is marked by voicelessness of the last syllable of the macrosegment, which always ends with a short vowel. The other is marked by voicing and high stress (and pitch?) on the last syllable, which, in the case of a certain number of interjection-like words, ends in a long vowel, otherwise in a short vowel. Nothing is known of the PLs of Fox—if any. Work in the summer of 1952 with two related languages, Shawnee and Arapaho (the first quite close to Fox) seemed to show only two PLs, and this may be the case for Fox as well.

There is, of course, no reason why an intonational system must always be built out of the types of elements which it is convenient to recognize in English and in Sierra Popoluca, and certainly no reason why the pitch of the voice should function as the principle phonetic raw-material for every intonational system. On the other hand, a language which makes phonologic use of pitch in other ways is not necessarily precluded from using it intonationally. Two examples deserve brief mention. In Mandarin, the pitch contours required by intonation are spread through the succession of syllables which individually carry pitches or contours of an accentual system (§2321), so that the actual pitch at any point is a sort of geometrical sum of the two factors. Thus the tones and stresses are identical in /tùi ma?/ 'Is that right?' and in /tùi le./ 'That's right,' both of which have been falling tone, and loud stress, on the first syllable, no tone and no stress on the second. But in the first of the two the fall of pitch is only to middle register, and the second syllable is pronounced in the middle register; in the second of the two, the fall is all the way to low register, and the second syllable is pronounced in the low register; this difference is intonational. In Mazahua Otomi the situation is quite different. Roughly speaking (a definitive purely phonologic analysis is not yet available), the last syllable of each "word" is reserved for pitches which constitute part of the intonational system, while all preceding syllables of each "word" carry pitches which are part of an accentual system.

All-or-none features, logically like the English /^/, are known in some instances where the other details of the intonational system remain obscure. The French phenomenon traditionally called the *accent d'insistence* is of this sort. This manifests itself, when present, on the first syllable of a macrosegment which begins with a consonant—thus not necessarily on the initial syllable, which may not begin with a consonant; it lengthens the consonant and places greater articulatory force both on the consonant and on the following vowel. Thus the word *impossible*, pronounced as a macrosegment with this feature, has a lengthened *p*, and the *-po-* is stressed and (probably always) has higher pitch.

Some of the above information is, of course, not very reliable. Investigators have been attempting intonational studies for a fairly long time, but earlier reports are so different in approach that they are hard to interpret, and the most recent studies show a variety of technique which clearly reflects differences among the investigators as much as, or more than, differences among the languages studied. This is all to the good, since only by trying many alternative techniques of analysis can we ever hope to develop a unified technique which will both yield valid results in individual cases and also render cross-language comparisons easier. One of the most interesting of the newer approaches is that used by Martin for Korean: he simply precedes each syllable by /↑/ if it is higher in pitch than the preceding syllable (or, if directly after pause, if it contains a rise in pitch) and by /↓/ if it is lower in pitch than the preceding (or, if directly after pause, if it contains a fall in pitch). It is impossible to judge, without extensive independent work, whether this device actually covers all the intonational contrasts of the language. In any case, quite obviously the time for a general typology of intonational systems has not yet arrived.

22. *Syllables and Juncture.* In §210 we made our initial IC-cut of macrosegments (presumably in any language) into an intonation and what we informally called a "remainder." The term "remainder" is so awkward that we shall now make a terminological shift, using henceforth the term "macrosegment" itself for what we have previously been calling a "macrosegment" *minus* its intonation. In theory, the material with which we are now to deal has been completely extricated from its accompanying intonational matrix, and we cannot be concerned even with any "side-effects" of the latter. In practice, it is of course impossible to "lift off" intonations completely unless the intonational system has been thoroughly analyzed, so that the intonationless macrosegments with which we shall now deal may in some cases include unrecognized features that are actually parts of intonation. This is the sort of risk which must be entailed if we are to proceed at all.

In every known language, a macrosegment (now and henceforth in the new, more limited, meaning) consists of one or more smaller structural units to which, by a generalization of its meaning, we shall assign the term *syllable*. It is not to be assumed that "syllables" in all languages are comparable to those of English— or to what are usually interpreted as syllables in English. In our generalized sense of the term, it will turn out that the so-called syllables of English indeed conform to the broader definition, but in other languages we will find strikingly different units which also conform to the definition.

A preliminary survey of syllables in English will serve to introduce a number of terms which will be needed in our survey of types of syllable structure.

Consider the following utterance, which in our traditional conception of English would be called monosyllabic:

Hot!   /³¹hat↓/

Lifting off the intonation leaves what we can transcribe (though not pronounce) as /hat/ (the omission of a stressmark is intentional: the transcription subsumes what is customarily called "primary" or "loud" stress; see §2311). This is a single syllable, and consists of three constituents: an *onset*, /h/; a *peak*, /a/; and a *coda*, /t/. Whether these three constituents are to be regarded as structurally on a par with each other (three ICs), or whether some two of them go together more closely and the combination in turn goes with the third, is a matter which will be taken up in §2222. As a second example, consider

$$Hot\ day! \qquad /^2hat + {}^{31}dey\!\downarrow/$$

Here there are two syllables, and each consists of onset, peak, and coda. Between the two peaks occurs a sequence of material consisting of a coda which goes with the first peak and an onset which goes with the second, and, further, an *internal open juncture* (or simply *juncture*) which marks clearly the line of demarcation between coda and onset—the point of division between the successive syllables. Successive peaks in English are not always so separated, as can be seen by comparing the following two familiar disyllabic utterances with each other:

$$Nitrate. \qquad /^{31}naytrèyt\!\downarrow/$$
$$Night\text{-}rate. \qquad /^{31}nayt + rèyt\!\downarrow/$$

In both, the first peak is /ay/, the second /èy/. In the second example, the first peak is followed by a coda /t/, and the second is preceded by an onset /r/, with an intervening juncture. But in the first example, the consonant sequence /tr/ cannot be broken into a combination of coda and onset. Rather, it constitutes another type of structural unit which we must recognize in English: an *interlude*. An interlude is coda-like and onset-like at the same time, and structurally it belongs *both* to the syllable which contains the preceding peak *and* to that which contains the following peak. When two successive syllables in a language like English are linked by an interlude, there is no "point of syllable division" between them. Typographical rules governing how to break a word between the end of one line and the beginning of the next are largely arbitrary in such cases— at least in their relation to pronunciation. Certain special styles of singing introduce a clear break; for example, in singing such a two-syllable sequence on two successive notes, one would usually sing *nitrate* as *ni-trate* or as *nite-trait*. But what this special style does is to *introduce* a juncture, at the indicated point, which is not there in normal speech.

The terms of importance introduced in the above brief discussion are "onset," "peak," "coda," "interlude," and "juncture." The best starting-point for a classification of phonologic systems as to syllable type seems to be to divide them all into two groups: those having juncture and those not having any such phenomenon. The absence of a juncture necessarily implies that there can be no contrast between medial interlude and medial coda-onset sequence; however, we shall see that it is in some cases more convenient to speak of interludes (to the exclusion of coda-onset sequences) and in other cases the reverse; in still others, the choice of terminology seems not to matter.

In the treatment of specific examples, we shall have to supply terms for structural classes of units: for example, in discussing Mandarin, we shall use the term "semiconsonant" for a set of three units which may either constitute a whole syllable (except for tone and stress, if any), or occur as onsets in syllables that include other material as well. Later on, in §242, a number of terms of this sort will be assigned rather sharp meanings for purposes of cross-language discussion and comparison. For the present, however, the terms will be defined separately for each language, with no necessary consistency in their precise use from one language to another.

221. *Systems without Juncture.* Systems of this kind fall into four subtypes: the *peak* type, the *onset-peak* type, the *onset* type, and, standing rather apart from these first three, the *duration* type. The difference (for the first three) lies in the constant or most nearly constant constituents of syllables: in the peak type, for example, every syllable, or every syllable save for a definable and limited subclass, contains a peak which contrasts positively with other possible peaks.

2211. *Peak Type.* Systems of this type are further differentiated by the nature of the phonologic material which defines (and constitutes) a peak. The following varieties, at least, are worth distinguishing: peak defined by *vocoid*; by *tone*; by *vocoid and stress*; by *vocoid and duration*.

22111. *Peak Defined by Vocoid.* In Fox there are eight contrasting peak units: /i i· e e· a a· o o·/. Every syllable peak consists of one of these eight vocoids, and every occurrence of any one of the eight constitutes a syllable peak. All other vocoids which occur in Fox are of the glide type (§165). This exact matching of syllable-peaks and a specific set of units, all of them vocoids, is what leads us to say that peaks are definable in terms of vocoids.

Initially (in a macrosegment) a peak may be preceded by no distinctive onset, or by one of the set /p t č k s š m n/, or by one of the pair /w y/, or, with some limitations, by an onset consisting of one of the first set followed by one of the pair. In final position, only the four peaks /i e a o/ occur with the most frequent TC (involving terminal devoicing; §212), but all eight seem to occur with the other TC. No final syllables have codas. Successive peaks are in all cases separated at least by an onset for the second. This onset may be any of those which occur initially, or /h hw hy/. There are also interpeak sequences consisting of /h/ plus /p t č/ or /k/, with or without a following /w/ or /y/, and of /š/ plus /k/, with or without a /w/ or /y/. Phonetically, such sequences with /h/ as the first element strike ears accustomed to English as having /h/ as a coda for the preceding peak, the remainder as an onset for the following. But structurally, since there is no possible contrast between coda-onset sequence and interlude, it does not matter which terms we use.

Senadi represents a rather different variety. Here there are seven vocoids every occurrence of which constitutes a syllable peak: /i e ɛ a ɔ o u/ There are also four nasal continuants, /m n nʸ ŋ/, which do not constitute peaks when immediately before a vocoid of the first set, but do otherwise. (These nasals are reanalyzed in §252212.) Peaks of the latter type are never preceded by distinctive onsets, but those of the former type may be so preceded or not. For five of the vocoids, /i ɛ a ɔ u/, when preceded by an onset which is not itself nasal, there is a further contrast between oral and nasal; after onsets /m n nʸ ŋ/ there is no contrast, all seven of the vocoids occurring and being nasal.

Unlike Fox, peaks may occur in immediate succession, with no intervening onset—there are no distinctive codas at all. In addition to the above, there are three *tones*, respectively high, mid, and low. The number of tone-occurrences in a macrosegment, however, does not agree with the number of syllables, since although each syllable peak bears at least one tone, a few are accompanied by a succession of two (different) tones.

Senadi borders on the variety of syllabic system in which peaks are defined by duration (or at least jointly by vocoid and duration, §22114), and might be so classed. Thus the essential difference between a two-peak sequence /àá/, the first with low tone and the second with high, and a single peak /ǎ/ with two successive tones, lies in the fact that the former takes approximately the same length of time as a sequence like /tàká/, while the latter takes approximately the same length of time as /à/ or /á/.

22112. *Peak Defined by Tone.* Bariba apparently has a system which is a kind of reversal of that in Senadi. The vocoid system (other than nasal continuants) is much the same as in Senadi. Nasal continuants /m n/ occur both as peaks and as onsets, but which is the case is not predictable in terms of what precedes and follows: /m n/ are peaks when accompanied by a tone, otherwise not. The essential ingredient of a syllable peak is thus a tone, of which Bariba has five, high, mid, low, rising, and falling; all take about the same length of time to produce. There are as many syllables in a macrosegment as there are tone-occurrences. Each peak includes, in addition to the tone, a nasal continuant /m/ or /n/ or one of the seven other vocoids. Peaks not consisting of tone plus /m/ or /n/ may have no distinctive onset or any of a number of contrasting onsets; there are no codas.

Thus both in Bariba and in Senadi sequences such as /àá/ and /ǎ/ contrast. But while in Senadi the former and the latter both include two tone-occurrences, spread differently over vocoids the presence of which marks the occurrence of a syllable peak, in Bariba the former has two successive tone-occurrences, accompanied by the same vocoid, while the latter has a single tone (the rising one), and it is the number of tone-occurrences which tells how many syllables there are.

22113. *Peak Defined by Vocoid and Stress.* In Spanish there are five *stressed* vocoids, /í é á ó ú/, which constitute syllable peaks wherever they occur. There are also five unstressed vocoids, /i e a o u/, two of which constitute syllable peaks only in certain environments. Unstressed /e a o/ occur only as peaks. Unstressed /i/ and /u/ constitute peaks except in the following cases: (1) when flanked, on either side, by a stressed vocoid or by /e a o/; (2) in the sequence /iu/ or ui/. In this latter case the sequence counts as a single peak, but it is very hard to tell, phonetically, whether the first or the second is the more prominent. That is, it is hard to tell whether a form such as *muy* 'very' (/mui/), in a context in which neither vocoid is stressed, should be interpreted as [muy] or as [mwi]. From the point of view of counting syllables, this indeterminacy does not matter.

The conventions of Spanish poetry introduce a complication into this picture. If these conventions can be regarded as sufficiently artificial, then their implications can be ignored, but this conclusion requires careful investigation. In verse, a sequence /ea ae oa ao/ or of /e/ or /o/ flanked on either side by a stressed vowel, counts as two syllable peaks if within a single word, but when a word boundary occurs between the /e/ or /o/ and the /a/ or stressed vowel, the /e/ or /o/ is not counted as a separate syllable. Thus *veo* (/béo/ 'I see') is two syllables in poetry, but *sé olvidar* (/séolbidár/ 'I know how to forget') would count as only three, not as four. Now there is no convincing evidence for an internal open juncture in Spanish. Thus if such contrasts are genuine for ordinary speech, it becomes necessary to distinguish between peak unstressed /e/ and /o/ and glide-vocoid /ȩ/ and /ǫ/, even though no such contrast exists for the high vowels /i/ and /u/.

22114. *Peak Defined by Vocoid and Duration.* In Fijian there is a set of five vocoids, /i e a o u/, which occur only and always as peaks; and every peak consists of one or another of these five. Any peak, initial or medial in the macrosegment, may be preceded by no distinctive onset or by one of sixteen contrasting onset consonants. The element of duration enters because the only difference between /a/ and /aa/, or /i/ and /ii/, or the same contrast with any other vocoid, is that the second takes approximately twice as long to say as the first. That is, the word /βaa/ 'four' takes about as long as /saβa/ 'clean', where each peak is accompanied by an onset, or /βia/ 'wish', where the two peaks differ in vocoid quality; but /βaa/ has approximately the same unchanging vowel color throughout after the /β/, with no pulsation between the two /a/'s, and this vowel color is approximately the same as that of a single /a/ followed by a syllable beginning with an onset consonant.

The difference between Fijian and Fox is instructive. Fox has both short and long vocoids, but the structure is such that a long vocoid clearly constitutes the peak of a single syllable, not two successive peaks of the duration type. In Fijian, a sequence of two identical vocoids is structurally quite like a sequence of two different vocoids. The Fijian macrosegment is marked by some differences of stress from syllable to syllable, seemingly determined in a mechanical way in terms of the positions of the various syllables relative to beginning and end of the macrosegment. In particular, the next to the last syllable is stressed (if there are at least two in the macrosegment); if the last two syllables contain identical vocoids not separated by an onset consonant, then this stress stretches through both vocoids. This statement about the location of stress in the macrosegment can only be made efficiently in terms of the syllable-peak analysis given above. To treat Fijian as having "vowel length" like Fox (or, worse, like our current impression, perhaps in part false, of Latin) is to deal with the facts very inefficiently.

2212. *Onset-Peak Type.* In all the systems so far discussed the only syllable-constituent constantly found in all syllables has been a peak, itself of one or another structure. Because of this, we would say that in each of these systems the peak is the *nucleus* of the syllable, and that any other syllable-element present in one or another instance is a *satellite*. Thus in Fijian a syllable-onset consonant is a satellite to the nuclear peak; in Cree, which resembles Fox except that some syllables have codas, a coda is a satellite to the nuclear peak.

In systems of the onset-peak type, on the other hand, every syllable contains at least both an onset and a peak. In this case, neither of these two can be interpreted as satellite to the other; the construction is, so to speak, *coordinate*. Codas, when they occur, are satellites to the onset-peak combination.

The simplest variety of onset-peak system is one in which there are no codas, so that macrosegments uniformly consist of one or more syllables each including onset and peak. Examples are not very common, but Mazateco has such a system.

Onsets are *simple*, consisting of one or another of some eighteen or twenty *consonants* (fewer before loan words were introduced from Spanish), or *complex*, consisting of certain clusters of some of these consonants. Onset clusters may contain as many as three consonants, but in most of these the cluster seems to consist of two immediate constituents, one of which in turn consists of two consonants. Peaks always involve at least one of four vocoids and one of four tones, so that the combination of vocoids and tones is coordinate; in addition, the peak may be nasalized (not distinctively after nasal onset consonants or certain other simple or complex onsets), and nasalization is to be interpreted as satellite to the vocoid-tone combination. The vocoid part of the vocoid-tone combination may consist of up to three vowels in succession, and the tonal part may consist of up to three tones in succession, but there is little coordination between the number of vowels and the number of tones. Regardless of complexity, a syllable lasts approximately the same length of time—the duration of peaks being somewhat more consistent, perhaps, than that of onsets.

Yawelmani presents a system with far fewer layers of immediate constituents, but with codas. Peaks are one or another of a set of ten vocoids, five short /i e a o u/ and five long /iˑ eˑ aˑ oˑ uˑ/; these vocoids occur only as peaks. Onsets are one or another of thirty-three contoids or glide vocoids; any of these may also occur as a coda, though a few are very rare in that function. Thus every macrosegment begins with an onset unit followed immediately by a peak unit; medially, one consonant (contoid or glide vocoid) between two peaks constitutes an onset for the second peak and the preceding syllable has no coda, while two consonants are split between the two syllables; in final position, one may have either a peak or any of the possible codas. Although there is no contrast between an interpeak coda-onset sequence and an interlude, the occurrent material between successive peaks is more easily described—and with complete phonetic accuracy—in terms of codas and onsets.

A great many phonologic systems resemble that of Yawelmani in all details except for the exact matching of onsets and codas. Often, only some of the consonants which occur as onsets also occur as codas; sometimes codas include, in addition, some sequences of two or more consonants. Except by virtue of such complex codas, it is rare to find a greater variety of codas than of onsets. Thus in Taos there are twenty-seven different onsets; nine of these are voiced, and occur also as codas, while the rest do not; there are no complex codas at all.

Nootka resembles Yawelmani save for the occurrence of long codas. Of the thirty-four consonants that appear as onsets (initially or medially, whenever a vowel immediately follows), at least twelve occur neither as nor in codas. But the consonants which do so occur turn up singly or in long strings with relatively few limitations on sequence. It may be, therefore, that Nootka should be classed with the onset type, which we are about to discuss; this possibility will be considered after an unambiguous instance of the onset type has been presented.

2213. *Onset Type.* This type of syllable structure is most unusual from our Western point of view, but seems to be undeniably attested at least in one case: Bella Coola. This language was the subject of a paper by Boas half a century ago, which is said to have been rejected by the editor of a German philologic journal on the grounds that, as "everyone knows," it is impossible to have words without vowels. Bella Coola proves that this nineteenth-century belief is false.

The key feature of Bella Coola syllable structure is that while every (or almost every) syllable has a distinctive onset, many syllables contain no other syllable-element distinctively. Some contain a distinctive peak, some a distinctive coda, and some both. Whatever occurs in a syllable in addition to the onset is to be regarded as satellite thereto; if both peak and coda are present, they stand in a coordinate construction, and the combination is then satellite to the onset.

Thus there is a set of units, *full consonants*, which constitute onsets wherever they occur, and are therefore nuclei of syllables on every occurrence. One or two of these full consonants (which total thirty) are *defective*: they occur only in syllables containing also a distinctive peak or coda. There is a set of three *semiconsonants*, /m n l/, which function now as onsets, now as codas, depending in a fairly complex but perfectly determinate way on the environment. Finally, there is a set of *vowels*, /i a u/, which occur singly or, it would seem, in sequences of two, and which constitute (singly or in pairs) syllable peaks wherever they occur.

We give some examples of Bella Coola macrosegments to show how these differently constituted syllables can occur in sequence relative to each other. A hyphen is inserted to show the point of syllable division; the hyphens are not part of the systematic notation, since their position is predictable in terms of the other symbols used, and they are included only for clarity of exposition. In /ɬ-k'ʷ-t-xʷ/ 'make it big!' there are four syllables, each consisting of onset unaccompanied by any distinctive peak or coda. Furthermore, this entire macrosegment is voiceless. The same is true in /k'-x-ɬ-c/ 'I looked'. In /s-k'l-xl-x-c/ 'I'm getting cold', two of the syllables have a distinctive coda (/l/); an automatic murmur vowel between the onset and the /l/ functions phonetically as the peak, but is phonologically predictable in terms of the onset consonant and the coda. In /ka-c'an/ 'tail' the second syllable contains both distinctive peak and distinctive coda. In /nm-nm-k'/ 'animal' and /mn-k/ 'excrement' we see semiconsonants functioning as onsets (those written initially, or immediately after a hyphen) and as codas (those written before a hyphen); here, also, there is a predictable murmur vowel as peak. The first syllable of /m-tm/ 'sea-egg' is the one variety in Bella Coola which seems not to involve a distinctive onset: that is, a syllable consisting of a preconsonantal semiconsonant initially in the macrosegment. In this connection there remain some problems of analysis; it may be that here, too, a distinctive onset has to be recognized (perhaps /ʔ/).

The clinching factor in forcing us to this interpretation of Bella Coola is the occurrence of whole macrosegments in which all the syllables consist, structurally, of distinctive onset only (cf. the first two examples given in the preceding paragraph). Supporting this is the fact that if we interpret successions of such syllables simply as "consonant clusters," then there seem to be virtually no limitations on the sequences in which consonants can occur in clusters. In every language where the peak or peak-onset interpretation suggests itself, there are such limitations, few or many (save for an occasional case of complete matching of *simple* onsets with codas, as in Yawelmani).

Yet in some cases where the second situation occurs, unaccompanied by the first, we may still prefer the onset interpretation. Let us describe Kota as though this interpretation were to be accepted. Kota has a set of eighteen full consonants, which occur only as onsets, and five semiconsonants /m n ṇ ŋ ṣ/ which occur also as codas (/ṣ/ only as coda, after a vowel before a retroflex stop /ṭ ḍ/). There are also onsets consisting of one or another consonant plus /y/. There are five vowels, /i e a o u/, and five long vowels /i· e· a· o· u·/, which occur only as peaks; all peaks consist of one of these ten, but there are syllables with a peak and syllables without. Initially in a macrosegment, syllables occur consisting of a peak without an onset—that is, vowels occur initially—and this is one structural difference from Bella Coola. Any full consonant followed immediately by another full consonant constitutes a syllable of the isolated-onset type. Phonetically, such a consonant is followed by "loose transition" to the next, producing a murmur vowel, an aspiration, or the like; phonetically, but not phonologically, this may be taken as a syllable peak. By this interpretation, the form /anžrčgčgvdk/ 'because of the fact that (someone) will cause (someone) to terrify (someone)' would not consist of one syllable, containing a peak followed by a long and complex coda, but of ten syllables, /an-ž-r-č-g-č-g-v-d-k/, most of them of the isolated-onset type.

The major structural difference between this and Bella Coola lies in the fact that every Kota macrosegment contains at least one syllable with a distinctive peak. This is apparently true also of most of the Salishan languages other than Bella Coola, which otherwise resemble the latter, particularly in having long and complicated sequences of consonant phonemes with few limitations. (Georgian also belongs here; no doubt there are others.) Such a situation implies another factor of hierarchic structure in the macrosegment: since every macrosegment contains at least one syllable with a distinctive peak, a syllable of that kind constitutes a nucleus, and any other syllables which are present are satellites to it.

This does not tell us, of course, what to do in the case of macrosegments which contain several distinctive-peak syllables. But this structural situation is very familiar though it usually turns up in the context of rather different phonologic raw-material. For example, it often happens that at least one syllable in a macrosegment must bear stress, so that in a macrosegment containing one and only one stressed syllable, any other syllables are satellites to it; if the macrosegment contains more than one stressed syllable, then we are faced with just the problem of IC-analysis stated above. This problem will be dealt with in §23.

Now we can turn back to the Nootka system. Nootka seems to occupy an ambiguous position between the onset-peak type with some codas (Yawelmani) and the onset type of Kota (if we so interpret it) rather than that of Bella Coola. There are rather more limitations on "consonant clusters" than in Kota or a Salishan language, so that it might not be too difficult to describe what occurs in terms of long and complex codas; yet certainly the relative complexity of these "clusters," despite the limitations on sequence, is reminiscent of the typical situation in Kota or Salishan. No doubt a further refinement of our typology can provide a neater categorization.

2214. *Duration Type.* Japanese has a set of vocoids, /i e a o u/, which occur only and always as syllable peaks. The statements which we made about Fijian (§22114) apply in part here: the sequence /aa/ is two syllables, rather than a single syllable with a long peak /a·/, even though phonetically what one hears for /aa/ is [a·]; the reasons are quite comparable to those stated for Fijian. In addition, however, there is a nasal continuant /ñ/ (the diacritic is arbitrary), which varies in position of oral closure depending on environment, but which is always a syllable peak: a syllable with this peak has neither onset nor coda. And, finally, there is a set of voiceless stops and spirants, /p t k c č s š x/, and an /h/, which occur both as syllables in their own right and as onset consonants. The members of this set are syllabic in the position before any other member of the same set (not all of the sequences occur); otherwise they are onsets. Thus /nippoñ/ 'Japan' takes just about the same length of time to utter as does /sayonara/ 'goodbye', where all the syllables contain onset and peak; the syllables of the first are /ni/ (onset plus peak), /p/ (acoustically a silence of approximately syllabic duration), /po/ (onset plus peak) and /ñ/ (syllabic nasal).

We cannot class this Japanese system in any of the other three types (peak, onset-peak, or onset), because the Japanese syllable is defined fundamentally in terms of duration and nothing else. A syllable consisting of a lone /p/ or /š/ cannot be broken down into anything like onset and peak; it simply lasts the proper length of time to fulfil the requirement of syllabicity.

In terms of hierarchic pattern, a Japanese syllable consisting of /ñ/ or of a voiceless stop or spirant is a satellite, since every macrosegment contains at least one syllable with a vocoid peak. /ñ/ occurs only initially before an onset consonant or medially after a vocoid; stop and spirant syllables occur only between successive syllables with vocoid nuclei, of which the second must have an onset consonant.

222. *Systems with Juncture.* The recognition by the analyst of an internal open juncture may be brought about in a number of different ways, and the methodology will be discussed later (§324). Even where juncture either must be recognized or is merely extremely convenient to recognize (and we do not insist that these two situations are distinct), there may or may not be any contrast between medial coda-onset sequences and interludes. Where there is no such

contrast, then we do not speak of interludes at all, and the juncture may be called *syllable juncture*. We shall take up this sort of situation first, and then turn to that in which interludes must be recognized.

By definition, we shall assume that the boundary of a macrosegment entails open juncture, since this renders description easier. In some instances this may be a mode of speaking rather than a phonemic conclusion.

2221. *Systems without Interludes.* Our first example here is Cantonese. In a macrosegment there are as many syllables as there are segments bounded by successive syllable junctures. Each syllable contains a single peak, which may or may not be preceded by distinctive onset, and may or may not be followed by distinctive coda. Furthermore, each syllable includes one tone.

A number of vowels, including /a/, occur only as peaks. Two units, /i/ and /u/, occur as peaks, as codas, and as onsets (or as parts of complex onsets). Three units, /m n ŋ/, occur as onsets and as codas, and also as peaks, but in the latter case only when they stand alone in the syllable except for the tone (this limitation does not apply to /i/ and /u/ as peaks). Of the consonants, /p t k/ occur both as onsets and as codas, while the rest occur only as onsets. Writing a hyphen for syllable juncture, it is possible to get such contrasts as the following:

/. . .an-a. . ./
/. . .a-na. . ./
/. . .a-n-a. . ./

—to say nothing of /. . .an-na. . ./,/. . .an-n-a. . ./,/. . .a-n-na. . ./ and the like. In the first three, we see that whether /n/ between two successive vowels is a syllable, or a coda, or an onset, depends on the number and location of syllable junctures.

This is one of the distinctive things about the Cantonese system. Since a syllable is defined by its boundaries, and since each syllable contains one and only one peak, it turns out that there is no contrast between, say, glide-vocoid [y] and peak-vocoid [i], or between onset [n], coda [n], and syllabic (peak) [n]. The unit /i/, for example, will be an onset, or part of a complex onset, if it is followed by a vowel like /a/; a coda if it is preceded by such a vowel; but will itself be the peak if the syllable which contains it does not also contain a vowel. The point of syllabic division is not predictable from the sequences of vocoids and contoids, as it is in Yawelmani; but, contrariwise, given the points of syllable division, the location of peaks is predictable.

However, this property of Cantonese is not exclusively to be found in systems with syllable juncture. The occurrent sequences of vocoids and contoids in some languages without open juncture, perhaps for example in Ojibwa, may be such that [y] and [i] are not in contrast. Nor do all systems with syllable juncture necessarily have this property. Burmese, which is in some ways much like Cantonese, has distinct and contrasting /y/ and /i/, /w/ and /u/.

The Apachean languages represent a different variety of system with syllable juncture, particularly in the functioning of tones. The fundamental description of the Cantonese syllable applies here—as it does, necessarily, in any syllable-juncture system. We supply details for Chiricahua. A syllable may have no onset, or any of twenty-nine simple onsets, or any of four complex onsets /mb nd sd šd/. It may have no coda, or any of eight simple codas /ʔ h z s ž š ł l/, or any of three complex codas /ʔs ʔš ʔł/. The three complex codas occur only before syllables beginning with an onset. The peak consists of one vocoid /i e a o/ or of certain sequences of two of these, including the geminates /ii ee aa oo/ and /ea ai ei oi ao eo/. The whole peak can be oral or nasal. Each individual peak vocoid is accompanied by one or the other of two tones (high and low pitch). There are also syllables with no onset or coda consisting of the consonant /n/ or /m/ with one of the two tones, or of the geminate cluster /nn/ or /mm/, each with one of the two tones. A syllable containing two vocoids lasts about twice as long as a syllable containing one. We may therefore introduce the term *mora*: a syllable contains one or two moras. There is no need for this term (in addition to "syllable"), save when a language shows both types of unit, as Chiricahua seems to.

The tones here function differently from any case cited heretofore. There is an exact matching between number of tone-occurrences and number of vocoid or syllabic nasal occurrences, and the duration of a syllable depends on both equally. There are more limitations as to what variety of syllable can precede or follow what other type than there are in Cantonese; one such limitation was stated in the preceding paragraph. The position of the syllable juncture is in many cases predictable in terms of the sequence of tones, vocoids, and contoids, but there is a sufficient body of exceptions to justify recognition of the syllable juncture as a separate functioning entity. Thus, in such a sequence as /. . .V-tV. . ./, there has to be a syllable juncture and it necessarily comes before the /t/; therefore a notation which left out any mark for the juncture would still be unambiguous. But in /łì-bá-í/ 'those who are gray' versus /sáí/ 'sand', one has a contrast between /a/ and /i/ in two successive syllables and the same sequence within a single syllable, and this contrast would be obliterated if the symbol for syllable juncture were omitted from the notation.

The writer knows of no case of a system with syllable juncture which does not also have tones of one kind or another. Burmese, Thai, Vietnamese, many dialects of Chinese (but not all), and a good number of less well-known languages resemble Cantonese both in the presence of syllable juncture and in having tones with whole syllables as their domain. The Apachean situation may recur in the Northern Athabascan languages. Certain of the West Coast Athabascan languages are reported to have no tones; if, apart from this, they have the kind of syllable structure typical of Apachean, then they illustrate the possibility mentioned at the beginning of this paragraph.

2222. *Systems with Interludes.* A system which has both interludes and internal open juncture necessarily has some segments flanked at both ends by that juncture, or by margin of macrosegment, but containing more than one syllable. Such we shall call a *microsegment,* and the variety of internal open juncture which bounds microsegments we shall call *microjuncture.* Syllable juncture is, then, simply a variety of microjuncture; we use the former term when microsegments and syllables are identical.

Mandarin falls, somewhat marginally, into this type. In many ways Mandarin is like Cantonese. The tones of Mandarin, like those of Cantonese, have as their domain whole microsegments. Unlike Cantonese, some Mandarin microsegments carry no tone; since in any macrosegment (with rare, interjection-like exceptions) there is at least one microsegment bearing a tone, toneless microsegments are satellites to those with tones. Also unlike Cantonese, there are a fair number of microsegments in Mandarin containing two peaks instead of just one, with an intervening interlude. Thus /srə́mə/ 'what' carries a single tone (rising), and is flanked by microjuncture but contains none; but it has two peaks, both consisting of the mid vowel /ə/, the first preceded by an onset /sr/, and the two separated by an interlude /m/. This /m/ goes with both the preceding and the following peak in a way which is, phonetically as well as structurally, much like the way the medial /m/ of English *hammer* goes both with the preceding stressed vowel and the following unstressed vowel.

Mandarin interludes are all fairly simple, and they are not numerous; in the flow of speech /m/ is probably the most frequent. Furthermore, there are apparently never more than two peaks in a single microsegment. Despite this more complex structure, it is possible, as in Cantonese, to predict the location of peaks in terms of the location of microjunctures and the intervening sequences of contoids and vocoids. Thus there is a class of two *vowels*, /ə a/, which are always peaks; there is a class of *semivowels* /i u r ü/, which occur as peaks in syllables containing no vowels, but as parts of onsets or of complex peaks when flanked by a vowel; there is a class of *semiconsonants* /s c c‛/ which occur as onsets with a distinctive peak, but which also occur as the only constituent of a microsegment save for the tone (if any), and which in the latter case are followed by an automatic peak vowel of the [ɨ] type; and there is a larger class of *consonants*, which occur only as onsets, parts of onsets, or (in a few instances) as parts of complex peaks.

There is some evidence to suggest that Mandarin has an internal open juncture of an opener variety than microjuncture—call it, say, *mesojuncture*, since if it really exists and occurs within macrosegments its occurrences break a macrosegment into one or more *mesosegments*, each in turn composed of one or more microsegments. But it is possible that a more thorough investigation of Mandarin intonation will show that the difference between this intermediate type of open juncture and either microjuncture or macrosegment-boundary, and the location of apparent mesojuncture occurrences, are both subsumable within the intonational picture. In any case, this possible mesojuncture does not materially bear on our problem here.

English is another instance of a system with both internal open juncture and interludes; the details differ greatly from those in Mandarin. In the first place, English microsegments have no unity-marking constituent comparable to the Mandarin tones. In the second place, there may be any number of peaks in an English microsegment, from none up to perhaps six or eight, though the upper extreme is not common.

A microsegment with no peaks at all does not occur as the only one in a macrosegment. Such a microsegment consists of a single consonant flanked on both sides by microjuncture. In *She's going with us* (said with emphasis on *she*), there is most usually no microjuncture between the *she* and the *'s* (/z/), but the latter is normally followed by one. But if we replace the pronoun by a proper name, say *Bea*, giving *Bea's going with us*, then there is frequently (though not always) a microjuncture both before and after the *'s*. A closer contrast is between this latter and what normally happens in *Bea's going with us was a surprise*, where the "genitive particle" /z/ added to *Bea* is seldom if ever separated from it by a microjuncture. In *He owed me ten-odd dollars* we have sequences /owd/ and /ad/, flanked by microjunctures; in one common way of saying *He oh'd and ah'd* we have, instead, the sequences /ow-d/ and /ah-d/, so that the /d/ in each of the latter instances is bounded by microjunctures. In *yacht* one has /ya . . . /; in *Well, y'oughta* one often hears /y-ɔ . . . /.

We can say either that this marginal kind of microsegment contains no syllables at all, or we can say that it consists of a single syllable of a special type, the *isolated consonant* type. The latter is probably systematically preferable, since it permits us to say that a microsegment includes one or more syllables; the former, however, makes it easier to state some of the things that need to be said about all *other* microsegments, and we shall therefore adopt it.

Every English syllable contains a peak, either *simple* (one of a number of *vowels*) or *complex* (a vowel plus a *semiconsonant* /y w h/, perhaps in some cases /r/). The vowels occur only as, or as part of, syllabic peaks, so that, as in Fox, syllables are defined by peaks and peaks by vowels. Initially in a microsegment a syllable may have a distinctive onset (*man, snow, scrimp*), or none (*each, ouch, apple*). Finally in a microsegment, a syllable may have a distinctive coda (*man, scrimp, glimpse, sixths*) or none (*day, idea*). Such a final syllable, if stressed, has either a complex peak or a coda or both; if unstressed the peak may be simple and not be followed by any coda.

Onsets consist of from one to three consonants and semiconsonants; the clusters of two and three are relatively limited. Codas consist of from one to four consonants (not semiconsonants): *thing* (1), *think* (2), *thinks* (3), *jinxed* (4). One consonant which occurs as a coda—/ŋ/—does not occur as or in any onset; another—/ž/, *rouge*—is very rare as an onset. All the consonants which occur as onsets, however, occur also as codas.

Interludes range from zero (*layer*), providing the peak of the preceding syllable is complex, through one (*manner, hammer, fatter*), two (*faster, milking, asking*), three (*pantry, empty*), to four (*subscribe*), and possibly, very rarely, more. In the case of the simplest interludes, the contrast between an interlude and a coda-onset sequence is quite clear: *minus : slyness, nitrate : night rate : dye trade*. With longer interludes the contrast is not so clear, probably largely because the forms which may contain them are pronounced now with, now without, a microjuncture at some point, even by a single speaker, with no particular functional importance.

All interludes can be divided, in at least one way, into two successive parts, the first of which occurs also as a coda, the second of which occurs also as an onset. Thus the interlude /m/ of *hammer* occurs also both as coda and as onset, and so does zero, so that this interlude can be divided either into /m/ and zero, or into zero and /m/. Similarly, the /ntr/ of *pantry* can be divided either into /nt/ and /r/ or into /n/ and /tr/. The /bskr/ of *subscribe*, on the other hand, can be divided only into /b/ and /skr/, and the /ml/ of *hemlock*, which is at least sometimes pronounced without microjuncture, can be divided only into /m/ and /l/. As has already been pointed out, the possibility of such division does not mean that an interlude can be interpreted as a coda plus an onset; thus the fact that the /tr/ of *nitrate* can be broken either into zero and /tr/, or into /t/ and /r/, does nothing to eliminate the contrast between that interlude and the coda-onset sequences of *night rate* and *dye trade*.

But phonetically the divisibility has an important implication. In interludes where only one division of the kind described above is possible, the phonetic point of syllable division is quite clear: everyone would agree that it falls between the /b/ and the /skr/ of *subscribe*, between the /m/ and the /l/ of *hemlock*. Where multiple division is possible, the phonetic point of syllable division is obscure or variable. In *pantry*, one sometimes seems to hear the /n/ as syllable-final and the /tr/ as initial, whereas at other times the point of syllable division seems to fall in the middle of the /t/. Now, structurally, the point of syllable division in an interlude is irrelevant. The purpose of this and the preceding paragraph is to show that as a phonetic phenomenon, even if partly impressionistic, both unambiguous, and ambiguous or variable, points of syllable division at interludes can be accounted for in structurally relevant terms.

Other Germanic languages have syllable patterns largely similar to that of English, though English interludes and codas perhaps become somewhat more complex.

Some of the Slavic languages also have partially similar systems. In Russian, at least, the similarity reaches the point of having some microsegments, not standing alone in the macrosegment, which consist of an isolated consonant; e.g. /v-górad^{y}i/ 'in the city', /v-aknó/ 'through the window', /s-útk^{y}i/ 'from a duck', /g-góradu/ 'towards the city'.

Finnish has a microjuncture with a special kind of phonetic marking: microjuncture is a point of onset of loud stress. Every macrosegment thus begins with loud stress, and any loud stress in the middle of a macrosegment starts at a definite place and constitutes an occurrence of microjuncture. By "at a definite place" is meant that in a medial sequence of vowel, consonant (say /n/), vowel, there are three clearly contrasting situations: /...VnV.../, with no loud stress during the particular stretch, /...V-nV.../, where loud stress begins with the /n/, and /...Vn-V.../, where loud stress begins after the /n/, with the second vowel. Microsegments consist of one or more vowel-peak syllables; onsets (by definition involving microjuncture) are relatively limited, codas even more so, but interludes achieve some complexity. Apparently the phonetic point of syllable division in an interlude is normally quite clear; but it is not possible, as for English, to divide every interlude into a part which occurs also as a coda and a part which occurs also as an onset.

23. *Accentual Systems*. At a number of points during the discussion of §22, we had occasion to refer to features present in every macrosegment of a language (or in all save a few clearly marginal ones), or to a feature or type of structure which occurs only in macrosegments which contain also some other given feature or structure. Our aim now, for the moment, is to discuss this sort of thing in greater detail.

The syllables of a system often fall into a number of mutually exclusive structural types: e.g., in Bella Coola, syllables may have only an onset, or they may include peak or coda or both; in English a syllable bears loud stress, or medial stress, or none at all. If, in any such case, a whole macrosegment may consist exclusively of (one or more) syllables of one type, that type is *isolable*; otherwise it is *non-isolable*. A type is *strongly isolable* if a whole macrosegment may consist of a single syllable of that type. In a language which has microsegments larger than syllables but smaller, on the average, than macrosegments the same terms apply to mutually exclusive structural types of microsegment

Thus in Bella Coola both onset syllables and those involving other material are isolable: witness the macrosegments /lk'ʷtx̣ʷ/ 'make it big!', /kac'an/ 'tail'. But onset syllables are not strongly isolable, and it is doubtful that peak-or-coda syllables are. In Nootka, if we interpret the system as of the onset-syllabic type (§2213), syllables with a peak are isolable, perhaps strongly so, but syllables consisting only of an onset are not. In Yawelmani, where all syllables have onset and peak, both the type with a coda and the type without are isolable. In English, syllables with loud stress are strongly isolable, but those with medial stress or with none are not isolable at all. In Cantonese, where all syllables can be classed according to which tone is present, apparently all the types are isolable. But in Mandarin, where some macrosegments have no tone, only the type with a tone is isolable.

In some cases of this kind, we are confronted with an *accentual system*. In other cases we are not. It seems very difficult to define formally the line of demarcation between the two situations. We should like a definition of "accentual system" which would include the tones of Cantonese and Mandarin, the stresses of Mandarin, English, Spanish, and perhaps the syllable peaks of Nootka. But we should not like to include also the difference between micro-segment-initial syllables with and without an onset in English, although those constitute two clearly distinguishable and mutually exclusive structural types, both of them strongly isolable. Whether or not the tones of Apachean, Mazateco, Senadi, or Bariba should be subsumed under the definition seems uncertain. The tones of these languages are encountered at a later point in the progressive IC-analysis from large to small: they are not ICs of syllables as wholes. But this is true also of the stresses of English and Spanish, which we definitely want to include. Any definition of "accentual system" in terms of the kind of articulatory material involved—say as systems involving contrasts of pitch, volume, or duration—would be of little use, since intonational systems involve such raw material, and systems of the kind we want to call "accentual" sometimes involve other types of raw material.

Instead of attempting to give a formal definition of "accentual system," therefore, what we shall do is to give, classified by several criteria, a number of examples of systems which probably ought to be subsumed under any definition finally formulated, and leave the formulation itself to the future.

We classify the systems to be described as *linear* and *non-linear*, and as systems *with* or *without zero*.

231. *Linear Systems.* In a linear system, the contrasts which are involved constitute points or regions along some single scale of articulatory or acoustic property: for example, two or more different pitches, or two or more degrees of prominence or stress, or, conceivably, presence versus absence of nasalization, glottalization, or the like.

2311. *Linear Systems with Zero.* If one of the contrasting elements of a linear system is isolable and the others are not, the system falls into this classification. Beyond this, classification can be made into two-termed, three-termed, and so on (if there are in fact any systems of this kind with more than three terms), depending on the number of contrasting points along the scale.

Spanish and Italian, for example, have isolable syllables with loud stress, and non-isolable syllables with soft stress. Many languages are like Spanish and Italian; others are like English and German, which have isolable loud stress, non-isolable medial stress and soft stress.

In the case of a two-term system, we can define one of the two as involving the *presence* of a particular structural unit, and the other as marked by the *absence* of that same unit. In a three-termed system, we can define two of the three as involving the presence of one or the other of two different units, and the third as marked by the absence of both. The usual way to do this is to say that loud stress in a language like Spanish is a positive unit, while soft stress is its absence; or that loud and medial stresses in a language like English are positive units, soft stress their absence. If we mark loud and medial stress by accents /''/ and /'/ over vowels, then our marking stands in direct relationship to this usual interpretation. Such a notational convention usually has the advantage of minimizing the number of accent marks which have to be written, since unstressed vowels, in Spanish for example, are considerably more frequent than stressed ones. And it is because of the possibility of such as interpretation that we speak of "linear systems with *zero*."

However, it is also perfectly possible, and for some purposes more useful, to regard the *absence* of loud stress as the positive entity, rather than the other way around. (The notational conventions described above can still be retained: they simply stand in a less direct relationship to the phonologic interpretation.) In English, for example, a word such as *cat* as a whole macrosegment would then consist entirely of its vowels and consonants; only in polysyllabic macrosegments would the positive entities of secondary and weak stress make their appearance. One advantage of this alternative is that accents as positive entities would only be mentioned (and transcribed, if transcription followed phonologic interpretation) in those environments in which contrasts are possible. There is no secondarily or weakly stressed *cat*, as a whole macrosegment, to contrast with the one with loud stress: secondary and weak stress are non-isolable. There are also, as it happens, some clear advantages of a morphophonemic and grammatic nature, but we cannot strictly be concerned with them in the present manual.

It is tempting to propose a general methodologic rule at this point: to prescribe that, in any linear accentual system with zero, the isolable, or strongly isolable, member be the one which is zeroed out. In our treatment of English in this monograph we shall do this, and our phonologic notation for English will accord with the interpretation: /a/ means the vowel with loud stress, /à/ the vowel with medial stress, and /ă/ the vowel with soft stress. But we are not actually proposing the suggested methodologic legislation, because it involves a degree of arbitrariness which we want to avoid. The typologic fact of importance is only that in a linear system with zero such "zeroing out" of one term is *realistically possible*, whereas in a linear system without zero it seems not to be; this will be further demonstrated shortly.

In either a two termed or a three-termed system, the occurrent arrangements of the various types of syllables so differentiated may vary a great deal. In English there is at least one loud stress in a macrosegment, and there may be more; there is at most one loud stress in a microsegment, but there may be none. A microsegment may contain secondary stresses whether or not it also contains a loud stress, and also weak stresses whether or not it contains either secondary stresses or a loud stress. The possible arrangements are very numerous, though not unlimited.

In Spanish there is at least one loud stress in a macrosegment; if the macrosegment is four syllables in length or longer, then at least one of the last four contains a stressed vowel, and most usually it is one of the last three. More than two stresses in immediate succession is very rare, if it occurs at all, but two is fairly common. Unstressed syllables are satellites to stressed syllables: those preceding the first stress of the macrosegment are satellites to that one, and those following the last stress of the macrosegment are satellites to that one, but those between two successive stresses cannot be definitely assigned, on the phonologic level, to either. Rather, they go with both, like the planets of a double star.

In some languages the first syllable of a macrosegment is always stressed; in others the last, or the last but one, always bears stress. The location of other stresses, however, remains distinctive. Finnish is not a system of this kind, since in Finnish loud stress is part of what constitutes microjuncture. But some languages differ from Finnish only in the following way: every macrosegment begins with stress, and some stresses occur medially, as in Finnish; whereas in Finnish there is a medial contrast between /...V-nV.../ and /...Vn-V.../, with the second V stressed, in these other languages there is no such contrast, the consonant immediately before a stressed vowel necessarily syllabifying with it. However, even in such a system as this we are at least able to say that unstressed syllables are uniformly satellites to the nearest *preceding* stressed syllable.

Often enough a system has predominantly a stress on every macrosegment-initial syllable, or on every macrosegment-final syllable, or in some other statable position, but with some small numbers of exceptions. Thus Hungarian always has a stress either on the first or on the second syllable of the macrosegment, and the former is the case in a much larger number of *different* macrosegments, though the text-frequency of the latter is not particularly low.

2312. *Linear Systems without Zero.* If neither (or none) of the contrasting elements of a linear system is isolable, or if both (or all) are, then the system falls into this classification. But these two situations need to be differentiated. One may imagine a language with two stress levels in which neither is isolable because the shortest macrosegment consists of two syllables, one of each kind. Logically this situation is different from that in a linear system with zero, but one suspects that in any such case the system might work, in all other respects, like one of the latter. The cases with which we shall deal here are all of the other kind: those in which both or all of the contrasting elements are isolable. Here, as in the case of systems with zero, a further classification can be made into two-termed, three-termed, and so on.

If we choose to interpret Apachean tones as an accentual system, then they constitute a two-termed system (low versus high pitch) without zero. High tone is strongly isolable: a macrosegment may consist of a single one-vowel syllable with high tone, as (Chiricahua) /tó/ 'water'. Low tone is likewise strongly isolable: /ł̩/ 'smoke'. In longer macrosegments we cannot regard occurrences of either tone as in any way satellite to some occurrence of the other tone. However, there is doubt as to whether Apachean tones ought to be interpreted as constituting an accentual system. Precisely the structural statements just made about high and low tone would apply also to the contrast between high vowel and low vowel, or to that between front vowel and back vowel: it is probably preferable to regard the two tones, the two tongue heights, and frontness versus backness of tongue position, as three contributing factors in the differentiation of vowels. The only reason to doubt this is that the two tones do also occur as differentiae with syllabic nasals, whereas the tongue positions occur only for the vowels. On the level of whole syllable peaks, of one or two units length, it would be equally valid to interpret oral versus nasal as an accentual system of the two-termed type without zero.

Loma is representative of a large number of languages with a two-termed accentual system without zero: the terms are high and low tone, as in Apachean, but seemingly these appear at the level of syllables rather than at the lower IC-level on which they function in Apachean. Senadi and Mixteco have three-termed systems (low, mid, and high tones); Mazateco has four; Trique is reported to have five, which is, so far, the maximum.

It is interesting to note that linear systems without zero seem uniformly to involve tone, rather than stress, as the predominant raw material. There may be fundamental reasons for this. Pitch levels, as used in phonologic systems, are always relative matters: a woman's pitches are all higher than a man's, and even in one person's speech some structurally low pitches can be higher than some structurally high ones. Yet there is such a thing as "absolute pitch" in the musical sense—the ability of an individual to identify in terms of the musical scale, and thus indirectly in terms of number of vibrations per second, a tone that he hears, or to produce a tone of a prescribed pitch quite accurately. Different voices, and even different concomitant circumstances of the kind that may lead a speaker to raise or lower his whole register of pitches, fall into recognizable categories, and a syllable of a tone language pronounced in isolation can usually be identified as to its structurally relevant pitch level, not only by another speaker of the language, but even by analysts who have had extensive experience with languages of the kind. The loudness scale is apparently much more purely relative, not only in speech but generally. The relative loudness of a syllable, or of any other sound, can be measured and judged only relative to the noise-level of the background in which it is presented. However, whether these considerations prove ultimately relevant or not, it is none the less a fact that stress systems, so far as is now known, are always of the type with zero, while pitch systems never are.

From a purely logical point of view it would be possible, in these systems as in those discussed in §2311, to "zero out" one of the contrasting terms. As a matter of notation, it is certainly possible to omit any positive *mark* for one of the contrasting terms. In some cases even other notational conventions are used, in order to economize on diacritics. Thus in some two-toned languages of West Africa investigators have adopted the convention of marking the first high tone in a sequence flanked by spaces in transcription (the spaces are usually nonphonologic, which does not concern us here) with an acute accent mark, and of writing acutes and graves thereafter only on a syllable which differs in tone from the preceding one. A graphic segment all on low tone then needs no mark; one all on high tone, or with no low tones after its first high tone, needs only one mark.

But we must distinguish between possible notational devices and the phonologic pattern which is represented by them. In a linear system without zero there is no structural basis for deciding which terms are positive, which term negative: one term of the set is just as positive as another. This is all the meaning that need be read into our labels "with zero" and "without zero." And this difference remains even for those analysts who, following slightly different predilections, insist that English weak stress is just as much a "positive" phonologic entity as medial or strong stress.

232. *Non-Linear Systems.* In a system of this kind the contrasts cannot be lined up along some single scale of articulatory or acoustic property. Sometimes two or more points along one such scale are involved, together with differentiations of some other kind that partly intersect. If the intersection is complete or nearly so, then instead of speaking of a single non-linear system it may be better to speak of two intersecting systems, each linear or not as the case may be. But complete intersection is rare.

A *non-linear system with zero* is one which involves contrasts along one scale, at least, some of which are non-isolable; that is, such a system looks like a partial intersection of a linear system with zero and some second system. A *non-linear system without zero* is then any other kind of non-linear system.

2321. *Non-Linear Systems with Zero.* In many Scandinavian dialects, including standard Norwegian and Swedish, there is an accentual system largely reminiscent of that in English or German: loud, medial, and weak stresses, with much the same privileges of occurrence relative to each other as in the latter languages. There is, however, a further complication: loud stresses are of two types, differing in tonal contour. Loud stress with "simple" tonal contour (the phonetic details vary from one form of Scandinavian to another) is strongly isolable; loud stress with "compound" tonal contour is not isolable at all. Every macrosegment includes at least one loud stress, but this may be that with either tonal contour, save in the case of a monosyllabic microsegment, which, as already indicated, will have the simple contour. In Norwegian, /bö·nər/ 'peasants' has the simple-contour loud stress on the first syllable; phonetically the stress is accompanied by a pitch lower than that on the following weak stressed syllable. /bô·nər/ 'beans' has the compound-contour loud stress on the first syllable; phonetically the stress is accompanied by a downwards glide in pitch, starting and ending at least somewhat lower than the pitch on the following weak stressed syllable.

A linear system with zero can be graphed as shown on the left below; the system chosen is that of English, and parentheses mean non-isolability. The Scandinavian non-linear system with zero can then be graphed as shown on the right:

	English		Norwegian
	´		´ (ˊ)
	(ˋ)		(ˋ)
	(ˇ)		(ˇ)

The transverse contrast at primary stress level in Norwegian does not force us to "zero out" weak stress; we can still proceed as in English (§2311), taking the strongly isolable ['] as phonologically nothing, the other three as positive entities. The type of contrast between ['] and /ˆ/ still remains different from that among ['], /ˋ/, and /ˇ/.

Such a diagram is the best way to present the much more complex stress-and-tone system of Mandarin, though some of the symbols require description. For the stress levels we use, in this diagram, the marks used above for English stress levels. For the tones we use, here, superscript numbers, to the right of the stress marks. /¹/ is a level tone, not low; /²/ is a rising tone, not low; /³/ is a low tone, rising terminally in some environments; /⁴/ is a falling tone; /⁵/ is a rising tone which starts and ends lower than /²/ and is accompanied by a diminuendo of force, rather than the crescendo which normally accompanies /²/. /⁵/ is quite limited, and for some speakers does not contrast with /³/ or /²/. Absence of any of these tones is represented by /⁰/:

´1	´2	´3	´4	(´5)	
(ˋ1)	(ˋ2)	(ˋ3)	(ˋ4)	(ˋ5)	
(ˇ1)		(ˇ3)	(ˇ4)		(ˇ0)

It should be remembered that the domain of a tone in Mandarin is the microsegment, not the syllable; this is true also of the stresses.

Burmese has a simpler non-linear system with zero. There are four tones, and, in context only, some toneless syllables, but apparently no stress contrasts. The system is non-linear because the tones are not simply points along the scale of pitch, but rather, as in Mandarin, fairly complex contours of level, rise, and fall, the latter at different tempos. A diagram of the system would look like this, where we number the tones arbitrarily:

$$1 \quad\quad 2 \quad\quad 3 \quad\quad 4$$
$$(0)$$

—the non-isolable weak type is put in a different line because of the non-linearity of the system.

Another system of this kind is found in Taos, where the situation resembles a partial intersection of two linear systems, one without zero (three pitch-levels) and one with (three stress-levels). Numbering the pitches from bottom to top, we can diagram thus:

$$'1 \quad\quad '2 \quad\quad '3$$
$$(`1) \quad\quad (`2) \quad\quad (`3)$$
$$(ˇ0)$$

The presence or absence of a syllable peak in Nootka can be interpreted as an accentual matter; if so, then the different vowel qualities constitute an intersecting system without zero. We can interpret vowel length as part of the accentual system too, and thus arrive at the following diagram:

$$i\cdot \quad e\cdot \quad a\cdot \quad o\cdot \quad u\cdot$$
$$i \quad\; e \quad\;\; a \quad\;\; o \quad\;\; u$$
$$(0)$$

Syllables of the non-isolable type (with no vowel as peak) occur only in sequences of one or more preceded by one of an isolable type, so that they can be regarded as satellites thereto.

The point of this last example is not, of course, to insist on the interpretation, but simply to show that the structural situation, despite its manifestation in markedly different phonetic material, is quite comparable to obvious instances of accentual systems.

2322. *Non-Linear Systems without Zero.* In Tangsic (a Wu-type dialect of Chinese) there are three tones: level, rising, and falling. All are isolable; their domain, as in Cantonese, is the whole syllable; also as in Cantonese, there are no toneless syllables.

In various other languages one can find three, four, five, six, or more contrasting tones, all or most of them isolable, constituting non-linear systems without zero. Bariba has five (§22112); Vietnamese has six; some varieties of Cantonese have eight, others nine.

In any such case the possibility must always be considered of the sort of reduction achieved for Mazateco (§2212). There, if one were simply to count the total number of tonal contours which occur distinctively on the peaks of syllables, one would end up with a system of fourteen tones. Four of these are level; eight more are rising or falling; two involve a rise followed by a fall. But the pitches at the endpoints of the rises and falls can be identified with the four level pitches, reducing the system to one of four tonemes which occur not only alone but also in sequences of two and three.

This sort of reanalysis will not work for Tangsic, since there two of the tones involve change of pitch; and only one is level. Nor would it work conveniently for Bariba, since although there are three level tones to which the endpoints of the rising and falling tones could be related, there is contrast between the rising or falling tone, on a single vowel, and a sequence of two level tones, on two successive vowels: the rising and falling tones are irreducible because they last the same length of time as any of the level tones and contrast with (reducible) contours which last longer.

There are also more complex systems for which such a reduction is, if not impossible, at least of no particular profit; and this seems to be true even of such a many-termed system as Cantonese. However, it is quite possible that further investigation into such more complex systems will change our interpretation.

24. *Syllable Peak Systems.* All languages have at least some syllables with peaks composed of distinctive and contrasting material. Quite apart from accentual matters, the syllable peaks of a language constitute a system of one kind or another, and the investigation of such systems is our program in this section. First we shall deal more systematically with the matter of *simple* and *complex* peaks: these terms were occasionally used in §22, but require refinement. Then we shall be ready to introduce the term (*segmental*) *phoneme* and labels for structural classes thereof. Then we shall survey the various kinds of peak systems which involve complex as well as simple peaks. Finally we shall classify vowel systems.

241. *Simple and Complex Peaks.* In an English microsegment like *bet*, we say that the onset is /b/, the peak /e/, and the coda /t/. In *bent*, we have the same onset and peak, but coda /nt/. In *bait* /beyt/, however, we do not speak of peak /e/ and coda /yt/, but rather of a complex peak /ey/, and coda /t/ as in *bet*. And in *bay* /bey/ we recognize the same complex peak, with no coda at all. Similarly, in microsegments such as *baying* /beyiŋ/, *bating* /beytiŋ/, *painting* /peyntiŋ/, we do not recognize interludes /y/, /yt/, and /ynt/ after a simple peak, but instead speak of a complex peak /ey/ and interludes zero, /t/, and /nt/.

The choice in such cases stems from a simple and well-known criterion in the analysis of hierarchic structures. We investigate both possible cuts between peak and coda, or peak and interlude, and see what the results would be if either were adopted definitively. Suppose that in all English syllables we were to cut immediately after the vowel. The codas (and interludes) thus tentatively recognized would fall into four sets: those beginning with /y/, those with /w/, those with /h/, and those with none of those three units; and the members of these four sets would line up, with random exceptions, like this:

/yz/	/wz/	/hz/	/z/
faze	*rose*	*gauze*	*is*

/yt/	/wt/	/ht/	/t/
beet	*loot*	*ought*	*it*

/ynd/	/wnd/	/hnd/	/nd/
fiend	*loaned*	*spawned*	*end* .

On the other hand, we would discover the most whimsical limitations as to what peaks were followed by what codas (or interludes). Peak /i/, for example, would turn out to be followed quite freely by codas of the type listed in column four above, and by codas beginning with /y/, but hardly ever—for some speakers never—by codas beginning with /w/ or /h/.

If, on the other hand, we assign postvocalic /w/, /y/, and /h/ uniformly to the preceding vowel as part of a complex peak, then the limitations on peak-coda or peak-interlude sequences become far less whimsical. It is still perfectly true, of course, that the sequence /iw/ or /ih/ is rare or nonexistent: analysis cannot fill a pigeonhole which is in fact empty, or force symmetry where there is none. But such limitations can now be covered in a simpler way. Instead of having to make long lists or complex descriptions of codas which do not follow certain peaks, one can describe all the limitations within the discussion of peaks themselves.

The criteria do not always give such clearcut answers. In the Middle-Western American variety of English, postvocalic /r/ presents a problem. Something is gained by considering the /ər/ of *fur, first, furred, firze, Bert* as a complex nucleus rather than as involving codas beginning with /r/. But there is less neatness in the overall picture when this is done than there is in the case of postvocalic /y/, /w/, and /h/. Furthermore, the case is not at all convincing for other sequences of vowel and /r/. Again in microsegments like *cute, pure, few, spew*, one may hesitate between dividing into onset /k p f sp/ and peak /yu. . ./, or onset /ky py fy spy/ and peak /u. . ./. The former suggests itself because /y/ does not occur after a microsegment-initial consonant before all vowels, but only (or largely) before /u/. On the other hand, assigning the /y/ to the onset has the advantage of pointing up the partial parallelism between onset clusters with last member /y/, /w/, /r/, and /l/.

Such vacillations between alternative ways of making a cut between ICs are not unusual. They stem not solely from inadequate methodology (though there is always room for further sharpening and clarification), but at least in part from the tremendous complexity of the object of analysis—a kind of object in which we have no right to expect absolute neatness of pattern.

In Russian, sequences such as /ay ey oy/ occur as they do in English. But the same criteria give a different answer. The "privileges of occurrence" of such sequences in Russian do not particularly resemble those of simple nuclei like /a e o/; they are much more like those of such sequences as /et em ap an/. Therefore we do not speak of complex peaks in Russian; instead, we assign postvocalic /y/ to an interlude or coda.

In some cases it does not seem to matter which way we interpret the evidence. In Cantonese, such syllable-final postvocalic consonants as /p t k/ set us up with a phonetic prejudice in favor of interpreting /. . .ap/, /. . .at/, /. . .ak/ and the like as peak plus coda, rather than as complex peak: having made this decision, then other post-peak elements must also be called codas (e.g., the /m/ of /. . .am/ or the /i/ [y] of /. . .ai/). In Mandarin, our preference is rather for treating the second elements of prejunctural /ai au ar an aŋ am əi əu ər ən əŋ əm in iŋ ün uŋ/ uniformly as parts of complex peaks—there are no syllable-final stops. But in both cases either terminology would do, since there is no contrast. (In §22 we followed the preferences just indicated.)

Distinct from these instances where the choice of terminology does not matter are cases where, logically, the question should simply not arise. For example, the presence in Fijian of articulations which sound to our ears like long vowels (such as [a·]), or like diphthongs (such as [ay], does not present us with a problem of complex peak versus peak-plus-coda. The status of these segments is solved by logically prior criteria: they turn out to consist of successive vowel units, each one of which is the peak of a syllable. In the actual chronology of analytical work, of course, one may be led to a temporary assumption that things like [a·] and [ay] in Fijian are within single syllables, and so attempt to determine whether they are peaks plus codas or complex peaks. But in due time their structurally disyllabic status should become clear, and the irrelevant question be abandoned.

242. *(Segmental) Phonemes and their Structural Types.* As most usually used in American linguistics, the term "phoneme" subsumes several classes of units: junctures, accents, and intonational features such as PLs and TCs, are all called phonemes, along with units which are of the vowel-or-consonant type. Phonemes which are not junctural, accentual, or intonational are grouped together as "segmental." Segmental phonemes are structural units of larger average size than ultimate phonologic components, but smaller average size than syllables. Generally speaking, a "simple" onset, peak, coda, or interlude consists of what is ordinarily called a single "segmental phoneme," whereas a complex one consists of two or more. Thus in English /bet/, the onset /b/, the peak /e/, and the coda /t/ are all single "segmental phonemes"; in /streŋkθ/ the onset and the coda each consist of three "segmental phonemes."

European usage sets up essentially the same sorts of different classes of units, but the term "phoneme" is used in a different way. The European "phoneme" equates, by and large, with what in America is called a "segmental phoneme," and American "suprasegmental" or "non-linear" phonemes are given other terms.

In this manual, we shall follow the European usage, not because it necessarily has any greater merit for linguistic purposes in general, but because the particular nature of our discussion renders it more convenient to use the one-word term "phoneme" instead of the longer phrase "segmental phoneme." We have already dealt with all the phonologic features of the sort which in American usage would be called "suprasegmental" or "non-linear" (§§21, 22, 23), and when subsequently we have occasion to refer to them it will always be possible to speak specifically of a juncture, an accent, a PL, or the like. Furthermore, our cover term "ultimate phonologic constituent," taken in the context of the thoroughgoing IC approach which is here being attempted, and in the context of a sort of relativism of phonemic units (§323), tends to render irrelevant most of the arguments by which proponents of either the American or the European usage have supported their ways of speaking.

The phonemes of a language fall into various structural classifications, based on similarities and differences of privilege of occurrence. It is impossible to supply any general classificatory frame of reference from which terms can be drawn in a completely consistent way for the discussion of every individual language. But some approach to this can be attempted. In a language which has only simple syllable peaks, it is usually important to know whether a given phoneme occurs only as a peak, only otherwise, or as a peak in some environments and otherwise in others. Instead of "otherwise," we can say "as *margin*," which is then shorthand for occurrence as, or as part of, either onset, coda, or interlude. General terms for the possible types of phonemes in such a case are the following:

| | occurs as: | |
	peak	margin
vowel	yes	no
consonant	no	yes
semivowel	yes	yes .

Fijian phonemes are all vowels or consonants; Senadi has also semivowels /m n nʸ ŋ/.

If a language has both simple and complex peaks, then a given phoneme in a given environment may be a simple peak, or the *nucleus* of a complex peak, two situations which we will class together; or it may be a *satellite* in a complex peak; or it may be marginal. A given phoneme may be restricted to one of these three functions, or, in different environments, it may have differing functions. The following set of terms includes three neologisms, of which one at least is not particularly apt; but some terms are needed:

| | occurs as: | | |
	peak nucleus	peak satellite	margin
vowel	yes	no	no
covowel	no	yes	no
consonant	no	no	yes
semivowel	yes	yes	no
demivowel	yes	no	yes
semiconsonant	no	yes	yes
omnipotent	yes	yes	yes .

English has vowels (e.g., /i e/), consonants (e.g. /p t m n/), and semiconsonants (/y w h/). German is similar, but has only two semiconsonants, /y h/; /w/, as in *Haus* /haws/, is a covowel. Mandarin has vowels /a ə/, consonants /p t/ etc., semiconsonants /m n ŋ/, a demivowel /ü/, and three omnipotents /i u r/. (Our generalized terminology, it will be noted, supplies no term for the special class /s c c'/ mentioned in §2222.) Spanish has vowels /e a o/, consonants, and semivowels /i u/—providing we interpret such sequences as /éi/, /ié/, /uéi/ (*rey, tierra, buey*) as complex peaks.

This terminology is inadequate for a few rare systems in which one finds what might be called *hypercomplex* peaks: an example (Totonac) will be described in the next section. It is likewise unsatisfactory for systems in which complex peaks involve a coordinate construction of two units rather than a construction of nucleus and satellite: this is the interpretation which seems preferable for the double vowels (and triple vowels) in Mazateco (§2212). But in such cases a satisfactory terminology can usually be obtained by a slight extension of meaning of the term "vowel," throwing out the terms "semivowel" and "covowel."

243. *Systems with Complex Peaks.* If complex peaks involve nucleus and satellite, then three situations can be distinguished in theory: those in which a satellite always follows the nucleus; those in which it always precedes; and those in which it either precedes or follows, though not necessarily both in the same complex nucleus. The second of these does not seem to be attested. A third actually attested situation has coordinate construction in complex peaks.

Some systems can be interpreted in more than one way. Many systems have "long vowels," for example, which can be interpreted either as short vowel phoneme plus satellite length, or as a coordinate construction of two identical short vowels in sequence. Sometimes there is clear indication as to which of these interpretations is preferable, but sometimes there is not. When there is not, then the fact that either interpretation is possible is the typologically relevant consideration. However, it is easy to jump to the conclusion that choice of interpretation is irrelevant when a more thorough examination of the facts would show that it is not. Such conclusion-jumping is naturally to be avoided; when, in the examples given below, there seems to be reasonable doubt, this is indicated.

2431. *Satellites Follow Nucleus.* An extremely widespread system is that with exactly equal numbers of simple and complex peaks, in which the phonetic difference lies primarily in quantity: simple peaks are short, complex peaks are monophthongal and long. In such a system there is approximate matching of vocoid color between a paired short and long, though there may be minor differences. For example, the four short vowels /i e a o/ of Fox are roughly [ɪ ɛ ʌ ʊ]; the corresponding longs are [i· æ· a· o·]. The proper pairing is quite obvious: two of the shorts are high, and two low; two of them are front, and two back; and the same classifications apply to the longs. The short high front and the long high front, then, belong together.

This still does not tell us, however, whether [i·] should be interpreted as /i·/, with a covowel /·/, or as /ii/, a presumably coordinate construction of identical vowel phonemes. If the former interpretation can be justified, then Fox belongs in the category now under discussion—complex peaks with satellite following nucleus. If it cannot, or if there is no more evidence for one interpretation than for the other, then some other classification is preferable.

If we take the longs to be the shorts plus a covowel phoneme of length $/\cdot/$, then the latter has what can be described as two phonetic shapes. Since [i·] differs from [ɪ], which we are asserting it contains as one constituent, by being longer and higher, the phonetic shape or *allophone* of $/\cdot/$ when it accompanies [ɪ] is that of a *raising lengthener*: both the greater height and the greater length of the long peak are assigned to the $/\cdot/$. But with the other three shorts, $/\cdot/$ appears as a *lowering lengthener*, since [æ· a· o·] are not only longer but also lower than the corresponding shorts. We are justified in saying that the $/\cdot/$ "follows" the vowel it accompanies, not just in terms of symbolism but also structurally, since there is one structurally definable position—final in normally-intoned macrosegments—in which only the shorts occur, not also the longs. By saying that $/\cdot/$ follows the vowel, we are able to state that the limitations on consonant-vowel sequence are the same everywhere. If we wanted to interpret the covowel as preceding the vowel, then we would have to say that a consonant-covowel-vowel sequence occurs only non-finally, and the limitations on sequence (e.g., the non-occurrence of $/y/$ before both $/i/$ and $/i\cdot/$) would be harder to state. It is not $/\cdot/$ which does not follow $/y/$; it is $/i/$, whether itself followed by $/\cdot/$ or not.

If we take the longs to be geminate (coordinate) clusters of vowels, then it is important to note that only *geminate* clusters of vowels occur as peaks, not also clusters of different vowel phonemes. Each vowel, in this interpretation, has two allophones: $/i/$ is somewhat higher when flanked by itself, on either side, than when not; the other three vowels are all somewhat lower as members of geminate clusters than otherwise.

Still a third interpretation is possible: the contrasts of length of nucleus can be taken as accentual. Since both short and long are isolable (though not strongly so), the system would be a two-termed linear system without zero.

So far as the writer can see, there is no convincing evidence in favor of any of these interpretations, and if this is true then that in itself is a typologic fact about Fox. An uncritical reading of the literature would yield far more examples of this type of system than are actually to be so classified. No English dialect is of this type; nor is German, nor any other modern Germanic language; nor is Latin or Greek or Sanskrit; nor is Czech or Polish or Finnish; nor is any Polynesian dialect, nor Fijian; although the literature on many of these languages and families of languages is full of talk of "short and long vowels." But even when greater care is taken there are still many genuine instances: Alabama, Badaga(?), Chitimacha, Choctaw-Chickasaw, Chontal(?), Creek-Seminole, Delaware, Fox, Hitchiti-Mikasuki, Hopi(?), Hungarian(?), Karok, Koasati, Kota, Kutenai, Miwok (Sierra and Western), some Nahuatl (Matlapa), Nootka, Oneida, Seneca, Shawnee, Tojolabal, Tonkawa, Tubatulabal, Wichita(?), Yokuts, Yuchi, Yuma, Zuni.

Sierra Popoluca has a more complex, but very symmetric, system. A simple peak is one of the six vowels /i e a o u ɨ/. A complex peak has one of these vowels as nucleus, followed by one of two satellites: a covowel /·/ or a semiconsonant /ʔ/. The parallelism of function of these two leads one to interpret long vowels as short vowel plus a covowel, and to say that the covowel /·/ structurally follows its vowel. Virtually the same codas and interludes are possible after a simple peak and after either type of complex peak. A single /ʔ/ between vowels is onset (or interlude), but /ʔ/ after a vowel, before a consonant or at end of macrosegment, is part of a complex peak. The following three examples show minimal contrast and part of the parallelism: /ʔihíkpah/ 'he dries it up' : /ʔihí·kpah/ 'he pulls it' : /ʔihíʔkpah/ 'he permits it'. Note that coda /y/ can follow complex peak with /ʔ/ : /ʔíškuy/ 'eye' : /krúʔyčih/ 'quail'.

Totonac has a more complicated system. Simple peaks consist of one of the three vowels /i a u/. Complex peaks consist of any of these plus a covowel /·/, satellite to the vowel. *Hypercomplex* peaks consist of a nucleus which is either a vowel or a vowel plus /·/, and a following satellite /ʔ/, which, as in Sierra Popoluca, is a semiconsonant, since it occurs also as an onset. The codas and interludes which can follow these various types of peaks are subject to very few limitations in terms of what type of peak precedes. Phonetically, /ʔ/ as a satellite in a peak colors the preceding vowel or vowel plus /·/, which is pronounced with glottal stricture.

All the systems so far described in this section manifest a kind of symmetry which is not by any means always to be found. For example, if we interpret the Fox system with a covowel /·/, then the peaks can be displayed in a table:

simple	complex
i	i·
e	e·
a	a·
o	o· .

Totonac peaks can be shown in a table which, though it has more pigeonholes, still has all of them filled:

simple	complex	hypercomplex	
i	i·	iʔ	i·ʔ
a	a·	aʔ	a·ʔ
u	u·	uʔ	u·ʔ .

But now let us consider Plains Cree. We begin with a table, which shows clearly the lacks of symmetry, and then describe the phonetics:

simple		complex	
i	iˆ	iˇ	iy
a		aˇ	ay
u		uˇ	uy .

The three vowels, as whole peaks, are approximately [ɪ ʌ ʊ]. /ˆ/ is a raising lengthener (covowel), so that /iˆ/ is [i·]. /ˇ/ is a lowering lengthener (covowel), so that /iˇ aˇ uˇ/ are [e· a· o·]. /y/ is a semiconsonant: /iy ay uy/ are [ɪy ʌy ʊy].

Or consider Menomini, which has six vowel phonemes and eight complex peaks, and allows of three differing interpretations. Phonetically the vowels, as whole peaks, are [i ɪ ɛ ʌ ʊ u]; the complex nuclei are [i· e· æ· a· o· u· iə̯ uə̯]. These can be lined up as follows:

simple	complex	
i	i·	iə̯
e	e·	
ɛ	ɛ·	
a	a·	
o	o·	
u	u·	uə̯

—in which /·/ is a covowel with two allophones: a *scalar lengthener* (neither raising nor lowering) after /i u/, and a lowering lengthener with the other four; and /ə̯/ is a covowel which appears only as a centering glide. Alternatively, the second allophone of /·/ could be grouped with the centering glide, which still gives two covowels. A third alternative interprets the eight complex peaks as two-vowel clusters: /ii ee ɛɛ aa oo uu/ and /ia ua/. This third is not very desirable, since it chooses the vowel /a/ for a special honor, and /a/ is not otherwise special—for example, /a/ is not a single low vowel, neutral as to front and back, set off from the other vowels which come in pairs including a front member and a back member, but is rather, specifically, the low *back* vowel, contrasting with /ɛ/ just as /o u/ contrast with /e i/. But between the other two interpretations there seems little choice. One sensible way to describe this situation is simply to say that there are three satellite elements, only two of which contrast.

In one variety of standard German we find an interesting system which can be diagrammed as follows (the peaks covered by the chart and description are those in stressed syllables):

simple	complex		
i	iy		
e	ey		eh
a	ay	aw	ah
ü	üy		
ö	öy		
u		uw	
o	oy	ow	

The vowel phoneme /a/, which is low central unrounded but not extremely low when it constitutes a peak by itself (as in *Mann* 'man'), occurs in three contrasting complex peaks: with a glide towards high-front-unrounded position in *mein* 'my', with a glide towards high-back-rounded position in *Haus* 'house', and with a lowering lengthener in *man* 'one'. This means that the system involves at least three contrasting satellites in complex peaks. Since there is no other case of greater than two-way contrast with a given vowel as nucleus, and some cases of no contrast at all, there is leeway for various interpretations. The interpretation indicated by the chart is as follows. We set up a satellite /y/

which has two allophones. After /a/ the only allophone is that already described; likewise after /o/. After /i e ü ö/ what one hears sometimes seems to be a glide towards high-front position (rounded or unrounded depending on whether the vowel is /i e/ or /ü ö/), but more often seems to be simply a raising lengthener: /iy/ usually begins and ends higher than /i/ as whole peak, and so on for the others. The ambiguity of hearing between these two allophones makes no structural difference under the interpretation we have chosen. Since /y/ occurs also as an onset, it is a semiconsonant. We set up a satellite /w/ which likewise has two allophones: after /a/ only that already described, after /o u/ either this or a raising lengthener, with the same ambiguity as for satellite /y/ after /i e ö ü/. This unit /w/ occurs only as satellite in complex nuclei, and so it is a covowel. Finally, we set up a satellite /h/ which appears after vowels only as a lowering lengthener; this unit, however, occurs as onset in forms like *Hand, Haus* 'hand, house', and so, like /y/, is a semiconsonant.

The system of any one personal variety of English is apt to show asymmetries reminiscent of those found in Cree, Menomini, and German. The writer's English could' be charted as follows:

simple	complex		
/i/ .*sit*	/iy/ *seat*		/ih/ *museum*
/e/ *set*	/ey/ *sate*		/eh/ *can* (aux.)
/æ/ *sat*	/æy/ *ash*		
/ɨ/ *just* (adv.)			
/ə/ *cup*			/əh/ *the* (stressed)
/a/ *cop*	/ay/ *sigh*	/aw/ *cow*	/ah/ *spa*
/u/ *book*		/uw/ *new*	
/o/ *wash*	/oy/ *boy*	/ow/ *no*	
/ɔ/ *calm*			/ɔh/ *law*

All three satellites are semiconsonants: cf. their occurrence as onsets in *yes, hue, well, when, hot* (/y hy w hw h/). The allophones of /h/ as satellite in complex nucleus include scalar lengthener, lowering lengthener, and centering glide.

2432. *Satellites Precede or Follow Nucleus.* In Winnebago there are five vowels which occur as simple peaks: /i e a o u/. There are five homogeneous long vocoids among the complex peaks; for reasons which we shall see in a moment, we interpret them as geminate clusters /ii ee aa oo uu/. The other complex nuclei are all considerably rarer, and a few may occur in addition to those of which we are sure enough to list. The nucleus precedes the satellite in /ae ai oe oi ei ui/: in these, /e/ and /i/ are glides not only *towards*, but *to*, the region of peak-nucleus /e/ and /i/, but are less prominent than the preceding vowel. The satellite precedes the nucleus in /oa ua ea ia uo eo io ie/: the second element is more prominent. As our transcription implies, all of these complex nuclei are interpreted as sequences of two vowel phonemes. Very occasionally more than two vowel phonemes occur in sequence: the point of division between the successive syllables is always statable. Thus in the postconsonantal sequence /ioi/, the first /i/ is a simple peak, the /oi/ a complex peak of the variety listed above. Instead of classifying the vowels to account for their behavior as nuclei or as satellites in clusters, we need only list the five of them in order of decreasing "strength": /a o u e i/. If two different vowels are present in a peak, then the "stronger" one is the peak, the other the satellite.

This picture is complicated by nasalization, which manifests itself in a peculiar way. We shall represent nasalization by a superscript /^{n}/ before the first vowel-letter of a peak: the nasalization effects not only the peak but, in some cases, the preceding onset or part of it. If the onset is /m/, then /^{n}/ is necessarily present. If the onset is /r/, then /^{n}/ may be present or not: the consonant which we are representing as /r/ is [n] when within the domain of /^{n}/, but [r] (a tap or very brief trill) otherwise. The peak influenced by /^{n}/ is nasalized as a whole, whether it includes one vowel or two, except that /e/ and /o/, occupying any position within a peak, remain oral. Thus there is no contrast between, say, /ke/ and */k^{n}e/: only the former occurs. Nor is there any contrast between */me/ and /m^{n}e/: only the latter occurs, phonetically [me] (with nonnasal [e]). But /re/ and /r^{n}e/ contrast, phonetically [re] and [ne]; and /ka/ and /k^{n}a/, or /kea/ and /k^{n}ea/, contrast, the former pair phonetically [ka] and [ką], the latter [kęa] and [kęą]. Possibly the contrast between nasal and nonnasal should be interpreted as accentual in character.

It may be that Spanish should be classed here; the problem of cutting between peak and onset, coda, or interlude is difficult (or meaningless?), but it is possible that such sequences as /ué/ in *bueno* or /ié/ in *viene*, /áu/ in *náutico*, /uéi/ in *buey*, should be interpreted as complex peaks. If so, then the satellite in a complex peak is unstressed /i/ or /u/, occurring either before or after the nuclear vowel, or both.

2433. *Coordinate Construction in Complex Peaks.* In a number of languages, complex peaks seem best interpreted as involving coordinate constructions of two units, usually members of the same structural class. In Taos the vowel phonemes which compose simple peaks are as follows:

oral		nasal	
i	u	į	ų
e	ə	ę	ǫ
a	o	ą	

These have been presented tabularly to show the lack of parallelism between the oral and the nasal set. Complex peaks are all oral or all nasal, and consist of two vowels in sequence: /ie ia uo əo įę/ (rarely /ue/, perhaps only in unassimilated Spanish loans). We are told that usually there is little difference in prominence between the two vowels of a complex peak, and that a syllable containing one takes only about as long to pronounce as one with a simple peak in the same stress and pitch circumstances.

In Apachean (Chiricahua), as we saw in §2221, a syllable peak may consist of a single vowel phoneme /i e a o/, oral or nasal, or of /n/ or /m/; a complex peak contains a geminate cluster of any of these, or a non-geminate cluster /ea ai ei oi ao eo/, oral or nasal as a whole. All the complex peaks are perhaps best interpreted as two phonemes in a coordinate construction.

Just as it is not always easy to decide, in the analysis of a hierarchically organized system, where to cut between obvious ICs, so, when the cut has been made, it is by no means always obvious whether the construction in which the immediate constituents stand is coordinate or subordinate. In the preceding section and the present one we have chosen Winnebago as the most likely candidate for vowel clusters within peaks, standing in a subordinate construction, and Taos as a likely candidate for vowel clusters within peaks, standing in a coordinate construction. The difference lies largely in the fact that in Winnebago there is reputedly a clear difference in prominence between one and the other part of the complex peak, whereas in Taos the report states, to the contrary, that normally the two constituents are about equally prominent. These may be very tenuous grounds for the differentiation; it is possible that structurally no such distinction should be made.

The problem presents itself in a more complex way in Mazateco. Setting aside the tonal constituent of a peak, and then lifting from the remainder the contrast between oral and nasal, which applies to the peak as a whole, we are left with vocalic constituents as follows: simple /i e a o/; more complex /ai ao ie ia io oi oe oa/; most complex /iai iao oia oai oao ioa ioi/. The variation in relative prominence among the constituents of these complex nuclei is extremely complicated, seeming to depend partly on which position is occupied by a particular vowel and partly on which vowel occupies the position. If the choice between subordinate and coordinate must be made, it seems best to regard all the complex nuclei—even those of three vowels—as coordinate.

244. *Vowel Systems.* In a language which has only simple peaks, there is a set of phonemes, either just vowels or vowels and semivowels, which occur as peaks. In a language which has both simple and complex peaks, we find after analysis some set of phonemes which occur as simple peaks, or as the nuclei of complex peaks, or as members of complex peaks where the construction is coordinate: these phonemes, again, may be just vowels, or may include semivowels, demivowels, or omnipotents. In any case, the set of phonemes which occur as peaks, or as nuclei in complex peaks, or as coordinate members of complex peaks, form one or more systems in terms of the ultimate phonological constituents which compose them.

To determine whether the phonemes in question constitute a single system or more than one system it is necessary to survey their privileges of occurrence, as or in peaks, under varying accentual and other conditions. In Yuma there are five vowels which occur as peaks or peak nuclei in stressed syllables; all of these occur also in unstressed syllables, but in addition there is a sixth vowel, found only in unstressed syllables, in contrast with all of the five and with zero. Here we can segregate the set of five which occur in stressed and unstressed syllables and treat them as a single system; the sixth vowel constitutes a special system in its own right. Quite similarly, the French schwa ("e muet," /ə/) seems not to pattern as one of the ordinary vowels, but as an element apart from all the rest, even though in this case it is not stress differences which are involved, but positions of occurrence relative to surrounding segmental phonemes. Where nasalization applies in some way to whole peaks or whole syllables (as in Apachean or Winnebago), it is necessary in the first instance to examine the system which occurs without nasalization and the system which occurs with it; one may find parallelism, in which case one can speak of a single system, or lack of parallelism, in which case it is often necessary to speak of two systems. The latter is the case in Taos, where oral nuclei involve six vowels in one pattern, whereas nasal nuclei involve only five vowels in quite a different pattern.

Nasal continuants (/m n/ etc), which are semivowels in some languages, seem regularly to be marked as constituting separate subsystems in their occurrences as nuclei. Thus in Chiricahua Apache nasal continuants occur as syllable peaks only in syllables with no distinctive onsets or codas, and in complex peaks only in geminate sequences, not in mixed sequences with a vowel. In most of the cases where laterals or trills are semivowels or demivowels, they are similarly ear-marked as special; this is not true, however, of the retroflex high omnipotent /r/ of Mandarin, which forms part of the regular peak system.

By a "vowel system," then, for the purposes of the present survey, we shall mean the system formed by the phonemes which occur as peaks, or as peak-nuclei, in any given language, or any one such system when there are two or more. We shall set aside subsystems represented by nasal continuants, laterals, or trills, when these occur as semivowels or demivowels, since there seems to be very little relation between these and the systems formed by the other relevant phonemes. But the term "vowel" will be used here in the sense just described, larger than the limited sense of §242.

Vowel systems can be classed in terms of the dimensions of contrast involved in them and the number of contrasting points in each dimension. The one dimension that is always present is that of tongue-height, and attested vowel systems involve two, three, or four contrasting heights. We shall therefore use this as the primary criterion for our classification. A second dimension in many cases consists of the two-way contrast between front-unrounded and back-rounded. Sometimes the contrast is only front-back, with rounding secondary; occasionally the second contrast is fundamentally rounded-unrounded, with frontness and backness secondary. When three points are involved in the second dimension, there are two cases: front-unrounded versus front-rounded versus back-rounded, involving both the factors of lip-rounding and tongue frontness and backness but only in three combinations; and front-unrounded, back-un-rounded, and back-rounded, involving the same factors but in a different set of three combinations. Sometimes central occurs rather than front in the first type, or instead of back in the second.

Such a second dimension of contrast may apply at all the tongue-heights, or only at some of them. With rare exceptions, the number of contrasts along the second dimension is never greater for a lower tongue-height than for a higher one.

If more than three contrasts are involved at any tongue-height, then one has not a single added dimension, but two: tongue frontness and backness and lip rounding or spreading working independently. To this generalization, how-ever, Mandarin is probably an exception.

By no means all the systems which are theoretically possible with the raw materials just described are actually attested. In our survey below we have assigned no system to the type with three high and three low vowels. Some systems, with /i ü u e a o/ or /i ɨ u e a o/, might be so classed, but the /a/ in any such case is typically lower than the /e o/, and we have been led to choose an interpretation with three heights. Yet such a minor difference in height is not always decisive: we class Fox as a two-by-two system despite the fact that the vowel classed as low back, /a/, is typically lower than that classed as low front, /e/. It is perhaps arbitrary to have insisted on a three-height interpretation for the systems first mentioned when allowing a two-height interpretation for languages like Fox. In the survey that follows there are doubtless various cases of arbitrary decision, and perhaps some of indisputably wrong classification.

2441. *Systems with Two Heights.* A 2+1 system (this type of coding will explain itself as we proceed) of the shape

$$\text{i} \qquad \text{u}$$
$$\text{a}$$

is reasonably common; it is reported for Arunta, Cree, Eskimo (most dialects, perhaps not all), some Arabic dialects (including Iraqi), Salishan (except Coeur d'Alene; some of the languages may have a neutral /ə/ as a separate system), Muskogean (except Creek-Seminole), Ojibwa, Kechua before the introduction of Spanish loans, Totonac, Lak, and Wishram. In Wishram, /i u/ are apparently semivowels, so that only /a/ is a "pure" vowel in the sense of the definitions of §242. The subsystem of unaccented vowels in Russian and Tunica, or of nasalizable vowels in Winnebago, Iowa-Oto, Osage, and Temoayan Otomi, is also of this type.

A 2×2 type is almost equally widespread:

$$\text{i} \qquad \text{o}$$
$$\text{e} \qquad \text{a .}$$

In Rutul the high back vowel is sometimes rounded, sometimes not, depending on environment. In the other attested cases it is always rounded: in Fox and Shawnee the low back vowel is usually unrounded, but rounded in certain environments. This system is reported, in addition to the cases already mentioned, for Apachean, Campa, Chatino nasal vowels, many dialects of Nahuatl (not Tetelcingo), Creek-Seminole (/e/ rare and limited to occurrence before /y/), and Wichita; it was probably the system of Proto-Germanic, and almost certainly that of Proto-Central Algonquian.

A 3+1 system is reported for Amahuaca:

$$\text{i} \qquad \text{ɨ} \qquad \text{u}$$
$$\text{a}$$

though the /ɨ/ may be lower than /i u/, placing Amahuaca rather with Ilocano and others (§2442).

3+2 systems occur in two varieties:

$$\text{i} \qquad \text{ü} \qquad \text{u}$$
$$\text{e} \qquad \text{a}$$

in Tabassaran and Kyuri; but with /ɨ/ instead of /ü/ in Huichol.

Turkish has a 2×2×2 system:

$$\text{i} \qquad \text{ü} \qquad\qquad \text{ɨ} \qquad \text{u}$$
$$\text{e} \qquad \text{ö} \qquad\qquad \text{a} \qquad \text{o}$$

with tongue-height, frontness-backness, and rounding-unrounding all working independently. We might describe the Apachean system as $2\times2\times2$, the third dimension being tone:

í   ó   ì   ò
é   á   è   à

but the pitch components are not confined to occurrence within this system of eight units, since the languages also have syllabic nasal continuants with one or the other of the tones. Therefore we extract the tones and regard them as separate elements, leaving merely a 2×2 system of vowels.

2442. *Systems with Three Heights.* A $1+1+1$ (or 1×3) scheme is reported for Adyge and possibly for Abkhaz and Ubykh:

ɨ

ə

a .

This is the only known type in which only tongue-height is involved. All of the vowels in the Adyge version of this system have variants which are relatively more front or back, and relatively more or less rounded, but such variations are dependent on the environment, not a part of the vowel itself.

Ilocano, Dibabaon, and perhaps some other Filipino languages have a $2+1+1$ pattern:

i   u

ə

a .

The mid vowel /ə/ has fronted variants, and also higher variants (central or back without rounding). Spanish loans have rendered the situation more complicated for some speakers.

Potawatomi has a $2+1+2$ pattern:

i   o

ə

e   a .

The mid central vowel /ə/ varies more widely from one environment to another than the other four, but there is no reason to set it off as constituting a special subsystem by itself. Nevertheless, the system resembles a 2×2 pattern with an added neutral vowel in the middle.

Probably the commonest pattern of all—certainly the most familiar—is the $2+2+1$ scheme:

i   u

e   o

a .

In Spanish, and many other cases, the second dimension for the mid and high vowels is front-unrounded versus back-rounded. For Russian, however, the second dimension is rounded versus unrounded: /i/ has central and front allophones, and /u/ back and central (or even front) allophones, and there is similar, though less marked, variation for /e o/. In Keres, likewise, the second dimension is rounded-unrounded: /i/ and /e/ are central or back, and front allophones are rare if they occur at all.

A 2+2+1 scheme, of one or another of these varieties, is reported for Awar, Badaga (with an added contrast between retroflex, partly retroflex, and non-retroflex), Chatino oral vowels, Chitimacha, Chontal, Coeur d'Alene, Czech, Erzya, Fijian, Greek (modern and early Classical, but not late Classical), Georgian, Hausa, Huasteco, Iowa-Oto oral vowels, Japanese, Keres, Kota, Latin, Miwok, Nootka, Osage oral vowels, Polish, Polynesian, Kechua (with Spanish loans), Russian stressed vowels, Spanish, Serbo-Croatian, Saho, Tagalog (the /i/:/e/ and /u/:/o/ contrasts relatively weak), Tojolabal, Tonkawa stressed vowels, most dialects of Yokuts (including Yawelmani), and Zuni. In Malay and Yuma such a system is accompanied by a neutral vowel /ə/, found in Yuma only in unstressed syllables; this was probably the pattern in Chaucerian Middle English. In Taos, Terena, Bariba, Supide, and Senadi the vowels of nasalized peaks have this pattern, those of nonnasalized peaks some larger pattern.

Cebuano Bisayan, and perhaps some dialects of Tagalog, have a system which can only be realistically set up as follows:

$$\left\{\begin{array}{ll}[i] & u \\ [e] & o\end{array}\right.$$
$$a\,.$$

[i] and [e] are both heard as allophones of a single vowel, while their parallel back vowels are phonemically distinct. Any rearrangement to show just the four vowel phonemes seems highly unrealistic from the phonetic point of view.

The 2×3 pattern is rarer:

$$\begin{array}{ll} i & u \\ e & o \\ \varepsilon & a\,. \end{array}$$

Chipewyan, Dargwa, Menomini, Persian, Ukrainian, and Yuchi have this system. Taos vowels in non-nasal peaks have a pattern differing only in phonetic details, mainly the fact that the mid back vowel is unrounded.

A 2+3+1 pattern appears in Oneida:

$$\begin{array}{lll} i & & u \\ e & ə & o \\ & a\,. & \end{array}$$

/ə/ and /u/ are nasal, the other four oral, but there seems to be no better way of setting them up. No distributional characteristics set /ə/ and /u/ up as over against the other four.

A 2+3+2 pattern appears in Lifu:

$$\begin{array}{lll} i & & u \\ e & ə & o \\ æ & a\,. & \end{array}$$

The 3+2+1 pattern is attested in two versions, depending on the combination of front-back and rounded-unrounded found in the "central" high vowel:

$$\begin{array}{lll} i & ü & u \\ e & & o \\ & a & \end{array}$$

in Taki-Taki, late Classical and early Medieval Greek; but

i ɨ u
e o
a

in Cashibo, Bulgarian, Mazahua Otomi nasal vowels, Mixteco, Sierra Popoluca, and Zoque.

3+2+2 pattern occurs in some Bulgarian dialects and perhaps in Votyak:

i ɨ u
e o
ɛ a .

The other version of this (with /ü/ instead of /ɨ/) is not attested.

The 3+3+1 pattern with /ü/ is fairly common:

i ü u
e ö o
a

in German, Dutch (some dialects, and overall pattern for standard Dutch), Hungarian (some dialects), French (some dialects, particularly in the south), Zyryan. In Terena the vowels of oral syllables have the other version, recurrent in Maidu and Romanian:

i ɨ u
e ə o
a .

Votyak may belong here rather than in the 3+2+2 type. In Terena the seven-way contrast appears only before /h/; in all other environments (as for the vowels of nasal syllables) /ɨ/ and /ə/ are lacking, and the system reduces to the 2+2+1 type.

Both versions of the 3+3+2 pattern are attested: Finnish and some Hungarian dialects have

i ü u
e ő o
æ a ,

while Cuitlateco and perhaps some dialects of Korean have

i ɨ u
e ə o
a ɔ .

If Korean dialects have this pattern, the low vowels are front /æ/ and back /a/, rather than unrounded /a/ and rounded /ɔ/ as in Cuitlateco.

The symmetrical 3×3 pattern is apparently also attested in two versions. In Trukese, Thai, Temoayan and Mazahua Otomi, and English:

i ɨ u
e ə o
æ a ɔ ,

but in Esthonian:

i ü u
e ö o
ɛ ɔ̈ ɔ .

In Mandarin there appears a 4+1+1 system in which front-back and round-ing-unrounding do not function separately:

i ü r u

ə

a .

/r/ is a high strongly retroflexed vocoid, which, like the other three high vowels, occurs both as a peak and in margins. The mid and low vowels vary from front (unrounded) to back (with or without rounding) depending on environment.

Koibal, Karagin, and possibly some dialects of Korean have a system describ-able as 2×(2+2+1):

i   ü   ɨ   u

e   ö   ə   o

æ   a .

Standard Korean is skew in lacking the /ü/, though the remaining vowels fall obviously into this pattern. (Cf. the skewness of Cebuano Bisayan, above.) In some dialects the /ü/ may occur as a separate phoneme; in others it is known that both /ü/ and /ö/ are lacking, which places those dialects in the 3+3+2 pattern.

There is some evidence suggesting that certain dialects of Old English had the following scheme:

i   ü   ɨ   u

e   ö   ə   o

æ   a   ɔ .

As displayed, this would be describable as (2+2+1)+(2×3). Naturally, details are obscure: in particular, it is not clear whether the vowel listed as /ɔ/ was rounded or merely back.

2443. *Systems with Four Heights.* A 2+1+1+1 system is reconstructed by Fairbanks for the Old Slavic of the Zographensis manuscript (oral vowels only):

i   u

ə

ʌ

a .

The higher-mid, lower-mid, and low vowels all have variants differing as to front-back or rounding or both, dependent on environment. Thus /ʌ/ after a palatal consonant was (roughly) [e], but after a plain consonant was [o]. This system is not attested for any language known through direct observation, but it is sufficiently reminiscent of the 1×3 system of Adyge, the 2+1+1 system of Ilocano, and the 4+1+1 system of Mandarin to qualify easily as a "realistic" reconstruction.

The 2+2+2+1 system is reasonably frequent:

i   u

e   o

ɛ   ɔ

a

in Italian, late Latin (?), some dialects of Portuguese (oral vowels), Tunica stressed vowels, Loma, Kiowa, Tetelcingo Nahuatl, and the oral syllables of

Bariba, Senadi, and Supide. In Loma the second dimension of contrast is unrounded and rounded: /i e ɛ/ have both front and central (or possibly back) allophones, whereas /u o ɔ/ are always rounded and back. In the other cases /i e ɛ/ are front unrounded.

Different Polish dialects are said to represent both versions of the 2×4 scheme:

i	u		i	u
e	o	and	e	o
ɛ	ɔ		ɛ	ɔ
æ	a		a	ɒ ;

in the first, the fundamental second-dimension contrast is between front and back, while in the second it is between rounded and unrounded.

Some Portuguese dialects have a 2+2+3+1 pattern in oral syllables:

i		u
ɵ		o
ɛ	ʌ	ɔ
	a .	

With nasalization, /ɛ a ɔ/ do not occur, and the system simplifies to 2+2+1. In other dialects the contrast between /ʌ/ and /a/ is lacking and one has a 2+2+2+1 pattern in nonnasal syllables.

The Lyster dialect of Norwegian is reported to have a 3+3+3+1 system:

i	ü	u
e	ö	o
ɛ	œ	ɔ
	a .	

Some conservative French dialects, and perhaps some dialects of Danish and Norwegian, have a 3+3+3+2 pattern resembling that just displayed except that the bottom row includes /æ/ and /a/. Still other Danish dialects seem to have a symmetric 3×4 system, the bottom row /æ a ɑ/. The crosswise contrasts for the lowest vowels in this case is not the same as those for the higher vowels: /æ/ is front, /a/ central, and /ɑ/ back but perhaps not rounded.

2444. *Skew Systems.* Uncertainties of classification, such as for Votyak, and holes in otherwise neat patterns, such as the absence of /ü/ in varieties of standard Korean which have an /ö/, are normal enough. But there are also some reports which apparently describe completely skew vowel systems which will fit into no classification of the sorts worked out above. We must suspend judgment in these cases: perhaps the investigator has erred, but perhaps he is quite accurate and really skew systems indeed exist.

One example is Hopi. Whorf sets up six vowel phonemes. Two, /i/ and /a/, are fairly clear. There is an /e/ which varies between mid and low front unrounded. And there are three vowels which vary between mid and high: central unrounded /ə/, front rounded /ö/, and back rounded /o/.

Another example is Chahar Mongol, for which the report gives: lower high /i/, /ɨ/, /u/; higher mid /ö/; mid /o/; higher low /ə/, /ɔ̆/, /ɔ/; low /a/; intersecting this, front unrounded /i/; unrounded central to back /ɨ/, /ə/, /a/; rounded front /ɔ̆/; rounded central /ö/; rounded back /u/, /o/, and /ɔ/.

2445. *Double and Multiple Systems.* In §§2441-3 we separated subsystems, such as that in stressed and that in unstressed syllables, and treated each independently. Here we summarize the types of multiple systems which are attested.

The contrast of nasal and oral exactly doubles the number of vowels in Apachean (2×2, all either oral or nasal) and in Yuchi (2×3, all either oral or nasal). In no instance are there more nasal than oral contrasts. In Winnebago, Iowa-Oto, and Osage, the oral vowels form a 2+2+1 system and the nasalized (or nasalizable) vowels a 2+1 system. In Bariba, Supide, and Senadi the oral vowels form a 2+2+2+1 system and the nasal (or nasalizable) vowels a 2+2+1 system. The same holds for some dialects of Portuguese; others have a 2+2+3+1 system for oral vowels. In Terena, oral vowels before /h/ form a 3+3+1 system, but elsewhere, and with nasalization, the back unrounded vowels are lacking and the system is 2+2+1. In French the ratio of oral to nasal vowels is quite high (the number of the former depending on dialect); some dialects have a 3+1 nasal system /ę/, /œ̨/, /ǫ/, /ą/, others a 2+1 system without the /œ̨/. French is quite unique in that the nasal system involves only relatively low vowels; in most languages where nasal vowels occur, at least the highest and lowest of the oral vowels are matched fairly closely by nasal vowels.

Taos, Chatino, and Mazahua Otomi stand apart in that the nasal vowels cannot in any sensible way be paired off with oral vowels, but must be taken as constituting a totally different pattern. Thus Taos has a 2×3 oral system, but a 2+2+1 nasal system; Chatino has a 2+2+1 oral system but a 2×2 nasal system; Mazahua Otomi, finally, has a 3×3 oral system but only a 3+2+1 nasal system.

Badaga is the only language for which contrasts of retroflexion are attested as playing a major role; the three-way contrast exactly intersects the 2+2+1 basic vowel system.

It is rather common for fewer vowels to occur in unstressed syllables than in stressed: Russian has 2+2+1 in stressed syllables, but only 2+1 in unstressed; Tunica 2+2+2+1 in stressed, but only 2+1 in unstressed. But it also happens that a language may have more contrasts in unstressed position. Yuma has a 2+2+1 set of vowels stressed or unstressed, and a /ə/ only unstressed; Middle English was perhaps the same.

French and Malay both have a /ə/ in addition to their principal vowel systems. This is not separated from the principal vowel system by occurrence relative to stress, because neither language has any accentual system, but in both cases certain special phonetic and distributional features mark the /ə/ off.

2446. *Hierarchical Structure in Vowels.* In any simple vowel system, or any simple subsystem of a double or multiple system, there seems no reason to regard the construction in which the ICs stand as other than coordinate. That is, in a 2×3 system, for example, we regard the frontness and the height of /i/ as of coequal importance, rather than taking either as a satellite to the other.

On the other hand, in a double or multiple system there is often reason for regarding the members of all subsystems but one as involving an attributive construction. Thus in Yuchi, where there is a 2×3 system of oral vowels and an identical system of nasal vowels, we would interpret /į/ as nucleus /i/ and *simultaneous* satellite /./; in Badaga we would regard any half-retroflexed or fully retroflexed vowel as consisting of a non-retroflex vowel as nucleus and the degree of retroflexion as satellite.

This also applies in any case where the phonetically more complex subsystem forms a neat selection of some of the possibilities of the phonetically less complex. Thus the fact that Winnebago /e o/ are not subject to nasalization does not prevent us from regarding /i a u/ as consisting of /i a u/ under the influence of a nasalization factor (§2432). However, where the two subsystems are incommensurate, as in Taos, this particular type of componential analysis is not possible.

Following this clue, we might decide to treat Russian stresses in the same fashion in which we decided, in §2311, to treat English stresses: set up a phoneme of absence of stress, for example on the second vowel of /gorát/ 'city', rather than a phoneme of stress on the first vowel (/górat/). Doing this does not render unstressed vowels phonetically more complex, but it renders them by fiat *structurally* more complex, and paves the way for saying that only /i a u/ can be modified by the simultaneous satellite /ˇ/, just as in Winnebago only /i a u/ can be modified by nasalization. A consistent following of this procedure would then require us to describe Yuma with a phoneme of stress, since of the six vowels which occur unstressed, only five (all but /ə/) occur stressed.

Simultaneous satellites in vowels then come to occupy a status structurally comparable (in part) to sequential satellites in complex peaks (§243). This is particularly desirable because in some instances what is phonetically a simultaneous satellite turns out to be in complementation with something else, just as the directional glide in English complex peaks /ay ey oy/ is in complementation with the onset glide vocoid in *yes*. Some French dialects, particularly in the south, have no contrast between [ę] and [en]; the nearest approach to the latter is [enə], and it is advisable to treat the former as structurally /en/, the latter as /enə/ (similarly, of course, for the other nasalized vowels of the dialect). This treatment does not destroy the distinction between (phonetic) simultaneity and successivity, but it capitalizes on a complementation and portrays the actual network of contrasts more efficiently; /en/ remains a complex peak, not a simple peak followed by a coda.

25. *Syllable Margin Systems.* By the two classifications of phonemes in §242, the phonemes which occur as margins (as or in onsets, codas, or interludes) in a language which has only simple syllable peaks are either consonants or semivowels; and, in a language which has both simple and complex peaks, either consonants, semiconsonants, demivowels, or omnipotents. We wish now to consider the systems into which these phonemes, in any one language, enter, *in their marginal roles*, regardless of whether they also occupy other roles in other environments. For this purpose we shall generalize the term "consonant" to subsume any phoneme which occurs in or as a margin, when so occurring—with one exception: glide vocoids which are allophones of phonemes which occur as syllable peaks or as nuclei in complex syllable peaks (Chinese /i u ü r/) are excluded. These have already been covered in our survey of vowel systems, by the special definition of "vowel" used for that purpose. It will be noted that

covowels were not covered in that survey and are also not covered here: they occupy a special sort of status, where they occur at all, dealt with adequately in §2431.

The consonants (in our generalized sense) of any one language fall into various *distributional classes* depending on their privileges of occurrence relative to each other in simple and complex onsets, codas, and interludes. The determination of these distributional classes goes hand in hand with the examination of the variety of structure found in margins. The same consonants fall into certain *constitutional classes* depending on the ultimate phonologic constituents of which they are composed. In analytic work these two matters have to be investigated together, since otherwise one cannot tell, for example, whether an affricate [c] is a unit phoneme or a cluster /ts/ or /ty/, or whether a glottalized consonant, say [k'], which occurs as an onset, is to be interpreted as simple (one phoneme) or as complex (a cluster of /k/ and /ʔ/). However, the methodology will concern us later; it need only be pointed out here that questions of this sort are not always equally important—though they must always be asked, for one cannot even discover that they are unimportant without asking them.

251. *Distributional Classification.* No general typology for distributional classes of consonants can be offered. In some languages this matter is extremely simple, in others extremely complex, and the complexities vary from one case to another in the most whimsical way. We shall, however, give several examples (beyond the hints in §221).

2511. *The Simplest Situations.* In Fijian, all onsets consist of a single consonant, and consonants occur only as whole onsets. Therefore the only distributional classification of consonants is into a class which includes them all. This is the case, or nearly so in a good many other languages, including some which have codas or interludes as well as onsets. In Yokuts, for example, any consonant may occur as an onset or as a coda; the only limitation is that the glottalized sonorants /m' n' l' w' y'/ occur only directly after a vowel. This sets these aside as a special distributional subclass; otherwise all are in the same class.

In Fox the occurrent onsets and interludes can be charted as follows:

p	t	č	k	s	š	h	m	n	
pw	tw		kw	sw	šw	hw	mw	nw	w
py			ky			hy	my	ny	y
hp	ht	hč	hk						
hpw	htw		hkw						
hpy			hky						
			šk						
			škw						
			šky						

All of these occur as interludes; those in the first three rows, except /h hw hy/, occur also as onsets. It seems reasonable to call the single-phoneme units *simple* margins; to call the two-phoneme units in which /w/ or /y/ is the second *complex* margins, with the /w/ or /y/ a satellite to what precedes; and to call the units in which /h/ or /š/ precedes a stop (whether a /w/ or /y/ follows or not) *hyper-complex* margins, with the /h/ or /š/ satellite to the simple or complex unit that follows it. The labels ("simple, complex, hypercomplex") are of no importance, but the assertion that the clusters are of the subordinating type rather than co-ordinate, and that the direction of satellite-nucleus relationship is of one kind rather than another, is roughly in keeping with our general habits of usage of these terms in the analysis of hierarchic structures. We break a three-termed cluster such as /hpy/ first into /h/ and /py/ because of the greater freedom of occurrence of the latter—initially in macrosegment as well as medially.

A first distributional classification of Fox consonants would then be: (1) /p t č k/, which occur after a satellite; (2) /s m n/, which occur before but not after a satellite; (3) /š h/, which occur before but not after a satellite, but also as preposed satellites; (4) /w y/, which occur as postposed satellites. A finer-grained distributional classification would ultimately set up a separate class almost for each consonant, since no two (save only /m n/) have exactly identical privileges of occurrence.

Mazateco has only onsets, but these attain a fair degree of complexity. *Simple* onsets include all the single consonants, a few of which occur only in this role (e.g., /p b/, only in Spanish loans). The consonants which occur both as simple onsets and in complex ones are /t k c č ç v y m n nʸ s š h ?/. *Complex* onsets are /nt nk nc nč nç sk št šk šn/. Since there is greater variety in the second member of these than in the first, we may perhaps say that the first is satellite to the second; for /šn/ this is dubious, and perhaps it should be taken as coordi-nate. *Hypercomplex* onsets consist of a simple or complex unit preceded or fol-lowed by /h/ or /?/: /ht hk hc hč hç hv hy hm hn hnʸ hnt hnk hnc hnç/, /th kh ch čh çh vh mh nh sh šh nth nkh nch nčh nçh/, /?v ?y ?m ?n ?nʸ ?nt ?nk ?nc ?nč ?nç/, /t? k? c? č? ç? v? y? m? n? nʸ? s? š? nt? nk? nc? nč? nç? sk? št? šk?/. Here we interpret /h/ or /?/ as satellite. There are also two onsets, /hc? hč?/, which we interpret as nuclear /c č/ with a satellite on either side. Rougher or finer distributional classifications can be deduced from these data.

2512. *More Complicated Cases.* All of the above examples are fairly simple. In a language which has, in addition to onsets, fairly complex codas or interludes or both, the situation can become extremely complex, even if the total number of individual consonant phonemes is not very large. This is true, for example, in English. Often, despite the complexity, certain generalizations can be made as to what occurs and what does not. In many languages which have a contrast such as that between voiced and voiceless for some consonants, it will happen that only voiced consonants, or only voiceless consonants—of those that pair off—will occur in a single onset, coda, or interlude. This is almost true in English: it holds for onsets, but there are codas /dθ/ (*width*) and /dst/ (*midst*) in which it does not hold, and many such interludes. Some speakers pronounce these words with /tθ/ and /tst/, and for them the generalization holds for codas. In standard Polish and in Portuguese the statement holds throughout. In Russian it holds save for the pairs /f v/ and /fʸ vʸ/: the voiced members of these pairs occur both after voiced phonemes and after voiceless phonemes (of those that pair).

Another commonly found limitation applies in clusters in which the first member is a nasal continuant and the next is a stop: only such clusters occur as have continuant and stop in the same position of articulation. This applies in Spanish and in many other languages.

In any such case it is often convenient to set up one's phonologic units differently. Since voicing and voicelessness apply not individually to the paired consonants, but to any sequence of one or more flanked by other phonemes (unpaired consonants, vowels, junctures), one may halve the number of consonant phonemes and recognize voicing, or voicelessness, as an additional phonemic unit, having as its domain that which we have just described. If we do this in Polish, for example, we set up "voicing" as a sort of accentual phoneme; writing this with a diacritic /ˇ/ after the string of consonants affected, we write /. . . asa . . ./, /. . . asˇa . . ./ (instead of /. . . aza . . ./); /. . . atfa . . ./, /. . . atfˇa . . ./ (instead of /. . . adva . . ./); and so on. There is the additional advantage that /ˇ/ is never written before microjuncture, and this automatically covers the fact that voiced consonants, of those that pair off as voiced and voiceless, never occur before microjuncture. There are, of course, other ways to state this structural fact, but this way seems to subsume as many different relevant structural considerations as possible at once.

2513. *Correlation between Constitution and Distribution.* We must note also that the distributional classification of consonants often correlates, at least in part, with the constitutional classification. In Fox even the finest-grained distributional classification leaves /m/ and /n/ together: constitutionally, this is the class of nasal continuants. A looser classification leaves /w/ and /y/ together, but isolated from all the other consonants: /w/ and /y/ form the constitutional class of glide vocoids in Fox. /p t č k/ form a distributional class in that /h/ can precede any of them as satellite: /p t č k/ is the constitutional class of stops and affricates. In Mazateco, /h/ and /ʔ/ are members of a single distributional class, and they go together constitutionally as "glottalic" consonants.

It is only when there is some correlation, of this kind, between distributional and constitutional classes that a change of phonemicization, of the sort proposed above for paired voiced and voiceless consonants in Polish, can be undertaken. And often there is at least some lack of correlation. English has a constitutional class of nasal continuants, /m n ŋ/: the former two go together fairly well distributionally, but /ŋ/ stands quite apart, since /m n/ occur as onsets and in complex onsets, while /ŋ/ does not.

Let us see what the correlation is in Mandarin. Distributional class (1), /p pʻ m t tʻ/, includes those consonants which occur alone or with following /i/ or /u/ in onsets. Class (2), /n l/, go alone or with following /i u ü/. Class (3), /c cʻ s/, go alone or with following /i u ü r ru/. Class (4), /f k kʻ x/, go alone or with following /u/. Class (5), /ŋ/, goes only alone. Now (1) includes labial stops and nasal, and also apical stops, but not the apical nasal. The two members of (2) are both apical continuants, and there are no others. (3) contains all the sibilants: two affricates and one spirant. Class four includes the dorsal stops and spirant—but also the labial spirant. Thus there is some correlation, better in some spots than in others, but far from complete and exact.

The correlation is worst—or best—when no distributional classification is possible at all; that is, when all the consonants occur in all possible positions, as in Fijian or Yawelmani. It is at its worst in the sense that there are no distributional considerations to aid the analyst in deciding just how to distinguish between simple and complex margins (e.g., in the case of a [c] which may be a unit /c/ or a cluster /ts/). It is at its best in the sense that there are no distributional considerations to interfere with a decomposition of the consonants into ultimate phonologic constituents and a classification of the consonants on the basis of those constituents: the constitutional classification is the only one that counts, and some possible questions about "unit or cluster" lose their meaning. We will illustrate this with Fijian.

Fijian onsets include /t k ᵐb ⁿd ⁿg β ð m n ŋ s r ⁿr l w y/. Four of these, /ᵐb ⁿd ⁿg ⁿr/, sound like clusters to speakers of English. They could be so interpreted: the first three let us say as phonemically /mp nt ŋk/, setting up /p t k/ as phonemes which are everywhere stops but are voiced or voiceless depending on environment, or else as /mβ nð ŋγ/, setting up /β ð γ/ as phonemes which are everywhere voiced but are stops or spirants depending on environment. The first of these requires adding a /p/, which does not occur otherwise in Fijian (save in the speech of some, in recent loans). The second requires adding a /γ/, which does not occur at all (save as a free variant of /k/). Either of these interpretations, or the one originally indicated which takes the prenasalized consonants as units, does no violence to the system: the choice has to be based purely on considerations of esthetics or "elegance," which reside in the analyst, not in the data, or else has to be suspended. The only reason that we do not like to suspend the choice is that our current terminology and techniques render it difficult to describe a system which is determinate just to the point to which Fijian is, but in which further questions of the "phoneme or cluster" type are irrelevant.

But this apparent indeterminacy is encountered only because all the Fijian consonants belong to a single distributional class. If /ᵐb ⁿd ⁿg/ occurred only medially, not initially and medially, then they would form a separate distributional class of consonantal entities, and the cluster interpretation would have more to support it—even if /m n ŋ/, like all other consonantal units, did not occur otherwise save before a vowel.

252. *Constitutional Classification.* Consonantal systems are highly varied and, in some cases, quite complex. It does not seem feasible to handle them as wholes for constitutional classification; it seems better to develop some manner of breaking them up into subsystems. Of course, the particular way in which we shall do this is in no sense the sole "correct" way, and can no doubt be improved on.

In order to illustrate our approach, let us tabulate the consonants of Ossetic:

p	t	c	č	k	
pʻ	tʻ	cʻ	čʻ	kʻ	
b	d	ʒ	ǯ	g	ʔ
f		s	š	x	
v		z	ž	γ	
m	n				
w	y	r	l		

In the upper left-hand box we have included all consonants which are stops, affricates, or spirants in at least some environments. This set constitutes the *obstruent system* of the language. In the lower left-hand box we have included nasals, semivowels, laterals, and trills—the *sonorant system* of the language. The upper right-hand box includes all consonants produced in pharynx or glottis —in this case, just one consonant. We shall use the already physiologically meaningless term *laryngeal* as a cover term for these last.

A generalization of this yields our organization for most consonantal systems. We include among the obstruents not only all stops and affricates and most spirants, but also, in some cases, a [y]-like, [w]-like, or [l]-like consonant if it fits neatly into the scheme, and if distributional facts do not militate against such a treatment. On the other hand, a [v]-like spirant sometimes seems to pair off distributionally with a [y]-like glide, and so may belong to the sonorants. In a few cases a simple two-way partition of all consonants (apart from laryngeals, if any) does not fit the facts, and a more complicated set-up is required.

Sometimes one or more of the laryngeals count as *manner consonants*, in the sense that they match one or another of the styles of delivery found for obstruents. For example, in Nootka /ʔ/ matches the obstruent set /p' t' c' č' ƛ' k' k'ʷ q' q'ʷ/, while /h/ matches the obstruents /s š ł x xʷ x̣ x̣ʷ/. Occasionally a manner consonant is not a laryngeal: for example, the /y/ of Russian, which matches the whole set of palatal consonants as over against the plain consonants.

In a few cases all the consonants, apart from manner consonants (if any), must be otherwise dichotomized in the first instance, the classification into obstruent and sonorant coming second. To illustrate this we tabulate the Lifu system:

p	t		ṭ	č	k	
f	θ	s		š	x	h
M	N			ɲ	Ŋ	
W	L					
b	d		ḍ	ǯ	g	
v	ð	z		ž	γ	
m	n			ɲ	ŋ	
w	l					

Here the contrast between voiceless and voiced is operative throughout the system except for /h/; the latter is a manner consonant and pairs off with the whole set of voiceless obstruents and sonorants. Distributional classification supports the constitutional grouping indicated above: only voiced consonants (and all of them except /w ŋ g γ v/) occur finally. (An alternative, worthy of serious consideration, is to regard the voiceless set as clusters of the voiced set and /h/; one could then say that /h/ occurs finally neither after a vowel nor after a consonant.) Syllable structure is almost as in Fijian: vowel, or consonant plus vowel, except for the sprinkling of final consonants.

We shall begin our survey of the constitutional classification of consonant systems with obstruents; then we shall deal with sonorants; then with manner consonants and laryngeals.

2521. *Obstruent Systems.* The usual classification of obstruents is according to *manner* and *position*. Thus, in the table of Ossetic obstruents in §2520, all those in a single row (say /p t c č k/) share a manner (voiceless unaspirated, sometimes glottalized), while all those in a single column (say /p p‘ b f v/) share roughly the same position (labial). Similarly, we could tabulate the obstruents of either Lifu half-system as follows:

$$p \quad t \qquad \underset{\cdot}{t} \; č \quad k$$
$$f \quad \theta \quad s \qquad š \quad x \; .$$

A simple way to classify obstruent systems would be to tabulate each system in this way, with rows and columns marked. There would then be several relevant typologic considerations: (1) the number of columns; (2) the position or range of positions for each column; (3) the number of rows; (4) the manner or range of manners for each row; (5) holes—as, in Ossetic, the lack of any spirants to match the apical stops.

We are going to follow a slightly more complicated procedure, though it is not certain that the information gained by it is either clearer or better. As one point of reference we shall be concerned with the number and variety of positions of articulation for *stops*; positions for spirants will be judged against this. But before dealing with manners we shall first perform another operation.

This preliminary operation consists in deleting from the tabular array of obstruents those which will leave a rectangular array with all pigeonholes filled, and listing the deleted obstruents separately. In each case, we shall do this in whatever way yields the largest rectangular array. In Ossetic, for example, we could obtain a rectangular array of three rows of five entries each by deleting the eight spirants; but we can obtain an array of five rows of four columns each by deleting the three apical stops. The latter is a larger array than the former (20 pigeonholes in the 5×4, only 15 in the 3×5), so we choose the latter rather than the former. If the consonants deleted in this initial operation allow of a second comparable operation, we perform the operation again. In Ossetic the leftovers do not allow any reapplication of the procedure, but in some cases they do.

Any rectangular array obtained in this way is a *symmetric set*. A number of obstruent systems include no symmetric set at all; at least one consists of a single symmetric set. The number of non-intersecting symmetric sets included in an obstruent system, and the size of the largest, relative to the whole number of obstruent phonemes, are a rough measure of the symmetry of the system.

In surveying manners, we shall be concerned only with the nature of the manner-contrasts within a symmetric set. This yields results somewhat at variance with what might otherwise be obtained. In Yawelmani, for example, it is possible to find a four-way manner-contrast recurring in the set /c c’ c‘ s/, in

/ç ç' ç' ş/, and in /k k' k' x/. However, the largest symmetric set which can be excised from the obstruents of Yawelmani does not include /s ş x/, which are, instead, the leftovers. Therefore we are concerned only with a three-way manner-contrast in the language.

In a few cases symmetric sets of equal size can be drawn from the whole obstruent system in either of two ways. This is the case for Latin, Takelma, Sierra Popoluca, Hungarian, Supide, and Georgian. Each of these will be dealt with in both of the possible ways, since our criteria, as stated above, afford no grounds for choice.

Systems like Lifu, where some single contrast in effect doubles the number of consonants, will be treated here in terms of "half-systems"—that is, the obstruents of whichever half includes more. But systems in which it is necessary to make a three-way primary classification of non-laryngeal consonants, in place of the two-way grouping into obstruents and sonorants, will be left until after our discussion of sonorants.

25211. *Stop-Position Systems.* All known languages have at least some consonants which are stops at least in some environments. In the survey of stop-positions which follows, we shall use the symbols usually associated with voiceless stops ("p," "t," "k," and so forth) to represent positions; it is not to be deduced from this that the languages in question necessarily have *voiceless* stops, or even that they necessarily have stops at all listed positions for all manners.

We shall take up, first, systems in which there occur only "pure" stops. A great many languages have phonemes which are phonetically affricates but which obviously go with the "pure" stops as additional "positions." Systems of this sort we shall consider second. Some languages have affricates which are single phonemes rather than clusters, but which count as manners rather than as additional positions; these, of course, will be dealt with in conjunction with our discussion of manner systems.

Apart from affricates functioning as "positions," some languages have what we shall call color-modified stops (labialized velars and the like). When these are units rather than clusters, they invariably function as additional "positions."

Finally, some languages have coarticulated stops, which likewise seem always to function as "positions" rather than as manners.

252111. *Pure Stops Only.* There is but one known language which has only two positions: Hawaiian, with bilabial /p/ and lingual /k/. There is evidence that some decades ago the latter was pronounced freely either as [t] or as [k], and this is why we characterize it merely as "lingual." Today, the dorsal closure is apparently regularly used, which is why we choose the symbol "k." We might also describe the two stops as labial and non-labial. So described, the contrast recurs in the nasals, /m/ and /n/, though the latter is regularly apical. There is no manner of articulation (for obstruents or sonorants) for which more than two positions are in contrast. We may therefore safely chart the stop-position system thus:

p   k .

In Samoan (barring recent loans), only the stops /p/ and /t/ occur, and in

Fijian (with the same proviso) only /t/ and /k/. However, the situation in these languages is not like that Hawaiian, since a three-way position contrast appears elsewhere in each system: Samoan /m n ŋ/, Fijian /m n ŋ ᵐb ⁿd ⁿg/. Our chart of stop positions for Samoan should then be

$$p \quad t \quad —$$

and for Fijian,

$$— \quad t \quad k \,,$$

where the dashes indicate a position which occurs distinctively somewhere in the system, though not for stops.

A three-position system of the pattern

$$p \quad t \quad k$$

is of course extremely widespread; it is attested for Breton, Cheyenne, Dibabaon, Dutch, Finnish, French, German (standard and the dialect of Brienze), Ilocano, Latin, Maidu(?), Marshallese, Portuguese, Tagalog, Takelma, Taki-Taki, Terena, Isthmus Zapotec.

Four-position systems are not so common. South Greenlandic Eskimo has

$$p \quad t \quad k \quad q \,;$$

Keres and Campa have

$$p \quad t \quad t^y \quad k \,;$$

and Bororo has

$$p \quad \d{t} \quad t \quad k \,,$$

where the second position is apico-labial. The recent report of this is the only reliable evidence to show that such a position of articulation functions in speech anywhere.

Five-position systems are extremely rare. Kota has

$$p \quad \d{t} \quad t \quad \d{t} \quad k$$

(/t̪/ interdental); but it also has a pair of phonemes which are sometimes spirants and sometimes affricates: [s]∼[č] and [z]∼[ž]. We may not be justified in setting these aside; perhaps properly we should treat Kota in the next subsection.

252112. *Systems with Affricates as Positions.* We classify these with a pair of numbers, the first specifying the number of pure stop positions and the second that of affricate positions.

A 2-1 system is found in Oneida, Seneca, and Cherokee:

$$t \quad k$$
$$c \,.$$

In Seneca and Cherokee /c/ varies between apico-alveolar (like /t/) and lamino alveolar; in Oneida it is always [č]. These languages lack all labial phonemes, and the 2–1 scheme looks like part of the far more widespread 3–1 scheme which adds a bilabial stop. Four main varieties of 3–1 system can be distinguished. Supide has

$$p \quad t \quad k$$
$$\hat{f} \,,$$

the only clearly attested labial affricates (i.e., voiced and voiceless) as unit phonemes—and there is residual doubt even here. The other three systems all have a tongue-front affricate of some sort, but we can distinguish between

apico-alveolar, lamino-alveolar, and a type which varies (as in Seneca). Thus
we have

$$p \quad t \quad k$$
$$c$$

in Kiowa;

$$p \qquad t \quad — \qquad k$$
$$č$$

in Fox and English;

$$p \qquad t \quad — \qquad k$$
$$[c] \sim [č]$$

in Menomini and Cree.

These last three cannot always be distinguished from our reports. Languages
which have one or another of the three include: Alabama, Amahuaca, Arapaho,
Arunta, Burmese, Chickasaw-Choctaw, Cree, Creek-Seminole, Crow, Dakota,
Delaware, English, Fox, Hidatsa, Hitchiti-Mikasuki, Iowa-Oto, Kaingang,
Karok, Kiowa, Koasati, Korean, Kraho, Mandarin, Menomini, Ojibwa, Osage,
Potawatomi, Shawnee, Spanish, Thai, Tunica, Winnebago, Chukchansi Yokuts.

One 3–2 system is quite common:

$$p \qquad t \quad — \qquad k$$
$$c \quad č$$

in Armenian (East and West), Chitimacha, Georgian, Italian, Japanese, Ossetic,
Mesquital Otomi, Polish, Romanian, Shipibo, Tarascan, Tojolabal, Tsotsil,
Tubatulabal, Tzeltal; and perhaps in Russian (this depends on how we break
the whole Russian consonant system into half-systems; see §25224).

A second 3–2 system is reported only for Motilone:

$$p \qquad t \quad — \quad — \qquad k$$
$$č \quad ̧č .$$

Several 3–3 systems are attested. Mazateco has

$$p \qquad t \quad — \quad — \qquad k$$
$$c \quad č \quad ̧č ;$$

Serbo-Croatian may have the same, though the descriptions would lead us to
list the affricates rather as /c cʸ č/. Chiricahua Apache, and perhaps Yuchi, have

$$p \qquad t \quad — \quad — \qquad k$$
$$c \quad č \quad ƛ ;$$

and Tillamook, with no labials, has

$$t \quad — \quad — \quad k \quad q$$
$$c \quad č \quad ƛ .$$

4–1 systems are of six types. Unaaliq Eskimo and Kutenai have

$$p \quad t \quad k \quad q$$
$$c ;$$

Cuzco Quechua has rather

$$p \qquad t \quad — \quad k \quad q$$
$$č ;$$

Turkish has

$$p \qquad t \quad — \quad ķ \quad k$$
$$č ;$$

Zoque has

$$p \quad t \quad t^y \quad k$$
$$\check{c} \; ;$$

Sanskrit has, and Lifu (half-system), Badaga, and Chawchila-Choynimni-Gashowu Yokuts have

$$p \quad t \quad — \quad \underset{.}{t} \quad k$$
$$\check{c} \; ;$$

finally, Sierra Miwok has

$$p \quad t \quad \underset{.}{t} \quad k$$
$$\underset{.}{\check{c}} \; .$$

The Sanskrit /č/ may, of course, have been a pure stop [t^y].

4–2 systems are also of several types. Sui, Totonac, and perhaps some Kechua (Callejon de Huaylas) have

$$p \quad t \quad — \quad k \quad q$$
$$c \quad \check{c} \; ;$$

Hungarian has

$$p \quad t \quad — \quad \underset{\ast}{k} \quad k$$
$$c \quad \check{c} \; ;$$

Czech and Sierra Popoluca have

$$p \quad t \quad t^y \quad k$$
$$c \quad \check{c}$$

(though in Sierra Popoluca affrication can alternatively be interpreted as a manner rather than as two added positions); Western Miwok, Pashto (?), and Wikchamni Yokuts have

$$p \quad t \quad — \quad \underset{.}{t} \quad k$$
$$c \quad \check{c} \; ;$$

and Yawelmani Yokuts has

$$p \quad t \quad \underset{.}{t} \quad k$$
$$c \quad \underset{.}{c} \; .$$

The evidence about Yuma is not entirely clear, but a 6–1 pattern seems to fit:

$$p \quad t \quad t^y \quad \underset{.}{t} \quad k \quad q$$
$$c \; .$$

Our report lists also /k^y k^w q^w/, but a distributional analysis suggests that these three might better be taken as clusters. A consonant of the [t^y] type can also easily be a cluster in many languages, but the distributional facts for Yuma are not the same for this as for the velars and it seems best to regard it as a unit /t^y/.

In the above survey we have distinguished between some systems which might well be classed together: e.g., the Sui situation with /p t k q/ and the Hungarian situation with /p t ḵ k/. In one structural sense the phonetic difference between these two may be irrelevant. There are other contexts, however, in which it is not, so that it has seemed preferable to keep them apart in the first instance; regrouping can be undertaken by anyone who so wishes.

252113. *Systems with Color-Modified Stops as Positions.* All attested systems with color-modified stop "positions" also have affricate "positions." Furthermore, with just one exception, the basic position to which the coloring is added is dorsovelar (or two contrasting dorso-velar positions, one fronted and one back), and with no exceptions at all the color-modification is produced by lip-rounding. This last point is due largely, or perhaps wholly, to the way we have organized matters for our discussion: palatal modification sometimes appears for dorsals, or for apicals or laminals, but this seems to result in a somewhat different basic position of articulation, so that the results have been treated in preceding sections. When palatal modification runs through a whole system (sonorants as well as obstruents), as in Russian or Marshallese, then we have the sort of phenomenon discussed earlier for Lifu, and the results will be treated in §2523.

We classify with three numbers: the first for the number of "pure" stops, the second for the number of color-modified positions, and the third for the number of affricate positions.

2–2–1 systems are rare. But Wichita has

$$t \quad k$$
$$k^w$$
$$c \,,$$

and Cuicateco has

$$t \quad - \quad k$$
$$k^w$$
$$\check{c} \,.$$

It has been suggested that in such cases, there being no labials, the labialized dorso-velars be assigned the structural position of an ordinary bilabial, placing the system therefore in the same category as the three-one type dealt with in §252112.

3–1–1 systems: Comanche, Isleta, Sandia, Taos, Picuris, and Tonkawa have

$$p \quad t \quad k$$
$$k^w$$
$$c \,;$$

Cuitlateco, Mixteco, and Villa Alta Zapotec have rather

$$p \quad t \quad - \quad k$$
$$k^w$$
$$\check{c} \,.$$

Trukese has our one instance of a color-modified stop which is not dorsal:

$$p \quad t \quad k$$
$$p^w$$
$$c \,.$$

There is only one attested 3-1-2 system, found in Bannock, Cashibo, Hopi, Huasteco, Huichol, Olmeca and Sierra Nahuatl, Mazahua and Temoayan Otomi, Sierra Zapotec, and Zuni:

$$p \quad t \quad - \quad k$$
$$k^w$$
$$c \quad \check{c} \,.$$

There is also only one attested 3-1-3 system, found in Navaho and in Nahuatl dialects other than the two mentioned just above:

$$p \quad t \qquad - \qquad k$$
$$k^w$$

$$c \quad \lambda \quad \check{c}\,.$$

3-1-4: Chipewyan:

$$p \quad t \qquad\qquad - \qquad k$$
$$k^w$$

$$\hat{\theta} \quad c \quad \lambda \quad \check{c}\,.$$

3-2-2: Coeur d'Alene:

$$p \quad t \quad - \quad - \quad q$$
$$k^w \quad q^w$$

$$c \quad \check{c}\,.$$

3-2-3: Kalispel:

$$p \quad t \quad - \qquad\qquad - \quad q$$
$$k^w \quad q^w$$

$$c \quad \check{c} \quad \lambda\,;$$

and Tlingit:

$$t \quad - \qquad k \quad q$$
$$k^w \quad q^w$$

$$c \quad \check{c} \quad \lambda\,.$$

4-1-2: Santa Clara Tewa:

$$p \quad t \quad t^y \quad k$$
$$k^w$$

$$c \quad \check{c}\,.$$

4-2-2: Bella Coola and Kwakiutl:

$$p \quad t \qquad k \quad q$$
$$k^w \quad q^w$$

$$c \quad \lambda\,.$$

4-2-3: Nootka, Duwamish, and Snoqualmie:

$$p \quad t \quad - \qquad k \quad q$$
$$k^w \quad q^w$$

$$c \quad \check{c} \quad \lambda\,.$$

252114. *Systems with Coarticulation.* One other device by which a position-system is sometimes filled out is by the use of coarticulated stops. In Bariba, for example, there are /p/, /t/, and /k/, and also a type of stop produced by simultaneous closure of the lips and of dorsum and velum. This last is not a cluster /pk/ or /kp/, for much the same reasons that a /c/ or a /k^w/ is often not a cluster: it patterns like a unit, and occurs in contrasting voiceless and voiced manners as do the three simple stops. It is a little puzzling to know where to place the symbol representing such a phenomenon in charts like those we have been presenting. If one uses a single line, then where in sequence should it be listed? If one uses a separate line, should it be entered under /k/ or under /p/? We are told that in Bariba the coarticulated stops are more apt to be mistaken for velars than for labials, so that perhaps we can regard them as types of dorso-velar stops with labial modification, rather than the reverse. It is further worthy of note that systems with a coarticulated /kp/ "position" do not have, in any known case, a contrasting /kʷ/, and that all known coarticulated stops involve bilabial and dorso-velar closure, never any other combination. So we can chart the Bariba system thus:

$$p \quad t \quad k$$
$$kp \ ;$$

this recurs in Loma, Kpelle, Mende, Yoruba, Mano, and Jukun. Gourma and Senadi have a 4-1 system:

$$p \quad t \quad t^y \quad k$$
$$kp \ ;$$

and one dialect of Jukun has a 3-1-1 system:

$$p \quad t \quad k$$
$$kp$$
$$c \ .$$

25212. *Manner Systems.* Here we summarize the types of contrast of manner which are attested, naming in each case one or two languages where the type is found, but without listing the obstruents in question; in §25213, where we tabulate whole obstruent systems in terms of symmetric sets, positions, and manners, fuller examples are given.

Except when especially listed, affricates count in the following as stops.

Two-way manner contrasts are of the following types:

(1) (voiceless) stop versus (voiceless) spirant: Samoan, Fox.

(2) (voiceless) stop versus spirant which is voiced or voiceless depending on environment: South Greenlandic Eskimo.

(3) (voiceless) stop versus voiced spirant: Yuma. (In a system of any of the above three kinds, the stops may be always voiceless, or may be voiced in some environments.)

(4) voiceless versus voiced stops: Tagalog.

(5) nonglottalized stop (sometimes slightly voiced or slightly aspirated, depending on the language) versus glottalized stop: Huasteco.

(6) unaspirated stop versus aspirated stop: Tarascan, Chitimacha. In the latter, the unaspirated stops are sometimes glottalized.

(7) voiceless versus voiced spirant: Hungarian.

In each of the above we have named first the less positively characterized or "unmarked" manner, except that in a few cases there is no particular reason for selecting either manner for this special status. In more complicated manner systems there usually is good reason for such a selection.

Three-way manner contrasts are of the following types:

(1) stop, affricate, and spirant (all voiceless): Keres.

(2) unaspirated stop (sometimes voiced), aspirated stop, and voiceless spirant: Mandarin.

(3) voiceless and voiced stops, voiceless spirants: standard German.

(4) voiceless stops; weak obstruents which vary between voiced stop, voiced non-fricative spirant, and voiceless non-fricative spirant; and strong voiceless spirants: Spanish.

(5) nonglottalized stop (sometimes aspirated), glottalized stop, voiceless spirant: Tillamook.

(6) nonglottalized stop (sometimes voiced), glottalized stop, and obstruents which are aspirated stops in some positions, voiceless spirants in others: aboriginal Cuzco Quechua.

(7) voiceless stop (sometimes aspirated), glottalized stop, and voiced stop: Western Miwok.

(8) voiceless unaspirated stop, aspirated stop, and voiced stop: Thai.

(9) voiceless unaspirated stop (sometimes glottalized), aspirated stop, and voiced stop: Georgian.

(10) unaspirated stop (sometimes slightly voiced), aspirated stop, and glottalized stop: Yawelmani.

Four-way manner contrasts are of the following types:

(1) stop versus spirant and voiceless versus voiced (or, in some cases, fortis versus lenis): French, Dutch. This is far and away the commonest type.

(2) voiceless stop, voiced stop, voiceless affricate, and voiceless spirant: Sierra Popoluca.

(3) voiceless nonglottalized unaspirated stop, glottalized stop, aspirated stop, and voiced stop: Sandia.

(4) voiceless stop (sometimes aspirated), glottalized stop, voiced stop, and voiceless spirant: Kwakiutl.

Five-way manner contrasts are of two types:

(1) voiceless stop (unaspirated, sometimes glottalized), aspirated stop, voiced stop, voiceless spirant, and voiced spirant: Georgian, Ossetic.

(2) unaspirated stop (sometimes voiced), aspirated stop, glottalized stop, voiceless spirant, and voiced spirant: Chiricahua Apache.

Many languages, of course, have no contrasts of manner at all: Hawaiian, Korean, Cree, Terena, Huichol. This does not imply that such a language cannot have both stops and spirants, or even two different manners of stops: under our criteria, as expounded in §25210, it means only that the obstruent system includes no symmetric set.

Many languages are reported as having more manner contrasts than are here recognized. Apparent manner contrasts are sometimes due to allophonic variation, as in Ojibwa, where /p t č k s š/ are voiced in certain surroundings, otherwise voiceless. It is not difficult to eliminate cases of this sort. It is somewhat harder to be sure of eliminating all cases in which apparent contrasts of manner are better taken as the difference between single obstruents and clusters of one kind or another. We shall discuss here several instances in which we have preferred a cluster interpretation (and so obtained fewer genuine manner contrasts), plus a number where we have not chosen the cluster interpretation though perhaps one should do so.

A rather common situation is for there to be a medial, or otherwise limited, contrast between short and long obstruent. In Finnish the contrast is found only medially, and the obvious interpretation is that the longs are geminate clusters— /pp tt kk ss/ comparable to non-geminate clusters /pt tk ps ts ks sp st sk/ and to geminate /mm nn rr ll/. Ojibwa has both medial and final longs, but the geminate interpretation is again fairly obvious: /pp tt čč kk ss šš/, comparable in distribution to /mp nt nč nk/. We choose a similar interpretation in most other cases.

In Potawatomi the long fortis stops and spirants cannot be interpreted as geminates, since such geminates as /pp tt čč kk/ occur, often with each consonant released separately, but in any case lenis rather than fortis. However, it seems best to extract a feature of fortisness from all the single fortis obstruents or fortis clusters of obstruents, as something which occurs or does not occur as a property of the whole obstruent sequence (of one or more). One then has the contrast between /nteptan/ 'I obtain it' and /ntept·an/ 'I hear it', where the fortis feature /·/ spreads through the whole cluster /pt/. This is comparable to the extraction of voicing proposed in §2512 for Polish and Portuguese.

In Delaware, also, the geminate interpretation does not at first seem possible. One finds medial sequences such as [k'k], in which the first stop is released with an aspiration just as in a non-geminate cluster [k't]. However, it turns out that this aspirate release can be set up as one allophone of a special vowel, for which we shall use the symbol /i/, and which also has murmur-release as an allophone in certain environments. Having done this, the two "clusters" listed above can be treated as /kik/ and /kit/, so that the medial long stops can be taken as genuine geminates /pp tt čč kk/. These four are then the only geminates which occur; all other apparent longs involve /i/.

Korean has an apparently somewhat complicated situation. Initially one finds voiceless and slightly aspirated [p t č k s], voiceless and strongly aspirated (with pharyngeal constriction) [p' t' č' k'], and voiceless fortis long [p' t' č' k' s'] pronounced with glottal constriction. Medially one finds short and often voiced [b d ǯ g], short voiceless aspirated [s], voiceless and strongly aspirated [p' t' č' k'], and long voiceless (not fortis and without glottal constriction) [p· t· č· k· s·]. Finally one finds only short voiceless unaspirated (often unreleased) [p t k]. The simplest interpretation is in terms of five obstruents /p t č k s/ and an /h/; all of which occur initially and medially and three of which occur finally; the strongly aspirated initials and medials are clusters /ph th čh kh/; the initial and medial long stops and spirant are /pp tt čč kk ss/.

In Tonkawa there occur glottalized stops which can best be interpreted as clusters of the simple stops and /ʔ/: /pʔ tʔ cʔ kʔ/. This is supported by the occurrence of /kʷʔ/, where the stop is released before the glottal catch is formed, and by distribution: none of these clusters with /ʔ/ occur finally.

The last two examples show that we are especially led to suspect a cluster interpretation when there is some key environment (in both of the examples, final position) in which only one manner of obstruents, or of stops, occur. This does not mean that a cluster interpretation is always possible under these distributional circumstances, or that, if possible, it always represents a gain in clarity over an interpretation in terms of contrasting manners. But in some cases one or both of these latter points do seem to hold.

In Winnebago, for example, only aspirated stops [p' t' č' k'] occur finally. These also occur initially and medially. In initial and medial clusters of two consonants, with a few exceptions, the second member of the cluster is voiced:

we have, thus, medial [p'g] and [k'b]. We therefore interpret the aspirated stops as single phonemes /p t č k/; the two listed clusters are /pk/ and /kp/, where the voicing (and lack of aspiration) of the second member is allophonic. What appear to be initial and medial unaspirated and slightly voiced stops are clusters of /p t č k/ and a phoneme /h/, which is voiced in this position according to the general rule. What appear to be initial and medial glottalized stops are clusters of /p t č k/ and /ʔ/—which, contrary to the rule (and not surprisingly, considering the physiology of production of a glottal catch) is not voiced.

In Takelma we find initial and medial contrast between voiceless, voiced, and glottalized stops; but finally only the voiceless ones occur, plus clusters of /ʔ/ and a stop in which the releases are separate. We can interpret initial and medial [p' t' k' c'] as clusters /ʔp ʔt ʔk ʔs/; all four of these clusters then also occur finally. A similar reinterpretation of initial and medial postvocalic [b d g] as /hp ht hk/ finds some support in the other habits of clustering, but seems a bit far-fetched. The reduction thus leaves us with two stop manners instead of three—but not with just one, as for Winnebago.

Sanskrit, and certain modern languages such as Hindustani, are often said to have four types of stops: voiceless and voiced, intersecting unaspirated and aspirated. But in both named cases the aspiration (be it voiceless or voiced) is raᵗher patently simply the phoneme /h/, which recurs elsewhere: this leaves just a two-way manner contrast.

Sui presents a complicated system of syllable-onsets which need not simply be taken as separate unit phonemes, though cluster interpretations do not eliminate the fairly great amount of skewness shown by the system. The onsets include voiceless unaspirated stops [p t c č k q], voiceless aspirated stops [p' t' c' č' k' q'], voiced stops [b d], preglottalized voiced stops ['b 'd], voiceless spirants [φ s š x], voiced spirants and nonspirantal glides [w z y γ ɣ], and preglottalized voiced spirants or glides ['w 'y 'ɣ]. The onset system also includes /h/ and /ʔ/, and we can reanalyze the obstruent onsets as follows: /p t c č k q/, /ph th ch čh kh qh/, /b d/, /ʔb ʔd/, /hw hz hy hγ/, /w z y γ ɣ/, /ʔw ʔy ʔγ/.

Similar reductions could be undertaken in other cases: say in Mandarin, Yawelmani, or Chiricahua. In Mandarin all that we could do would be to regard the aspirated stops as clusters of the unaspirated stops and /x/; this last varies between dorso-velar and mere aspiration, but seems to pattern distributionally (other than its participation in the clusters just mentioned, if they be recognized) as a dorso-velar obstruent rather than as a laryngeal. For this reason we here reject the reinterpretation.

In Yawelmani we cannot reinterpret the aspirated and glottalized stops as clusters of the plain stops and /h/ and /ʔ/ unless we also recognize syllable juncture, changing our classification of Yawelmani as to syllable-type. If we did not do the latter, then the notation /. . . VkhV . . ./ would be ambiguous for [. . . Vk'V . . .] and [. . . VkhV . . .], where in the former the [k'] begins a new syllable, in the latter the [k] ends one syllable and the [h] begins another. But if we write syllable-juncture with a hyphen, then we can distinguish the two as /. . . V-khV . . ./ and /. . . Vk-hV . . ./, and so on in the many other similar cases. The choice is trivial: the language allows of either treatment, and forces neither. We can choose a cluster interpretation, with syllable juncture; or a componential interpretation of the more complex consonants, without syllable juncture. More or less arbitrarily, we reject the reanalysis.

The case is not so clear for Chiricahua (and Navaho). Apparently we are already forced to recognize syllable juncture, and only one stop-type occurs terminally in syllables, so that one does not have the sort of balance between onset and coda that one finds in Yawelmani. One could reinterpret syllable-initial [c č ƛ k] as clusters with /h/, and [c' č' ƛ' k'] as clusters with /ʔ/; this would still leave two manners of spirants, which seem to be related to the voiceless unaspirated stops just as closely as are the aspirated and the glottalized stops, but which cannot be reinterpreted as clusters of the "basic" stops and anything to be found elsewhere in the system. Here, again, we have rejected the cluster reinterpretation.

25213. *Tabulation of Whole Obstruent Systems.* Having now discussed, separately, positions and manners, we are ready to classify and tabulate whole obstruent systems. We shall begin with the simplest and procede to the most complex, using the number of manner contrasts as principle criterion, the kinds of manner contrasts as subordinate criterion.

252131. *No Symmetrical Sets: No Manner Contrasts.* Hawaiian has only two obstruents: /p k/. Kapauku and Marshallese (half-system) have only three: /p t k/. Arunta has four: /p t č k/. These are the only languages known to have no spirants at all.

Many Polynesian dialects (not Hawaiian or Samoan), and many Finnish dialects (not formal standard Finnish) have three stops and one spirant: /p t k s/. Oneida has the same ratio, but the stop positions are different: /t č k s/; and in Cherokee, /t c k s/.

Korean has four stops and one spirant: /p t č k s/. Cree and Menomini agree except that the affricate /c/ and spirant /s/ vary between apical and laminal. Wichita also agrees, but with different positions: /t c k kʷ s/.

Standard Finnish has /p t k d s/.

Terena has three stops /p t k/, two spirants /s š/ which are voiceless or voiced depending on environment, and one spirant /v/ which is always voiced.

Comanche has five stops and one spirant: /p t c k kʷ s/.

Cuicateco has four stops /t č k kʷ/, one always voiceless spirant /s/, and two always voiced spirants /β ð/.

Huichol has six stops and one spirant: /p t c č k kʷ s/.

252132. *Two-Way Manner Contrast.* We shall subdivide on the basis of the type of contrast of manner found in the largest symmetrical set.

2521321. *Stop Versus Spirant.* Several languages have a two-by-two set

p   t

f   s

with various leftovers: Samoan /v/; Trukese /pʷ c k/; Creek-Seminole and Hitchiti-Mikasuki /č k ł/; Alabama and Koasati /č k b ł/.

Many have

$$\begin{array}{cc} t & \check{c} \\ s & \check{s} \end{array}$$

with leftovers: Fox, Ojibwa, Potawatomi, Tunica /p k/; Seneca /k/; Motilone /p č̣ k/.

Shawnee has leftover /p k/ and

$$\begin{array}{cc} t & \check{c} \\ \theta & \check{s} \, . \end{array}$$

Sierra Miwok has leftover /p ṭ k/ and

$$\begin{array}{cc} t & \c{c} \\ s & \c{\check{s}} \, . \end{array}$$

Cheyenne has leftovers /p š/ and

$$\begin{array}{cc} t & k \\ s & x \, ; \end{array}$$

Amahuaca has the same with leftovers /p č k θ/—or, perhaps, /θ/ and /s/ should be interchanged. Kutenai has the same plus /p c q ł/.

Hidatsa has leftovers /p t/ and

$$\begin{array}{cc} \check{c} & k \\ \check{s} & x \, . \end{array}$$

A number of languages have

$$\begin{array}{cc} c & \check{c} \\ s & \check{s} \end{array}$$

with various leftovers: Hopi and Olmeca Nahuatl /p t k kʷ/; Totonac /p t k q ł/; Sierra Nahuatl /p t k kʷ g/; other Nahuatl dialects /p t ƛ k kʷ/; Cashibo /p t k kʷ ṣ̌/ (and a /β/ which may belong to the obstruent system); aboriginal Mazateco /t č̣ k/.

Choctaw-Chickasaw has a two-by-three set

$$\begin{array}{ccc} p & t & \check{c} \\ f & s & \check{s} \end{array}$$

with leftover /k b ł/.

Crow, Winnebago, and Delaware have leftover /p/ and a different two-by-three set

$$\begin{array}{ccc} t & \check{c} & k \\ s & \check{s} & x \, . \end{array}$$

The Swiss-German dialect of Brienze has still a different two-by-three, with leftover /š v/:

$$\begin{array}{ccc} p & t & k \\ f & s & x \, . \end{array}$$

Tonkawa has leftover /p t/ and

$$\begin{array}{ccc} c & k & kʷ \\ s & x & xʷ \, . \end{array}$$

Yuma has a two-by-three set

$$\begin{array}{ccc} c & tʸ & k \\ s & \check{s} & x \, , \end{array}$$

plus four random leftovers /ṭ q ł łʸ/, and four which fit a subsidiary symmetric set:

$$p \quad t$$
$$v \quad \delta \, .$$

Here, also, the contrast is stop versus spirant, but the two spirants are always voiced, whereas the three of the major symmetric set are voiceless. This difference in allophonic behavior leads us to keep the two sets separate. A similar reasoning leads to the following set for South Greenlandic Eskimo:

$$p \quad k \quad q$$
$$\beta \quad \gamma \quad \gamma$$

with leftovers /t s ṣ/ (instead of including /t/ and /s/ in the symmetric set).

Lifu and Karok have two-by-four sets:

$$p \quad t \quad č \quad k$$
$$f \quad \theta \quad š \quad x \, ,$$

Lifu with leftover /ṭ s/, Karok only with /s/. In both cases, possibly the assignments of /s/ and /θ/ should be reversed.

In the two-by-five set of Sui the contrast is between voiceless stop and voiceless spirant or nonspirantal glide; the leftovers are /b t d/:

$$p \quad c \quad č \quad k \quad q$$
$$w \quad z \quad y \quad \gamma \quad \gamma \, .$$

2521322. *Voiced Versus Voiceless Stop.* Several languages have a two-by-three set

$$p \quad t \quad k$$
$$b \quad d \quad g$$

with various leftovers: Tagalog, Ilocano, Dibabaon /s/; Latin (alternative treatment) /f s/; Kiowa /c s z/; Takelma (alternative) /s ł x/.

The set

$$p \quad t \quad č \quad k$$
$$b \quad d \quad ǯ \quad g$$

is found in Burmese (leftovers /s z θ̂ ž/) and Japanese. The latter has leftovers /c x/ and four which form a smaller symmetric set,

$$s \quad š$$
$$z \quad ž \, .$$

Sierra Popoluca (one alternative) has

$$p \quad t \quad tʸ \quad k$$
$$b \quad d \quad dʸ \quad g$$

and symmetrical leftovers

$$c \quad č$$
$$s \quad š \, .$$

Supide (one alternative) has

$$p \quad \hat{f} \quad t \quad k$$
$$b \quad \hat{v} \quad d \quad g$$

and symmetrical leftovers

$$f \quad v$$
$$s \quad z \, .$$

Bariba has asymmetrical leftovers /f s z/ and

p	t	k	kᵖ
b	d	g	gᵇ .

Mazahua and Temoayan Otomi have

p	t	k	kʷ
b	d	g	gʷ

plus a smaller set of leftovers

c	č
s	š
z	ž .

Sanskrit and Badaga show two-by-five symmetrical sets of the shape

p	t	ṭ	č	k
b	d	ḍ	ǰ	g ,

the former with leftovers /s ṣ š/, the latter with /s/ and perhaps /š/.

Tubatulabal and Italian have

p	t	c	č	k
b	d	ʒ	ž	g ,

the former with leftover /š/, the latter with /f v s š/.

Hispanized Zoque has

p	t	tʸ	č	k
b	d	dʸ	ž	g ,

and adds /f s š/, plus /c/ which varies between voiced and voiceless.

Cuitlateco has leftovers /s š/ and

p	t	č	k	kʷ
b	d	ž	g	gʷ .

The Kota system is probably best set up as a symmetrical two-by five

p	ṭ̣	t	ṭ	k
b	ḍ̣	d	ḍ	g

with leftovers /s z ṣ/.

Hungarian (one treatment) has a two-by six

p	t	c	č	ḳ	k
b	d	ʒ	ž	ĝ	g

plus symmetrical leftovers

f	s	š
v	z	ž .

Bannock also has a two-by-six, but with one leftover, /s/:

p	t	c	č	k	kʷ
b	d	ʒ	ž	g	gʷ .

2521323. *Plain Versus Glottalized Stop.* Tojolabal, Tsotsil, and Tzeltal have a two-by-five

p	t	c	č	k
p'	t'	c'	č'	k' .

Tojolabal leftovers are /s š/; Tsotsil /s š/ and a peculiar bilabial phoneme (analysis uncertain); Tzeltal /b d s š/.

Huasteco has leftovers /p θ š/ and /b/ ([b∼β]), and a different two-by-five:

```
p    t    č    k    kʷ
p'   t'   č'   k'   k'ʷ .
```

Zuni has leftovers /s š ł/ and a two-by-six:

```
p    t    c    č    k    kʷ
p'   t'   c'   č'   k'   k'ʷ .
```

2521324. *Plain Versus Aspirated Stop.* This is attested only for Tarascan and Chitimacha, with the same symmetrical set:

```
p    t    c    č    k
p'   t'   c'   č'   k' .
```

Chitimacha leftovers are /s š/; Tarascan /b d g s š/. In Chitimacha the plain stops are sometimes glottalized.

252133. *Three-Way Manner Contrast.* Here, again, we subclassify on the basis of the types of manners involved.

2521331. *Stop, Affricate, and Spirant.* This is attested in Keres and Campa, with leftover /p k/:

```
t    tʸ
c    č
s    š .
```

2521332. *Two Stop Manners, One Spirant Manner.* Mandarin has unaspirated and aspirated stops, and voiceless spirants:

```
p    c    k
p'   c'   k'
f    s    x ,
```

with leftover /t t'/.

A good number of languages have voiceless and voiced stops, plus voiceless spirants. Takelma (alternative) has leftover /p b ł/ and

```
t    k
d    g
s    x .
```

Latin (alternative) had leftovers /k g/ and

```
p    t
b    d
f    s .
```

All other cases have three-by-three sets. Taki-Taki and German:

```
p    t    k
b    d    g
f    s    x ,
```

the former with leftover /v z/, the latter with these and /ž/. Mesquital Otomi has rather

```
p    t    k
b    d    g
f    θ    x ,
```

with an odd /z/ and a secondary symmetrical set

$$c \quad č$$
$$s \quad š.$$

Dagur Mongol has

$$t \quad č \quad k$$
$$d \quad ǯ \quad g$$
$$s \quad š \quad x,$$

with /p b/. Finally, Breton has

$$p \quad t \quad k$$
$$b \quad d \quad g$$
$$\phi \quad s \quad x$$

with an uncertain set of leftovers: /ϕ· v z š ž/, of which all but /z/ perhaps form a subsidiary symmetrical set (or else the same result with /ϕ/ and /ϕ·/ interchanged).

Spanish belongs marginally to the type of German and Taki-Taki listed above, with leftovers /č ǯ/ (some dialects only /č/, others also /θ/). But Spanish /b d g/, and /ǯ/ when present, have weak spirantal allophones as well as stop allophones, which can even be voiceless in some environments.

The Loma system deviates, with voiced and voiceless stops but with voiced spirants:

$$p \quad t \quad k$$
$$b \quad d \quad g$$
$$v \quad z \quad \gamma,$$

plus /kᵖ gᵇ b' f s/ and a lenis voiced labio-dental spirant in contrast to /v/.

A number of languages have plain stops (sometimes aspirated), glottalized stops, and voiceless spirants. Tillamook:

$$c \quad č \quad λ \quad k \quad q$$
$$c' \quad č' \quad λ' \quad k' \quad q'$$
$$s \quad š \quad ł \quad x \quad x̣,$$

with leftover /t t'/. Bella Coola:

$$c \quad k \quad kʷ \quad q \quad qʷ$$
$$c' \quad k' \quad k'ʷ \quad q' \quad q'ʷ$$
$$s \quad x \quad xʷ \quad x̣ \quad x̣ʷ$$

with leftover /λ' ł/ and a two-by-two set

$$p \quad t$$
$$p' \quad t'.$$

Coeur d'Alene:

$$c \quad č \quad kʷ \quad q \quad qʷ$$
$$c' \quad č' \quad k'ʷ \quad q' \quad q'ʷ$$
$$s \quad š \quad xʷ \quad x̣ \quad x̣ʷ$$

and leftover /ǯ gʷ ł/ plus a three-by-two

$$p \quad t$$
$$p' \quad t'$$
$$b \quad d.$$

Kalispel:

$$
\begin{array}{cccccc}
c & č & \lambda & k^w & q & q^w \\
c' & č' & \lambda' & k'^w & q' & q'^w \\
s & š & ł & x^w & x̣ & x̣^w
\end{array}
$$

with a leftover two-by-two like that of Bella Coola above. Duwamish has the same three-by-six, with a left-over two-by-three like that of Coeur d'Alene. Nootka and Snoqualmie have a three-by-seven:

$$
\begin{array}{ccccccc}
c & č & \lambda & k & k^w & q & q^w \\
c' & č' & \lambda' & k' & k'^w & q' & q'^w \\
s & š & ł & x & x^w & x̣ & x̣^w
\end{array}
$$

to which Nootka adds the two-by-two of Bella Coola and Kalispel, while Snoqualmie adds the three-by-two of Coeur d'Alene and asymmetric /ʒ ž gʷ/.

Similar to the above are several systems in which plain stops and glottalized stops contrast with a series for which aspiration and spirantization must be regarded as structurally equivalent. Aboriginal Cuzco Kechua, for example, had an odd /s/ and the following three-by-five:

$$
\begin{array}{ccccc}
p & t & č & k & q \\
p' & t' & č' & k' & q' \\
p' & t' & č' & k' & q',
\end{array}
$$

where the members of the last row were aspirated stops in certain environments, voiceless spirants in others. Picuris and Taos are similar, except that the aspirated stops fill out the pattern for certain positions, the spirants for others:

$$
\begin{array}{ccccc}
p & t & c & k & k^w \\
p' & t' & c' & k' & k'^w \\
p' & t' & s & x & x^w.
\end{array}
$$

Picuris adds /ł/, Taos /ł b d g/.

2521333. *Three Stop Manners.* The Yokuts languages (or dialects?) contrast plain stops (sometimes slightly voiced, more in some of the languages than in others) with aspirated stops and with glottalized stops. Chukchansi has

$$
\begin{array}{cccc}
b & d & ž & g \\
p & t & č & k \\
p' & t' & č' & k'
\end{array}
$$

plus /s ṣ x/. Chawchila-Choynimni-Gashowu has

$$
\begin{array}{ccccc}
b & d & ḍ & ž & g \\
p & t & ṭ & č & k \\
p' & t' & ṭ' & č' & k'
\end{array}
$$

plus /ṣ š x/. Wikchamni has

$$
\begin{array}{cccccc}
b & d & ḍ & ʒ & ž & g \\
p & t & ṭ & c & č & k \\
p' & t' & ṭ' & c' & č' & k'
\end{array}
$$

and /ṣ s x/. Yawelmani has

$$
\begin{array}{cccccc}
b & d & ḍ & ʒ & ǯ & g \\
p & t & ṭ & c & ç & k \\
p' & t' & ṭ' & c' & ç' & k'
\end{array}
$$

and /s ṣ x/.

Georgian (alternative) contrasts plain stops (voiceless, unaspirated, sometimes glottalized) with aspirated stops and voiced stops:

$$
\begin{array}{ccccc}
p & t & c & č & k \\
p' & t' & c' & č' & k' \\
b & d & 3 & ǯ & g ,
\end{array}
$$

with a voicing-variable /v/ and a secondary two-by-three system

$$
\begin{array}{ccc}
s & š & x \\
z & ž & γ .
\end{array}
$$

Where the Western Miwok system fits in is not clear. Ostensibly there are voiceless, glottalized, and voiced stops:

$$
\begin{array}{cc}
t & ṭ \\
t' & ṭ' \\
d & ḍ ,
\end{array}
$$

plus odd /p b č č' š/ and a secondary two-by-two

$$
\begin{array}{cc}
c & k \\
c' & k' .
\end{array}
$$

/c' k'/ show an environmentally conditioned variation between glottalized stop and voiceless spirant [s x]. In the case of the major symmetrical set, it is not clear which of the three manners is the "unmarked" type.

Thai, however, obviously contrasts voiceless unaspirated, voiceless aspirated, and voiced—like Georgian, except that the first set do not tend to be non-distinctively glottalized:

$$
\begin{array}{ccc}
p & t & k \\
p' & t' & k' \\
b & d & g
\end{array}
$$

plus /č č' f s/.

252134. *Four-way Manner Contrast.*

2521341. *Voiced and Voiceless, Stop and Spirant.* French and Brazilian Portuguese have

$$
\begin{array}{cc}
p & t \\
b & d \\
f & s \\
v & z
\end{array}
$$

plus /k g š ž/. Continental Portuguese is the same except that /b d g/ have weak spirantal allophones.

Supide (alternative) has

$$
\begin{array}{cc}
f̂ & t \\
v̇ & d \\
f & s \\
v & z
\end{array}
$$

with a leftover two-by-two

$$
\begin{array}{cc}
p & k \\
b & g .
\end{array}
$$

Dutch has a four-by-three with no leftovers:

$$p \quad t \quad k$$
$$b \quad d \quad g$$
$$f \quad s \quad x$$
$$v \quad z \quad \gamma \,;$$

/g/ is quite rare (except in loanwords).

English, Turkish, Czech, Serbo-Croatian, and Romanian have the same main symmetrical set:

$$p \quad t \quad č$$
$$b \quad d \quad ž$$
$$f \quad s \quad š$$
$$v \quad z \quad ž \,,$$

to which English adds /k g θ ð/ (and one might interchange the assignment of /s z/ and /θ ð/); Romanian adds /k g c/. Turkish adds a second set

$$ḳ \quad k$$
$$ĝ \quad g \,;$$

Czech adds /c x/ and a second set

$$t^y \quad k$$
$$d^y \quad g \,;$$

Serbo-Croatian adds /c/ and a second set

$$c^y \quad k$$
$$ʒ^y \quad g \,.$$

Polish and Hungarian (alternate) have

$$p \quad c \quad č$$
$$b \quad ʒ \quad ž$$
$$f \quad s \quad š$$
$$v \quad z \quad ž \,,$$

to which Polish adds /x/ and a two-by-two

$$t \quad k$$
$$d \quad g \,,$$

while Hungarian adds a two-by-three

$$t \quad ḳ \quad k$$
$$d \quad ĝ \quad g \,.$$

Senadi has

$$p \quad t \quad t^y$$
$$b \quad d \quad d^y$$
$$f \quad s \quad s^y$$
$$v \quad z \quad z^y$$

and a subsidiary set

$$k̓ \quad k^p$$
$$ʒ̓ \quad g^b \,.$$

The Russian half-system, finally, has /c/ and

$$p \quad t \quad č \quad k$$
$$b \quad d \quad ʒ \quad g$$
$$f \quad s \quad š \quad x$$
$$v \quad z \quad ž \quad \gamma \,.$$

2521342. *Other Four-Way Contrasts.* Sierra Popoluca (alternative) contrasts voiceless and voiced stops, voiceless affricates, and voiceless spirants:

$$t \quad t^y$$
$$d \quad d^y$$
$$c \quad \check{c}$$
$$s \quad \check{s}$$

with a two-by-two second set

$$p \quad k$$
$$b \quad g \; .$$

Saho, Santa Clara Tewa, and Kwakiutl contrast voiceless, voiced, and glottalized stops and voiceless spirants. Saho:

$$t \quad k$$
$$d \quad g$$
$$t' \quad k'$$
$$s \quad x$$

plus /č' z ž/ and a two-by-two

$$b \quad \check{\mathrm{3}}$$
$$f \quad \check{s} \; .$$

Santa Clara Tewa:

$$p \quad t \quad \check{c} \quad k$$
$$b \quad d \quad \check{\mathrm{3}} \quad g$$
$$p' \quad t' \quad \check{c}' \quad k'$$
$$f \quad \theta \quad \check{s} \quad x$$

plus /t^y/ and a three-by-two

$$c \quad k^w$$
$$c' \quad k'^w$$
$$s \quad x^w \; .$$

Kwakiutl:

$$c \quad \lambda \quad k \quad k^w \quad q \quad q^w$$
$$\mathrm{3} \quad \lambda \quad g \quad g^w \quad \underline{g} \quad \underline{g}^w$$
$$c' \quad \lambda' \quad k' \quad k'^w \quad q' \quad q'^w$$
$$s \quad \dagger \quad x \quad x^w \quad \underline{x} \quad \underline{x}^w \; ,$$

with a three-by-two subsidiary set

$$p \quad t$$
$$b \quad d$$
$$p' \quad t' \; .$$

Sandia and Isleta have four manners for stops: voiceless unaspirated, glottalized, aspirated, and voiced:

$$p \quad t \quad k$$
$$p' \quad t' \quad k'$$
$$p' \quad t' \quad k'$$
$$b \quad d \quad g \; .$$

Isleta adds /c c' k^w s š ł/; Sandia adds /s š ł/ and a two-by-two

$$c \quad k^w$$
$$c' \quad k'^w \; .$$

252135. *Five-Way Manner Contrast.* In Georgian (one alternative treatment)

Ossetic, and East Armenian, the five-way contrast is between plain stop ("un-marked": voiceless, sometimes glottalized), aspirated stop, voiced stop, voiceless spirant, and voiced spirant. Georgian:

$$
\begin{array}{ccc}
c & č & k \\
c' & č' & k' \\
\mathfrak{z} & \check{\mathfrak{z}} & g \\
s & š & x \\
z & ž & \gamma
\end{array}
\quad + \quad
\begin{array}{cc}
p & t \\
p' & t' \\
b & d
\end{array}
\quad + \quad v \, ,
$$

where /v/ is weak and varies as to voicing. The voicing contrast which is not phonemic for Georgian /v/ establishes separate phonemes in Ossetic and East Armenian, so that the system is

$$
\begin{array}{cccc}
p & c & č & k \\
p' & c' & č' & k' \\
b & \mathfrak{z} & \check{\mathfrak{z}} & g \\
f & s & š & x \\
v & z & ž & \gamma
\end{array}
\quad + \quad
\begin{array}{ccc}
t & t' & d
\end{array} \, .
$$

In Athabascan (Chiricahua, Navaho, Chipewyan), on the other hand, the five-way contrast is between plain stop ("unmarked": unaspirated and unglot-talized, but sometimes slightly voiced), aspirated stop, glottalized stop, voiceless spirant, and voiced spirant. Chiricahua has the simplest system of the three languages:

$$
\begin{array}{cccc}
\mathfrak{z} & \check{\mathfrak{z}} & \lambda & g \\
c & č & \check{\lambda} & k \\
c' & č' & \check{\lambda}' & k' \\
s & š & \dlj & x \\
z & ž & l & \gamma
\end{array}
\quad + \quad b\,d\,t\,t' \, .
$$

Navaho adds to this the leftovers /kʷ xʷ γʷ/; the last is often simply [w]. These additions do not yield any subsidiary symmetric set. Chipewyan has the same four leftovers as Chiricahua, but a larger main set:

$$
\begin{array}{cccccc}
\hat{\eth} & \mathfrak{z} & \check{\mathfrak{z}} & \lambda & g & g^w \\
\theta & c & č & \check{\lambda} & k & k^w \\
\theta' & c' & č' & \check{\lambda}' & k' & k'^w \\
\theta & s & š & \dlj & x & x^w \\
\eth & z & y & l & \gamma & \gamma^w
\end{array} \, .
$$

As in Navaho, /γʷ/ is often [w]; note that the /y/ and /l/ of Chipewyan, like the /l/ of Navaho and Chiricahua, belong to the obstruent system.

2522. *Sonorant Systems.* The sonorant system of a language is defined nega-tively: a pheneme is a sonorant if it is not (1) part of the obstruent system (like the /y l/ of Chipewyan), (2) part of the vowel system (like the /i/ of Mandarin or Italian, which has an allophone [y]), or (3) a laryngeal or a manner consonant (English /h/, Menomini /h ?/, Russian /y/). Sonorants uniformly turn out to be nasal continuants, laterals, trills, or glide vocoids, but, of all these, only sounds of the first sort seem always to be sonorants. For that reason, we shall deal first with nasal systems (as subsystems of sonorant systems), then with nonnasal sonorants, and then with a handful of sonorant systems where the nasal-nonnasal contrast is lacking or requires special handling.

As in dealing with obstruent systems, we shall handle "half-systems" in cases like Lifu, Marshallese, and Russian, where an overriding contrast breaks almost all the consonants into two subsets each of which includes obstruents and sonorants.

Some languages have two manners for sonorants, one of which resembles one of the manners found for obstruents, without yielding any neat breakdown of all the non-pharyngeal and non-glottal consonants into two sets. Nootka, for example, has /m m' n n' w w' y y'/, where the glottalization recurs (in slightly different form phonetically) in one manner of obstruent; but there is no exact pairing between glottalized and non-glottalized, because of the spirants in the obstruent system. Plain versus glottalized sonorants are found not only in Nootka, but also in Kwakiutl, many of the Salishan languages (Coeur d'Alene, Bella Coola, Kalispel and others, but not Duwamish, Snoqualmie), Yokuts, and Navaho. In these cases, the following sections will deal with the "half-system" obtained by deleting the contrast between plain and glottalized. There seems to be no other contrast which works in just this way.

25221. *Nasal Systems.* The number of nasal phonemes (differentiated solely by position of articulation) which appear in various languages ranges from none at all to four. Two generalizations can be made, neither of them perfect. The number of positions of articulation for nasals exceeds the number for stops only very rarely: Samoan is a case, with /m n ŋ/ but only /p t/. The only languages with but a single nasal have an /n/, and usually have no labial consonants at all; for example, in Iroquoian; but Winnebago and Senadi are exceptions of a peculiar sort (§252212 below).

252211. *No Nasals.* This is reliably reported for Quileute, Duwamish, and Snoqualmie; probably also in a few other southern Coast Salishan dialects. In all of these cases, it is known that the languages at an earlier period in their histories had nasals, which have become voiced stops.

252212. *One Nasal.* Tillamook, and most or all of the Iroquoian languages (Seneca, Oneida, Cherokee, Mohawk), have no labial consonants, and only one nasal, /n/. Arapaho also has only an /n/, though its stops include /b t č k/.

Winnebago has only one sonorant that is always a nasal: /m/. [n] and [r] contrast only in a way which is tied up with oral and nasal vowels; we extract a nasalization feature (§2432), which leaves /r/ as a sonorant undefined as to nasality.

There are some languages where at first one is led to recognize two or more nasals, but where on further examination a different solution presents itself. Senadi, for example, has nasal continuants [m n nʸ ŋ]. It also has both oral and nasal vowels: in vowel sequences, either all are nasal or all are oral. After a nasal continuant onset, only nasal vowels occur. After other onsets both nasal and oral vowels occur. There are syllabic nasals, with a tone, but these do not contrast as to position of articulation, since each occurs only before a homorganic stop or spirant. All of this can be handled with a single nasal phoneme, /n/. This unit occurs, with a tone, as a syllable, but only directly before a consonant-initial syllable, and the position of articulation of the /n/ is that of the following consonant. Thus we have /ńbá/, /ńdá/, /ńdʸá/, and /ńgá/, which are phonetically [m̃bá], [ńdá], [ń^yd^yá], and [ń́gá]. /n/ occurs, secondly, without a tone, but immediately followed by /b d d^y/ or /g/ and one or two vowels: in this case the /n/ nasalizes both the stop and the vowel or vowels. Thus /nbá ndá nd^yá ngá/ are [mą́ ną́ n^yą́ ŋą́]. Finally, /n/ occurs directly before a vowel or two vowels, in which case it is represented only by the nasalization of the vowel or vowels: /bná dná d^yná gná tná/ are [bą́ dą́ d^yą́ gą́ tą́]. This reanalysis is not a trick: it is an attempt to extract in the most economic way those factors which are maximally independent of each other in their occurrence, non-occurrence, and cooccurrence. Some of the other languages which we shall deal with below in other ways would perhaps allow of some such reinterpretation, but many of them do not.

252213. *Two Nasals.* All systems with two or more nasals have an /n/, and all with more than two have both /m/ and /n/. Thus systems with just two nasals have /m n/.

This is reported for: Alabama, all Central Algonquian, Amahuaca, Arunta; Bariba, Bella Coola; Chipewyan, Chiricahua, Chitimacha, Choctaw-Chickasaw, Coeur d'Alene, Crow, Cuicateco, Cuitlateco; Dakota, Delaware; German (of Brienze), Georgian; Hawaiian, Hitchiti-Mikasuki, Hopi, Huasteco, Huichol; Kalispel, Karok, Kiowa, Koasati, Kutenai, Kwakiutl; Latin; Western Miwok, Motilone; Nàhuatl, Navaho, Nootka; Ossetic; Polish; Romanian, Russian; Saho; Takelma, Terena, Tiwa, Tojolabal, Tonkawa, Totonac, Tsotsil, Tunica, Turkish, Tzeltal; Yokuts (except Wikchamni); Sierra Zapotec, Zuni.

252214. *Three Nasals.* There are three patterns for three nasals: /m n ŋ/, /m n n^y/, and (quite rare) /m n n̠/.

The first, with /ŋ/ more limited in distribution that /m n/, is reported for: Creek-Seminole, Dutch, English, Finnish, German, Japanese, Korean, Taki-Taki. There seems to be no distributional limitation in: Bannock, Burmese; Cantonese; Dibabaon; Ilocano; Kraho, Loma; Mandarin, Sierra Miwok; Samoan, Supide; Tagalog, Tarascan, Thai, Tubatulabal; Wikchamni.

The second: Campa, Cashibo, Czech; French; Hungarian; Italian; Keres; Mazateco; Otomi; Portuguese; Santa Clara Tewa, Serbo-Croatian, Spanish; Yuma.

The third is reported for Breton and for Badaga, though the latter may have also a phonemically separate /ŋ/.

252215. *Four Nasals.* All languages with four nasals include /m n ŋ/.

The fourth is /n^y/ in: Lifu (half-system), Senadi (but see reanalysis in §252212), Cuzco Kechua, Sui, and Zoque.

The fourth is /m^w/ in Trukese, matching the stop /p^w/.

The fourth is /n̠/ in Kota (and possibly Badaga has these four).

South Greenlandic Eskimo distinguishes between fronted /ŋ/ and backed /ŋ̠/, as for its stops.

25222. *Non-Nasal Sonorants.* A few systems have only glide vocoids among their non-nasal sonorants, and a few have no glide vocoids at all. We deal with these first, then with the commoner situation in which system involves both glide vocoids and other types of non-nasal sonorants.

252221. *Glide Vocoids Only.* Chiricahua Apache and Navaho have only a /y/. Bannock has only a /w/. /w **y**/ occur in Arapaho, Chitimacha, Plains Cree, Fox, Kraho, Menomini, Motilone, Nootka, Ojibwa, Potawatomi, Seneca, and Wikchamni. Winnebago has /w y/, plus the nasalization-indifferent /r/.

252222. *No Glide Vocoids.* /r/ only: Chipewyan, Crow.

/l/ only: Cantonese, Mandarin, Samoan, Sui, Kiowa.

/l r/: Georgian.

/l ḷ r/: Breton.

/l lʸ r/: Italian.

/l r r·/: some Spanish dialects.

/l r ɽ/ (the last a retroflex flap): aboriginal Tarascan.

/l lʸ r r·/: Castilian Spanish, Portuguese.

/l r ɽ r·/: Hispanized Tarascan.

252223. */w/ and Others.* /w l/: Hawaiian, Telelcingo Nahuatl, Lifu (halfsystem).

Cashibo has /β/, probably to be classed as a sonorant, and /r/.

/w l r r·/: some Spanish (e.g., southern Mexican).

/w l r ɽ/: Sierra Zapotec (the second trill is not described; this may be like southern Mexican Spanish).

/w l r γ γʷ/: Coeur d'Alene (the last two are dorso-velar voiced spirants which seem to belong to the sonorant system).

252224. */y/ and Others.* /y l/: South Greenlandic Eskimo.

/l r y/: Sierra Popoluca, some French; standard German (in which /w/ is a covowel and thus not a part of the marginal system); Russian.

/l r rʸ y/: Czech (/rʸ/ is an apical trill accompanied by a laminal spirant).

/l r r· y/: Mazateco.

/l lʸ r y/: Turkish, Serbo-Croatian.

/l ḷ r ɽ y/: Kota (plus /v/ which perhaps belongs to the sonorant system).

252225. */w y/ and Others.* The commonest scheme is /w y l/, found in Alabama; Bella Coola, Burmese; Cherokee, Choctaw-Chickasaw, aboriginal Cuitlateco, some Cree dialects, Creek-Seminole; Duwamish, Dakota, Delaware; Hitchiti-Mikasuki, Hopi, Huasteco; Koasati, Kutenai, Kalispel, Kwakiutl; Loma; Miwok; Nahuatl (except Telelcingo); Oneida; Snoqualmie, Shawnee, Supide; Tillamook, Takelma, Tonkawa, Totonac, Tubatulabal; Yokuts (except Wikchamni); Zuni.

/w y r/: Amahuaca, some Cree, Isleta, Japanese, Keres, Sandia, Santa Clara Tewa, Trukese.

Karok and Campa have /β y r/.

Korean has /w y/ and a retroflex /l/ which is sometimes lateral and sometimes not.

/w y l r/: Arunta, Bariba, Dibabaon, Dutch, English, German (Brienze), Huichol, Ilocano, Hungarian, Ossetic, Otomi, Picuris, Romanian, Taos, Terena, Tojolabal, Tunica, Tzeltal, Tagalog, Taki-Taki, Thai. Finnish and Tsotsil have /v/ or /β/ instead of /w/.

/w y l r r·/: Hispanized Cuitlateco, Hispanized Zoque.

/w y l r ɽ/: Saho (the /ɽ/ is a retroflex flap, sometimes sounding like [ɖ]).

/w y l ḷ r/: Badaga.

/w y l lʸ r/: Yuma, Cuzco Kechua.

252226. *More than Two Glide Vocoids.* Some dialects of French have both /w/ and /ɥ/ phonemically distinct from /u ü/, yielding a system /w ɥ y l r/.

25223. *Symmetric Sets of Sonorants.* The exact doubling of sonorants through the contrast of nonglottalized and glottalized (§2522) of course places them all in a symmetric set. Apart from this, symmetric sets of sonorants are rather rare, but the following cases appear:

Italian, Portuguese, Castilian Spanish, Serbo-Croatian, Yuma, and Cuzco Kechua have

$$
\begin{array}{ll}
n & n^y \\
l & l^y .
\end{array}
$$

Czech has rather

$$
\begin{array}{ll}
n & n^y \\
r & r^y .
\end{array}
$$

Breton and Badaga have

$$
\begin{array}{ll}
n & ṇ \\
l & ḷ .
\end{array}
$$

Kota has a larger set:

$$
\begin{array}{ll}
n & ṇ \\
l & ḷ \\
r & ṛ .
\end{array}
$$

25224. *Unitary sonorant Systems.* A few languages have well-defined sonorant systems which cannot be divided into a nasal system and a nonnasal system. Winnebago, which we treated in §252212, might also be classed in this way. A closely related language, Hidatsa, must be: there are two sonorants, /w r/, but these are oral [w r] in some environments, nasal [m n] in others.

Wichita also has just /w r/; the /r/ varies as does that of Hidatsa, but the /w/ is apparently always oral.

The situation in Fijian is similar, but we defer its treatment to §2523 because it does not have a well-defined sonorant system.

2523. *Systems Not Marked by Obstruent-Sonorant Dichotomy.* Here we shall discuss two types of situation: (1) that represented by Lifu, where the whole set of consonants, apart from laryngeals, is more or less neatly halved by some overriding contrast; (2) the situation in which a neat dichotomy of non-laryngeal consonants into obstruents and sonorants is impossible.

Isthmus Zapotec is reminiscent of Lifu:

p	t	k		b	d		g
	s	š			z	ž	
(m)	N			(m)	n		
W	L			w	l	r	y .

The consonants in the left-hand set are voiceless fortis; those in the right-hand set voiced and lenis. It will be noted that the matching is not exact: there are no fortis opposite-numbers for /r y/, and /m/ is fortis or lenis depending on environment (for which reason we have entered the same symbol on both sides). There are, in addition, a long apical trill /r·/ which occurs in a handful of native words as well as in Spanish loans, and a bilabial trill which occurs in just one word.

Marshallese affords another example, but the basis of overriding contrast is plain and palatal:

p	t	k	p^y	t^y	k^y
m	n	ŋ	m^y	n^y	$ŋ^y$
l			l^y		
r			r^y .		

Other details are not clear. It is not certain whether there is a manner consonant /y/ going with the palatals, but if there is it is apparently not feasible to treat the palatals as clusters.

The last comment applies to Russian. In the following table we list what may be taken as the basic "half-system" of Russian, apart from the manner consonant /y/; a hyphen before the symbol means that the consonant in question occurs in the plain variety, and a hyphen after it means that it occurs in the palatal variety. Contrast is thus certain only for those which are both preceded and followed by hyphens. Some of the contrasts are very rare; in any case, individual speakers vary, and it is possible that we have provided too much or too little—or both, for different speakers:

-p-	-t-	-c	č-	-k-
-b-	-d-		ž̌-	-g-
-f-	-s-		-š-	-x-
-v-	-z-		-ž-	-γ(-)
-m-	-n-			
	-l-			
	-r- .			

Many Slavicists operate under the impression that most (or all) of the Slavic languages have the same sort of fundamental set-up of largely paired plain and palatal consonants. But in many of the languages (not Russian, and possibly not Polish) it is perfectly feasible to regard most of the "palatal" units as clusters with /y/. Our option of this latter treatment for Serbo-Croatian and Czech may be no less arbitrary than a Russian-like treatment, but it is also certainly no more arbitrary.

Iraqi Arabic has a system in which the contrast of plain and pharyngealized cuts across the obstruent-sonorant dichotomy, but only in a very irregular and partial way. The largest symmetrical set which can be drawn from the obstruents is

p	t	č	k
b	d	ǯ	g
f	s	š	x .

To this must be added the non-pharyngealized obstruents /θ ð z/, and the non-pharyngealized sonorants /m n r l/. Four of the obstruents are matched by pharyngealized ones: /ṭ ḳ ṣ ð̣/; there is also a /γ/ which is unmatched by any plain obstruent. Only one of the sonorants is paired: /ļ/. The manner-consonant going with the pharyngealized consonants is /ʕ/, a voiced pharyngeal spirant which is sometimes a stop. There are, in addition, /ʔ h/ and a pharyngeal /ḥ/ which can be regarded as a pharyngealized partner to /h/. /w y/ may be separate phonemes, or may be only allophones of vowels.

Next we consider Fijian and Chatino, where no simple obstruent-sonorant dichotomy is feasible. A trichotomy is possible in Fijian:

Pure Obstruents:		t	k
	β	ð	
		s	
Mixed obstr-sonor:	ᵐb	ⁿd	ⁿg
Pure Sonorants:			
Nasals:	m	n	ŋ
Mixed nasal-nonnasal		ⁿr	
Nonnasals:		r	
		l	
	w	y .	

A similar treatment is possible in Chatino:

p	t	k		ʔ h
b	d	g		
	s š			
ᵐb	ⁿd	ⁿg		
m	n			
w y r l				

In neither of these cases does there seem to be any justification for forcing the prenasalized voiceless stops into the classification of "pure obstruents" or of "pure sonorants." However, it is possible in Chatino (not in Fijian) that they should be treated as clusters. Mixteco resembles Chatino in general outline.

2524. *Manner Consonants.* Often, in analyzing a language, one hesitates for a long time between interpreting certain consonantal elements as units or as clusters. This is of course true of affricates, but it also happens for consonants of contrasting manners: one may seem to have the choice between recognizing two or more manners, or just one manner, the consonants of the other manners being clusters.

The cluster interpretation is impossible if there is no appropriate element in the system which can function as the "modifying" element of each cluster. Thus a [pʻ] can be a cluster providing there is also a [b] cr [p] and an independently occurring /h/, but if there is no independent /h/ then an interpretation as /ph/ is precluded.

However, even if this first condition is met, the weight of evidence may be against the cluster interpretation, or, indeed, such an interpretation may be downright impossible. For example, a [p'] cannot be /ph/ if there is a contrasting cluster /ph/ in the system—unless, of course, it should turn out that the latter is efficiently interpretable as /p-h/, with an intervening juncture.

In those cases in which the first condition is met, but in which the cluster interpretation is nevertheless rejected, we propose to speak of *manner consonants*. If [p'] is a unit phoneme /p'/ (paralleled by similar units at other positions of articulation), and there is an /h/ in the system, then (other things being suitable) we say that /h/ is a manner consonant, going with the aspirated stops.

/h/ would seem to be a manner consonant, under this definition, in Chitimacha, Thai, Kechua, Lifu, and perhaps others. English and German /h/ is a different matter: its syllable-margin allophone [h] might be said to parallel the voiceless aspirated stops (though the latter are not aspirated in all positions), but its postvocalic allophone (in complex peaks: scalar or lowering lengthener or centering glide) is voiced and does not fit. In Kechua, the obstruent series paralleling /h/ are sometimes voiceless aspirated stops, sometimes voiceless spirants. In Lifu, /h/ parallels the whole voiceless half-system.

/ʔ/ would seem to be a manner consonant in Huasteco, Western Miwok, Tojolabal, Tsotsil, Tzeltal, and Zuni, where the paralleling obstruents are glottalized stops. The same applies in Coeur d'Alene and Snoqualmie, where we would be led to expect also a manner consonant /h/—but /h/ does not occur.

In Czech there is a voiced /ɦ/ which perhaps can be taken as a manner consonant going with the voiced stops and spirants.

In Iraqi Arabic the pharyngeal /ʕ/ can be taken as a manner consonant going with the various pharyngealized consonants.

In Russian, /y/ is certainly a manner consonant going with all the palatalized consonants. The same holds in Marshallese—if the language has a /y/.

Both /ʔ/ and /h/ are manner consonants in Bella Coola, Duwamish, Kalispel, Tillamook, Nootka, and Kwakiutl (perhaps others), where the former goes with the glottalized stops and sonorants, the latter with the spirants. In Chipewyan, Chiricahua, Yokuts, Navaho, and Santa Clara Tewa, /ʔ/ goes with the glottalized stops (in Navaho also with the glottalized sonorants), while /h/ goes with aspirated stops. In Tiwa, /ʔ/ goes with the glottalized stops, /h/ with both the aspirated stops and with voiceless spirants, there being no minimal contrasts (both manners at the same position) for the latter.

It will be noticed that the only non-laryngeal manner consonant is the Russian /y/. This is partly due to our method of analysis. Since one hesitates between the unit and cluster interpretation in such cases as [kʷ qʷ xʷ x̣ʷ], it may be that, if a system includes a /w/ but analysis of labialized stops and spirants as clusters with /w/ is impossible, /w/ should be called a manner consonant. However, never does one find such extensive parallel sets with and without [w]-type modification.

2525. *Laryngeals*. A good number of languages have no laryngeals at all: Arunta, South Greenlandic Eskimo, Fijian, most dialects of French, Italian, Kota, Latin (early Latin an /h/), Loma, Mandarin, Marshallese (?), Polish, Portuguese, Spanish, and Trukese.

Many have only an /h/: Badaga, Bariba, Breton (?), Burmese, Cherokee, Cree, Crow, Delaware, Dutch, Finnish, Fox, some dialects of French, German, the German of Brienze, Hungarian, Korean, Lifu, Muskogean Nahuatl (Matlapa, Sierra Nahuat, Tetelcingo), Kechua, Romanian, Sanskrit, Serbo-Croatian, Shipibo (?), Taki-Taki, Tarascan.

Many have only an /ʔ/: Cashibo, Chontal, Coeur d'Alene, Dibabaon, Hopi, Ilocano, Motilone, Nahuatl (Milpa Alta), Ojibwa, Potawatomi (/h/ in interjections), Samoan, Senadi, Snoqualmie, Supide, Tagalog, Terena, Totonac, Yuma, Sierra Zapotec and Villa Alta Zapotec.

Shawnee has a single glottalic phoneme which is [h] before vowels, [ʔ] before consonants.

Czech has only its voiced /ɦ/.

Georgian and Ossetic have a pharyngealized glottal catch /ʔ/, which apparently sometimes has a very far back dorso-velar closure.

A great many languages have /h ʔ/: Amahuaca, Bannock, Bella Coola, Campa, Chatino, Cheyenne, Chipewyan, Chiricahua, Chitimacha, Comanche, Cuicateco, Cuitlateco, Dakota, Duwamish, Hawaiian, Hidatsa, Huasteco, Huichol, Iowa-Oto, Japanese (/ʔ/ very limited and perhaps tied up with intonation), Kalispel, Karok, Keres, Kiowa, Kraho, Kutenai, Kwakiutl, Maidu, Mazateco, Menomini, Sierra Miwok, Western Miwok, Mixteco, Nahuatl (Olmeca, Ixcatepec), Oneida, Osage(?), Otomi, Picuris, Seneca, Sierra Popoluca, Sui, Takelma, Taos, Thai, Tillamook, Tojolabal, Tonkawa, Tsotsil, Tubatulabal, Tunica, Turkish, Tzeltal, Wichita, Winnebago, all Yokuts, Isthmus Zapotec, Zoque, Zuni.

Tangsic has /h/ and a voiced /ɦ/; possibly (but probably not) a glottal catch /ʔ/.

Navaho, Santa Clara Tewa, Sandia, and Isleta have /ʔ h hʷ/.

Saho has /h ḥ ʕ/, the second a voiceless pharyngeal spirant, the third a voiced pharyngeal spirant.

Nootka has /ʔ h ʔ ḥ/, the latter two pharyngealized.

Iraqi has /ʔ h ḥ ʕ/.

26. *Ultimate Phonologic Constituents.* Some macrosegments (in some languages) consist of a single syllable. Some syllables consist of a lone peak, or of a lone onset; some peaks, onsets, codas, or interludes consist of single phonemes. In just this same way, some phonemes consist of a single ultimate phonologic constituent (or *component* or *feature*), while most of them, in any single language, consist of bundles of several ultimate components.

The elements of an intonational system are quite apt to be impervious to further analysis. The three PLs of English intonation are at once intonation elements ("suprasegmental phonemes" in American jargon) and ultimate constituents. Of the three TCs, it may be that / ↑ / can be regarded as consisting of two components, /|/ and "rise," and / ↓ / similarly of /|/ and "dying-away fall"; this leaves /|/ itself as consisting of a single ultimate constituent.

The elements of a linear accentual system, likewise, are usually not further divisible: medial and soft stress in English are both ultimate phonologic constituents. In non-linear accentual systems a further breakdown is often possible.

It is among (segmental) phonemes, however, that one-constituent units are rarest and multiple-constituent bundles commonest. The degree of indeterminacy which has characterized our statements all the way through our large-to-small survey is not destined to disappear as we approach the lowest hierarchic level. In surveying peak and margin systems we often found it necessary to indicate alternative classifications of phonemes. This automatically implies an indeterminacy as to the ultimate phonologic components found in the phonemes so classified. For, in one sense, the constitutional classification of some set of phonemes, and the breakdown of the same phonemes into their ultimate phonologic constituents, are simply two ways of doing the same thing. If we describe a five-vowel system

$$i \qquad u$$
$$e \qquad o$$
$$a$$

by saying that two of the vowels are high, two mid, and one low, and that the high and mid vowels are respectively front unrounded and back rounded, this is tantamount to saying that /i/ *consists* of the ultimate components "high" and "front-unrounded," and so on. The difference is largely in the grammar of our statements: (1) "/i/ is high and front-unrounded" describes /i/ with *adjectives* "high" and "front-unrounded," while (2) "/i/ consists of the features high and front-unrounded" analyzes /i/ in terms of things named by *nouns* "high" and "front unrounded." Obviously, then, any indeterminacy as to the constitutional classification of phonemes is at the same time an indeterminacy in the analysis of phonemes into ultimate constituents.

Yet this does not imply that the task of extracting and listing ultimate phonologic components can be completed by a simple mechanical transformation of our statements about constitutional classification. The discussion and examples which follow will demonstrate this.

We shall do two things in this section. First we shall take certain phonetically defined features, and show how in different languages they can be of relevance in any of many different ways—or even not at all; we shall be interested particularly in showing how the hierarchic level at which a given feature makes its appearance can vary. Then we shall give several examples of componential analysis of specific languages, to show the degree of indeterminacy which still characterizes our joint professional efforts along this line.

261. *Sample Features.* We shall consider first nasality and then tone.

2611. *Nasalization.* In a very few languages, as we have seen (e.g., Quileute), nasalization plays no role at all. In most it plays some role, but this is highly variable: we can distinguish at least its function in Fox (or English), Oneida, Taos, Cashibo, Chiricahua, Winnebago, Hidatsa, and Senadi.

In Fox (or English, or any of many other languages), nasalization functions as an ultimate phonologic component for consonants only: Fox /m n/ are nasal (and voiced), /p t/ oral (and usually voiceless); in English only nasalization distinguished /m n ŋ/ and /b d g/.

In Oneida, one consonant is nasal (/n/); in the single vowel system, two of the six vowels have nasality as a secondary characteristic.

In Taos, again, nasalization functions for consonants, but also, and quite independently, for vowels. The situation for consonants is much as in Fox or English. For vowels, nasalization is a component which participates on a par with tongue and lip position: /į/ is a coordinate construction of simultaneous high, front unrounded, and velic open. There is only one other possibility: to take the nasalization as nucleus, and the tongue and lip position as satellite. This is suggested by the fact that in the few one-syllable sequences of two vowels, it is the whole sequence which is nasal or oral. It will be remembered that the nasal vowels cannot be regarded as some subset of the oral vowels with added nasalization (§2446); this is why the nasalization cannot be regarded as a simultaneous satellite to the remainder.

In Cashibo, nasalization functions for the consonant system as in Taos, Fox, or English, but quite differently in the vowel system. All the vowels may be modified by adding nasalization, and this satellite feature applies separately to each vowel-occurrence: sequences such as /ai/, /ąi/, /aį/, and /ąį/ all contrast.

In Chiricahua, consonantal nasalization is once again about the same; the additional fact is that a nasal sonorant can occur as satellite to a tone, yielding a mora, one or two of which constitute a syllable (/ḿ/, /m̀ḿ/). In syllables with vowels as peaks, nasalization occurs as satellite to the whole remaining peak, be it one vowel or two. When the nasalization, if present, is removed, the remainder consists of one vowel or two, each with a tone, and the tongue and lip positions are satellite to the tone. In Mazateco, likewise, nasalization makes its appearance at the level of the whole syllable peak, simple or complex, not for the individual vowels.

In Winnebago we find the first trace of interdependance between nasalization for consonants and for vowels (§2432). In Hidatsa we find a further step in this direction: nasalized vowels occur, in contrast to oral vowels, after all consonants, but nasal consonants are allophones of oral sonorants in position before nasalized vowels: /wa wą ra rą/ are [wa mą ra ną].

In Senadi, finally, nasalization is a "long component" which stretches either through one or two vowels (/kⁿá/, /kⁿáá/, bⁿá/) or through a stop consonant /b d dʸ g/ and the vowel or vowels that follow it (/ⁿbá ⁿbáá/ = [mą́ mą́ą́]) (§252212).

This survey shows, at least, that it is trivial merely to ask of a language "does it have nasal vowels?" The possible answers are not just "yes" and "no," but manifold.

2612. *Tone.* Setting aside the use of pitch in intonation, we still find a variety of ways in which tone can function in a phonologic system.

In Chiricahua, a tone-occurrence forms the basic unit of duration: anything which is simultaneous with the tone-occurrence is satellite to it; a syllable (defined by syllable juncture) includes one or two tone-occurrences.

In Senadi the basic unit of duration is more complicated: a vowel, or a nasal continuant with a tone. A vowel is accompanied by a simultaneous satellite consisting of one tone or of two in sequence, but the single vowel-occurrence lasts about the same length of time whether it carries one tone-occurrence or two.

On this basis, we may say that a syllabic nasal has the nasality as nucleus and the tone (always just one) as satellite.

In Bariba the tone-occurrence is not only the basic unit of duration, but actually defines the syllable—there are as many syllables in an utterance as there are tone-occurrences. The vowel color or nasal sonorant which accompanies a tone-occurrence is therefore satellite to it, as in Chiricahua.

In Mazateco a sequence of one, two, or three tone-occurrences stands in a co-ordinate construction with a sequence of one, two, or three vowels to form a peak, to which, in turn, nasality may be added as a satellite; the number of tone-occurrences does not correlate with the number of vowel-occurrences.

Finally, in Mandarin, Cantonese, Burmese, Thai, and the like, the domain of a tone is the microsegment: in most of these languages the microsegment is simply a syllable (defined by syllable juncture), but in Mandarin it may include a simple interlude.

Phonologically, then, it is just as unrigorous to speak of "tone languages" as it would be to speak of "nasalized vowel languages."

262. *Examples of Componential Analysis.* Our first example will be Fox. The phonemes which we shall assume are /p t č k s š h m n w y i o e a ·/. It may be that /w y/ are in complementation with /o i/, but for the sake of simplicity we shall assume that this is not the case, so that these constitute four phonemes, not two.

/p t č k s š h m n w y/ occur only marginally, whereas /i o e a ·/ occur only in or as peaks. We might at first seek to find some feature present in all of the first group and in none of the second, or else vice versa, which correlates with this: say a feature *nonsyllabic* versus a feature *syllabic*. But in the case of /p t č k s š h m n/ the other features which are bundled together imply necessarily (for Fox) the presence of the so-called *nonsyllabic* feature; in the case of /e a ·/ the other features which are bundled together imply with the same necessity the presence of the *syllabic* feature. It is only in the case of /w y/ versus /o i/ that the difference might be said to lie in the presence of *nonsyllabic* versus *syllabic*. It will be more economic if we can detect some other articulatory characteristic in /w y/ versus /o i/, and set this up as the primary determinant of the contrast, regarding the matter of *nonsyllabic* and *syllabic* as a resultant of it. Now the factor which seems primarily to render /w y/ nonsyllabic, as over against the similar /o i/, is a factor of timing: /w y/ do not last as long as /o i/; they are glide-vocoids rather than peak-vocoids (§165). They are also usually a bit higher, and perhaps normally pronounced with less force than /o i/. All of this we will summarize (since the various factors are not separable) by saying that /w y/ contain a feature *shortness* which is not present in /o i/.

/w y o i/ all contain a feature *high* (referring to tongue-height), while /e a/ contain a contrasting feature *low*. /w o a/ contain a feature *back*, while /y i e/ contain *front*. These features obviously are paired: each of the set /w y i o e a/ contains *high* or *low*, and also *front* or *back*, while other phonemes do not contain any of the four. Similarly, while /w y/ contain *shortness*, and /o i/ distinctively lack it—we may say they contain *nonshortness*—no other phoneme (not even

/e a/) contains either shortness or nonshortness; this pair of features is operative only for bundles of features which include *high*.

/·/ in any given occurrence will contain *high* or *low*, and *front* or *back*, but this will depend on environment (*high* and *front* when /·/ follows /i/, and so on). We can interpret /·/ in either of two ways. One is as a phoneme which is not composed of articulatory features, but purely of a timing factor: /·/ means "more of the same." By this interpretation, /·/ is like punctuation in music: the note itself represents all the "features" (pitch and so on) while the dot has to do entirely with timing. But we do find one feature constantly present in /·/, and so a second interpretation is possible: /·/ is always *voiced*, and is the only phoneme of which this is true. We will choose this second interpretation, set up a feature *voiced*, and say that /·/ contains this feature and only this one.

For /m n w y i o e a/ this last feature, *voiced*, is present or not depending on environment, and so neither *voiced* nor its opposite, *voiceless*, is a distinctive component. But /p t č k s š h/ are apparently always voiceless, so that we can recognize *voiceless* as one feature in each of those bundles.

/p t č k s š/ are obstruents, and /m n w y/ are sonorants. However, we cannot set up a feature *obstruent* or *sonorant*; doing so would imply that all obstruents have some clear articulatory characteristic in common which differentiates them from sonorants and other nonobstruents. When the terms "obstruent" and "sonorant" were introduced (§2520) it was necessary to give first a rough cross-language definition, which defined "obstruent" as stop or spirant; and then it was necessary to indicate that in one or another language some spirants function not as part of the obstruent system but with the sonorants (e.g., the /v/ of Finnish, working like a /w/), while some apparent sonorants function as part of an obstruent system (e.g., the /y/ of Chipewyan, which pairs with voiceless /š/ as /z/ pairs with /s/). And in Fox it is simply not the case that /p t č k s š/ share some articulatory feature absent from all other phonemes. We will be able to define the class of Fox obstruents, and the class of Fox sonorants, in terms of the features we do extract, but not vice versa.

/p t č k m n/ all involve some complete oral closure: we will call this feature *stop* (which in this context obviously does not imply concomitant velic closure). /m n/ contain also the feature *nasal*, defined as velic open. Since *nasal* is present only when *stop* is, we regard *nonnasal* as distinctively present in /p t č k/, but outside of these six phonemes the contrast between nasal and nonnasal is irrelevant.

/p m/ contain *labial*, a "position of articulation" feature. /t s n/ contain *apical*; /č š/ contain *laminal*, and /k/ contains *dorsal*. /č/ has spirantal offglide, and this recurs in /s š/, perhaps in /h/, but we do not have to set this up as a separate feature, since we can predict when it will occur. For /s š/ also contain a feature *spirant*; we can say that any bundle containing *laminal*, or *spirant*, or both, automatically has spirantal offglide.

The features *stop* and *nasal* apply only when a "position of articulation" feature is present in a bundle, and *nasal*, moreover, only in a bundle containing *stop*. However, a bundle containing a "position of articulation" feature need not contain *stop*; it may contain *spirant* instead. We can interpret *stop* and *spirant* as opposites, as are *nasal* and *nonnasal*, or *high* and *low*.

However, one possible interpretation for /h/ is that it contains only *spirant*, not also any "position of articulation" feature. In medial clusters like /hp ht hč hk/, there is sometimes some local friction in the mouth for the /h/, at the position of the following consonant; this is no constant feature of /h/, which occurs also in a good many other forms: as voiceless glottal spirant (in which form a macrosegment-final voiceless or whispered /. . . a*hwa*/ differs from /. . . a*wa*/, where the italicized portion indicates the portion pronounced voicelessly), and as a voiceless vocoid in the position of a following voiced vowel. *Spirant* (liberally interpreted), without position of articulation, seems a better common denominator for this range of allophones than a possible alternative: that of taking /h/ as containing *voiceless* as its only constantly present positive feature.

One other feature which occurs quite regularly need not be regarded as primary: rounding. /w/ and /o/ are rounded, and no other phonemes are. We can say, however, that any bundle which contains *high* and *back* also contains, as a secondary implied concomitant, the feature of rounding.

We have now itemized the following sixteen features, in six pairs and one set of four mutually exclusive ones:

shortness	:	*nonshortness*
high	:	*low*
back	:	*front*
voiced	:	*voiceless*
stop	:	*spirant*
nasal	:	*nonnasal*

labial : *apical* : *laminal* : *dorsal* .

We began with sixteen phonemes, and have discovered sixteen primary ultimate phonologic components, which means that there has been no achievement of any greater "economy" of any kind. However, despite some inclination to think in this direction among current linguists, this is not the point of the analysis of phonemes into ultimate phonologic components. The point is to find out, in as determinate a way as possible, what actually distinct types of articulatory events do in fact comprise the stock of ultimate phonologic components of a phonologic system, and the various interrelationships in which they stand. Above we have merely a list. The ways in which these sixteen components participate in the bundles we have called the Fox phonemes can be shown by a table. In the table, the first line is for the four "position of articulation" components, the relevant presence of which is indicated by the abbreviations la ap lm do. The remaining lines are for the six pairs of mutually exclusive components: a plus indicates the presence of the one listed at the left above, and a minus the presence of its opposite.

	/p	t	č	k	s	š	h	m	n	w	y	o	i	a	e	·/
pos.	la	ap	lm	do	ap	lm		la	ap							
stop	+	+	+	+	−	−	−	+	+							
nasal	−	−	−	−				+	+							
shortness										+	+	−	−			
high										+	+	+	+	−	−	
back										+	−	+	−	+	−	
voiced	−	−	−	−	−	−	−									+

If we had accepted the other proposed analysis for /·/ (as a timing feature), then that phoneme would be omitted from the table and the last line would be left out, since *voiced* and *voiceless* would be completely determined by the other features in a bundle plus the position of that bundle in the macrosegment and relative to /·/.

By the analysis presented in the table, there is a single phoneme (/·/) which consists of a single distinctive feature; three, /h a e/, which consist of two; eight, /s š m n w y o i/, which consist of three; and four, /p t č k/, which consist of four. By the alternative analysis of /·/, one phoneme consists of a single feature, /h/; four of two, /s š a e/; and ten of three, /p t č k m n w y o i/.

We transcribe two brief utterances, /ihkwe·wa/ 'woman' and /newa·pama·wa/ 'I see him, her', each said as a macrosegment with the most usual intonation pattern. In each row we put plusses and minusses in parentheses when that feature is present for that particular occurrence of the phoneme because of its environment.

	/i	h	k	w	e	·	w	a/
pos.			do					
stop		−	+					
nasal	(−)	(−)	−	(−)	(−)	(−)	(−)	(−)
shortness	−			+			+	
high	+			+	−	(−)	+	−
back	−			+	−	(−)	+	+
voiced	(+)	−	−	(+)	(+)	+	(−)	(−)

The /·/ in the transcription of /ihkwe·wa/ is low and front because it accompanies a vowel which is; that vowel, /e/, is voiced because it precedes /·/. The terminal /wa/ is voiceless as part of the normal intonation.

	/n	e	w	a	·	p	a	m	a	·	w	a/
pos.	ap					la		la				
stop	+					+		+				
nasal	+	(±)	(−)	(−)	(−)	−	(±)	+	(±)	(±)	(−)	(−)
shortness			+								+	
high		−	+	−	(−)		−		−	(−)	+	−
back		−	+	+	(+)		+		+	(+)	+	+
voiced	(+)	(+)	(+)	(+)	+	−	(+)	(+)	(+)	+	(−)	(−)

The plus-or-minus sign in the nasal row in the transcription of /newa·pama·-wa/ represents optional partial nasalization of a vowel adjacent to a nasal continuant.

We give as an additional example an analysis of Nootka phonemes into ultimate phonologic constituents, but without preliminary discussion. For Nootka we will interpret /·/ as a "timing" feature, not composed of any concatenation of articulatory positions or motions, and will therefore omit it from consideration. The distinctive features are:

> *labial, apical, laminal, lateral, front dorsal, back dorsal* (the "position of articulation" features);
> *spirant, glottal, nasal, spirantal release;*
> *pharyngeal constriction;*
> *rounded, front;*
> *shortness;*
> *high, mid, low.*

Shortness applies only in the presence of *high*, as in Fox. In conjunction with *high* or *mid*, *front* and *rounded* pair off, *front* implying unrounded and *rounded* implying back. *Pharyngeal constriction* applies only in bundles containing *spirant* or *glottal* and not containing a "position of articulation" feature. A "position of articulation," unless accompanied by *spirant*, implies *stop*, which can thus be regarded as a secondary feature. *Spirant* implies *spirantal release*, but not vice versa, and minimum contrasts require the recognition of the latter as a separate primary feature. Voicing is always present when the bundle contains *high, mid,* or *low,* or when it contains *nasal,* and never present otherwise, so it is not a primary feature.

There are so many phonemes in Nootka that we present them in a succession of tables.

First the set involving *high, mid,* or *low* (hi, mi, lo on the table; "ro" = *rounded,* "fr" = *front*);

	/w	w'	u	y	y'	i	o	e	a/
height:	hi	hi	hi	hi	hi	hi	mi	mi	lo
ro : fr	ro	ro	ro	fr	fr	fr	ro	fr	
shortness	+	+	−	+	+	−			
glottal	−	+		−	+				

Next those involving *labial* or *apical* (la and ap on the table):

	/p	p'	m	m'	t	t'	n	n'	c	c'	s/
position:	la	la	la	la	ap	ap	ap	ap	ap	ap	ap
spirant:	−	−	−	−	−	−	−	−	−	−	+
spir. rel.	−	−			−	−			+	+	+
glottal	−	+	−	+	−	+	−	+	−	+	−
nasal	−	−	+	+	−	−	+	+	−	−	

Next the set involving *laminal* (lm) or *lateral* (lt):

	/č	č'	š	ƛ	ƛ'	ɬ/
position:	lm	lm	lm	lt	lt	lt
spirant	−	−	+	−	−	+
glottal	−	+	−	−	+	−
spirant rel.	+	+	+	+	+	+
nasal	−	−		−	−	

Next the set involving *front dorsal* or *back dorsal* (fd, bd):

	/k	k'	x	kʷ	k'ʷ	xʷ	q	q'	x̣	qʷ	q'ʷ	x̣ʷ/
position:	fd	fd	fd	fd	fd	fd	bd	bd	bd	bd	bd	bd
spirant	−	−	+	−	−	+	−	−	+	−	−	+
glottal	−	+	−	−	+	−	−	+	−	−	+	−
spir. rel.	−	−	+	−	−	+	−	−	+	−	−	+
nasal	−	−		−	−		−	−		−	−	
rounded	−	−	−	+	+	+	−	−	−	+	+	+

Finally, the laryngeals:

	/ʔ	h	ʕ	ḥ/
spirant	−	+	−	+
glottal	+	−	+	−
phar. constr.	−	−	+	+

Notice that the two consonants /ʔ/ and /h/ have been treated as containing a single (positive) distinctive feature each, respectively *glottal* and *spirant*; that these are mutually exclusive (we could have plotted them in a single line in the tables); and that each functions as a differential for a whole series of consonants. That is, many consonants which do not include *glottal* are paired by consonants identical save that they do; and similarly for *spirant*. /ʔ/ and /h/ are, of course, manner consonants in Nootka (§2524).

We transcribe a short Nootka utterance ('hunting wolves'?):

	/q'	a·	q'	a	n	a	ƛ'	a	ʔ	i·	ḥ/
position:	bd		bd		ap		lt				
sp : gl	gl		gl				gl		gl		sp
spir rel.	−		−				+				+
nasal	−		−		+		−				
phar constr									+	(+)	+
height:		lo		lo		lo		lo		hi	
ro : fr										fr	
shortness										−	

It is obvious that whole utterances or texts could be transcribed as we have transcribed a few words of Fox and one of Nootka, with a considerable range of possible conventions of symbolization. Such a transcription is comparable to the full score of a piece for orchestra, or even a piano piece written out on a grand staff; in contrast, our usual phonemic notation, consisting of an essentially linear sequence of symbols, with some diacritics, is comparable to a figured bass. There was a period in the history of music when the use of figured bass notation˙ was quite adequate: performers were adept at "realizing" a figured bass, at a keyboard instrument, in a way which might vary somewhat from one performance to another, but such that all variation fell within the range of what was "nondistinctive" relative to the musical tradition of the time. This was true in large part because the total number of permitted simultaneous bundles of notes was relatively small, and the sequences in which they were permitted to follow each other were likewise highly restricted. For more complicated music a figured bass is not adequate. That we are able to use essentially linear transcriptions for speech is due to precisely the factors that rendered figured bass a reasonable and usable notation earlier in the history of music: the total variety of combinations of articulatory motion, and the sequences in which the various combinations occur, are in every language relatively limited and small in number.

The comparison of "full score" componential transcription with a full orchestral score in music breaks down at one point, if we use for the former such componential analyses as those which have been presented above. In an orchestral score there is a line (a staff) for each instrument, and on it are placed the marks indicating at each moment what that instrument should be doing. Now the "instruments," in the case of speech, are certainly the various articulators in the mouth and the movable parts in the throat and at the back entrance to the nose. But we have not provided, in the "full scores" given above, a separate "staff" for each "instrument" in this sense: rather, since in both Fox and Nootka oral articulators function almost exclusively one at a time, we have specified, along one single "staff" of the "score," which articulator is to function, and along other "staves" what function it is to perform.

It is not too difficult to reanalyze the segmental phonemes of Fox or Nootka in order to achieve a "full score" notation more directly comparable to that in music. We shall do so for Nootka, which offers a bit more challenge in this connection.

We must have a staff for each of the following "instruments": the lower lip; the apex of the tongue; the blade of the tongue; the tongue as a whole; the front part of the dorsum; the back part of the dorsum; the velic; the pharynx; and the glottis.

For the glottis we must have two symbols for different functions: one for closure, and one for voicing. We shall use **k** for the former, **v** for the latter. Indication of voicing could be omitted, since, as we have already shown, its occurrence and non-occurrence are predictable in terms of what other features are present in a bundle, but it seems advantageous for our present purposes to work from the allophonic rather than the strict phonemic level. Where neither of these symbols appears on the glottis staff, the glottis is quiescent.

For the pharynx we need only one symbol: c for constriction. The absence of this mark means that the pharynx is relaxed and thus open. For the velic, also, a single symbol will do: o for open. We choose this rather than a positive symbolization for "closed" since it will save work: the velic is usually closed.

For the back and front dorsum we need two symbols: k for closed (stop closure), and s for spirantal approximation producing turbulence in the passing air. When neither of these is written, as usual, the articulator in question is doing nothing relevant.

For the blade of the tongue we have to distinguish between the following functions: k for closure against the alveolum and adjacent regions; s for spirantal approximation thereto; ks for closure followed by spirantal release; l for closure of the central part against the alveolum and adjacent regions but with spirantal approximation at the sides; kl for closure followed by this type of spirantal release. The symbol k will not occur along the blade staff save in these two combinations.

For the tip of the tongue the symbols k, s, and ks will suffice.

For the tongue as a whole we have to distinguish between high, mid, and low, and for the first two of those also between front and back: we will use i, u, e, o, and a for the five combinations.

For the lips we need two symbols, k for closure and w for rounding.

All these "instruments" are like percussion instruments in an orchestra in that they are individually capable of very few distinct roles. In an orchestral score an instrument which is confined, or virtually confined, to either making a sound or not—say a bass drum or a pair of cymbals—is scored not on a full staff of five lines but on a staff of a single line; if there are some few differences of function, different symbols on that single line are used. In our articulatory score we will use spaces between lines, instead of lines, as our separate staves, just as we did for the first analysis.

Two features of timing have to be symbolized. One is the "shortness" feature by the first analysis: we will put a breve over the symbol on the tongue-as-a-whole staff. The other is /·/, which we will indicate as in linear transcription with a postposed dot, also on the tongue-as-a-whole staff.

With these conventions, the "orchestral score" for the word transcribed earlier in another way looks like this:

	/q'	a·	q'	a	n	a	λ'	a	ʔ	i·	ḥ/
lips											
tongue		a·		a		a		a		i·	
tip			k								
blade							kl				
fd											
bd	k		k								
velic				o							
pharynx									c		c
glottis	k	v	k	v	v	v	k	v	k	v	

We show three more short utterances: 'thus much', 'three', and 'seven':

	/qʷ	a	m'	a·/	/q	a	č	c'	a/	/ʔ	a	ƛ	p	u/
lips	w		k										k	w
tongue		a		a·		a			a		a			u
tip								ks						
blade							ks					kl		
fd														
bd	k			k										
velic		o												
pharynx														
glottis	v	kv	v		v		k	v		k	v			v

The essential difference between the two methods of componential analysis which have been demonstrated lies in this: in one, positions and manners of articulation are alike regarded as features—all possible features are interpreted as constituting a homogeneous class, except insofar as privileges of occurrence with respect to each other serves to divide them up. In the other, positions of articulation (or, rather, actively functioning articulators) are regarded as items individually capable of two or more differentiated functions, some of those functions being the same for two or more organs, some of them not. There is no question as to "right" and "wrong" here: the two sorts of analysis produce mutually convertible results, and the fact that neither forces itself on us to the exclusion of the other is but another aspect of the relativism or indeterminacy of phonologic pattern.

Quite apart from the use of componential analysis in discovering the stock of ultimate phonologic constituents of a language (which can often be accomplished without resort to "articulatory score" transcription), the second kind of analysis is heuristically useful. If we begin with a large set of articulatory scores for a particular language, which include indication of all occurrences of any feature which may in some cases be phonologically relevant—including, say, the rounding of Fox /w/ and /o/, or the aspiration of Nootka plain stops not followed by a vowel, or the difference between the spirant and stop allophones of Spanish /b d g/—then careful examination of the combinations in which all these features occur, not only in simultaneous bundles but a' o in sequences, can be of material assistance in seeing the relative status of different features: that the presence of a particular feature implies, or is mutually exclusive with, the presence of another; that the occurrences of some particular feature are completely predictable in terms of others; that a particular feature is predictable in certain environments, but not in others; and so on. One is not likely to reach the point of such an examination without first having achieved at least a tentative phonemicization of the language and a tentative linear notation, but the examination can reveal interrelationships that are otherwise harder to detect, or which may otherwise even remain hidden altogether.

27. *Balance and Symmetry.* Problems of balance and symmetry are related, but distinguishable. Considerations of both kinds have come up in the course of our typologic survey, but some summarizing statements are needed, and some aspects have not come up at all.

271. *Balance.* We have found—using reasonably homogeneous analytic techniques from one language to another—vowel systems with as few as three members and with as many as twelve, and consonant systems with as few as eight (Hawaiian) and as many as forty-two (Kwakiutl). Some languages in the Caucasus are reported to have an even larger number of consonants, but we cannot be sure that the same principles were used, by those making the report, in deciding between single-phoneme and cluster interpretations. Now, speaking roughly in terms of "consonant" and "vowel," what are the ranges of possible *balance* between the number of consonants and the number of vowels in a single phonologic system? Can a language have eight consonants and three vowels? Can one have eight consonants and twelve vowels? Forty-two consonants and three vowels? Forty-two consonants and twelve vowels?

Obviously we cannot hope to answer such questions definitively, partly because there are too many chances for alternative interpretations of phonologic systems, but mainly because there are too vast a number of languages for which we have no reliable data. This is no reason not to give tentative and partial answers; perhaps we can at least discern some general tendencies. What we have done is to compute the ratio of the number of vowel phonemes to the total number of segmental phonemes for some sixty-odd languages on which our information is reasonably accurate. In this operation, covowels, such as the /·/ of Fox or the raising and lowering lengtheners of Cree, were counted with the vowel phonemes, but distinctions made by other than tongue and lip position, say nasalization, were omitted. The graph in Figure 12 shows the results. A vertical line appears at each point on the abscissa for which at least one language was found: that is, none of the languages examined had fourteen phonemes, or thirty-five. The lower curve shows the lowest ratios of vowel phonemes to all phonemes found in the different systems, while the upper curve shows the highest ratios.

In interpreting the graph it must of course be remembered that there were relatively fewer instances of systems with very few or very many phonemes than there were with an intermediate number. Despite this, we can probably safely read the following generalizations: The range of possible ratios of vowels to all phonemes is smallest in systems with very few or very many phonemes. The actual ratios tend to be lower in systems with very many phonemes than in those with very few. The greatest range of possible ratios is found in those systems with a moderate total number of phonemes.

Of the four theoretical extremes asked about earlier, we can with some safety conclude that only one is apt to occur—that with very many consonants and very few vowels. With as few consonants as eight or ten, we will not find the smallest number of vowels, nor the greatest number. And with very many consonants we will not find very large numbers of vowels.

Other questions can be asked about balance. What are the highest and lowest

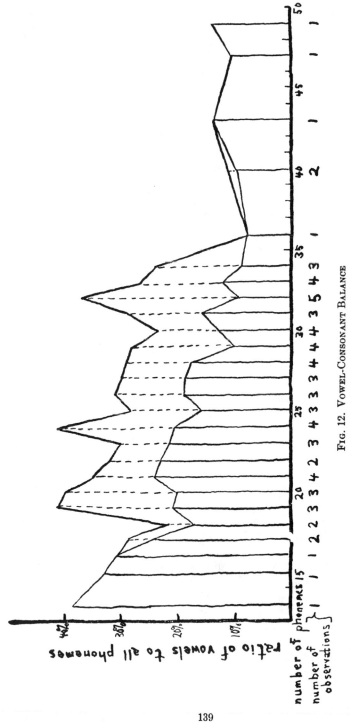

Fig. 12. Vowel-Consonant Balance

A vertical line shows the occurrence of at least one system with the indicated number of segmental phonemes (among the systems examined). The lower broken curve joins together the lowest ratios of vowels to all phonemes, and the upper broken curve the highest ratios. Total sample: 68 languages.

139

ratios of number of obstruents to number of sonorants? Some of the ratios are: Hawaiian .5, Marshallese .6, Samoan .8, Trukese 1.0, Hidatsa 3.0, Nootka 3.375, Chipewyan 11.33. Since fuller consonant systems are almost always built via a proliferation of obstruents, we can expect that the highest ratios will be found in the languages with the largest number of consonant phonemes; this is confirmed by the above examples since Hawaiian has 8 consonants, Marshallese 16, Samoan 10, Trukese 14, Hidatsa 10, Nootka 37, Chipewyan 39.

What are the highest and lowest ratios of stops and affricates to spirants? Of stops and affricates to nasals? Of nasals to non-nasal sonorants? A good many questions of this kind were asked, and tentatively answered, in the course of our survey of margin systems, and we need not repeat the data here.

272. *Symmetry*. The matter of symmetry is different. A set of four things is symmetric if in some sense a is to b as c is to d. There can be no question of symmetry where a and c are consonants and b and d are vowels, save in the limiting case where a and c are consonants of the type /w y/. Fewer than four things cannot manifest symmetry in this sense. It makes sense to say that English /t/ is to /k/ as /d/ is to /g/; it does not make sense to seek an x such that English /t/ is to /k/ as /p/ is to x.

Every phonologic system seems to have at least some symmetry, and at least some lack of symmetry. What are the symmetries of Fox phonemes? The four vowels constitute a symmetric set (/i/ is to /o/ as /e/ is to /a/, or, with a transformation, /i/ is to /e/ as /o/ is to /a/). The set /w y o i/ form another; by virtue of this, the set /w y a e/ do also. The four consonants /p t m n/ are symmetric, and the four consonants /t č s š/. Two consonant phonemes, /k/ and /h/, do not fall into any of these symmetries; likewise the covowel /·/ does not. Since there are sixteen phonemes in all, perhaps the ratio of three to sixteen can serve as a rough index of the *asymmetry* of the whole system. In Yawelmani Yokuts, with thirty-nine phonemes, only /a/ and /·/ stand unrelated; the ratio is about .05. Nootka, with forty-three phonemes, also shows just /a/ and /·/ standing outside. In Hawaiian, with thirteen phonemes, three, /a ? h/, participate in no symmetric set; this assumes that we can define /k/, /n/, and /l/ as *lingual* and say that /p/ is to /k/ as /m/ is to /n/ as /w/ is to /l/. This last example shows that it is not always entirely obvious whether a particular symmetry is to be recognized in a system or not.

Any "square," "rectangular," or "cubical" vowel system shows complete symmetry: the two-by-two system of Fox, the three-by-three system of English, the two-by-two-by-two system of Turkish. Any other vowel system involves lack of symmetry. Perhaps a three-plus-two-plus-one system, like the /i i u, e o, a/ of Sierra Popoluca, shows as little symmetry as one can find.

We can achieve a measure of the symmetry of obstruent systems by taking the ratio of the obstruents which belong to a symmetric set (§2521) to the total number. The raw-materials for this computation are at hand, for a number of languages, in §25213. Here are the results, for some of these languages, arranged in order of decreasing symmetry:

1.00 Kwakiutl, Sierra Popoluca, Hungarian, Senadi, Turkish, Dutch, Supide, Nootka, Duwamish, Isthmus Zapotec.

.95 Georgian (counting /v/ as an obstruent).
.94 Russian (half-system), Polish, Picuris, Serbo-Croatian.
.93 Aboriginal Cuzco Kechua.
.90 Snoqualmie, Bella Coola.
.89 Czech.
.88 Chipewyan, Coeur d'Alene, Tillamook.
.87 Ossetic.
.86 Yawelmani, Japanese, Crow, Winnebago, Delaware, Tagalog, Ilocano.
.84 Sandia.
.83 Chiricahua, Chitimacha, Cuitlateco.
.82 Taki-Taki, Spanish, Mandarin.
.80 Zuni, Lifu (half-system), Samoan.
.79 Taos.
.77 Sui.
.76 Kota.
.75 English, German, Keres, Campa, Tonkawa, the German dialect of Brienze.
.74 Navaho.
.73 Bariba.
.71 Huasteco, Hispanized Zoque, Italian, Yuma.
.69 Thai.
.67 Isleta, French, Portuguese, Western Miwok, Takelma, Tarascan, Burmese, South Greenlandic Eskimo, Choctaw-Chickasaw, Cheyenne, Hidatsa, Fox, Ojibwa, Potawatomi, Tunica, Shawnee.
.64 Breton.
.60 Loma.
.57 Sierra Miwok, Trukese, Creek-Seminole, Hitchiti-Mikasuki.
.53 Hausa.
.50 Mazateco, Hopi, Olmeca Nahuatl, Alabama, Koasati, Saho.
.44 Totonac, Sierra Nahuatl, most other Nahuatl dialects.
.00 Hawaiian, Kapauku, Marshallese (half-system), Arunta, most Polynesian, Finnish, Oneida, Korean, Cree, Menomini, Wichita, Terena, Huichol.

The jump from .00 to .44 is not surprising: an obstruent system can have no symmetry at all unless it includes at least four obstruents, and almost all systems with more than six or seven obstruents have four of them in symmetry. There is a rough tendency for systems with the largest number of units to have a greater degree of symmetry, but the range of variation is pretty wide.

Of especial interest is a "hole" in a system where one would expect an element because of predominating symmetric patterns. One such is in the vowel system of Korean. The vowels that do occur fit into a $2 \times (2+2+1)$ pattern, symmetrical for front and back, and, except for low, for unrounded and rounded. But this would imply ten vowels; the "high front rounded" spot is actually, for most speakers, simply not filled. Another example occurs among the obstruents of Bella Coola. Plain and glottalized stops and affricates pair off very neatly at various positions of articulation, and the dorsals and the tongue-front affricates are matched by spirants. However, among the laterals one finds only /ł/ and the glottalized stop /λ'/; there simply is no plain stop /λ/.

In the two instances just cited we are quite clearly dealing with a symmetric pattern where one position implied by the pattern is simply not occupied. This is a very different matter from an asymmetric pattern with all positions occupied, though it is not always easy to decide which situation confronts one in a given case. However, it is perfectly obvious that a three-vowel system /i a u/ is no example of a four-vowel symmetric system with one position not occupied; similarly an obstruent set-up with /p t k/ and /s/ is not a symmetric six-point pattern of three positions and two manners, with two holes. Either an asymmetric pattern or a symmetric pattern with a hole represents a degree of asymmetry, but of two somewhat different kinds.

273. *Frequency Aspects.* There is another point of view from which both the problem of balance and that of symmetry have to be examined. Up to this point we have been investigating these matters relative simply to the stock of phonemes (or other phonologic units) which occur in a language. But there is also the matter of relative frequency of the various units, or various kinds of units, in the actual stream of speech (text frequency).

It takes much more work to reach quantified conclusions along this line, for none can be obtained without extensive counting in actual texts. The percentage of vowels in the stock of phonemes of a language is one matter. The relative text frequency of vowels is a very different matter. In Hawaiian, where there are more different consonant phonemes than vowel phonemes, the latter occur somewhat more frequently than do the former—so much requires no counting, since a syllable always contains a vowel but only sometimes begins with a consonant. In the same way it can be proved without a count that, in Yawelmani, consonants must be more frequent than vowels, since every syllable contains at least one of each (as onset and peak) but some syllables also have a coda consonant; in Bella Coola the ratio must be in the same direction and even larger.

Relative frequency bears on the problem of symmetry in an interesting way. As a point of departure, let us consider the set of English spirants, /f v θ ð s z š ž/, which manifest symmetry in that /f/ is to /v/ as /θ/ is to /ð/, and so on. The relative text-frequencies of these eight consonants are as follows:

/s/	.279	/f/	.113
/ð/	.210	/š/	.050
/z/	.182	/θ/	.023
/v/	.140	/ž/	.003

That is, if a phoneme chosen at random from a long text is a spirant, then it will be /s/ with probability .279, and so on. It will be noticed, first of all, that while /s/ has a higher relative frequency than /z/, /f/ than /v/, and /š/ than /ž/, for the remaining pair the more frequent is the voiced member. Thus, although without regard to frequency we can assert that /s/ is to /z/ and /θ/ is to /ð/, if frequency is considered this is not the case.

Another interesting point stems from the extremely low relative frequency of /ž/. One could make a count in a very long English text and stand a reasonable chance of finding no occurrence of /ž/ at all. The difference between relative frequencies of .003 and of .000 is very slight. Yet just this is the difference between a symmetric pattern with one very low-frequency member and a symmetric pattern with a "hole." Now suppose that we had frequency figures for Taos obstruents, as indicated below (the figures given below are actually completely faked). We could describe the Taos system by listing twenty units, as follows:

b .005	d .013	ʒ .000	g .018	gᵂ .000
p .055	t .032	c .068	k .096	kᵂ .236
p' .177	t' .060	c' .024	k' .039	k'ᵂ .002
pʻ .001	tʻ .008	s .076	x .047	xᵂ .043 .

The two units to which we have assigned frequency .000 are the two which, so far as our reports show, do not occur in Taos at all. Yet this description perhaps portrays the Taos obstruent system quite as accurately as would a description which omitted /ʒ/ and /gᵂ/ from the table altogether.

Working purely from the stock of phonemes, then, a hole in a pattern appears as an asymmetry. Taking relative frequency into consideration, such a hole may be far less of an asymmetry than is some extreme deviation of the set of relative frequencies from some "most normal" distribution. For example, we would probably say that a situation in which one of a set of eight contrasting units accounted for eighty percent of the occurrence of any of the eight, while the remaining seven accounted about equally for the remaining twenty percent, was far more "skew" than the English spirants actually are, or than the Taos obstruents including a zero-frequency /ʒ/ and /gᵂ/ would be.

3. *The Principles of Phonologic Analysis.* In the taxonomic survey of §2 factual statements on this or that language were presented with a minimum of theoretic or methodologic comment. What justifies the claim that English has nine vowels? That Nootka has thirty-seven consonants? That glottalization is a positive "mark" in Nootka, but a negative device (equivalent to absence of the positive mark of aspiration) in Chitimacha? How does the analyst find out? Why, in some cases, should an analyst hesitate between alternative interpretations rather than making a forthright assertion? These are the sorts of questions which shall concern us here.

The process of phonologic analysis has two aspects: *gathering* and *collation.* We call these "aspects," rather than "steps," because it is not possible to do pure gathering first, pure collation afterwards—the two cannot altogether be *separated,* but they can be *distinguished.*

Analysis is undertaken under a wide variety of circumstances. At one extreme, an investigator does fieldwork of the observation-participation type in a community where a language is spoken. At the other extreme, there are no speakers, or they are unavailable, and one is forced to work via secondary sources, mainly written records. For linguistics, *any* sort of written record is a secondary source; the philologic and historical classification of some documents as "primary" and others as "secondary" is achieved from a different slant.

The fundamental assumptions are unchanged in these various circumstances, but the details differ a great deal. When one works from secondary sources—be they inscriptions several thousand years old or field reports from a contemporary colleague—some of the collation has been done, and cannot always be undone in order to try a different approach. Of course all the essential steps of gathering have been done in these cases, and although internal inconsistencies may lead the new investigator to question the accuracy of the gathering, he cannot do it over again unless he himself can work directly with native speakers. From the poorest of field-reports or surviving documentary evidence, sometimes virtually nothing can be deduced with any certainty. From the best, one can get something close to the whole story.

Usually the situation lies between these extremes: one can see fairly well the limits within which accuracy of reinterpretation is possible, though these limits may not be as narrow as one would wish. For example, from Boas's reports on Kwakiutl we can be sure that there is either a three-vowel system /i a u/ or a five-vowel system /i e a o u/, with contrast of length—not, say, some other sort of three- or four-vowel system or a system with eight or nine vowels. But one cannot with certainty choose between the three-vowel and the five-vowel system, and one cannot be absolutely sure whether there is, or is not, also an indeterminate /ə/. Sufficiently detailed examination of Boas's material can lead one to favor one or another of the alternatives, but only independent field work would settle the issue.

We shall now discuss gathering and collation in as separate a fashion as is realistically possible. In our discussion of gathering we shall assume that the circumstances are those first mentioned above: an investigator working directly with an informant. Most of the principles which apply under these circumstances are also as operative as conditions will allow when, at the opposite extreme, one's data are written records of forms of speech no longer current. Under the latter conditions there are also many special techniques, such as the various methods for dating manuscripts, the study of the development of writing-systems, and the use of information about earlier or more recent stages of the same language, on which we shall offer no comment. We refrain not because the special problems are not challenging and important, but because they would take us too far afield. In our discussion of collation we shall assume that the analyst has complete and accurate data—something which in the general case is true only after a great percentage of the process of collation has already been tentatively performed.

31. *Gathering.* The fundamental assumption in phonology is that, despite the wide variation of actual articulatory motion from one speech-event to another in a community, the speakers of a language themselves hear some speech-events as *the same*, some as *different*. To put this in a slightly different way: some speech events, under ideal hearing conditions (no background noise), *sound the same* to the native speaker, regardless of any variations in actual articulatory motion which the analyst may be able to observe, while others *sound different*. If two forms regularly sound the same (barring distortion by background noise) to the native speaker—say *meet* and *meat* in English—then when these forms occur as

whole utterances a speaker cannot tell, from the acoustic evidence alone, which of the two is being said. It is only rarely that one has to distinguish between two forms purely on the basis of the acoustic evidence; usually there is context. Thus, if A asks *What did you have for dinner?* and B answers *meat*, A knows that B has said *meat* rather than *meet*, not from the acoustic evidence, but because one does not have *meet* for dinner. At the same time, A knows that what B said was *meat*, rather than *potatoes* or *pork* or *company*, from the acoustic evidence and nothing else (and therefore, under poor hearing conditions, he may not be able to make the discrimination). Phonologic analysis, then, is concerned with the way in which utterances, under ideal hearing conditions, are kept apart *by virtue of acoustic evidence and it alone*; any other observations which an analyst makes are relevant only insofar as they contribute to this end.

To the field situation, the informant brings native control of his language, including the whole system of what "sounds same" and what "sounds different" to him. The investigator brings several things: (1) his understanding of the fundamental assumption, including an understanding of what it *means* for items to "sound same" or "sound different" to a native speaker; (2) some training in general phonetics, by which he will be able to tell, at least in part, what articulatory motions are probably responsible for any particular bit of speech-sound he elicits from his informant, and in terms of which he can put down in a written notation something which represents more or less accurately each elicited speech-event; (3) most important, his ability, as a human being, to be enculturated, to learn a new language, to *empathize*.

The basic problem in phonologic field work is to bring it about that there reside, in a single nervous system, both the native or native-like active control of the phonologic system, and the clear understanding of what is meant by "sounding same" and "sounding different." For, when this has been accomplished, it becomes possible to tabulate the various articulatory motions which differentiate utterances that sound different, ignore differences of articulation which do not make any such difference, and thus achieve a description of the phonologic system. Until the basic problem is solved, this is quite impossible: the investigator cannot be sure whether two items that sound the same to him actually sound the same to the informant, and cannot be sure that clear differences to his own ears have any relevance for the informant.

Obviously there are two ways, in theory, in which the basic problem can be solved: make the informant into an analyst, or make the analyst learn some of the language. It is a happy but rare event when the first of these alternatives is possible; usually the informant's concern with his own language is too purely instrumental and too subordinate to other interests. What would happen, for example, if one simply asked an English-speaking informant whether *meat* and *meet* sound the same or not? Experience shows that the answer is often wrong, not through any dishonesty or inability on the part of the informant, but because he does not understand the question. *Meat* and *meet* have different meanings; they occur in different contexts of other words; they are spelled differently (a consideration which is of course relevant only for some languages). It is very easy for an informant to say, and perhaps honestly to believe, that the two *sound* different because of these various other differences. I have seen in print the assertion that *grey* and *gray* "ought" to be pronounced differently.

This does not mean that one cannot address such questions to an informant, only that the responses require careful interpretation. The analyst is apt to have his own tentative opinion in any such matter: he thinks he hears a difference, or thinks that he does not. If the informant's answers in general agree with the analyst's opinion, then one can be fairly sure that the informant does understand the question as it is meant and is answering correctly. And in case of disagreement there is a simple test which can be performed, providing the psychologic factors in the field situation do not render it inadvisable.

For the test one needs two informants, A and B. A has claimed, let us say, that *meat* and *meet* sound different. It is arranged that B will produce ten or twelve utterances, each one of them *meat* or *meet*, in a random but prearranged order unknown to A. A is then asked to tell in each case which form he hears. If he can indeed tell in a significantly large proportion of the cases, then the investigator was wrong; if he cannot, then the investigator was right. Unless the informant's pride is injured by outcomes contrary to his claim, two or three tests of this kind can render him more effective as an informant, by showing him more clearly what the analyst means by "sounding same" and "sounding different." And the analyst, who of course has no pride to be injured, is aided because he discovers either that there is some subtle distinction which he has missed and which he must master, or else that he was indeed on the right track.

The converse of the *meet-meat* situation will also be encountered: for example, some speakers of English pronounce the word *root* sometimes with /uw/, sometimes with /u/. The analyst might not know, when he first noticed this fluctuation, whether it was a case of free variation within the bounds of a single phonologic unit, or a case of free alternation, for the particular form, between two distinct phonologic shapes. Perhaps ultimately the meanings of the two forms, *root* with /uw/ and *root* with /u/, are slightly different, but the degree of precision about meanings that can be achieved early in field work is not great enough to catch any such subtle difference in connotation—if indeed there is any—so that there would be no help from semantics. However, in due time the investigator would discover that /wuwd/ and /wud/ (*wooed, wood-would*), /kuwd/ and /kud/ (*cooed, could*), and a number of other pairs of obviously different forms, are kept apart precisely by the difference, /uw/ versus /u/, which appears in the two different pronunciations of *root;* and thereupon the answer would be clear: *root* varies in the way we call free alternation, not subphonemically.

The English examples which we have used above seem trivial, but this is because, knowing English, we know the answers. It must be remembered that problems of these kinds are encountered in the field when one is not yet thoroughly at home with the phonologic system which is being studied, in which circumstances examples of the kinds given are by no means trivial.

Whatever help the analyst is able to get by questioning his informant or using tests on him, sooner or later it is almost always necessary that the analyst acquire the ability to make for himself judgments of "sounding same" and "sounding different," not on any basis of general phonetics but in a way which matches closely the identifications and non-identifications which the native informant in fact makes. That is, the analyst must *empathize*, must to some extent learn the language with which he is working. We know of no set of procedures by which a Martian, or a machine, could analyze a phonologic system—an entity, that is, to which even the basic biologic and cultural common denominator of humanness would be alien and would require specification. The only procedures which can be described are rules for a human investigator, and depend essentially on his ability to empathize. To refuse to do this, to insist on avoiding it as much as possible in the name of a spurious "objectivity"—as, for example, Franz Boas did—is to place oneself in much the same position as that of a bacteriologist who would refuse to stain his slides. Obviously there are numerous pitfalls in the path of the investigator who seeks to enculturate to the phonology of a new language, but equally obviously we have reason to believe that the task can be accomplished. Any newcomer to a community, say a newborn child, in due time learns the language of the community, including its phonologic system: learns, that is, to identify and differentiate acoustic stimuli in much the same way as do those already in the community. The matching may not be exact, but apparently approximate matching is good enough, since the members of a speech community do in fact communicate via speech. All that we can ask of an investigator is that he do as good and precise a job along this line as a child does—but that he keep a record as he does it, so that we will have the materials to which to apply the other aspect of analysis, collation.

The fundamental assumption of phonology is really just that—an assumption, not capable of any kind of proof save the way in which it serves to coordinate and put sense into a wide variety of observations. Its logical status is much like that of, say, the particle theory in physics: particles are not observable in any direct way, but assuming them ties together a large number of matters which are directly observable. No one has yet proposed any alternative assumption which gives us a basis on which to work in phonology: without the fundamental hypothesis as we have stated it, the analyst is completely lost. No linguist ever approaches a new language with the intention of finding out whether that language has a phonologic pattern or not: its existence is necessarily taken for granted, and the analyst's aim is entirely one of discovering the specific details.

There is a second assumption involved in phonology which is closely related to the first but not deducible from it. This is the assumption that every utterance in some single language is composed wholly of an ordered arrangement of phonologic elements drawn from some strictly finite stock, which are the only ones of relevance for the language in question. If the total stock of actual and possible utterances in a language were finite, this second point would not be an assumption but would be a theorem provable on the basis of the fundamental assumption. For what one would do would be to compare the whole stock of utterances in pairs, listing the shared phonetic features and those which differentiate utterances, and continuing this until all possible pairs of utterances had been covered.

What the analyst actually does resembles this save for one point: the analyst can never observe more than a sample of the whole stock of actual and possible utterances, since in every language the whole stock is transfinite in number. As the investigator slowly enlarges the sample which he examines, the rate at which new contrasts are revealed steadily decreases; eventually he is forced to stop work and to predict that nothing new is going to turn up no matter how many additional observations are made. The steady decrease in new contrasts affords empiric support—though not logical proof—for this subordinate hypothesis.

Practically, what is usually assumed is that once one has tabulated everything which can differentiate *macrosegments*, one has tabulated everything. This implies that the total stock of actual or possible utterances of not greater than some maximum length is indeed finite, and that the only reason the whole stock of actual and possible utterances, regardless of length, is transfinite is because there is no arbitrary limit to the length of an individual utterance; it also implies that longer utterances will always consist of an integral number of macrosegments.

The procedure of the analyst in the field reflects all of these primary and secondary assumptions. One begins almost always by eliciting quite brief utterances, of approximately "word" length, for the practical reason that the investigator can hardly hope to hear with accuracy any much longer stretch of alien speech until he has had practice. Indeed, in some cases (perhaps not all) a new language sounds to an investigator for the first few hours or days like a completely confused and continuous flow of sound, entirely free of any segmentation. This fuzziness disappears in time, not because the investigator is trained especially in analytic techniques but simply because he is a human being; the analytic techniques cannot even be put to work until the fuzziness has gone away, and by that time some "problems" are already solved, without any conscious effort.

As work proceeds, one does not delay too long over indeterminate points. If one cannot decide whether a particular pair of forms sound "the same" or not, usually the best practical course is to pretend for the nonce that they do; further hearing of the language will often settle the matter, and one can always go back through one's notes and enter corrections.

Subject to such temporary decisions which may later be altered, one constantly tabulates what is turning up: vowels under stress (assuming that one hears a stress), consonantism between beginning of utterance and first vowel, consonantism between successive vowels, and so on. It is always possible to reach conclusions too soon. In particular, although sufficiently long utterances are assumed never to involve contrasting phonologic material which does not turn up in shorter ones, there are often features which are of relevance but which cannot appear in the very short "word"-like utterances with which one begins: junctural features and the like, and many intonational contrasts. This is a point on which we are more careful today than we were, by and large, ten or fifteen years ago: the older "Wortphonologie" constantly missed subtleties of some importance, or else brought them belatedly into the picture in a lopsided and disorganized way.

If it were possible to separate gathering and collation, we would say that gathering is completed when one is certain that new contrasts will no longer turn up, and when one has collected a large number of utterances, short and long, in an *allophonically* correct transcription. An allophone is a "target," as it were, at which a speaker aims as he produces an utterance: the /p/ of *spill* is an allophone, the /p/ of *pill* a different allophone, the /p/ of *stop* still a third. A transcription is allophonically correct if it differentiates, at each position in an utterance, between all the allophones which can contrast in that position. Thus such a transcription for English would have to differentiate between /p/ and /t/ and certain other possibilities in the position after initial /s/ before a stressed vowel, but it would not have to distinguish between the /p/ of *spill* and that of *stop*, because those fall in different environments; and it would not necessarily have to use the same symbol for, or in any other way imply some kind of identity between, the /p/ of *spill* and that of *pill* or *stop*, though in this case it probably would. Another kind of leeway in allophonically correct transcriptions has to do with the size of the unit taken as a single allophone. One might use unit symbols, rather than sequences of two symbols, for the syllable-peaks of English *beet, bait, bite*—or even unit symbols for *beet* and *boot*, *bait* and *boat*, but sequences of two for the peaks of *bite* and *bout*. It would not even matter, in fact, if one used a unit symbol for the /br/ of *bread*, so long as the items kept apart in one way or another matched those actually kept apart by speakers of the language, and so long as a reasonably accurate phonetic description of each "unit" symbolized in the transcription were at hand.

In other words, gathering is completed when all relevant distinctions are known and regularly indicated; the business of identifying elements in different environments as in some sense different occurrences of "the same" element is the task of collation. In practice, collation begins long before gathering is completed, but any identifications made before the completion of gathering are subject to revision. The total process may involve going back and forth between gathering and collation, but in the end the final results of collation are based on presumably complete gathering.

32. *Collation.* The purpose of collation is to determine what elements occur in distinctive contrast with each other, and the hierarchic arrangements in which those elements occur. Since the assumed point of departure for collation is an allophonically correct transcription (together, of course, with description of what each symbol in the transcription means), collation itself takes the shape of a readjustment of size of the units tentatively recognized in the allophonic transcription, and a readjustment in the identifications of units in different environments. The procedure is one of trial and error, of successive approximations, until finally a satisfactory portrayal is achieved.

The first matter which we shall discuss in connection with collation is the principles of IC-analysis. After our introductory discussion of this, we shall describe and illustrate some of the heuristic principles which were evolved and used before the hierarchic approach had been consciously introduced into phonologic work, and which are still by no means to be discarded. Then we shall show how certain recurrent types of problems which gave trouble under other approaches are often resolved—sometimes in surprising ways—by the hierarchic approach. Then we shall discuss the analysis of junctural phenomena, which require different procedures from those used in the bulk of phonologic analysis. Finally, we shall deal with the interrelationships of ultimate phonologic components.

321. *The Principles of IC-Analysis.* The questions that one must ask and seek to answer in IC-analysis can be posed if we assume that we are confronted by a recurrent or potentially recurrent unit of some kind—a macrosegment, a microsegment, a syllable-peak, or the like (a *constitute*)—the unity of which can be assumed, but which is to be broken into its ICs. If the unit in question is an ultimate phonologic constituent, then, of course, there is no problem of further breakdown. If it is a unit of only two ultimate phonologic constituents, then the breakdown is obvious. In any more complex case, one has to try various possibilities, comparing both the whole unit and the tentative ICs with what can be obtained from other comparable whole units. The questions that one asks and seeks to answer are as follows:

(1) How many ICs are there?

(2) Which portions of the unit belong to each IC?

(3) What is the physical arrangement of the ICs in the whole?

(4) In what construction do the ICs stand?

(5) Where else does each IC occur? What other elements have "privileges of occurrence" comparable to those of each IC of the given unit?

These questions cannot be discussed one by one, for they are interrelated in intricate ways. What we shall do is to discuss a number of examples (all in English), to show the possible answers which can be obtained, and the criteria on which one bases these answers.

(1) Consider first the English syllable *scrimp.* Phonetically, this syllable contains an onset, a peak, and a coda, respectively /skr/, /i/, and /mp/. Here, and generally, it is wise to follow the phonetic evidence unless there is very convincing reason to do otherwise, and in the present case there is not. So we assume that /skr/, /i/, and /mp/ (rather than, for example, /ri/ or /im/ or the like) are all units on some level of structure. But this does not answer the first question of those listed earlier. The ICs of the syllable may be these three smaller units; but it may also be that two of them belong together as one of two ICs of the whole. Examining English syllables in general, we find that while a great variety of microsegment-initial syllables occur with a peak not preceded by an onset, only certain special types of microsegment-final syllables have a peak not followed by a coda. The bondage of peak and coda seems to be slightly stronger than that between onset ·and peak. This may lead us to say that the ICs of /skrimp/ are the onset /skr/ and the peak-coda sequence /imp/, leaving the subdivision of the latter to a later step. The fact that peaks (or peak-coda sequences) occur without onsets, but not vice versa, leads us to say that the construction of the two ICs is *subordinate*, with the peak-coda constituent as *nucleus*, the onset as *satellite*. As for question (4), the answer is in this case quite

obvious: the subordinate onset /skr/ precedes the nuclear peak-coda combination /imp/. And question (5): /skr/ recurs as onset in other syllables (*scratch, scrape*), as an interlude (*describe, escrow*), and is comparable to other units which likewise have these and only these privileges of occurrence, e.g. /spl/ (*splash, display*), /skw/ (*squelch, esquire*), or /kr/ (*crate, acrid*). A unit such as /sk/ is not comparable, since it occurs also as a coda (*ask*). The other IC, /imp/, recurs and is matched by comparable units in much the same way.

(2) Next let us examine /imp/, extracted as one IC of /skrimp/, but also occurrent as a whole syllable. We have already seen that this consists phonetically of peak /i/ and coda /mp/, a guide to formal analysis which we will not reject unless forced to. But in this case formal considerations reinforce the phonetic guide. If we were to divide into /im/ and /p/, and to divide other sequences in a comparable way—say *ant* into /æn/ and /t/, (*f*)*ond* into /an/ and /d/, and so on—we would find ourselves with two types of units of little phonetic homogeneity and capable of occurring together in sequence only in a rather random manner. /im/, for example, would occur before /p/, but not before /t/ or /d/; /p/ would occur after /im/ but not after /æn/ or /an/. There is no possible division which will yield complete freedom of combination of the units obtained, but we can seek something as systematic as possible. The phonetically most realistic division, into /i/ and /mp/, /æ/ and /nt/, /a/ and /nd/, yields types of units which are at least freer in their combinations than the alternative proposed above: witness *imp, ramp, romp, hint, ant, aunt* (for some speakers), *sinned, manned, fond*. Furthermore, this way of cutting the whole yields units, like /mp/, of phonetic homogeneity: /m/ and /p/ are both bilabial, and in most (not all) nasal-plus-stop sequences in English the two are in the same position of articulation.

Since syllables do occur with a peak followed neither by coda nor interlude, we shall say that in /imp/ the second constituent, /mp/, is satellite to the first, /i/.

(3) Next let us consider a macrosegment, say

²*I don't* ³¹*want to* ↓

The ICs of this are the intonation and the remainder. This is phonetically the simplest analysis, and is supported structurally by the fact that every intonation occurs with a large variety of remainders, while many a sequence of "words" can be "intoned" in two or more ways. The physical arrangement of the two ICs is different from that in previous examples: the two occur simultaneously. This is not a sufficiently specific statement of the arrangement, however, since the same intonation and the same remainder might be joined together with the center at a different point—

²*I* ³¹*don't want to* ↓

The specification of arrangement, therefore, has to include indication as to where the center is. Here we have our first example—but not our last—of two ICs which can participate in a constitute in either of two (or more) arrangements, the resulting constitutes being distinct and in contrast with each other.

Since every macrosegment includes both an intonation and a remainder, the construction in which the two stand is presumably *coordinate* rather than subordinate. There is, in English, one phenomenon which suggests otherwise: we have an indefinite number of macrosegments of the type of

$$^{33}hm \uparrow$$
$$^{31}mm \downarrow$$
$$^{31}mm \uparrow$$

where the phonemic structure (vowels and consonants) is aberrant: in the writer's speech, the segmental "carrier" of the intonation is necessarily nasal and voiced, but the contour of the oral cavity is irrelevant. The intonational parts of these macrosegments, however, are like the intonations of any other macrosegment. This might lead us to say that in macrosegments in general, the remainder is a satellite to the intonation as nucleus.

(4) Take next the microsegment *believer* (as in, say, a macrosegment *He's a believer in modern ways*). Phonemically, this is /bĭliyvər/, with (nonphonemic) loud stress on the second syllable. Since loud stress is isolable, while weak stress is not, we conclude that the first and third syllables are satellites in some subordinate construction. It might still be that the first and second syllables should be taken as one IC of the whole, the third syllable as the other, or else the other way around. But weak-stressed syllables preceding a loud-stressed syllable in a microsegment are just as common as weak-stressed syllables following the strong stress; there seems to be no basis for a bipartite rather than a tripartite cut. So we recognize three ICs, the first and third each attributive to the second.

(5) In *believe* we have an interlude /l/ between two peaks. The first syllable is one IC of the whole, the second syllable the other, and the first is attributive to the second. But does the /l/ belong to the first IC or to the second (question 2)? The answer is that it belongs to both at the same time: it is a *shared constituent* or *pivot*. The breakdown can be indicated as follows: First, into /bĭ(l)/ and /(l)iyv/, where the parentheses indicate that there is just one /l/ but that it has to be assigned to both ICs. Second, /bĭ(l)/ into attributive /b/ and nucleus /ĭ(l)/; /(l)iyv/ into attributive /(l)/ and nucleus /iyv/. Third, /ĭ(l)/ into /i/ and /(l)/; /iyv/ into /iy/ and /v/; in both cases the second constituent is attributive to the first.

(6) The opposite of a pivot turns up in the form *slyness*, which is two microsegments, each a whole syllable. The first constituent is the whole syllable *sly*, and the second (subordinate) constituent is the whole syllable *-ness*. This leaves unassigned the juncture which separates the two constituents. Instead of arbitrarily assigning it to either IC, we regard it as standing apart from both, as a *marker* of the point of contact of the two; the physical arrangement is sequential with a *gap*.

(7) In such forms as *cats, cads, docks, dogs, nips, nibs, apt, act, ebbed, nagged* we find codas /ts dz ks gz ps bz pt kt bd gd/. Since in each case the coda as a whole is voiceless or voiced, it is useful to take as the ICs of the codas not that obtained by a vertical cut, e.g. /ts/ into /t/ and /s/, but rather a voice-irrelevant sequence of oral articulations on the one hand, and a voicing-component on the other. Representing the voice-irrelevant constituents with capital letters, voicelessness by /H/, and voicing by /A/, we thus break /ts/ into /TS/ and /H/,

/dz/ into /TS/ and /A/, and so on. The arrangement of the constituents, as in the case of intonation and remainder, is simultaneous, but unlike the intonational situation, there are no further specifications necessary. The construction in which /TS/ and /H/ occur in coda /ts/ is presumably coordinate, since the contrast between voicing and voicelessness is meaningless in English except in such a context, and the voice-irrelevant constituents occur only with one or the other of the two voicing-components. In the case of the coda of *width* (or *widths* or *midst*), we first divide /dθ/ (/dθs/, /dst/) into /d/ and /θ/ (/d/ and /θs/ or /st/), and then subdivide the constituents accordingly. In the case of the coda of *twelfths*, or any other coda, interlude, or onset which has both sonorants and obstruents in it, we similarly separate the sonorants from the obstruents (/lfθs/ into /l/ and /fθs/), and then proceed with the indicated analysis of the obstruents, the further analysis of the sonorants being another matter.

Now let us summarize the criteria which have emerged in the examples.

(1) We base our cuts between ICs on the phonetic facts except where there is overwhelming reason (stemming from other criteria) not to. No example has appeared in which there was such reason; the fact that we divide *imp* into /i/ and /mp/, but *Ike* into /ay/ and /k/ might seem inconsistent from the phonetic angle, but structural evidence supports the difference of treatment (see §241).

(2) When confronted with alternative possible cuts into ICs, we prefer that cut which yields elements of greater internal cohesion (/i/ and /mp/ rather than /im/ and /p/, because the common bilabial character of /m/ and /p/ constitutes "greater internal cohesion"), and with greater freedom of recombination (same example, or our treatment of codas /ts dz ks gz/ etc.). We try to cut in such a way that comparable limitations on recombination are dealt with on the same level. Since codas involving obstruents in general contain only voiced or only voiceless obstruents, it seems that the voicing or voicelessness is a feature of the whole sequence of one or more obstruents, rather than of each obstruent individually; we cut accordingly.

(3) A construction of two ICs is subordinate if one of the ICs is of a distributional class the members of which can appear without any member of the class of the other IC; it is *coordinate* if each requires the other, or, theoretically, if either can occur without the other.

To the five questions with which we began, clearly no general answers are possible: the answers depend on the details in each language. Yet we may note the range of possible answers to some of the questions. Question (1) is How many ICs are there? The answer is often two, sometimes three, and perhaps sometimes more than three. Question (2) is Which portions of the whole belong to each IC? We have seen, at least, that a cut may fall neatly between two contiguous but non-overlapping portions, or that there may be an overlap or *pivot*, or that there may be a *gap* and *marker*. Question (4) is In what construction do the ICs stand? For a bipartite form there are two answers: coordinate and subordinate. For a tripartite form the only possibility we found was one with a nucleus and two independent satellites, but there may well be other possibilities. Question (5) requires more expanded discussion, which will be given in the next section (§322).

There remains question (3): What is the physical arrangement of the ICs in the whole? We have seen instances of *sequential* arrangement, in immediate juxtaposition, or with a pivot, or with a gap; and we have seen instances of *simultaneous* arrangement, with or without necessary additional specification as to relative timing. A major point must be made here. It seems quite impossible, by any reasonable methodology, to treat the phonologic structure of an utterance (or of a macrosegment, or of any smaller unit) in the general case as merely a *combination* of elements in the mathematical sense; what we have, rather, is a *permutation*. That is: our working assumption is that any unit save an ultimate phonologic constituent, consists of smaller elements (ICs) *in a specific geometric arrangement*, and the matter of arrangement is as important as is the matter of the constituents themselves. Now there are of course exceptions. Thus, in Fijian, if one knows that a given consonant and a given vowel are to participate in a syllable, then there is no further choice of arrangement: the consonant must come first, as onset, and the vowel second, as peak. A similar, though more complex, predictability of arrangement applies for the constituents of any syllable in Japanese. But these are exceptions, not the rule. The intonation /2 31↓/ and the "words" *I don't want to* can combine in at least two contrasting arrangements. The /SK/ of *ask* consists of /S/ and /K/ in one linear order; in *ax* we have the same constituents in the reverse order.

There are certain matters of arrangement which are predictable, and hence not independently important, under the IC approach, but not predictable when one deals with whole utterances merely as intertwining strings of ultimate phonologic constituents. Thus in Fijian the units /k/, /a/, and /a/ can be combined into either of two disyllabic sequences: /kaa/ or /aka/; but if we follow the IC approach this indeterminacy and independence appears only for the whole syllables /ka/ and /a/ as units to be combined, and vanishes when we go down the size-scale to attack the structure of the individual syllables. Yet, as this example itself shows, the IC approach does not eliminate arrangement as an independent factor: it merely assigns contrasts of arrangement to one size-level or another.

322. *Older Heuristic Principles.* The fifth of the questions posed at the beginning of §321 implies that one has to make identifications of elements found in different environments: e.g., one says that the /skr/ of *scrimp*, of *scratch*, and of *describe* is "the same" element in three different environments. Many such identifications are obvious; many non-identifications are equally obvious. However, many languages seem to present also a residue of elements where the problem of identification requires more care.

As an example of a trivial identification, we may consider such English forms as *pep, tat, kick, bib, dead, gag*; one concludes immediately that English has elements /p t k b d g/ which occur both as onsets and as codas. The /p/ at the beginning of *pep* is "the same" element as the /p/ at the end of *pep*, and if there is any difference between them that difference is not part of the recurrent element, but part of the two differing environments. Confronted with *pill, bill, sill, spill*, it is likewise obvious that the /sp/ of *spill* is a more complex onset than the others, but that it contains, in one way or another, the same unit which occurs as whole onset in *sill*, and that it also contains a unit related somehow to the /p/ of *pill* or to the /b/ of *bill*—or to both—though the precise nature of this relationship is not so clear.

Many theoretically conceivable identifications are never considered. In many a language one will find, say, an onset [k] and a peak [a] in complementation (neither occurring in any environment where the other is found), but no one in his right mind would suggest that these two are "the same" unit in two different environments. The reason is that collation is not pure mathematics: it is an analytic process applied to empiric data of a certain kind, and worthwhile results are achieved only if we insist on hugging the phonetic ground closely.

Between the two obvious extremes just illustrated there are less trivial problems of identification. In German one gets contrasting onsets /p t k b d g/, but only something like [p t k] as codas. In this case what would it mean to say that those units occurrent as codas were "the same" as initial /p t k/, or, alternatively, "the same" as initial /b d g/? Could it make sense to deny both identifications or, in some way, to make both of them at once? The bilabial stop of English *spill* is not exactly like either the /p/ of *pill* or the /b/ of *bill*; we can ask the same questions in this case. Shall we count the onset of *chick* as simple or as complex, or does it matter?

Four heuristic principles have been proposed as guides in solving such problems; they are of unequal value, but all merit some discussion. One is the principle of *contrast and complementation*, one that of *phonetic realism* or *phonetic similarity and dissimilarity*; one that of *pattern congruity*; one that of *economy*.

3221. *Contrast and Complementation.* Segments which occur in identical environments are necessarily *phonologically different*: e.g., the /p/ and /b/ of English *pit* and *bit*. We say "phonologically different" rather than "different phonemes," because the contrasting segments may turn out to be either phonemes or phonemic sequences of some sort. Thus the pair *blown* and *groan* proves the phonologic difference of /bl/ and /gr/, both of which prove to be sequences of two phonemes. Even the /p/ and /b/ of *pit* and *bit* are phonologically complex, not simple: whether we call them "phonemes" or not depends in some measure on just how we choose to use that term (see §3231).

It is, of course, not implied that segments which are not in contrast—which are in *complementation* or *complementary distribution* in that one of them never occurs in any environment in which the other occurs—are necessarily phonologically identical. We may recall the hypothetic example of an onset [k] and a peak [a] in complementation as a case in point. Lack of contrast is a necessary but not a sufficient condition for phonemic identity.

In making use of this heuristic principle, it is necessary to work in terms of as much of the environment as may b ̃elevant, and no account can be taken of IC structure. In Fijian, [ia] and [ya] are distinct; therefore [i] and [y] are phonologically different. It is quite irrelevant that [ia] is two syllables and [ya] but one. But this proof of the distinctness of Fijian [i] and [y] is not yet sufficient to define the phonologic status of the two elements. If it were to prove convenient to recognize a syllable juncture in the language (which it does not), then the phonologic distinction between [i] and [y] could be ascribed to the juncture: [ia] would be /i-a/, and [ya] would be /ia/. Or if it should develop that there is an independently distinctive stress in the language, so that our original phonetic notations had to be amended to [ía] and [yá], then the distinction which the pair shows could be handled in terms of the stress: /ía/ versus /iá/ (this, also, does not turn out to be the case). The mere phonetic fact that [ia] is two syllables and [ya] one is not in itself sufficient to justify either of these two conclusions or any other. The pair proves the phonologic distinctness of [i] and [y]; a great deal more collation is necessary before we can decide realistically how to provide for the contrast. Nothing is commoner in the literature than conclusion-jumping along this line.

Another type of problem which is apt to arise, that presented by *multiple complementation*, will be dealt with below in §3232.

3222. *Phonetic Realism.* Segments which are in complementation are nevertheless phonetically distinct unless they resemble each other phonetically in such a way that the differencies can be extracted from the segments themselves and assigned, instead, to the environments, in some phonetically realistic way.

This principle bars the possible identification of onset [k] and peak [a] (or, at least, virtually all investigators feel that it does), but would certainly often allow an identification of onset (or coda, or complex-peak satellite) [w] and peak [u].

An example found in many languages involves voiceless stops [p t k], initially and finally, in complementation with voiced stops [b d g] medially between vowels or other regularly voiced sounds. There are two lines of approach which can be taken; they in general yield the same ultimate results, but their logic is somewhat different. One is the *method of allophones*, the other the *method of redrawing boundaries*.

First note that in any such case as that just described, there are two "phonetic similarities" in the picture: (1) the phonetic similarity between the sounds which are in complementary distribution; (2) the phonetic similarity of each of the sounds to the environments in which it occurs. In our example, initial and final [p] are phonetically similar to medial [b] in that both are produced with bilabial and velic closures; [p] is like its environment on at least one side in being voiceless (just as silence is voiceless), and [b] is like its environment on both sides in being voiced.

The method of allophones works in terms of essentially "vertical" cuts (transverse to the time axis). We find an allophone [p] in one set of environments, and a similar though phonetically different allophone [b] in another set of environments. We then set up a single phonemic unit /p/ which is, in a sense, a "class" of allophones, in this case including both [p] and [b], and we state the circumstances under which the single phoneme will be "represented by" or "actualized as" one or the other of its allophones. We have kept the requirement of phonetic realism in mind in that the allophone which represents phoneme /p/ in a given environment is phonetically similar to that environment. If the distribution of the two allophones were reversed, then the complementation would not be supported by phonetic realism and the identification would probably be rejected (I know of no language where such a peculiar distribution occurs).

The method of redrawing boundaries works differently. Instead of setting up a class-type "phoneme" which has two "allophones," what we do is readjust the boundary between "sound" and "environment." Specifically, we can delete the voicing of [b] from the [b] itself, leaving [p], and assign the voicing to the environment. This needs to be demonstrated graphically. For the purpose, let us consider a word which we have transcribed linearly as [pabap]. This transcription can be expanded as follows:

$$| V | V | V |$$
$$P | A | P | A | P,$$

where "P" means bilabial closure, "A" low central tongue position, and "V" vibration of the vocal cords. (Other symbols could be added—say an "O" for closure of the velic—but would be the same in all five columns and would not bear on the point at issue.) Now to say that [p] and [b] are in complementary distribution in this language is to say that the simultaneous bundle of "V" and "P" occurs only where both the preceding and the following bundle involve "V," and that "P" without "V" does not so occur. The vertical lines in the expanded transcription above represent the usual sort of boundaries between successive sounds. We can now redraw those boundaries as follows:

$$| V \quad V \quad V |$$
$$P | A | \overline{P} | A | P.$$

Having done this, we see that the element "P" recurs three times in the form, once in an environment of preceding, simultaneous, and following voicing, twice without such voicing. Instead of having two distinct units to deal with we have just one. By a rather easy definition, we can arrive at a linear transcription which shows all of this: /papap/.

Most operations involving the criterion of "phonetic realism" can be performed by this method rather than by the method of allophones. However, in examining our raw materials (utterances in allophonically correct transcription; §31), and searching for the specific items which call for this sort of readjustment, it is convenient to think largely in terms of block-like phones following each other without (structural) overlap. One looks for *phonetic* overlap, bearing in mind Pike's suggestive aphorism "Sounds tend to slur into their environments." Having found instances of what can be described in this rather non-rigorous manner, one can then optionally apply the method of redrawing boundaries.

There is rather general agreement about the application of the principle of phonetic realism, but there is much disagreement as to just what constitutes "phonetic similarity." Some investigators would like to say that phones cannot be phonetically similar unless they share one or more "distinctive features" (in our terms, ultimate phonologic components); this would also imply that ultimate phonologic components cannot be phonetically similar at all. This requirement was clearly met in our [pabap] example, but in general we cannot expect things to be so simple. There is often, apparently, some choice as to what ultimate phonologic constituents shall be recognized, and our choice along this line may go hand in hand with our choice of larger units which are to be taken as "phonetically similar."

Consider, for instance, the long syllable peaks of Fox: [i· o· æ· a·]. If we slice [i·] into two consecutive halves, then to what is the second half phonetically similar? Since the tongue position is high and front, it is like the first half of the same long peak, and also like the short peak [ɪ]. Since it adds to the length of the peak, it is phonetically like the second half of [o·], [a·], or [æ·]. Since it is vocalic, it is like the intervocalic [h] of Fox, the latter being a brief phase of voicelessness. Any of these phonetic similarities may be evoked in our analysis; our choice depends on distributional matters rather than on a decision that one of the phonetic similarities is somehow "closer" than the others; the particular way in which we view the ultimate phonologic constituents of the system will come about as a result of our choice.

It seems better, on the whole, not to insist on the stand taken by the investigators mentioned above, though wherever their requirements are easily met the ensuing steps are perhaps clearer. In dealing with the old Germanic languages, Moulton refuses to set up a phonemic identity between a prevocalic voiceless-vocoid onset [h] and a dorso-velar spirant [x], despite complementation, on the grounds that [h] and [x] share no distinctive feature. The particular identification, for the particular languages (e.g., Old English) may well not be suitable, but we should not bar it on the grounds given—especially when we find, in some languages, a single unit in a single position showing *free variation* through a range which includes [h] and [x] (e.g., the onset /x/ of Mandarin).

It should hardly be necessary to add that failure to see phonetic similarity can be induced by bad phonetics, particularly by an uncritical reliance on traditional use of phonetic descriptive terms. The initial [h] of English *he, haw, who* has often been called a "glottal spirant"; the association of the term "spirant" with sounds like [f θ s š x] can lead one to overestimate the phonetic difference between the [h] and the voiced postvocalic glide of *yeah, law, bah*.

There is one aspect of phonologic analysis where the usual principle of phonetic realism, in the writer's opinion, must be not merely suspended but almost reversed. This is in the search for junctures, to be discussed in §324.

3223. *Pattern Congruity.* Roughly speaking, this principle states that, of several alternative analyses which equally well meet other requirements, one should choose that which yields the greatest symmetry, both of phonemes and of allophonic variation with phonemes. Heuristically, all that the principle can do is guarantee that all the symmetries in the system be discovered and reported; it is important not to let the analyst's esthetic preferences distort the facts and "find" greater symmetry than is actually there. In gathering data, one makes, and constantly revises, tables showing the segments which occur in contrast with each other in apparently relevant environments—as onsets, as codas, and so on. If in one such table one has, let us say, voiceless and voiced stops in three positions of articulation, but glottalized stops only in two of the three, one suspects that perhaps—not necessarily, but *perhaps*—the third glottalized stop will turn up, rounding out the pattern. Now this "turning up" can come about in several ways. A form not previously recorded may turn up and contain the "missing" unit. Or a form already recorded may turn out to have been heard wrongly, and upon correct hearing may show the missing unit. Or, if neither of these events comes about, the analyst may conclude that something which he has been dealing with in other terms actually belongs in the empty pigeonhole.

It is at this point that the danger of forcing one's data becomes greatest; many systems, as we saw in §2, do have holes. Yet the analyst has every right to play around with any notions of the kind which occur to him: they may prove fruitful. An example is Taos, with five voiceless unaspirated stops (and affricates), five glottalized ones to match, and only two voiceless aspirated ones. It may make sense to "fill out the pattern" by regarding /pʻ tʻ/ and the three spirants /s x xʷ/ as a third obstruent type, matching the other two in all positions. This does not make aspirated stops out of /s x xʷ/, nor spirants out of /pʻ tʻ/. What it does is to treat, say, /x/ as differing from /k/ *primarily* in the presence of a certain feature in /x/ lacking in /k/, /pʻ/ as differing from /p/ *primarily* in the presence versus absence of this same feature. There is still a difference between /pʻ/ and /x/: in the former, the arrangement of the /p/ and the added feature is sequential, whereas in /x/ the arrangement is simultaneous. This difference of arrangement, however, is relegated to secondary status.

Pattern congruity is also appealed to as a guide in cases of multiple complementation. The unaspirated voiceless stops of *spill, still, skill* are in complementation both with the aspirated voiceless stops of *pill, till, kill,* and with the unaspirated voiced stops of *bill, dill, gill.* This is an example we have given before, and which will come up later for what the writer believes to be the most satisfactory treatment. For the moment, let us assume that we must insist on identifying the unaspirated stops either with the aspirated ones or with the voiced ones, with no third alternative. Now we have already seen that, by and large, clusters of obstruents as codas are voiced or voiceless as wholes: /st/ *past* and /zd/ *razzed,* but not /sd/ or /zt/. The /s/ of *past* is surely the same as the /s/ of *sill* or of *spill, still, skill.* In codas it is /p t k/ which go with /s/, /b d g/ going rather with /z/. Therefore, for the sake of neatness of pattern, we conclude that the stops in *spill, still, skill* are phonemically /p t k/.

Pattern congruity is also evoked when one confronts a decision between single phoneme and cluster: e.g., a [kʷ] which may be /kʷ/ (unit) or /kw/; a [č] which may be /č/ or /tš/ or /ty/; an [aˑ] which may be a unit or a cluster of /a/ plus something (another /a/, a covowel /ˑ/, a semiconsonant). A [č] cannot be interpreted as /tš/ if there is a [tš] in contrast, of course (the principle of contrast and complementation); but in some cases there is only one segment of the kind and still there may be grounds for one interpretation or the other. In German, [č] is a cluster /tš/, because a whole series of clusters of stop plus spirant occur: /pf ps ts tš ks/. In Fox, [č] is usually taken as a unit because it parallels closely the pattern of positions of occurrence of obviously unitary /p t k/, and because treating it as a cluster /tš/ or /ty/ gives less parallelism—less "pattern congruity." We shall have more to say below about this type of problem also, and the above examples should not be accepted as definitive discussions.

3224. *Economy.* The general law of parsimony applies in phonologic analysis as it does elsewhere, but in actual practice it is of remarkably little help. No one sets up fifty phonemes by dealing with, say, onsets and codas in complete independence, when the number can be halved by identifications of elements in onset position and in coda position. Sometimes an investigator will establish two separate entities where the recognition of one actually eliminates the necessity of the other: this is unparsimonious and subject to correction, providing the evidence is all in. However in the course of analysis it is often very wise to recognize more items than will probably ultimately be proved independent. Thus in working with Cantonese it would be wise at first to keep syllable-juncture and also to indicate the distinction between onsets /y w/ and peaks /i u/. In due time, however, it turns out that, given syllable juncture, [y] and [i] are in complementation, as are [w] and [u]. Whenever one becomes sure of such a situation, one reduces the number of recognized elements.

Parsimony is sometimes evoked where it is not relevant. Some analysts prefer to list a large number of, say, consonant "phonemes," and have few or no clusters to deal with; others prefer to treat as many segments as possible as clusters, giving a smaller number of "phonemes." The latter group cannot rightly evoke parsimony in defense of their position. The difference lies entirely in the level of complexity at which the term "phoneme" is applied. If "phoneme" refers to anything of a higher status in the hierarchic pattern than that of ultimate phonologic constituents, then part of the total task of description is the specification of the constituent elements of the phonemes themselves. The worker who sets up a larger number of "phonemes" has to present more information of this kind, and less at the "superphonemic" level (clusters etc.); the worker who sets up fewer "phonemes" must cover less "subphonemically" but correspondingly more "superphonemically." Quite obviously, equally accurate descriptions can be presented either way, and there is no way to show that one way is any more economic than the other.

Recognition of this relativity in the size-level at which one introduces the term "phoneme" should knock the wind out of the sails of the proponents of all sides of the argument about the "phonemic" status of English syllabics. One group argues that the syllabics (that is, in our terms, the peaks, simple or complex) of *beat, boot, bate, boat, bite, bout, Hoyt,* and so on, should all be called single "phonemes," along with those of *bit, bet, bat, book, buck, bock, wash.* A second group argues for the breakdown of the syllabics in the first list into two "phonemes" each. Still a third group wants to call the peaks of *beat, boot, bate, boat, fa, law* all single "phonemes," but recognize two each in the peaks of *bite, bout, Hoyt.* Now the position of the first group can be defended as a consistent use of the term "phoneme" to cover all the units which appear distinct and in contrast when a certain level has been reached in working down the IC scale; it remains for them to show the complex structure of some of these "phonemes" in terms of ultimate phonologic features, in simultaneous or successive bundles. The position of the second group can likewise be defended as a consistent use of the term "phoneme." Only the position of the third group is indefensible, and that not because they use the word "phoneme" in a slightly different way but because they mix IC-levels. We shall see a more thoroughly worked-out example of this sort of thing shortly.

323. *Crucial Problems.* There are three types of problems which have recurred

constantly in phonologic work and theory. One is that of *phoneme versus cluster*; another that of *multiple complementation*; the third that of *marked and unmarked*. In each case, most systems of phonologic analysis have erred by providing for fewer alternative possible answers than the facts seem to require, thus forcing arbitrary decisions. The strict IC approach by no means eliminates all the difficulty, but it seems at least to afford greater flexibility.

3231. *Phoneme Versus Cluster.* The very way in which this question is usually posed indicates misplaced emphasis. The phraseology implies that a [č]-type phone, for example, must either be a unit phoneme or a cluster of an integral number (presumably two) unit phonemes. By any one precise set of rules for the use of the term "phoneme," this is perhaps true, but this simply shifts the arbitrariness to the rules instead of to their application. The question "phoneme or cluster?" is only apt to be asked of a segment which seems in some ways to work like items that have already been accepted as unit phonemes, in other ways like items that have already been interpreted as clusters. What the IC approach adds to this is primarily a recognition that the ICs of a unit occur in that unit *in a specific arrangement*, and that the arrangement itself may be a matter of primary concern. The IC approach also allows greater flexibility in that there is no insistence on exhausting all possible "vertical" cuts between ICs (cuts transverse to the time axis, giving ICs in sequential arrangement) before cuts of other kinds, yielding other arrangements, are made.

We shall illustrate by presenting, first, a typical discussion of the status of [č] in Fox, followed by a statement in IC terms.

Traditional Statement. The Fox segment [č] occurs as an onset, as an interlude, and as part of an interlude [hč]. These positions of occurrence are shared by /p t k/. Unlike /p k/, [č] does not occur before /y/; this is shared by /t/. Unlike /p t k/, it does not occur before /w/. By the use of slant lines we have indicated that these other segments are all being interpreted as unit phonemes; it is only the status of [č] which is in doubt. [č] also shares with /p t k/ the privilege of occurrence before any vowel. /y/ does not occur before /i i·/, and /w/ does not occur before /o o·/.

There are three phonetically realistic alternatives to be considered. One is to take [č] as a unit phoneme /č/; a second is to take it as a cluster /tš/; a third is to take it as a cluster /ty/. Either the second or the third interpretation involves, naturally, some redefinition of /t/ and of /š/ or /y/. If we treat [č] as /ty/, then we must consider a parallel treatment of /š/ before a vowel; /š/ in the clusters /šk šky škw/ may complicate this.

Unit interpretation yields distributional results already stated above.

Interpretation as /tš/ means that this is being recognized as the only cluster in the language consisting of stop plus spirant; this throws /t/ out of parallelism with /p k/, and /š/ out of parallelism with /s/.

Interpretation as /ty/ yields a neat pattern for stops, since we now have, as occurrent margins, /p t k/, /py ty ky/, /pw tw kw/, /hp ht hk/, /hpy hty hky/, /hpw htw hkw/. This is a clear gain in "pattern congruity." On the other hand, the revised /y/ which is involved in the interpretation has a peculiar distribution;

/y/ now occurs before /i i·/ providing that the /y/ is itself preceded by /t/ (or by /s/, if we also interpret prevocalic [š] as /sy/), but not otherwise. There is nothing else in the distributional pattern of the system which resembles this.

It is hard to be sure what conclusion would be drawn from the above considerations; it would depend in part on the preferences of the analyst. The writer's own preference, within the limitations of the "phoneme *or* cluster" approach, is to settle for a unit phoneme /č/. Another possible answer is "it doesn't matter." This answer is not bad if it is given *after* the examination of the possibilities and what they imply; it is bad if it is given in advance and shortcuts the investigation. For, in a way, what counts is not so much the interpretation which one accepts as *the evidence on which that interpretation is based.* The most fruitful aspect of the lengthy discussions of the "phoneme or cluster" problem in the literature has been the careful examinations of distributional facts which were undertaken; they have posed as a byproduct, but only because we were really asking the wrong question.

Before passing on to an IC approach to the Fox problem, let us first indicate that the choice of notation is a separate matter and should not be confused with what we are discussing. Fox [č] has to be indicated somehow in a transcription, by a unit symbol, or by /tš/, or by /ty/; any of these three, or some other notation, would do perfectly well in that there would be no ambiguity. And with any choice of notation, the problem of the structural status of [č] would remain.

IC Statement. Working from large to small in Fox, we eventually come to a listing of all those elements which occur as onsets, as interludes, or both. At the moment, no matter what notation we use for these, they are all on a par. The full list is given in §2511 (we now call this List A). When we proceed to break the elements of this set into their own ICs, we first break twelve of the set down as follows:

$$
\begin{array}{llll}
/hp/ &= /h/ + /p/ & /hpw/ &= /h/ + /pw/ \\
/ht/ &= /h/ + /t/ & /htw/ &= /h/ + /tw/ \\
/hč/ &= /h/ + /č/ & /hkw/ &= /h/ + /kw/ \\
/hk/ &= /h/ + /k/ & /šk/ &= /š/ + /k/ \\
/hpy/ &= /h/ + /py/ & /šky/ &= /š/ + /ky/ \\
/hky/ &= /h/ + /ky/ & /škw/ &= /š/ + /kw/ \, .
\end{array}
$$

The first ICs, /h/ and /š/, appear also on our original list (List A) as whole margins; the various second ICs also all appear on List A. This first breakdown therefore leaves us with the following lower-level elements which must in turn be analyzed if possible (List B):

p	t	č	k	h	s	š	m	n	w	y
py			ky	hy			my	ny		
pw	tw		kw	hw	sw		mw	nw .		

The recurrence of some elements on both List A and List B, where other elements appear on List A but not on List B, is typical of what happens in the analysis of any hierarchic organization. A list of all members of the clergy of the Church of England would include the names of all bishops, archbishops, and primates. A list of all the bishops would still include the names of all archbishops and primates. A list of the archbishops would still include the names of all primates. A list of all primates would include but one name. An analogy in terms of the areas spiritually ruled by these various members of the clergy would be even closer.

The next IC cut applies to twelve of the elements in List B:

$$/py/ = /p/ + /y/ \qquad /pw/ = /p/ + /w/$$
$$/tw/ = /t/ + /w/$$
$$/ky/ = /k/ + /y/ \qquad /kw/ = /k/ + /w/$$
$$/hy/ = /h/ + /y/ \qquad /hw/ = /h/ + /w/$$
$$/sw/ = /s/ + /w/$$
$$/my/ = /m/ + /y/ \qquad /mw/ = /m/ + /w/$$
$$/ny/ = /n/ + /y/ \qquad /nw/ = /n/ + /w/ .$$

Once again all the first and all the second constituents are elements which already appear on List B. That is, we state that the /y/ of /py/ (whether the latter is a whole margin or is occurring as one IC of the more complex interlude /hpy/) is the same element as the /y/ which occurs as a whole margin; and so forth. However, we have not, in this step, broken /č/ down any further, precisely because of the difficulty in "pattern congruity" which is encountered if we reinterpret /č/ as /ty/ in a way *exactly* paralleling the breakdown of /py/ into /p/ and /y/. After the second IC cut, we are left with the following elements (List C):

> p   t   č   k   h   s   š   m   n   w   y .

In the first and second cuts, the plus-sign has had a very simple meaning: "followed by." That is, we meant to state that the unit /hp/ consisted of the lower-level unit /h/ *followed by* the lower-level unit /p/, and so on. We are now going to cut in a different way—at a different angle, as it were—though we shall for simplicity use the plus-sign again (third breakdown):

$$/č/ = /t/ + /y/ \qquad /š/ = /s/ + /y/ .$$

Here the plus-sign means something like "simultaneous with" or "partly overlapping." Once again we identify the ICs with elements already in our list (List C), but the *arrangement* in which the ICs /t/ and /y/ participate in /č/ is different from the arrangement in which the ICs /p/ and /y/ participate in /py/. Our residual list is now (List D):

> p   t   k   h   s   m   n   w   y .

Further cuts will necessarily be other than "vertical," and will for the most part yield constituents which are not already on the list—constituents such as stop closure, bilabial position, and so on (§262).

This treatment deals with /č/ as different both from /p t k/ (which appear on List D as well as on all earlier lists) and from /py ky/ (which appear on Lists A and B but not on those from C on). Such a treatment matches the distributional facts, which show a set of privileges of occurrence for /č/ which resemble both those of /p t k/ and those of /py ky/, but differ from both in some ways.

Comment. Now is /č/ a unit phoneme or a cluster? We have not used the term "phoneme" in our IC analysis, since we do not know where to introduce it. One could logically call all the elements in List A "phonemes," or all those in List B, or all those in List C, or all those in List D. If we introduce the term "phoneme" in connection with List A, B, or C, then /č/ is a phoneme—except that in the first case (List A) it is both a phoneme and also a part of the larger phoneme /hč/. In the last case (List D), /č/ would be a cluster—but a different *kind* of cluster from /py/, /ky/, and the like. We see that the question "is /č/ a phoneme or a cluster?" is too narrow and not properly fruitful; a more productive question to ask is "on what hierarchic level, or levels, does the given element function, and at what step, working down the IC scale, does it break down into smaller constituents?" These are the questions which we have tried to answer above; the *term* "phoneme," and just how to use it, is regarded as of subsidiary importance.

A similar approach may be revealing in other cases of the kind which have supplied the ammunition for discussions of phoneme-or-cluster. Let us consider, very briefly, English /č/ and /ǯ/ (or, what amounts to the same thing, the voicing-irrelevant unit which can be extracted from these two). In some dialects, these units contrast with clusters /tš/ and /dž/ : *pitcher* : *won't ya*; *ledger* : *did ya*. In some of these same dialects, /č ǯ/ contrast also with /ty dy/ : *choose* : *tune*, *teutonic*; *juice* : *dune*, *deuteronomy*. The customary conclusion, that /č/ and /ǯ/ are "therefore" unit phonemes, misses the main point. Neither /č/ nor /ǯ/ participates in more complex onsets, while the most similar other elements, /p t k b d g/, all do. /č/ and /ǯ/ seem to occupy a position in the hierarchic scale midway between elements like /p t k b d g/ (which remain unbroken further down the scale) and elements like /pr tr kr br dr gr pl kl bl gl/ (which are broken into smaller constituents at an earlier step). Perhaps we must regard /č/ and /ǯ/ as something like *close* or *intimate* sequential clusters of /t/ and /š/, /d/ and /ž/, in contrast to the "normal" (though much rarer) clusters /tš dž/. This would involve a recognition of two kinds of sequential arrangement (intimate and "normal"), not contrasting in most cases; and, of course, one's notation would have to indicate the difference—perhaps precisely by writing the intimate clusters with the symbols /č ǯ/.

3232. *Multiple Complementation.* On this type of problem the Americanist and the Praguian traditions have supplied different machinery. The Americanist position has been that in English, for example, the stop after /s/ in *spill*, *still*, *skill* must be "the same" phonemically either as those of *pill*, *till*, *kill*, or as those of *bill*, *dill*, *gill*. On this assumption, we showed in §3223 that the identification with the stops of *pill*, *till*, *kill* is neater. One result is that /b d g/ are somewhat *defective* phonemes: they occur for the most part in positions paralleling those of /p t k/, but do not occur in initial clusters after a spirant.

The Praguian tradition affords greater flexibility in the treatment of such problems. In Prague terms, a pair of phonemes, say English /p/ and /b/, which differ in some one constituent feature but are otherwise identical and composed of features not all of which occur in any other phoneme, constitute an *archiphoneme*. In certain positions both phonemes of an archiphoneme occur, in contrast. In positions where the contrast is irrelevant, one does not say that what occurs is either one phoneme or the other; rather one says that it represents the archiphoneme, the contrast in that position being *neutralized*.

This is a neat way to avoid a spurious identification: instead of insisting that the bilabial stop of *spill* simply *must* be either /p/ or /b/, one has a way of saying that it is both and neither: it is what /p/ and /b/ have in common, without the distinguishing features of either as opposed to the other. The way is not available in all cases of multiple complementation. In English, /p k b g/ all occur in onsets before /l/ (*plain, clay, blare, glare*), whereas /t d/ do not. But one cannot speak, say, of neutralization of the contrast between /p/ and /t/ before /l/, since /p/ and /t/ do not constitute an archiphoneme, nor do /t/ and /k/. /p/ and /t/ have in common a manner of articulation, and differ as to position; but the manner is shared by /k/. On the other hand, one may sometimes recognize three-way neutralizations. There are dialects of Chinese which have a three-way stop distinction initially, /p t k/, but only one stop finally ([t] or [ʔ]); since /p t k/ differ as to position but are otherwise identical, and since their common features are not shared by any other phoneme, the three can be regarded as constituting an archiphoneme, and the contrasts can be said to be neutralized finally. (Similarly in Burmese.)

Now what the Americanist and Praguian traditions have in common is an insistence that vertical cutting be completed before any other kind of cutting into ICs be attempted, and that once one has shifted to any sort of "decomposition" of segmental units into simultaneous components, no more vertical cuts be allowed. In our discussion of IC-procedure (§321) we made no such blanket rule, and, indeed, did otherwise in a number of examples. One of the examples was that of clusters of obstruents in English. We broke such codas as /ts dz ps bz st zd pt bd/ first into ICs /TS PS ST PT/ (voicing-irrelevant constituents) and /H/ or /A/ (voicelessness and voicing). Only after this did we proceed to break /TS/, by a vertical cut, into a voicing-irrelevant apical stop /T/ and a voicing-irrelevant spirant /S/, in that order.

Let us examine the onsets of *spill, still, skill* in this light. These are, respectively, /SP/, /ST/, and /SK/ plus /H/; the first ICs then break into /S/ and, respectively, /P/, /T/, and /K/. There is no question of neutralization between /p/ and /b/ after /s/: /sp/ contains neither /p/ nor /b/, but /SP/ and /H/, and the first of these in turn contains neither /p/ nor /b/, but the voicing-irrelevant stop /P/. However, there is a question of limited distribution: the elements /SP ST SK/ in onsets are never accompanied by /A/, always by /H/. If neutralization is to be spoken of here, it is a neutralization between /H/ and /A/. But /H/ and /A/ are not phonemes that have something unique in common and otherwise differ: they have nothing at all in common phonetically (that is, though they are both effects produced by differing functions of the glottis, they cannot be broken down into smaller constituents such that some of the smaller constituents occur in both, others in just one or the other). The basis for the Prague terminology is therefore lacking.

It is important to recognize the difference between an environment in which a particular contrast is relevant and one in which it is not. The Americanist tradition does this in terms of phonemes and full or defective distributions. The Praguian tradition does it somewhat more neatly in some cases, in terms of phonemes, archiphonemes, and neutralization, but some cases are not subject to this treatment (non-occurrence of initial /tl/, for example, in English), and for them one has to revert to a procedure like that used in the Americanist tradition for all cases. The IC-approach cannot eliminate defective distributions, but with care it is possible to perceive them on the proper hierarchic level. Thus in English there are no microsegments of the shapes /gliyt/, /tlip/, or /zdil/. But these three lacks are of three different kinds. /gliyt/, if it occurred, would be composed of an onset /gl/, which occurs, a peak /iy/, which not only occurs but occurs after /gl/ (*gleam*), and a coda /t/, which not only occurs but occurs with onset /gl/ (*glut*) and with peak /iy/ (*eat*). The "hole in the pattern" is obviously at a fairly high size-level. /tlip/, if it occurred, would involve an otherwise unobserved onset /tl/; the sequence /tl/ does occur elsewhere (for some speakers: *rattling*). The "hole in the pattern" in this case is not at the syllable level, but specifically at the level of onsets. The non-occurrence of /zdil/ is at an even lower level: the onset /zd/ does not occur, but /st/ does, which means that /ST/ occurs in onsets but not in the company of /A/. An even lower-level "hole" is the non-occurrence of a spirant /x/ or /γ/, which would involve a simultaneous cluster of a position of articulation which does function in the language (/k g/) and a manner which also functions (/f v s z/).

In any case of multiple complementation the aim of the IC approach is fundamentally to determine the hierarchic level on which the hole appears. If this, as it seems to the writer, is the important issue, then both the Americanist and the Praguian traditions have tended to obscure the problem.

3233. *Marked and Unmarked; Simple and Complex.* In connection with the terminology of neutralization, the Praguian approach calls one member of certain archiphonemes the *unmarked* member, the other or others *marked*. In Russian /p b/, for example, /p/ is the unmarked member, while /b/ has the positive marking of voice. Our partial rejection, in §3232, of the theory of neutralization does not invalidate this way of speaking, which is very useful. Rather more generally, we may distinguish between contrasting units (perhaps clusters rather than single phonemes) where one is phonologically *simpler* than the other or others. The analytical problem, under an IC approach, is to know which member of a contrasting set is to be regarded as the simplest. The stock of ultimate phonologic components may differ depending on how we answer this question in any one case.

There are two criteria which can be used realistically in solving this problem; the two never seem to conflict, but in some cases neither affords an answer.

One is that, if one of two or more matching sets of units has a wider distribution than the others, the former is phonologically simplest. This applies for Russian /p b/, /t d/, and so on: the voiceless obstruents occur before juncture (at the end of a macrosegment), while the voiced obstruents do not. In Winnebago we find the aspirated stops initially, medially, and finally; the unaspirated and glottalized stops do not occur finally. We conclude that the aspirated stops are phonologically simplest; and it turns out that the others can all be regarded as clusters or as the result of allophonic variation (§25212). In Korean we find the short stops /p t k/ finally, while other varieties occur only initially or medially or both; once again, it is possible to set up /p t č k/ as single phonemes, and handle all the other varieties as clusters (§25212).

The other criterion is that, if one of two or more matching sets of units has a wider range of non-distinctive variation than the other or others, the former is phonologically simplest. In Nootka the nonglottalized stops are unaspirated before vowels, aspirated finally or before consonants; the glottalized stops and the spirants show no such variation. We conclude that the plain stops are the simplest set, and that the glottalized stops and the spirants are more complex. Since in this case all three turn out to be unit phonemes rather than clusters (at least in the sense that /p'/, for example, cannot be reinterpreted as a cluster /pʔ/), we call the plain series unmarked, the other two series marked. The first criterion in part supports this conclusion, and in no way goes against it: glottalized stops do not occur after a vowel before a consonant or at end of macrosegment. But in Georgian the same criterion gives phonetically different results. One series of stops shows a variation between voiceless unaspirated and voiceless unaspirated glottalized; a second is always aspirated, and a third is always voiced. The first series, then, is unmarked, and the other two have aspiration and voicing as positive marks. Here, also, there is some distributional support. There are few limitations on occurrence in sequence of Georgian consonants, but it is true that only the series of stops which we take as unmarked occur before /ɿ/.

The decision is not always easy to make, and perhaps in some cases we must suspend judgment. English /p t k/, it would seem, show more nondistinctive variation than /b d g/; but here the extraction of voicelessness as a "long component" (§3232) takes precedence, so that the question of marked and unmarked does not come up in quite the same way.

The bearing of simple and complex on the tabulation of ultimate phonologic constituents is easy to see. Our analysis of Nootka in §262 is based on the fact that /p'/ is more complex than /p/. Given exactly the same stock of consonantal units, but with a /p'/ which was sometimes glottalized, sometimes not, and a /p/ which was always aspirated, we should have to analyze /p t c č ƛ k kʷ q qʷ/ as involving the feature of which /h/ consists, and /p' t'/ etc. as involving one less feature than is recognized in §262; the spirants /s š ł x xʷ x̣ x̣ʷ/ could not be recognized as containing the feature which characterizes /h/. Furthermore, /h/ would remain a manner consonant, but /ʔ/ would cease to be one; the spirants would not be matched by a manner consonant.

324. *Junctural Analysis.* Junctures are in some ways a very different kind of phonologic entity from ordinary vowel or consonant phonemes (however one may choose to apply the term "phoneme" in the latter case). We can well enough call the English bilabial stop /P/ a phoneme: the /p/ of *pot* consists of /P/ and /H/; the /b/ of *bought* consists of /P/ and /A/; the /p/ of *clasp* consists of /P/ and part of an occurrence of /H/, which latter stretches also through the preceding /S/. Now all the articulatory events which we say constitute occurrences of this element /P/ involve velic and lip closure. An articulatory event does not constitute an occurrence of /P/ unless it does involve both of these features, and

if it involves them both it is by definition an occurrence of /P/; any accompanying articulatory motions or positions are not part of the /P/, but environmental. It is by and large typical of ordinary segmental phonemic units that all occurrences of them have something articulatory in common. This is a derivative of the heuristic principle of "phonetic realism" (§3222), and we said when discussing that principle that it had to be suspended in the analysis of junctures.

In *slyness*, the internal open juncture is represented by a drawl of the /ay/ in the first syllable, which is longer than an /ay/ in a form like *minus*, and comparable to the /ay/ which occurs in macrosegment-final in a sentence like *He's very sly*. The /n/ of *-ness* is accompanied by voicing which begins fairly weakly and increases (*crescendo* voicing); this is typical of a macrosegment-initial /n/ in a form like *Never do that*, and different from the fairly even voicing accompanying a medial /n/ as in *minus*. This voicing difference is subtle and perhaps not always present. When it is present, we say that the crescendo voicing—or, more precisely, the crescendo characteristic of the voicing—of the /n/ of *slyness* is part of the juncture, not part of the /n/ itself. The juncture of *slyness*, then, is composed of two features: one, always present, is the drawl on /ay/; the other, sometimes not present, is the crescendo of the voicing accompanying the /n/. In some utterings of the form *slyness* not only the second but also the first of these features may be missing; but when this is the case the form has been said in a phonologically different way, without any juncture, making it rhyme completely with *minus*.

In *night-rate* the juncture is composed again of two features. The first is the type of release accompanying the /t/ of *night-*; this /t/ is either inaudibly released or has slight aspiration. This is the nondistinctive range of variation of release of a final /t/, as in *He arrived last night*, and differs from the release of a medial /t/ as in *nitrate* or *bottom*. However, there is a range of variation here and this distinction is not always audible; it is like the evanescent distinction in voicing-contour between the /n/ of *slyness* and that of *minus*. The other is the full, slightly crescendo, voicing of the /r/ of *rate*, like that of an initial /r/ as in *Rates are high there*, and quite unlike the largely voiceless /r/ of *nitrate*. This feature is much more constant; on the rare occasion when the form *night-rate* is spoken with neither of these characteristic features, then, of course, it is being spoken just like *nitrate*, with no juncture.

In these two different environments of juncture (*slyness, night-rate*), the element is composed of almost completely diverse phonetic features. The contrast between this and the constant common denominator of a segmental unit like /T/ is obvious.

But why should we attempt to discover and recognize any such peculiar elements in a phonologic system? Why cannot one set of principles be used throughout? If we think of the heuristic principles of §322 as the fundamental operating principles of phonologic analysis, then junctures indeed stand out of line, and it is a fact that a phonologic system can be completely analyzed without recognizing any junctures at all. The contrast between *nitrate* and *night-rate* can be provided for by setting up two different [r]-like phonemes; that between *slyness* and *minus* by setting up /ay/ and, say, /ay·/, as different units, perhaps subsequently extracting the "drawl feature" /·/ as a lower-level unit.

However, if we think of the IC-approach as the fundamental orientation, and the principles of §322 as ancillary, then the recognition of junctures occupies an entirely logical place, despite the large difference which we have demonstrated. Confronted with long utterances as well as short, the IC-approach implies that we should break them down a bit at a time, in whatever way the facts allow. One of the things we look for in this connection is parallelisms between medial and terminal phenomena (where "terminal" subsumes both "utterance-initial" and "utterance-final"), versus phenomena which occur only medially. If we find a point in the interior of an utterance where articulatory motions are organized in a way typical of utterance-final and utterance-initial environment, in contrast with organizations occurrent only medially, we suspect that we have found an interior boundary of some kind at which the whole utterance can be broken into successive ICs. This suspicion becomes stronger if we find that either half of the whole utterance is identical with some shorter whole utterance, although such is not always the case. The technique of junctural analysis allows us to organize all such phenomena in a simple way, and affords an excellent structural point of departure for IC analysis of the whole system.

Sometimes no such special interior points are to be found. This would seem to be the case in Fox. The Fox phrase /e·howi·kičiwi·sahke·howi·yanoni·ča·nesahi/ 'It was when Wisahkeha was living with his wife and children' is uttered without any internal pauses. There is a smaller isolable segment (i.e., one which occurs as a whole utterance) /e·howi·kiči/, and likewise one /oni·ča·nesahi/, but if these two be extracted from the beginning and ending of the long phrase above, the remainder is not pronounceable alone. The "same" phrase (in terms of meaning, not phonology), pronounced a word at a time, becomes /e·howi·kiči, wi·sahke·ha, owi·yani, oni·ča·nesahi/; when said rapidly, the /a/ at the end of the second word and the /i/ at the end of the third disappear. The sequence /ičiwi·/ across the first "word"-boundary is not characteristic in any way whatsoever of sequences across "word"-boundary when the original long phrase is uttered, nor is the sequence /yanoni·/ across the last "word"-boundary. There are, true enough, certain medial sequences here which might be broken into a possible final portion followed by a possible initial portion, and other medial sequences which could not be so broken down. We can put a hyphen into the phrase to indicate each place where one might interpret in terms of occurrent final plus occurrent medial: /e·ho-wi·ki-či-wi·sahke·ho-wi·ya-no-ni·ča·ne-sa-hi/. No hyphen follows a long vowel, because long vowels do not normally occur finally. None follows a consonant, because consonants never occur finally. No hyphen precedes an /h/ or a cluster of /š/ plus consonant, because these do not occur initially. We find, however, no minimal contrasts between points where a break is possible and points where a break is not, and there is little positive correlation between the points where hyphens were inserted above and actual boundaries between segments which occur as whole utterances.

In this case, then, we say that there is no juncture in the language. There is no basis on which to divide the long Fox phase into some small number of ICs (once we have lifted off the intonation); we are forced to interpret the phrase as composed of as many ICs as there are syllables, namely seventeen.

The two English examples already discussed (*slyness*, *night-rate*) show clearly the difference between Fox and English in this respect. Let us give another example, which will also show how the extraction of certain features from certain contexts and their assignment to junctures renders the handling of ordinary segmental phonemes neater. In *Ben's here* we have an initial bilabial stop with crescendo voicing, which is the only kind of voiced stop found initially in English. In *Want a cab?* we have a final bilabial stop with diminuendo voicing, the only occurrent final variety. In *He's a cabby* we have a medial bilabial stop with even and fairly full voicing. In *I see Ben* we have a medial /b/ different from that in *He's a cabby*: the voicing is not full, but crescendo, like that in *Ben's here*. *There's a cab over there* has a medial /b/ like that of *Want a cab?* Medially, then, there are three kinds of voiced bilabial stop in contrast. We can assign the evenness of voicing of the /b/ of *He's a cabby* to the environment rather than to the phonemic unit /b/—the preceding and following sounds are of the always-voiced class in English. The crescendo quality of the voicing of the /b/ of *Ben's here*, and the diminuendo quality of the voicing of the /b/ of *Want a cab?*, can likewise be assigned to environment, since in the first case the /b/ is preceded by silence, in the second case it is followed by silence. But if we want to extract the crescendo of the voicing of the /b/ of *I see Ben* from the /b/ itself and assign it to the environment, to what part of the environment does it belong? It cannot simply be assigned to the preceding /iy/, since in *rebus* one has the fully voiced /b/ after /iy/. The only thing to do with the crescendo, if we don't want it to be a part of the /b/ itself, is to set it up in its own right as an element environmental to the /b/. The same argument applies to the diminuendo of the voicing of the /b/ in *There's a cab over there*.

Suppose we decide to write crescendo-voicing /b/ as /-b/, diminuendo-voicing /b/ as /b-/. In macrosegment initial and final we can omit the hyphen, since there is no contrast with anything else. But medially we will have to write it wherever our definition calls for it. If the three-way contrast for medial /b/ were the only set of features in the system which could be handled in this way, we would have accomplished nothing. But since medial /d/ and /g/, and others, manifest this same three-way contrast, and since many other medial elements manifest phonetically different but distributionally comparable contrasts, we can accomplish a great deal by extracting a large number of different features— all on the same basis of comparison with utterance-terminal phenomena—and setting them up as different allophones of a single structural unit: the English juncture.

It is also relevant that a great many, though not all, of the segments which thus come to be transcribed between successive occurrences of /-/ (or between macrosegment-initial and a /-/, or /-/ and macrosegment-final) are segments which occur, save for intonation, as whole macrosegments, including precisely the features indicated by the hyphen. One can say *I see Ben*; one can also say just *Ben.* One can say *There's a cab over there*; one can also say just *There's a cab,* or just *cab.* The correlation is not complete, but unless there were some correlation there would be little point in the analysis.

We said above that if the three-way contrast for medial /b/ were the only one capable of being handled juncturally in English there would likewise be little point in the process. A situation of this kind is found in some varieties of Caribbean Spanish. /n/ and /ŋ/ contrast in these varieties of Spanish only between vowels, and whenever /ŋ/ occurs before a vowel it happens that what follows the /ŋ/ also occurs as a whole macrosegment; where /n/ precedes a vowel, on the other hand, this is never true. One might propose that /ŋ/ be reinterpreted as /n-/, where the /-/ is defined as "dorso-velar position." Segments between successive /-/'s would then be isolable, as in the case of similarly bound segments (with a differently defined /-/) in English. But there would be no gain: one would in fact be stating the same situation with a different symbolism, which, because it is based only on a reanalysis of prevocalic /n/ and /ŋ/, could be stated just as well in terms of /n/ and /ŋ/ themselves.

In other words, juncture phonemes achieve their power precisely because of their phonetic heterogeneity. When we say of English that segments bounded by /-/ are in general isolable, we are covering a large number of specific facts: a segment which begins with crescendo voicing on a voiced stop or spirant, with clear voicing on a sonorant, with slight glottal catch (or at least clear point of syllable division) before a vowel, with a voiceless stop which is well aspirated, and so forth, and which ends with diminuendo voicing on a voiced stop or spirant, with drawl on a stressed vowel, and so forth, is in general isolable. It takes longer to describe all the allophones of a juncture, but once the juncture has been described it constitutes a powerful tool.

It should also be noted that the heterogeneity of the allophones of a juncture renders possible a much neater phonetic layout for "ordinary" phonemes, because one has withdrawn from the latter many of the messy marginal differences which would otherwise yield a very complex system. A /b/ which has to be defined as sometimes evenly voiced, sometimes having crescendo voicing, and sometimes having diminuendo voicing is a heterogeneous kind of a /b/. A /b/ which can be defined as always involving bilabial closure, velic closure, and some voicing (in contrast to /p/), is homogeneous. For that matter, if one were to reject junctural analysis in English, there could be no recourse to a heterogeneous /b/: one would have to establish at least evenly voiced /b/, crescendo-voiced /-b/, and diminuendo-voiced /b-/ as three different phonemes.

There is one way of speaking of juncture which retains phonetic homogeneity of all its allophones. This is Harris's way. Harris sets up a juncture as a "zero" phoneme—a phoneme having no phonetic properties at all (and, because of this, having identical phonetic properties in all environments). The only function of the "zero" phoneme, then, is to function as environment for ordinary phonemes: English /b/ is represented by different allophones when flanked by this "zero" phoneme and when not so flanked, and by different allophones depending on whether the "zero" phoneme precedes or follows. This seems to the present writer a most unfortunate and misleading kind of hocus-pocus; he feels that setting up junctures as always involving identifiable phonetic material, no matter how diverse, is much better. This choice is directly in line with the procedure recommended in §3222 for handling similar phones which are in complementary distribution (that is, removing part of one phone and assigning that part to the environment, so that what is left is identical with the other phone in question).

There is one potential source of error which ought to be avoided. Juncture phonemes are not recognized in order to show grammatic boundaries of one or another kind—say boundaries between words. It often happens that grammatic boundaries fall at open junctures, particularly grammatic word boundaries. It is easy to see why this should be so. Grammatic words are by definition ("minimum free form" or the like) units which are apt to occur in various different positions in utterances, including initial and final position, and in some languages grammatic words retain much the same phonologic shape regardless of their position (in other languages this is not true). It would be very peculiar indeed if the purely phonologic procedures for the determination of juncture which we have described did not reveal them at a good many such grammatic boundaries. But one cannot reverse this and simply assume that at grammatic boundaries of some sort there will necessarily be phenomena subject to junctural treatment. The Fox case shows this. The long phrase we cited earlier contains four words, hence three phrase-medial word boundaries, but nothing happens at those boundaries any different phonologically from what happens in word-interiors. In English there is some correlation, but it is not complete. On the one hand, whereas *she* and *is* are two grammatic words, even when the latter appears in shortened form, there is normally no juncture between the two in such a phrase as *She's a friend of mine*; *find her* in normal speech is homophonous with *finder*, once again with no juncture. On the other hand, some people pronounce *Cato* and *Plato* with juncture between the *a* and the *t*—a drawl on the /ey/ and a fully aspirated /t/, not the quick voiced-flap allophone found in *matter*. *Cato* and *Plato* are none the less single grammatic words, and perhaps even single morphemes. Yet *Cato* and *Plato* share with such juncturally segmented stretches as *padlock* and *playbill* the fact that the *phonologic* segments separated by the junctures can (with suitable adjustment of stress-level and intonation) stand as whole macrosegments: *Kay, play, toe, pad, lock, Bill.* Even this fails in the case of the isolated microsegment /z/ of *John's going*, which, given the definition of open juncture for English which our operations and the facts of the language force on us, has to be taken as both preceded and followed by /-/.

325. *Interrelationships Among Ultimate Phonologic Constituents.* There is as yet no general agreement on the proper way to decompose phonemes, junctures, accents, and intonational features into ultimate phonologic constituents—indeed, there is not even complete agreement that we should do so at all. Several alternative approaches were demonstrated or referred to in §262. Jakobson has used what is, at least in theory, a still different approach, based seemingly on impres-

sionistic acoustics. Harris has tried a technique which keeps only the vaguest tie with either acoustics or articulation. Our purpose here is not to legislate a choice between the possible procedures, but rather to show certain problems of an empiric and a logical sort which inevitably turn up when any of the possible procedures is followed. For this purpose, it will be feasible for us to keep to a relatively simple-minded sort of decomposition based firmly on articulation.

One of the problems is that of "determining" and "determined."

In French (§2521341) there are twelve obstruents: /p t k b d g f s š v z ž/. It is tempting to regard each of these as a bundle of three coequal ultimate constituents: a voicing-term (voiceless or voiced), an occlusion term (stop or spirant), and one of three positions (say front, central, and back). This requires seven ultimate constituents in all, and is in a purely logical sense quite impeccable. We can even redefine "front" in articulatory terms as "involving lower lip as articulator": then when "front" and "stop" co-occur, the upper lip is predictably the point of articulation, while when "front" and "spirant" co-occur, the upper teeth are predictably the point of articulation. "Back" cannot be redefined quite so simply in articulatory terms, but logically it is perfectly possible to say that the combination of "back" and "stop" produces dorso-velar, while the combination of "back" and "spirant" requires lamino-alveolar. It is possible seemingly to reinforce the argument by a claim that in some vague acoustic sense (probably purely impressionistic), /t/ is to /k/ as /s/ is to /š/. But this impressionistic-acoustic claim will be made only within the phonologic economy of French; it will not be made, say, for German, where obviously one must say that /t/ is to /k/ as /s/ is to /x/, leaving /š/ aside.

But there is another possible decomposition of French obstruents which is equally impeccable from a purely logistic point of view. This lines the obstruents up as follows:

p	f	t	s	š	k
b	v	d	z	ž	g.

Each obstruent is here regarded as a bundle of just two coequal ultimate constituents: a voicing term and one of six positions. The latter are bilabial, labiodental, apico-dental, apico-dental rill, lamino-alveolar, and dorso-velar. The contrast between stop and spirant is now regarded as determined rather than determining: if "bilabial," "apico-dental," or "dorso-velar" is involved in a bundle, then, automatically, one has "stop," whereas otherwise one equally automatically has "spirant." True enough, this interpretation requires eight ultimate constituents instead of seven, but that is a small difference, and the portrayal is just as realistic as the first; furthermore, if the roster of ultimate constituents is larger, the number which participate in each obstruent is smaller.

Both of these decompositions of the French obstruents have the odor of pure game-playing, an odor which is seemingly appetizing to some linguists. True enough, in each treatment we retain complete predictability of the actual relevant phonetic nature of the several obstruents (in the first, "front" and "stop" imply bilabial, whereas in the second, "bilabial" implies "stop"). But with such retention as a sole guide in decomposition, it is possible to be far more drastic, in a way which guarantees an absolute minimum of determining "features" for any system one may confront. Suppose that there are a total of sixteen phonemes, a through p. We list them in any order we wish, in a table like the following:

	a	b	c	d	e	f	g	h	i	j	k	l	m	n	o	p
A	x	x	x	x	x	x	x	x								
B	x	x	x	x					x	x	x	x				
C	x	x			x	x			x	x			x	x		
D	x		x		x		x		x		x		x		x	

The four "determining features" are A, B, C, and D. Each of the six-teen phonemes is now a bundle of from none to all of these four features. All of the actual articulatory features of all the phonemes are "determined." Thus if a is a low central vowel, then we say that these phonetic characteristics are automatically present whenever determining features A, B, C, and D are all present in a bundle; if, on the other hand, a is a voiced dorso-velar spirant, we say that *these* phonetic features are the automatic product of the fourfold con-catenation of determining features. There are 16! different ways in which we can list the 16 phonemes of the system across the top; there are therefore 16! dif-ferent ways in which the system can be decomposed in terms of just four deter-mining features.

In general, let a system involve n phonemes. Then let k be the integer such that 2^k is the smallest integral power of 2 not less than n. (Thus if n is 9, 10, . . . , 16, k is 4; if n is 17, 18, . . . , 32, k is 5; and so on.) The system can then be decom-posed in terms of as few as k different "determining features," but not in terms of any smaller number; and there are at least n! different ways of doing it.

In other words, any phonemic system—and, indeed, any finite set of things whatsoever—can be arbitrarily converted to a binary code, and there is at least one such conversion which requires a minimum number of binary digits for each element of the set.

The above is, I believe, a psychologic reductio ad absurdum. It should show us all that we are not properly concerned, in phonologic analysis, with any sort of purely arbitrary decomposition; indeed, we should like insofar as possible to avoid such arbitrariness altogether. The opposite of this sort of game-playing is what I mean by "hugging the phonetic ground closely."

And if we hug the phonetic ground closely, then neither of the portrayals of French obstruents given above can be accepted. The interpretation offered in §2521341 seems to be about as far as we can go.

Furthermore, it turns out that in general we cannot divide the ostensible ultimate phonologic constituents of a system neatly into "determining" and "determined," assigning the latter some sort of secondary status. In the actual complexity of speech, a given feature or difference turns up in some contexts as of primary relevance, in other contexts as subsidiary. We are forced by the lack of balance and neatness in the average language to recognize a larger number of ultimate phonologic constituents than would be called for in a purely arbitrary binary coding, and these features are more rigorously and arbitrarily limited in their privileges of occurrence relative to each other than would be the purely abstract ones set up by a binary coding.

Thus, for French obstruents, we have no choice but to recognize (1) two voicing terms; (2) two occlusion terms; (3) six combinations of articulator, point of articulation, and contour of articulator—ten features in all. Theoretically this would yield twenty-four distinct bundles; in fact it yields only half that number. The non-occurrence of bilabial spirants and labio-dental stops does not mean either that the choice of position of articulation governs that of occlusion term or the reverse; it is simply a limitation on privilege of occurrence.

The other matter which must be discussed is that of primary and secondary features. This is closely related to the problem of determined and determining, but not quite the same. Let us consider a typical 2+2+1 vowel system, in which the second dimension of contrast is primarily unrounded versus rounded: the /u/ and /o/ are always rounded, but in some environments are relatively front. Possibly the fronting environments are such that we can perform the sort of resurveying of boundaries (between item and environment) described in §3222; for the moment this does not matter. Generally, the occasional fronting of /u/ and /o/ would either not be mentioned at all, or it would be described as a "secondary" feature (or even as "nonphonemic"). Now the problem is this: would we be justified in ignoring the fronting altogether? Is it proper to exclude such "secondary" features from a strictly structural account?

Note that, by our description, there are probably some environments in which /i/ and /u/ differ both as to rounding and as to tongue frontness and backness. In such environments, it may sometimes be the backness, rather than the rounding, of an /u/ which tells a hearer that he has heard an /u/ rather than an /i/; it may sometimes be the frontness, rather than the absence of rounding, which tells a hearer that he has heard an /i/ rather than an /u/. Granting that this can occur only in some of the environments in which /i/ and /u/ are found, it would seem quite arbitrary of us, as analysts, to leave out of our account articulatory facts which the speakers of the language quite obviously do not ignore. It is most certainly appropriate for us to mention the constant factor first (the lip position), but we should include the occasional factor too.

Another good example of this is the three stop-types of Georgian (§2521333). The plain (unmarked) series lack both voice and aspiration—this is the primary feature. They are often, though not always (and not just in specifically delimitable environments), glottalized. This is a secondary feature, but it deserves mention.

Of course it is easy to miss some relatively subsidiary secondary features, and this obviously impairs our description of the phonologic system of a language less than it would to miss some clearly primary feature. But we should not *intentionally* overlook them.

4. *Structure, Pattern, and Abstraction.* Any utterance in a given language has a *phonologic structure*: it consists of ICs in a given arrangement; those ICs in turn consist of smaller ICs in a given arrangement; and so on until one reaches ultimate

phonologic constituents. Any utterance, or IC of an utterance, or IC of an IC, and so on, is a *phonologic element*; any phonologic element either has a phonologic structure (in terms of its own ICs) or is a single ultimate constituent. An arrangement of phonologic material which is not a phonologic element does not have a phonologic structure, even though it may occur. Thus the sequence /yt/ occurs in English, for example in *bait*; but /yt/ is not an element and has no structure, since the ICs of *bait* are /b/ and /eyt/, and the ICs of the latter are in turn /ey/ and /t/.

The above describes, in a summary way, our operating assumptions in the collation part of phonologic analysis; it does not imply that we can always decide unambiguously how to cut a given element into its ICs, or even that there always exists an unambiguous way if only we could find it. In §§2 and 3 we saw many cases of non-uniqueness, only some of which responded to our efforts to resolve the conflict between different bits of evidence.

The *phonologic pattern* (or *system*) of a language consists of a stock of ultimate phonologic constituents and a set of (hierarchic) arrangements in which they occur in one or another utterance. A given phonologic element (if not ultimate) *has* a structure; it *conforms* to the pattern. To one who has analyzed the system, structure is directly observable; pattern can only be deduced from the comparison of the structures of actual utterances. Pattern is *habit*, structure is *behavior*; pattern is *langue*, structure is *parole*; pattern is *culture*, structure is *behavioral manifestation of culture*. These successive statements are intended as approximately synonymous, and the reader can choose for himself which one, in terms of his own background, is most meaningful. Another statement of the same kind: structure is the spatio-temporal arrangement of the parts of a specific historical event; pattern is that to which structure more or less closely conforms. A dress has a structure—different pieces of cloth fastened together in a certain way; the "dress pattern" is a set of pieces of paper with a similar structure; the structure of the paper and of the cloth both conform to a single pattern in our sense.

The aim of the investigator in phonologic work is to discover and describe the phonologic pattern of a language. This is an empiric task, as we have insisted time and again: he must base his judgments on observations of actual speech (observations made by himself or by others); insofar as he can, he must identify and distinguish as the speakers themselves do; he must describe in terms of actual articulatory events, hugging the phonetic ground closely; if in the field, he must make predictions on the basis of partly collated evidence and change his portrayal if the predictions are not born out.

In due time, however, it becomes both possible and useful (and, as we shall presently show, necessary) to abstract the phonologic pattern, as a system, from the articulatory and partly acoustic framework in which the observed events occurred. Or, to express this in another way, it is worthwhile to invent a completely abstract mathematical system, manipulable in completely abstract mathematical terms, but which can be regarded as *exemplified* by the phonologic pattern in question. We shall first show more fully what it means to do this, and the difficulties which are encountered, and will then show why the operation is useful.

An abstract mathematical system consists of a set of elements, of completely unspecified characteristics, but bearing certain specified abstract relationships to each other. The set of all positive integers constitutes such a system. Any two different elements of this set bear an *order* relationship: if a and b are elements, then either a is greater than b or vice versa. Some ordered sets of three elements of the whole set (not necessarily all different) stand in the relationship that the sum of the first and second is the third; if this is true of a, b, and c, then it is also true of b, a, and c. Given any two elements, a and b, then one can always find an element c such that this relationship holds between a, b, and c. All of these relationships hold in various abstract sets, not only in the positive integers, but it is possible to establish a set of relations such that any set of elements for which they hold are either precisely the positive integers or else "might as well be."

As for abstraction: two oranges and two more oranges make four oranges; two apples and two apples make four apples; two oranges and two apples make four pieces of fruit. When, in grade school, we come to the point of saying simply "two plus two is four," without bothering to mention apples, fingers, oranges, or the like, we have abstracted. There is no implication that a statement like "two plus two is four" has any *truth* or *meaning* in its bare form: it is meaningless, in a sense, until we reinsert apples, fingers, oranges, or something else. But the abstract statement has a kind of derivative truth, or *validity*, in that if properly expanded into a reference to the actual world about us, it will be true, and in that expansions which will render it true are indeed to be found. This is what is meant by finding an *exemplification* of an abstract system: one for which no exemplification, by definition, can be found, either in the world about us or elsewhere in mathematics, is quite empty.

To abstract a phonologic pattern from the "phonic substance" in which it is made manifest in speech, we set up a number of abstract elements, paired off with the ultimate phonologic constituents of the phonologic pattern; or, if we prefer, we may pair them off with phonologic elements larger than ultimate phonologic constituents—say with phonemes, junctures, and the like. The relations which these abstract elements bear to each other are then similarly to be abstracted from the relations manifested by the phonologic elements: a and b both occur in environments $E_1, E_2, \ldots, E_n$, though not at the same time; c and d do not both occur in the same environment; e occurs before f; g does not occur before h; and so on. The abstract system which is constructed in such a manner for a given phonologic system will not bear much similarity to any of the systems with which mathematicians usually concern themselves, but that does not controvert their mathematical nature: mathematicians as a general rule confine their attentions to systems of a considerable degree of homogeneity, containing large, even transfinite, numbers of elements which "work" in much the same way, while a phonologic system is, comparatively speaking, highly heterogeneous.

Unfortunately it is possible to devise more than one mathematical system on the basis of any single phonologic system. This is in part true because of the indeterminacies, of various kinds and at various IC-levels, which we have already seen in numerous instances. We are forced to say that any two systematizations of a single phonology, so long a they subsume in one way or another exactly the same totality of phonetic facts, bear a certain kind of *equivalence* to each other; we shall call this kind of equivalence *mutual convertibility*. An analysis which treats Fox /č/ as composed of simultaneous laminal position and stop closure is mutually convertible with one which treats it as simultaneous cluster of /t/ and /y/—or, rather, *can* be mutually convertible therewith, providing in each case other matters are adequately covered. An analysis of English based on an opinion that initial voiceless stops are not aspirated is not mutually convertible with one based on an opinion that they are: here there is disagreement as to fact, not just as to collation.

The equivalence-relation of mutual convertibility carries over to the abstract mathematical systems based on phonologic patterns: we must say that any two mathematical systems which are exemplified in mutually convertible systematizations of a single phonologic pattern are likewise mutually convertible. Now on the abstract mathematical level it should be possible to analyze and describe precisely what constitutes "mutual convertibility." This has not yet been done, and it is not a simple task, largely because the systems involved are complex and finite. But it probably *can* be done, and the performance of this task should show us a great deal more clearly than we can now see just what kinds of differences there can be between different systematizations of a single phonologic pattern. Furthermore, if an ensemble of systems are related by some equivalence-relation, such as mutual convertibility, then there exists some abstract system, in the ensemble or not, composed of all those elements and relations which are *invariant* under any transformation from one of the systems to another. This invariant underlying system, when it can be discovered for a given language, will be the most accurate description obtainable of the phonology of that language, by definition maximally free from artifact-like results of the esthetic preferences of one or another investigator.

This in itself constitutes one of the large reasons for undertaking abstraction, and we may hope that in the next period of years enough work will be done to render phonologic work far less subject to personal whim than it is as yet. But there are several other reasons for abstracting.

One reason is because we cannot perform the operations of collation at all unless we do. The articulatory motions which constitute speech, and the auditory behavior which constitutes hearing speech, cannot themselves be manipulated and displayed. Collation has to be performed on some sort of a symbolic record of actual speech behavior, on the sheets and file slips of the investigator's notes. There are no phonologic forms in this book: there are only marks on paper which represent them. If we are going to talk about a phonologic system with a set of marks on paper assigned in some way to types of articulatory event in speech, then those marks on paper must in some way be defined as bearing relationships to each other abstractly like those between the articulatory events they represent. For greatest accuracy, the phonologic *pattern* must be manifested not only in "phonic substance" as speakers of the language speak, but also in the "graphic substance" which we use in describing the language or—more particularly—in transcribing words, utterances, and longer texts.

The very act of undertaking to analyze and describe a phonologic system therefore implies that we have assumed that the kind of abstraction we are talking about is both possible and necessary.

Finally, it must be recognized that the phonologic pattern of a language manifests itself, quite apart from the observations of any investigator, not only in articulatory motions, but also in characteristics of the sound-waves produced thereby, in the ear and associated tracts of the nervous system of a hearer, and, indeed, in the nervous system of the speaker as he speaks. We cannot assume any very great similarity between the articulatory system and the shape events take in these other media, but if a hearer understands what a speaker says—if, in particular, under good hearing conditions he can tell exactly what the speaker has said, phonologic unit by phonologic unit—then all the phonologic structure in the articulatory motions must also be represented somehow in the sound waves, and similarly it must all be in the nervous system. Now one cannot discern such matters as "dorsal," "apical," "voiced," and the like in sound waves or in nervous currents. Nervous currents are homogeneous in kind, and differ only in their relative spatial and temporal location within the central nervous system. The only way in which a phonologic system can be represented in these media as well as in articulation is for the system itself to be abstract.

An analogy will be useful. The unit symbols of the Morse Code, as used in old-fashioned telegraphy, consist of short voltage pulses ("dots"), long voltage pulses ("dashes"), and silences of two or three distinct durations. One can transmit messages, using exactly the same code, with waves of a flag: in one direction for "dot," in another direction for "dash," and in some third direction, once, twice, or three times, for the "silences." Or one can transmit messages in exactly the same code using dots and hyphens and spaces written from left to right on paper. There is no physical similarity between a dot on a telegraph wire, a dot in flag-waving, and a dot on paper, but the code is exactly the same regardless of the medium used. Abstractly, a dot in Morse Code can only be defined as a unit which contrasts with a dash or a silence. A unit Morse Code symbol, or an ultimate phonologic constituent, is nothing in itself: it can be defined only as something *different* from the various units which which it stands in contrast or in other relationship.

In other words, the phonologic *pattern* of a language (in contrast to the phonologic *structure* of specific elements as they occur) IS an abstract system. The main reason for abstraction away from the articulatory medium is that one cannot describe the phonologic *pattern*, in the last analysis, by any other means. We were wrong, earlier in this section, in referring to phonologic systems and matching abstract mathematical systems as two different things; we did so for a heuristic reason, but must now conclude that they are one and the same.

We pointed out in §04 that the terminology of phonologic description, while largely articulatory, is not completely so, being in part acoustic ("high" and "low" with reference to pitch) and in part of the "imitation-label" variety; and we indicated that this mixed frame of reference did not impair results for most purposes. We can now see why the latter statement is true: it is because, before we complete the portrayal of a phonologic pattern, we have abstracted the elements and relations in it from the primarily articulatory frame of reference used in making our initial observations. When we begin work on a system, the symbol [m] refers to actual articulatory events involving lip closure and open velic, the symbol [a] to articulatory events which we describe—perhaps with only "imitation-label" validity—in a certain way in articulatory terms. When we have completed our analysis, we may find ourselves using the symbols /m/ and /a/ (now bracketed between slant lines), and it may well be that each of these symbols refers back to certain recurrent articulatory events, whether we can describe those events with any complete physical accuracy or not; what counts when this point is reached, however, is no longer the physical manifestation or "exemplification" of the elements symbolized by /m/ and /a/, but only their abstract relations to each other and to other elements within the abstracted phonologic pattern. Theoretically we should be able to derive the same pattern by tapping the speech-communication channel at some other point—say in transit, as modulated sound, between speaker and hearer; or somewhere in the central nervous system of a speaker or hearer, as spurts of nervous energy. If we could, then our physical descriptions of /m/ and /a/ would be very different, but the network of abstract relationships between them and the other elements in the pattern would presumably be the same. We do not, in fact, know how to tap the channel in any way other than that currently used, but in one sense this is irrelevant or accidental.

In another sense it is not. It is foolish to think that, just because we must abstract a phonologic system from the articulatory-acoustic substance in which it is made manifest, therefore the former is our sole object of interest and the latter is beneath our dignity. The analyst is not the only person who must *start*, at least, with the overtly observable speech signal and motions of articulation. A child has this same point of departure in learning a language; an adult has this same point of departure in learning a new language. No comparison of abstract phonologic systems will tell us anything about the probable course of events when a speaker of language A is exposed to (and may have to learn some of) language B. For this we must make a careful comparison of the physical manifestations of the phonologic units of each language. Russian /p/ is abstractly not comparable with English /p/, because the two are defined by different interlocking sets of contrasts. But if a speaker of English hears a Russian word beginning with /p/, he will none the less interpret it as though it were an occurrence of his own English /p/. Abstraction must add; it must not leave behind.

5. *Acoustic Phonetics.* Our aim in this section is not to survey exhaustively all that has been accomplished so far in acoustic phonetics, but merely to define the field precisely in its relation to phonology, and to supply a frame of reference in terms of which the results of experiments in acoustic phonetics can be sensibly interpreted. The limitations of this aim should be clearly noted. The acoustics of speech is studied from a number of angles and with a number of purposes in view, of which acoustic phonetics is only one. Sometimes work directed towards some other goal is helpful to us, and sometimes it is not. Conversely, the phonologist sometimes can give useful advice to the acoustician and sometimes cannot.

It is a mistake to think that merely because telephone engineers—to take one example—are concerned with the transmission of speech, they need help from specialists in linguistics. Both linguists and engineers have made this mistake, and in some instances it has led to wasteful research programs.

51. *Sound and its Physical Analysis.* Sound is a form of energy; acoustics is the branch of physics devoted to its study. The sound produced by a speaking human—the *speech signal*—contains no physical ingredient not found in other sound: the techniques which acousticians have developed for the observation and description of sound in general can be applied to the speech signal, and there is no a priori reason why their investigation should miss anything essential in it. The proper terminology for use in the study of the speech signal is the terminology of acoustics as a branch of physics. We can add certain terms which seem particularly useful for our special interest (as over against, say, the study of bird calls or sonar design), providing that any new terms are hooked firmly, by measurement and demonstration, into the general terminology of acoustics—just exactly as, in the study of articulation, we can use the well-defined term "velic" despite its non-use by anatomists. But we cannot with impunity invent any fanciful impressionistic terminology and use it *in place* of the physicist's technical vocabulary.

511. *The Physical Dimensions of Sound.* When, in the course of phonologic work, we call, say, a voiceless dorso-velar stop a "speech sound" or simply a "sound," we are indulging in a convenient but inaccurate figure of speech. We might describe this figure as a kind of metonymy: "the source for the product." We use the same figure in everyday life. A particular sound from the next room will evoke the comment "I hear someone striking a match," rather than a description in terms of frequency, amplitude, harmonic structure, duration, and phase. It would be ridiculous to scorn this useful metonymy in either context, but when we propose to describe sound itself, we must carefully eschew it.

Sound is vibration, at the molar level, in a physical medium, of which the most important for our purposes is the air. The vibration of a *source* of sound sets the adjacent particles of air into vibration; these in turn jog those a bit further from the source; and so on; so that the sound travels in all directions from the source as waves, at approximately 1100 feet per second, their strength diminishing as the distance from the source increases. The familiar inverse-square law governs the decrease of energy-level of such energy spreading out unguided in all directions; besides, some energy is lost by conversion into heat, so that the overall weakening is swifter than the inverse-square law specifies. On the other hand, the inverse-square law does not apply to sound that is confined and guided, as within a stethoscope tube.

If the vibrations are regularly spaced in time, we hear a musical note of a definite pitch: the more rapid the vibrations (the higher the *frequency*, measured in *cycles per second*, "cps"), the higher the musical pitch. Doubling the frequency raises the pitch one octave. The range of frequencies on a piano tuned to concert pitch is from 27.5 cps to 4184 cps, which is just over seven octaves. The human ear hears lower sounds—down to 15 or 20 cps—providing they are loud

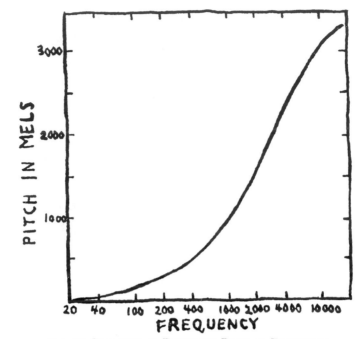

Fig. 13. Relation of Perceived Pitch to Frequency

The perceptual distance between two tones (as determined by psycho-acoustic experiments) of specified frequencies is proportional to the scale given on the right; "mels" are arbitrary units of measurement of perceived pitch, so designed that a 1000 cps tone has the pitch 1000 mels and a zero-mel tone is approximately at the lowest audible frequency. Redrawn from Stevens 40.

enough, and also somewhat higher sounds—up to 15 or 20 thousand cps—with the same proviso. The total range of a good ear is thus between ten and eleven octaves.

In our culture, at least in musical contexts, we are trained to hear octaves as equal intervals. Laboratory tests of pitch-differences have also shown that octaves are about equally large to untrained listeners over the middle of the range of audible frequencies, but that they sound smaller near each end of the range. Figure 13 demonstrates this. Since our crucial statements about frequency perceptions will all apply to the middle of the range, say from 200 cps to 4000 cps or so, it will be proper to say that the *perceptual* distance between two frequencies is proportional to their *musical* distance (measured in octaves and in fractions of an octave such as semitones); and this musical distance is of course proportional to the logarithm of the frequency ratio—that is, to the distance shown when the frequencies are plotted thus on a logarithmic scale. Figure 14 shows the difference between plotting frequencies linearly and logarithmically.

When the vibrations are not regularly spaced in time, we hear not a musical note but a noise of some sort. (This is the everyday sense of the word "noise," not to be confused with its special sense in communication theory, as in §02

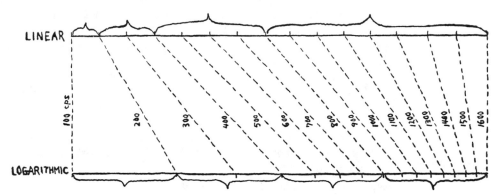

LINEAR

100 cps

200 300 400 500 600 700 800 900 1000 1100 1200 1300 1400 1500 1600

LOGARITHMIC

FIG. 14. LINEAR VERSUS LOGARITHMIC PLOTTING

Each brace encloses a one-octave interval. On the logarithmic scale octaves plot into line-segments of equal length; on the linear scale they do not.

and §6). Even noises, however, can often be classed roughly as higher or lower in pitch, as when we assert—quite correctly from the physical point of view—that the sound of a hammer striking a nail is higher in pitch than the sound of surf booming along a beach.

More technically, in a musical note almost all the energy is concentrated at a set of frequencies which are integral multiples of the basic frequency called the *fundamental*. If the fundamental is, say, 100 cps, then the energy will be concentrated at 100 cps, 200 cps (the *second harmonic*; the expression "first harmonic" is not used), 300 cps (the *third harmonic*), and so on. There need not be energy at all these frequencies, but it is essential that there be virtually none at, say, 150 cps or 220 cps. If the relative concentration at the different frequencies is altered, the difference is perceived as a change in *tone quality*. If the energy is all concentrated at a single frequency, the result is a *pure tone*.

In a non-musical noise, on the other hand, the energy is scattered more irregularly through a band of frequencies. If there is energy throughout the band from 100 cps to 300 cps, one hears a noise of indefinite but nevertheless relatively low pitch; if there is energy throughout the band from 1000 cps to 3000 cps, one hears a noise of indefinite but nevertheless relatively higher pitch. If the energy is spread evenly through all audible frequencies, the sound is called *white noise*.

At a given frequency, a greater amount of energy produces greater *amplitude*, and, other things being equal, the sound is *louder* than that involving a lower energy-level. Instead of speaking of amplitude, we can alternatively speak of *intensity*, which is by definition proportional to the square of the amplitude. Suppose that a violin string of fixed length vibrates in such a way that the point halfway between the ends passes back and forth through an arc one sixteenth of an inch in length. Then the sound will have twice the amplitude, and four times the intensity, that it would have if the arc were only one thirty-second of an inch in length.

We see from the above discussion that the physical dimensions of sound, in addition to *duration*, are *frequency* and *amplitude* or *intensity*; any other property of some specific sound can be expressed as a function of these three. There is one additional independent factor, *phase-relationship*, with which it will be more convenient to deal a bit later; but there is much evidence to show that human ears do not perceive differences of phase-relationship, so that it can hardly play any relevant role in the speech signal. For the sake of completeness, we had better mention also the three spatial dimensions in terms of which the source of a sound can be located—especially since binaural hearing does make it possible sometimes for us to localize the source of a sound, or at least its direction, without the evidence of other senses. But it is quite obvious that nothing further need be said along this line for our purposes.

512. *Laboratory Apparatus for the Study of Sound.* The acoustician can make "direct" observations of sound only with approximately the same apparatus which is built into all of us. For his purposes such observations are not sufficiently precise. Actually they are not "direct" at all, in one sense, since between the sound which impinges on his ears and the statements which he can make

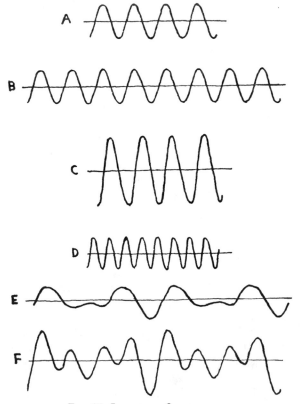

FIG. 15. IDEALIZED OSCILLOGRAMS

B lasts longer than A; C has greater amplitude than A; D has higher frequency than A. E and F differ from each other, and from A, B, C, and D, in harmonic structure.

about it there functions a complex, linguistically and culturally conditioned, apparatus which distorts his report in unknown ways—the common metonymy of "source for the product" playing a prominent but variable role. Therefore he turns to laboratory apparatus which will produce a visible record, of one sort or another, of the sound, and which can be calibrated with at least somewhat less difficulty than one can calibrate human beings.

The two chief devices currently used for acoustic study (at least of the speech signal) are the *oscillograph*, which dates back a number of decades, and the *spectrograph*, which was developed during World War II.

The oscillograph produces a visible record called an *oscillogram* which is, to within a measurable degree of accuracy, a kind of facsimile of the actual wave-motion which constitutes the sound. If the sound is not too complex, then it is relatively easy to measure off frequency, amplitude, and something of the harmonic structure. In Figure 15 we show, in a somewhat idealized way, how differences of frequency, amplitude, and harmonic structure appear on an oscillogram. Differences of phase-relationship also show up clearly in simpler cases: Figure 16 shows how, and at the same time will serve to explain what is meant by phase.

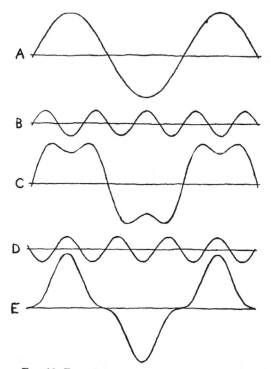

FIG. 16. DIFFERENCE OF PHASE-RELATIONSHIP

A and B are both pure tones; D is the same as B but "out of phase"—that is, D would have to be shifted to the left or right before it could be placed squarely over B. C is the sum of A and B; E the sum of A and D. C and E therefore are identical in harmonic structure, but differ in phase-relationships.

The spectrograph produces a different sort of visible record, which is proving to be more useful than that of the oscillograph for most aspects of analysis of the speech signal. As in an oscillogram, a *spectrogram* shows time along the length of the record, but here the resemblance ends. The up-and-down scale of a spectrogram shows frequency, so that the spectrogram does in a precise way what printed music does irregularly. The amount of energy present at a given time and frequency shows up as the degree of darkness of the spectrogram at the corresponding point. Thus a spectrogram is a three-dimensional portrayal, although the third dimension, shown by the light-dark scale, cannot be read very accurately. Figure 17 shows, in a highly stylized way, how differences of dura-

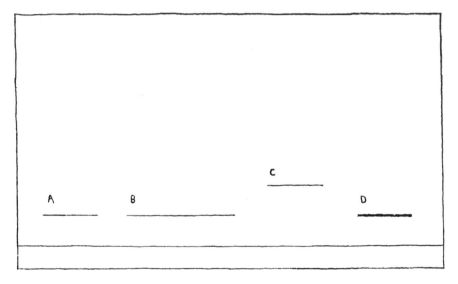

FIG. 17. IDEALIZED SPECTROGRAM

The spectrogram above shows exactly what the musical notation below does. The spectrogram shows difference of frequency by the height of the line; C is higher than A, B, or D. It shows difference of duration by length of the line: B is twice as long as A, C, or D. It shows difference of amplitude by heaviness of the line: D is more intense than A, B, or C. This last dimension is the hardest to read off accurately, just as in musical notation the marking of "p" and "f" is least precise.

tion, frequency, and amplitude appear. Like the human ear, the spectrograph does not respond to differences of phase-relationship.

Existing spectrographs will not produce a continuous record of a signal of indefinite length—such a machine is theoretically feasible, but the cost would be prohibitive. Instead, the existing machines will record a signal lasting not longer than two and four-tenths seconds, in two steps. First the signal is placed on a circulating band of magnetic material within the machine. Then it is played back repeatedly, within the machine, as a "band-pass" filter runs slowly up the frequency scale. This filter passes only the energy within a very narrow band of frequencies, and maps each narrow band in turn onto the spectrogram. Most spectrographs have two alternative settings, one of which will plot in terms of relatively narrower bands of frequencies, the other of which takes a broader band at a time. The difference is shown in Figure 18.

A real oscillogram does not look too different from our idealized specimens in Figures 15 and 16, but a real spectrogram of speech bears only the most super-ficial resemblance to the stylized drawings in Figure 17. There are lines, hatchings, and mottled or speckled areas all over the paper, and it requires considerable skill (plus sometimes a bit of artistry) to discern what is relevant. To a large extent, this fuzziness is the result of the awkward way in which energy-level is represented by the light-dark scale. Some help is afforded by a special circuit with which most spectrographs are now equipped, with which a different repre-sentation can be achieved. For any selected short segment of the input (as re-corded on the circulating magnetic band within the machine), this circuit pro-duces a two-dimensional graph measuring energy-level against frequency. This is

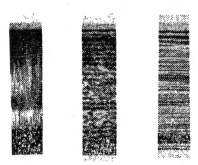

FIG. 18. DIFFERENCE IN WIDTH OF "BAND-PASS" FILTER

The figure on the left is a segment of a spectrogram made with a "band-pass" filter which passed a band 340 cps in width. That in the center was made with a filter passing a band 58 cps wide, and that on the right with a band passing 5.8 cps. All three are of exactly the same segment of the same signal. Note that with the broadest band frequency is smeared but time is precise, while with the narrowest band the time of a bit of energy is smeared and frequency is precise. No physical operation can eliminate such smear, but we can choose whether to smear time more and frequency less or vice versa. Reproduced, by permission, from Gordon E. Peterson, "Parameter Relationships in the Portrayal of Signals with Sound Spectrograph Techniques," Journal of Speech and Hearing Disorders 17.427–32, 1953.

equivalent to taking a narrow vertical slice out of a spectrogram and replacing the light-dark scale by a second dimension on the paper. The result is shown schematically in Figure 19. By making such a representation for a large number of successive narrow slices, and measuring the resulting graphs carefully, it is possible to build, out of some suitable material, a "spectrogram" in three spatial dimensions, a third spatial dimension replacing the light-dark scale. Examples will be found in Kersta; it would cost too much to reproduce a half-tone picture of one here. Furthermore, the process of preparing such a "solid spectrogram" is extremely tedious, and there is no reason to believe that it can yield results that cannot be obtained more easily by other methods.

Whenever a relatively musical tone is involved in the input to a spectrograph, the spectrogram shows a set of one or more approximately horizontal lines from left to right, representing concentrations of energy at the various harmonics of the tone. When the fundamental drops, the lines drop and move closer to-

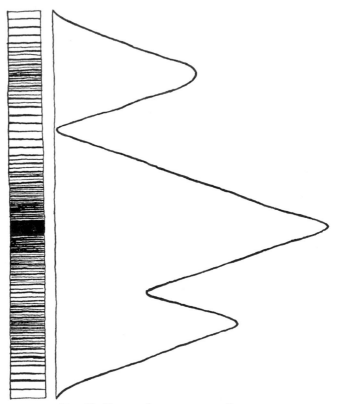

FIG. 19. ENERGY-LEVEL AGAINST FREQUENCY

To the left is shown (schematically) a short segment of a spectrogram. To the right is a curve in which the intensity of the signal at a frequency is shown by the height of the curve from the (vertical) base-line. Where the spectrogram is darker, the curve is higher, and conversely. To make the curve look like such curves usually do, turn the page ninety degrees counterclockwise.

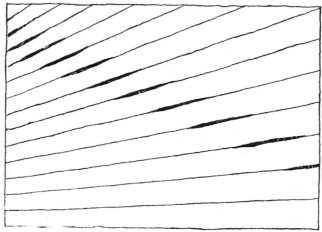

FIG. 20. HARMONIC STREAKS AND A FORMANT

gether; when the fundamental rises, the lines rise and move further apart. By careful measurement, under favorable conditions, it is possible to determine the frequency of the fundamental at any point where these *harmonic streaks* appear.

In addition to these, and often cutting across them, the eye seems to see rather broader and less distinct dark bands, called *formant lines*. Closer scrutiny reveals that these are not additional lines at all, but rather merely the result of variations in darkness of the individual harmonic streaks (though if the latter become dark and heavy enough, they may overlap and lose their distinctiveness). Figure 20 shows, with some magnification, a sheaf of upwards-sweeping harmonic streaks, each varying in darkness from point to point. When held at arm's length, the darker segments will seem to coalesce into a dark band curving downwards from left to right. Acoustically, all this means is that the amount of energy at a given time is concentrated more at certain harmonics than at others; a band of frequencies within which the harmonics are relatively intense constitutes a *formant*. A formant, thus, is not a fundamental feature of sound in addition to those itemized in §511, but simply the relatively great intensity of the harmonics at certain frequencies.

A third type of apparatus, developed very recently but already proving to be invaluable, is the *pattern playback*. This device will "read" a (photographically enlarged) spectrogram and produce the appropriate sound. Not all of the original input to the spectrograph is thus read out: the pitch of the fundamental is lost, so that speech comes out in a monotone. The greatest utility of this device has been in psycho-acoustic experiments. Rather than using an actual spectrogram, one can draw pseudo-spectrograms freehand, play them, and record the responses of subjects. Thus one can eliminate one or another feature of what appears on actual spectrograms, in order to test the relevance of what is retained.

52. *The Problem of Acoustic Phonetics.* The fundamental problem of acoustic phonetics—the problem which defines the field—can be described as follows: given the phonologic structure of utterances in a certain language, what are the acoustic correlates of the different phonologic elements?

This can be restated in terms of the discussion of §02 and the diagram in Figure 1. In §02 we defined the phonetic system of a language as the code by which an individual's Speech Transmitter transduces a discrete flow of phonologic units into a continuous speech signal, and by which an individual's Speech Receiver performs the inverse transduction to recover the discrete flow of phonologic units from the continuous speech signal. The problem of acoustic phonetics, then, is to determine and describe this code—to determine and describe the phonetic system of a language.

In attacking this problem there are certain general considerations to be kept in view—considerations which apply axiomatically to any study of any sort of transducer in any sort of communicative system. A transducer is a device (of hardware or of flesh) which converts an input signal into an output signal; the only transducers with which we are concerned are *non-singular*, which means that their output allows, by the application of a suitable second transduction, of the virtual recovery of the original input. The conventions according to which a given transducer converts input into output constitute a *code*. The physical construction of a transducer determines the code by which it works—in the sense that if one knows the former, one can determine the latter. The reverse is not true: transducers of varying physical construction can function according to a single code. However, one can define as *communicatively equivalent* all those transducers, real or possible, which operate or would operate according to a given code, and one can then be concerned with the code rather than with the transducer as a physical entity: in communicative theory, this is generally what one does, and in effect it amounts to treating the transducer itself as a "black box."

As between input, output, and code, there is a sort of two-to-one determinism: if the investigator knows any two of these three, the third can be predicted. Knowing input and code, one can predict what output will be produced by the input; knowing output and code, one can similarly predict (in a sort of inverse way) what input produced the output. Or, knowing input and output, one can describe the code. On the other hand, knowledge, no matter how complete, of just one of these three factors is equivalent to no knowledge at all, since nothing can be deduced about either of the others.

Often enough, the knowledge which is available at the beginning of an investigation falls short of complete information about two of the three factors, without amounting to knowledge of one of the three factors and no knowledge about either of the other two, In military cryptanalysis, for example, one may have (1) a fair sample of outputs (messages in encoded form); (2) general information as to the *sort* of input which might be responsible for the outputs (the messages certainly concern ship-movements, plans of attack, and so forth); and (3) some general information as to the *sort* of code which has been used. The "breaking" of the code—and the interpretation of the specific outputs—then involves a trial-and-error process; there is a well-developed mathematical theory of the conditions under which the trial-and-error can be successful, and much practical know-how for making the period of trial-and-error as short and effortless as possible. In theory, all that the trial-and-error process can ever lead to is a solution of a certain degree of probability—not to an absolutely certain solution. In practice, however, the degree of probability of correctness is often high enough to eliminate any reasonable doubt.

Let us apply this to our present problem. Oscillograms and spectrograms afford us as large a sample as we wish to obtain of the output of an individual's Speech Transmitter. By one of the principles stated above, this sample in itself is quite useless. But we can supplement it, theoretically, in either of two ways: (1) by obtaining information as to which utterances (of those of which we have the acoustic records) sound the same to a native speaker and which ones sound different. We then have precise information about output and statistical information about input, and can proceed to a probabilistic determination of the code. The logic of this is the same as the logic of ordinary methods of phonologic analysis (§3), except that acoustic specification of output replaces articulatory, impressionistic, and imitation-label specification; in theory, the procedure should yield in due time not only a probabilistic specification of the phonetic system (as a code), but also of the phonologic system itself, as an abstract network of elements; (2) by accepting the phonologist's description of a phonologic system (as attained by his ordinary methods, and perhaps as abstracted along the lines discussed in §4), as a presumably accurate description of the economy of the signals which are emitted by an individual's Phoneme Source and Speech Receiver. We then have precise information both about output and about input, and can proceed to a presumably precise (rather than probabilistic) determination of the code.

The first of these two procedures has never been used. Theoretically it should be possible, but there is serious reason to doubt its practicality. In any case, it would be vastly more difficult than the second procedure, and it is hard to see how it could possibly yield any information which the second, and much simpler, procedure cannot be made to yield. Thus, while it is not logically valid to say that the acoustician *must* accept the findings of the phonologist as a stable frame of reference, it is an empiric fact that doing so constitutes a practical short-cut that the acoustician would be foolish to reject.

521. *Methods of Attack.* There are two major lines of experimentation which can be followed in seeking an answer to the fundamental problem of acoustic phonetics, under the practical assumption, just discussed, that the acoustician will accept the phonologist's analysis as a stable frame of reference:

(1) A set of utterances is selected, each one clearly and completely identified in phonologic terms. The selection is such that each low-level phonologic element (each phoneme, each juncture, each intonation pattern, and the like) occurs in various different environments. A number of recordings are made of each utterance, perhaps as said on successive occasions by a single voice (at least this is a good way to start: the complication of differing voices can well be postponed).

Each recording of each utterance is then checked, by listening, to be sure that, as actually delivered, the phonologic structure is just as planned; deviants, in which the speaker has said the wrong thing, are discarded. Then acoustic records (particularly spectrograms) are made for each uttering of each utterance. This gives the analyst two sorts of material with which to work: the phonologic specification of each utterance; and the measurable acoustic record of each uttering of each utterance. The necessary procedure in searching through this evidence for the acoustic correlates of the phonologic elements is obvious in general outline, though tedious and very difficult in detail.

(2) The second line of investigation is quite different, and can be profitably undertaken only after some tentative results have been achieved by the first method. Subjects are selected who are native speakers of the specific language under investigation (and of the proper dialect of that language.) Hand-drawn pseudo-spectrograms are prepared, varying in some systematic way one or more of the features which have been shown, by experimentation of the first kind, to be of probable relevance. These are then played on the pattern-playback to the subjects, who are instructed to identify what they think they hear. The instructions given the subjects have to be phrased with great care, and their answers have to be carefully interpreted, since the frame of reference in terms of which the responses are to be evaluated (namely, their phonologic system) is one which they possess and use but about which they are not trained to verbalize accurately.

522. *General Character of Work Done So Far.* Almost all investigations so far reported in the field of acoustic phonetics have been of an essentially preliminary nature, and have involved certain simplifications which must be borne in mind. These simplifications are of three sorts:

(1) In work along the first line of experimentation, there has been a great deal of "spoon-feeding" of spectrographs: that is, inputs have consisted of utterances spoken very slowly and carefully, or even of pseudo-utterances such as artificially prolonged vowels. There are certain purposes (other than those of acoustic phonetics) for which this sort of spoon-feeding is legitimate. For example, if one is trying to work out a "visible speech" system for the deaf, it is legitimate to require especially careful articulation: if the system could be made to work only with this restriction, the small imposition thus made on anyone who wished to communicate via such apparatus with the deaf would be far more than counterbalanced by the gain. But for acoustic phonetics the results are only of the roughest preliminary value. Eventually, it is imperative that naturally flowing speech—which means rapid, carelessly articulated speech—be examined.

(2) Also in experiments of the first sort, there has in general been an inadequate understanding of the full complexity of phonologic systems. Studies have been made, for example, of the acoustic correlates of "English [æ]," with no realization that as used by the investigator this single symbol may have subsumed as many as four phonologically distinct English stressed syllable nuclei: /eh/, /æ/, /æh/, and /æy/. Eventually it is essential that such lumping be abolished. In the meantime, however, the results obtained are by no means to be discarded; they are of value, despite the lumping, for reasons connected with

functional load and with the difference between "frequency norm" and "clarity norm" phonology (both of which will concern us in §6).

(3) A similar oversimplification has been involved in work along the second line of investigation. Instead of taking the actual phonologic system of some real language as frame of reference, what the experimenters have done is to devise one or another miniature system—turning largely on a traditional misunderstanding of "IPA" and its "cardinal vowels." Thus one study of this sort, which we shall discuss later, used syllables beginning with [p t k] and ending with one of a set of seven "cardinal vowels" [i e ɛ a ɔ o u]. Fortunately, as shown by our survey in §2, the vast majority of known languages include a stop subsystem /p t k/, and a good many include vocalic or syllabic units which can be roughly identified with the seven "cardinal vowels" just listed. The latter comment applies even to English: the speaker whose system has not been modified by training in "general phonetics" of the IPA sort can identify the seven "vowels" with his /iy ey eh ah oh ow uw/.

The nature of the misunderstanding which leads to this sort of simplification and artificiality deserves brief comment here. What we may call the "IPA general phonetic" misunderstanding assumes that there is some strictly finite, even if large, total set of "speech sounds," as auditorily distinguishable units, from which each actual language makes some selection. The IPA "cardinal vowels" form part of this stock, and it is supposed to make sense to say that a given IPA "cardinal vowel," say [i] or [a] or [ɯ], occurs, or does not occur, in a given language. The Prague phonologists early pointed out the crucial error in this view, as did, more or less independently, such American linguists as Bloomfield and Sapir. A phoneme is functionally nothing at all—except insofar as it is *different* from other phonemes. A phonologic system is at bottom not a set of elements, but a network of contrasts: the elements are but the end-points of the contrasts. The entire discussion of this manual is based on this view.

Although the above remarks may seem sharply critical, we must in fact be thankful that acoustic phoneticians have forged ahead within their oversimplified frame of reference. Without the results achieved through oversimplification, we should be completely at a loss for what to look for in examining the acoustic properties of normal rapid speech. We perhaps should also be thankful that acoustic phonetic research has been carried out by speakers of Western languages, in which vowels are prominent and important. It is not easy to imagine what turn acoustic phonetic study would have taken were we speakers of a language like Bella Coola (§2213), but one suspects that the initial period of floundering-about and of repeated frustration would have been considerably prolonged.

53. *Tentative Results.* In the following subsections, we shall discuss the sorts of partial correlations which have so far been discovered. These do not constitute an answer to the fundamental problem of acoustic phonetics, but they are evidence pointing towards the answer.

531. *Formants and Vowels.* Work with spectrography quickly strengthens a theory first proposed on the basis of earlier experiments with cruder apparatus: the theory that vowels (and certain kindred types of unit, roughly "vocoids" or

"sonorants" or "resonants") are kept apart largely by the frequency-locations of formants. One version of this theory holds that vowels distinguished in articulation solely by lip and tongue position (setting aside retroflexion, and non-oral differentiating factors such as nasalization, glottal stricture, pharyngealization, and the like) are, or at least can be, distinguished completely by the two lowest formants.

This general theory (not necessarily the two-formant version) is reasonable when we examine the functioning of the speech tract in the production of voiced vowels. The vibrating glottis produces a musical tone exceedingly rich in harmonics. The particular conformation of the oral cavity as a resonance chamber, brought about by lip and tongue position, serves to reinforce the energy at and near certain frequencies and to damp out that at others. The reinforced frequency-bands are the formants.

5311. *Artificial Two-Formant Matching of "Cardinal Vowels."* In ordinary speech there rarely occurs anything which might be called a "steady state" vowel. The articulatory organs are in motion almost constantly, and therefore the formants are also constantly shifting their frequency-positions. This is just as true of phonemically simple (or, phonetically, crudely "monophthongal") vowels as it is of complex nuclei which involve an obvious glide, except that the rate of change may be rather less, or the direction of change less obvious, for the former. It is well known that any vowel sound, if prolonged indefinitely, soon loses its character as a "speech-sound": what is heard, in the context of speech, as a vowel color, comes to be heard, when the sound is prolonged, as a tone-quality. One need only think of humming, which involves the articulatory mechanism of an [m], but which does not for long continue to have any noticeable [m]-ness about it.

Nevertheless, it is possible to prolong fixed vowels or pseudo-vowels somewhat longer than they would normally be held in ordinary speech, without immediately having them lose their vocalic character. The first experiment which we shall report involved steady-state pseudo-vowels, produced by hand-drawn spectrograms played on the pattern-playback. A large number of these were prepared, and then a psycho-acoustic experiment was performed to determine the optimum two-formant matching of the sixteen Jonesian "cardinal vowels." If these sixteen "vowels" were a real vowel system, then in ordinary phonologic terms they would constitute a 4×2×2 system, charted as follows:

i	ü	ɯ	u
e	ø	ɣ	o
ɛ	œ	ʌ	ɔ
æ	a	ɑ	ɒ .

The subjects used in the experiment knew at least something of both French and English and had had some training in IPA phonetics. The testing procedure guaranteed in advance that the first (lower) formant would be identical for all four vowels of a given articulatory height. The most satisfactory pairs of formants proved to be the following:

[i] 250, 2900	[ü] 250, 1900	[ɯ] 250, 1050	[u] 250, 700
[e] 360, 2400	[ø] 360, 1650	[ɣ] 360, 1100	[o] 360, 800
[ɛ] 510, 2000	[œ] 510, 1450	[ʌ] 510, 1150	[ɔ] 510, 950
[æ] 750, 1650	[a] 750, 1300	[ɑ] 750, 1200	[ɒ] 750, 1100.

In Figure 21 we show the pseudo-spectrograms for these sixteen vowels, and in Figure 22 the sixteen pairs of formants are mapped in two dimensions, first formant against second. It has become customary, in this sort of representation, to plot the first formant vertically, the values increasing from top to bottom, and the second formant horizontally, values increasing from right to left. This is in three ways a reversal of the most usual conventions for graphs and charts, but it is just as correct mathematically, and has the property (a merit if not abused) that articulatorily high vowels place higher on the graph than low vowels, and articulatorily front vowels further left than back vowels. Both of the outer scales in Figure 22, and all scales in figures to follow, are logarithmic (see Figure 14).

However artificial the convention of the "cardinal vowels" may be for ordinary phonologic analysis, in acoustic phonetics it is highly convenient to have a frame of reference of this sort. We are going to adopt a sixteen-point grid as frame of reference, and we shall call the points (acoustic) cardinal points, but in doing so we shall modify slightly the sixteen discovered in the above experiment. Figure 22 shows lines adjoining the vowels of the same height and also the vowels of the same front-back quality and the same rounding-unrounding quality (all of this, of course, in articulatory terms). The line joining any four vowels of the same height is horizontal, since the first formant was prescribed in advance to be the same for all four. The more nearly vertical lines in Figure 22 also look straight, but they are not, as a larger-scale graph would show. However, by keeping the first formants as fixed by the experiment, and the second formants for the highest and ʾᴜwest vowels, but by making slight adjustments in the second formants for the ʾᴜgher-mid and lower-mid vowels, we can make the four vertiᴜal

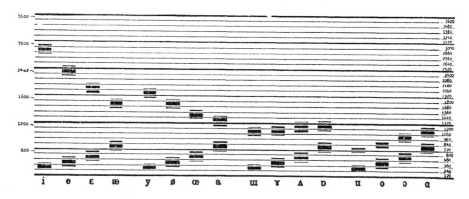

FIG. 21. PSEUDO-SPECTROGRAMS FOR ARTIFICIAL CARDINAL VOWELS

Reproduced with the permission of Haskins Laboratories. The phonetic symbols under the fifth-from-last and the last spectrograms should be interchanged.

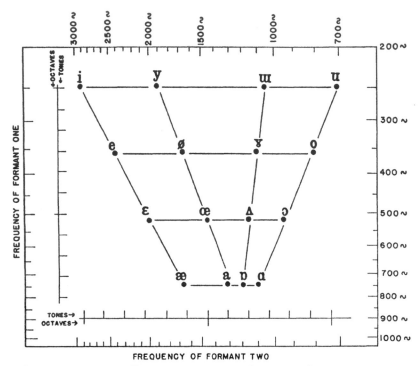

FIG. 22. FORMANT-BY-FORMANT PLOTTING OF ARTIFICIAL CARDINAL VOWELS
Reproduced with the permission of Haskins Laboratories. The two right-hand phonetic symbols in the bottom row should be interchanged.

lines straight. The new values for the higher-mid and lower-mid vowels are as follows:

[e] 360, 2411   [ø] 360, 1675   [ɣ] 360, 1098   [o] 360, 813.2
[ɛ] 510, 2011   [œ] 510, 1485   [ʌ] 510, 1145   [ɔ] 510, 938.4.

Figure 23 shows the resulting grid of straight lines: at each meeting-point or intersection of two lines there is one of our acoustic cardinal points of reference. The crosses mark the positions of the psycho-acoustically matched values where these deviate from those arbitrarily established for our grid. There is only one slight gain in making this readjustment: the grid is easier to draw on a graph. But this gain is not offset by any loss at all: the "cardinal vowels" are arbitrary to begin with, and, what is more, the very slight changes in second-formant frequencies would be scarcely detectable by ear.

5312. *French Vowels.* Spectrograms of French vowels spoken in isolation show general agreement with the cardinal points conventionally thought of as closest to them. There are two spurious reasons contributing to this. One is that the French vowel system played a major role in the development of the original "cardinal vowel" theory. The other is that in selecting first-formant frequencies for the first part of the psycho-acoustic tests for cardinal-vowel matching, resort

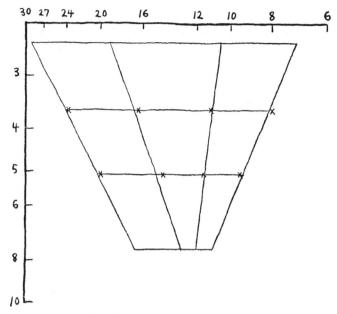

FIG. 23. ACOUSTIC CARDINAL POINTS

was made to measurements of French vowels. After the best second formants had been selected, these were held constant and the first formants varied, but except for the four lowest vowels the original values were finally settled on as more satisfactory than any alternatives.

However, the correlation between nine of the vowels of educated northern French (all but the two lowest in a 3+3+3+2 system) and our cardinal grid is nevertheless interesting; we display it in Figure 24. Perhaps the most striking deviation is the rather lower second-formant frequencies for the three French front unrounded vowels /i e ɛ/; we shall discuss the implications of this a bit later.

5313. *English Vowels.* Spectrograms have also been made of English vowel phonemes in isolation; there is more artificiality about this than for French, since the English vowel phonemes do not occur stressed before no consonant, nor prolonged, and we can therefore expect something a little wilder in the way of results. Figure 25 shows eight of the nine English vowel phonemes as measured in this artificial way; there are no data for the ninth. The frequency figures for the formants are as follows:

/i/ 400, 2100	/ɨ/ 300, 1500	/u/ 450, 1000
/e/ 500, 1800	/ə/ 600, 1300	/o/ 550, 900
/æ/ 650, 1700	/a/ 700, 1100	/ɔ/ —.

The arrangement may at first seem rather random, yet certain correlations appear. Considering any three vowels of the same articulatory height, the frequency of the second formant decreases as we pass from front to mid unrounded to back

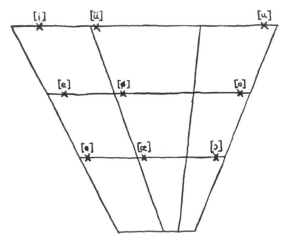

FIG. 24. MEASURED FRENCH VOWELS MAPPED AGAINST THE CARDINAL REFERENCE GRID

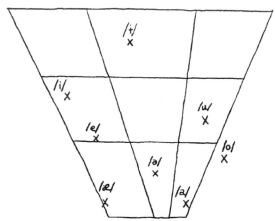

FIG. 25. ENGLISH VOWELS MAPPED AGAINST THE CARDINAL REFERENCE GRID

rounded (e.g., /i/ to /ɨ/ to /u/). Considering any three of the same front-back and lip position, the frequency of the first formant increases as we go from high to low (e.g., /i/ to /e/ to /æ/).

The measurements of /ə/ and /a/, as compared to the cardinal points on our grid, are interesting. Words such as *cup, but, luck* have /ə/ in most American English, but /a/ in southern British English, of the sort with which Daniel Jones usually deals. The Jonesian cardinal [ʌ] is supposed to be quite close to the British vowel in *cup, but, luck.* The test audience in the two-formant cardinal matching was obviously largely American, for their selection of a match for cardinal [ʌ] reflects an identification of that with their own /ə/, rather than with British English /a/, in the key reference words.

In Figure 26 we graph, against our reference grid, one occurrence each of /u/,

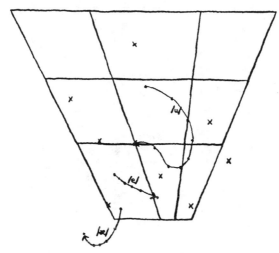

FIG. 26. THREE ENGLISH VOWELS IN CONTEXT
The x's locate the measured English vowels shown in Figure 25.

/e/, and /æ/ in clearly articulated, but rapid and natural, speech. The /u/ is from the word *understood*, the /e/ from *hotel*, and the /æ/ from *exactly*. Each vowel appears as a curve: there is an arrowhead at one end of the curve, and dots appear at various places along each. The dots represent actual measurements, via a spectrogram, taken at intervals of two hundredths of a second, throughout the duration of the vowel; the curves are then drawn in freehand. It will be noticed that the curve for /u/ passes fairly close to the point measured for an artificially prolonged /u/, and that that for /æ/ is even further down and to the left than the similarly measured point for an artificially prolonged /æ/. The curve for /e/, however, is quite a distance from the "point" /e/. This is presumably because of the very dark /l/ which follows it. Nevertheless, and despite the fact that the speaker for these three vowels was different from that for the steady-state vowel measurements, it is clear that there are very wide limits of tolerable variation which does not destroy the recognizable phonologic identity of the vowels in actual context.

If we were to make observations and measurements of, say, a thousand occurrences of each of the nine English vowels, in actual speech, and to draw curves for each occurrence of each in the style of Figure 26, we should expect to find a distribution of each of the nine around some most favored point; this is shown—quite hypothetically—in Figure 27. The relative darkness within the region for each vowel is supposed to represent the relative frequency with which that vowel shows formants at a particular point; the regions for the six vowels intersect, implying that some /i/'s, for example, pass through areas also passed through by some occurrences of /e/ or of /i/. Remember that Figure 27 is not based on actual measurements; it is only an attempt to show the sort of picture which we should expect actual measurements to yield.

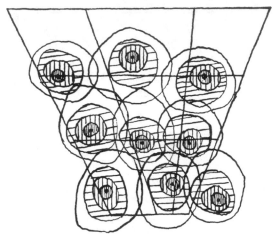

FIG. 27. HYPOTHETICAL GRAPH OF FREQUENCY-DISTRIBUTION OF ENGLISH VOWELS

This portrays what we should expect to find if we made measurements of vast numbers of occurrences of each of the nine English vowels. The portrayal is *not* based on actual data.

5314. *How Many Formants?* Although all of the experiments and observations reported on in the above have tacitly assumed the two-formant theory, it should be noted that the results do not in any sense constitute *proof* of that theory. Even for languages like French and English, we have demonstrated neither the necessity nor the sufficiency of two formants.

On the score of necessity, there is evidence that reasonably adequate matching of some vowel-colors can be achieved with but a single formant. Old disc records may fail to reproduce the lower formant of such high vowels as [i] and [u], without destroying the intelligibility of speech or even the distinctiveness of those two vowels. The same is true of obsolete telephones. A psycho-acoustic experiment for one-formant matching was carried out at the same time as the two-formant matching already reported, with suggestive results. It was discovered that the effect of an [a] can be achieved, more or less closely, not only by a pair of formants of equal loudness at 750 cps and 1300 cps, but also by a single formant at about 1200 cps. Similarly:

[i]   2760 cps or anything higher
[e]   about 2520 cps
[ɛ]   about 2160 cps
[æ]   about 1100 cps (poor)
[ɑ]   950 to 1050 cps (poor)
[ɔ]   510 cps (poor); about 720 cps (better)
[o]   360 to 480 cps
[u]   about 240 cps.

Now it must be recognized that the acceptability of such artificially simplified pseudo-vowels—not only the one-formant ones, but the two-formant ones described earlier—to a test audience, as equivalent to one or another natural vowel (or at least as more similar to one natural vowel than to others), depends on a sort of *complaisant* listening by the audience, which is conditioned by the test situation to hear vowel-like characteristics in the stimuli if at all possible. The acceptance of a single formant at about 240 cps as a sort of [u] means only that (1) this single-formant sound resembles an [u] more than it resembles any other "natural" vowel, and that (2) this particular single-formant sound resembles an [u] rather more than does any other single-formant sound (of those tested). Quite similarly, the acceptance of the two-formant [i] (250 and 2900 cps) as an [i] means that this stimulus was more [i]-like than any of the other two-formant stimuli which were tested, but in no sense implies that the artificial two-formant stimulus sounded as thoroughly [i]-like as does a "natural" [i], with some energy at various other (and higher) frequencies.

On the score of sufficiency, then, we can draw only some rather negative conclusions. Pseudo-speech, produced by playing back hand-drawn spectrograms in which vowels are represented by at most two formants and sometimes only by a single formant, ought to be intelligible providing that other factors (representation of consonants) are adequately provided for; experimentation has shown that this is indeed the case. Similarly, actual speech, reaching the ears of a hearer under noise conditions which effectively cancel out some of the natural formants for vowels, should not thereby lose all intelligibility. On the other hand, it is clear that under many hearing conditions vowel-sounds, as they reach a hearer, involve more than two formants, and we have absolutely no reason to believe that under such conditions the hearer automatically discards any information carried by the higher formants and bases his interpretation on the two lowest alone.

Some positive evidence for this is found in the extremely high second-formant frequencies which were required by the test audience in the artificial two-formant matching of "cardinals" [i e ɛ], as compared with the values for French /i e ɛ/ (Figure 24), or with other measured values for natural vowels of this general sort—usually around 2400 cps, 2000 cps, and 1800 cps respectively. The natural vowels have some energy at higher levels (above the second formant), which gives them an auditory quality which we may call "shrillness." The artificial two-formant vowels can achieve comparable "shrillness" only by having the second formants relatively higher than do the natural vowels.

We have, therefore, no reason to believe that in general the two lowest formants do all the work of identifying vowel colors in ordinary speech. Beyond this, it must be borne in mind that formants have not been completely specified when we state their number and the frequency-level of each. Apparently it is not necessary to add any specification as to the width of the reinforced band of frequencies which constitute a formant, since this seems to remain fairly constant, at something between 120 and 150 cycles: the mid-point of this frequency band is chosen as the representative frequency for the whole formant. But it is essential to pay attention to the relative intensities of the different formants. We do not know in full detail what effect rounding has on a vowel color (say the passage from [i] to [ü]), but it is at least clear that rounding somewhat weakens formant two and any higher resonances. When the higher formant of the artificial two-formant cardinal [i] was progressively weakened, the test audience described it first as taking on a sort of "dull" character, and then, with sufficiently great weakening, as becoming almost like an [u]. An [i] thus partially "dulled" can easily be heard as a sort of [ü], if the hearer is favorably inclined towards that interpretation.

5315. *Dimensionality and Formants.* In the light of all the above, we may venture a few rough tentative conclusions.

In the relatively rare case of a one-dimensional vowel system (§2442), the most important acoustic correlate will be the frequency of the first formant. Both the location and the relative intensity of the second formant, and of any higher resonances, will vary allophonically, as do, in articulation, the front-back nature and the roundedness of the vowel phoneme, depending on environment, and will, in a sense, constitute part of the environment rather than part of the vowel (§3222).

In the common case of an articulatorily two-dimensional vowel system, with no· more than two contrasts at any height (e.g. /i/ versus /u/, without either /ü/ or /ɯ/), our usual tabular arrangement of the vowels will correlate roughly with positions on a two-formant graph, with both relative intensities and any higher formants set aside: position of first formant will correlate with tongue height, and position of second formant with the other articulatory features. This, of course, does not mean that resonances higher than the second formant are performing no communicative function, and perhaps in due time we will discover some single function of the second formant and any higher resonances which correlates even more precisely with the articulatory features other than tongue-height and which can replace the second formant in our two-dimensional acoustic charts.

In the case of some two-dimensional systems with three contrasts at a single height (for example, quite possibly English), the statements just made about two-dimensional systems with at most two contrasts at a single height may well prove to apply. But in other two-dimensional systems (e.g., certainly French and German, with /i ü u/), and certainly in genuinely three-dimensional systems, a two-formant chart will not accurately portray the acoustic correlates. The full specification of the latter will require not only the frequencies of the two lowest formants, but also their relative intensities, or the location and intensities of one or more higher formants, or both.

Thus our best guess, on the basis of evidence so far available, constitutes at least a partial rejection of the two-formant theory: we are led to suspect that there will turn out to be a fairly close correspondence between the "dimensionality" of a vowel system, determined articulatorily, and the number of independent acoustic variables necessary for the specification of the individual vowels in the system:

one-dimensional system:	frequency of first formant;
two-dimensional system:	(1) frequency of first formant;

three-dimensional system:

(2) either frequency of second formant, or some single-valued function of this and higher resonances;

(1) frequency of first formant;

(2) frequency of second formant;

(3) some single-valued function of the intensity of the second formant and of the frequency and intensity of higher resonance-bands.

5316. *R-color and Nasalization.* Observations have led to the suspicion, partly confirmed through psycho-acoustic experiments, that the position of the third formant correlates with r-color and with nasalization. Just what connection there may be between this and the relevance of the third formant for other factors of vowel-color contrast is not yet known.

When the third formant is relatively close to the second—closer than it is (when it can be observed at all on a spectrogram) for a non-r-colored vowel—subjects report hearing r-color, and the closer the third formant is to the second the stronger is the r-color. In spectrograms of actual speech, the correlate of r-color does not always appear in sequence where the phonologist would insist it is: one speaker's word *phrases* had r-color throughout the /ey/, and most prominently at the end rather than at the beginning. One must assume that the hearer sorts out what he hears and puts each bit in "proper" chronological sequence on the basis of expectation.

The acoustic correlates of nasalization are not so clear. Formant three seems to be raised relatively higher for a nasalized vowel than for a corresponding oral vowel, but there are other differences too: often an additional band of reinforced resonance appears just above formant one. French is a poor language to use in testing this, since the French nasal vowels do not very closely match any of its oral vowels in tongue and lip position; we therefore suspect that the hearer of French identifies a nasal vowel not only on the basis of the direct acoustic correlates of nasalization, but also through the somewhat different location of first and second formants. French spoken with the velic closed save for the nasal consonants would still keep apart all the vowels (nasal and oral). Portuguese or Ojibwa, where the matching of oral and nasal vowels is closer, would be better languages to use in this connection.

The apparently opposite effects of r-color and of nasalization on the distance between formant three and formant two also raise some interesting problems. In Chinese one has (phonetically speaking: some of the sounds are phonemically clusters) vowels with neither nasalization nor r-coloring, vowels with nasalization without r-coloring, vowels with r-coloring but no nasalization, and vowels with both—the last, for example, at the end of the syllable *hengr*[2] 'horizontal stroke'. Thus r-color and nasalization are not mutually exclusive. Therefore one or the other, or both, must involve acoustic correlates in addition to the alteration of the distance between formants two and three.

532. *Noises and Noise Bursts.* Voiceless consonants show up in a spectrogram with no clearly-placed formants; rather, energy is spread more or less evenly through whole bands of frequencies. As in the case of voiced vowels (and other relatively resonant voiced sounds) this is entirely what we would expect from an examination of the articulatory motions involved—primarily because of the absence of the harmonically rich glottal tone.

Voiceless spirants appear as randomly distributed energy through a relatively wide frequency band, sometimes with points of relative concentration, but the latter seem to depend on the identity of the speaker. English /š/ yields the lowest band of frequencies, centering around 1800–3000 cps. English /s/ is higher, with some energy up to 4000–5000 cps. English /f/ and /θ/ are even higher, and considerably fainter (less total energy); on spectrograms made to cut off at 4000 cps they often do not show at all. We can be quite sure that in conversation under ordinary conditions the distinction between /f/ and /θ/ is often not heard, but is "read in" to fit the context, either on the basis of the sort of evidence discussed in §534, or, in some cases, perhaps even without that evidence. English is of course intelligible even if all four of these spirants are replaced in all occurrences virtually by silence: old-fashioned phonograph records, with a low cut-off frequency, can be understood, though the distortion is obvious. It is interesting to note that the distortion is more noticeable for /s/ and /š/—which are less affected—than for /f/ and /θ/; presumably we notice the greater distortion of the latter two less because we are fairly accustomed to not really hearing them much of the time anyway.

The rather common inaudibility of /f/ and /θ/ (and even of the voiced partners, /v/ and /ð/) can be observed without any apparatus: it is only necessary to listen for speech-sounds, rather than for meanings, during a conversation in noisy surroundings.

Genuinely voiceless stops (by which we mean to exclude, for example, the medial /t/ of a Middle Western *rattle*, even though the phoneme may be classed structurally as "voiceless") show a brief moment of complete silence (a blank vertical strip on a spectrogram). This serves to tell the hearer that some voiceless stop, or a glottal catch, has occurred, but does not tell which one. The silence in itself is quite identical for any voiceless stop or a glottal catch, but the way in which the preceding signal (if any) fades out, and in which the following signal (if any) fades in serves to differentiate them. Examination of spectrograms suggests that one or both of two features in the fade-out and fade-in may perform this differentiating function. One feature is a brief burst of noise spread over some band; the other is the rate and direction of change of the vowel formants next to the stop silence.

An extremely interesting psycho-acoustic experiment has been carried through to test the auditory effect of variously placed bursts of noise before various artificial (two-formant) vowels. A set of seven such vowels were used, as follows:

[i] 270, 2720	[u] 270, 600
[e] 360, 2200	[o] 360, 720
[ɛ] 540, 1830	[ɔ] 540, 960

[a] 720, 1320.

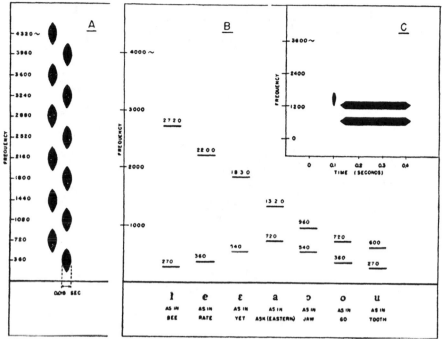

FIG. 28. ARTIFICIAL VOWELS AND NOISE-BURSTS
Reproduced with the permission of Haskins Laboratories.

These were hand-drawn to last .3 seconds. Figure 28 shows, on the right, the seven vowels; on the left, the twelve bursts of noise; and in the upper right, a typical combination of noise-burst and artificial vowel.

In the test, the subjects had already been familiarized with the artificial vowels; they were asked only to identify the preceding "consonant" as [p], [t], or [k]. As might be expected, there was not complete agreement in all cases, but for certain combinations agreement was very good, and in a few cases it was complete. Figure 29 graphs all the results at once. The most important individual conclusion to be deduced from Figure 29 is that one and the same burst may be interpreted fairly consistently in more than one way depending on the following vowel: the bursts centering around 1800 cps were interpreted generally as [p] before [i] or [u], but as [k] before [a].

533. *The Voice Bar.* In spectrograms made with a wide filter of carefully enunciated speech, a relatively low band of reinforced frequencies appears fairly regularly during all voicing. For voiced vowels this is simply the first formant, but for voiced consonants (particularly voiced stops and spirants) it is often called, instead, the *voice bar*; it is at the frequency of the fundamental of the glottal tone. Except for the presence of the voice bar, it is possible to think that one sees some vague similarity between the spectrogram of, say, [ba] and that of [pa], or that of [za] and that of [sa].

However, in all of these cases there is some question as to whether the main

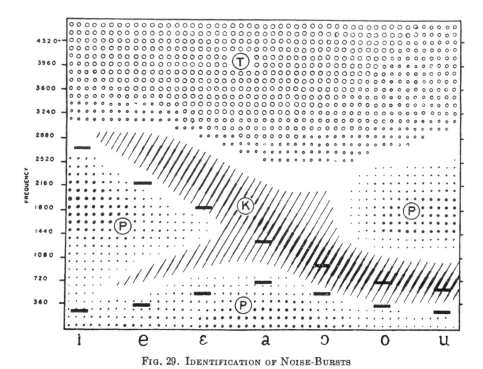

FIG. 29. IDENTIFICATION OF NOISE-BURSTS

The seven artificial vowels are plotted on the diagram. Dotted areas are those for a noise-burst usually identified as [p] when followed by the artificial vowel shown in the same strip; e.g., a noise-burst in the range of 1800 cps, followed by the artificial [i], was regularly identified as [p]. Slanted hatching marks the areas where the identification was [k], and circles the areas where the identification was [t]. The heaviness of the dots and hatching, and the size of the circles, is a rough index of the extent of agreement of the test audience in making the identifications. Reproduced with the permission of Haskins Laboratories.

acoustic clue really lies in the voice bar. It is known that the effect of voicing can be achieved, in hand-painted spectrograms, in either of at least two other ways. One of these consists merely in making a given configuration short enough: if one draws what is interpreted as [fa], and then makes the [f] part very short, one can lead subjects to hear [va]. The other way turns on the bending of vowel formants, which we shall now discuss in this connection and others.

534. *Initial and Terminal Bending of Formants.* We have already mentioned that acoustically steady-state vowels are very rare. Any spectrogram of natural speech shows this; and one may also compare Figure 26. Though the formants for, say, English /æ/ may pass through certain values which serve to distinguish this vowel from any other vowel in English, they come from certain other values, and go to certain other values, at varying rates, and the directions from which they come and towards which they move seem to depend on, and to help to identify, the surrounding consonants.

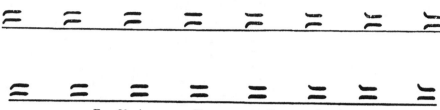

FIG. 30. ARTIFICIAL VOWELS WITH BENDING ONSETS
Reproduced with the permission of Haskins Laboratories.

This early suggested that much of the information as to what consonant precedes or follows a vowel might be carried within what would acoustically be called the vowel itself, rather than within what precedes or follows. Psychoacoustic tests have been made of this, some of them involving nothing more than a spectrograph. A syllable such as *back* is recorded on the spectrograph's internal storage band, and then everything is erased which would ordinarily be thought of as representing the /b/ and the /k/, leaving only the two twisting formants. When the tape, thus doctored, is played back, subjects usually report hearing *back* rather than any other English syllable. The erasing can be done progressively from the two ends, bit by bit, and it is remarkable how much has to be taken away before what remains becomes unidentifiable.

Experiments along this line have also been done with the pattern playback. A set of hand-painted spectrograms were prepared, each consisting of one of the seven reference vowels mentioned in §532 and charted in Figure 28, but variously modified by curved onsets; Figure 30 gives some examples. The results varied from one to another vowel in a fairly complicated way, and were not equally clear-cut for all of the vowels. The results with the artificial [a] were fairly sharp: when the first formant of the artificial [a] was kept the same in all samples, then a very low beginning for the second formant gave the effect of a preceding [b], an even or slightly high beginning sounded like a preceding [d], and a very high beginning was interpreted as a preceding [g]. It is interesting to note an apparent contradiction between these results for [a] and the psycho-acoustic stop-identifications of bursts of noise before the same artificial [a], as shown in Figure 29. Since a noise-burst at approximately the frequency of the second formant of the [a], or a little above, was identified as [k], and a relatively higher noise-burst as a [t], we should expect that an even or slightly high beginning for formant two would be heard as [k] and a very high beginning as [t]: but the experimental results are exactly the reverse.

There was more consistency in interpretation of curved beginnings for formant one, regardless of the vowel. A relatively low beginning tended to be interpreted as voicing of the consonant, while a level beginning tended to be interpreted as voicelessness.

Figure 31 shows nine syllables involving [a] and the essential correlation between initial (or terminal) bending of formants and the consonants. It will be noticed that the effect of a terminal nasal is not achieved by a downswing of the first formant, but by two separately placed formants, the lower of which is the "voice bar."

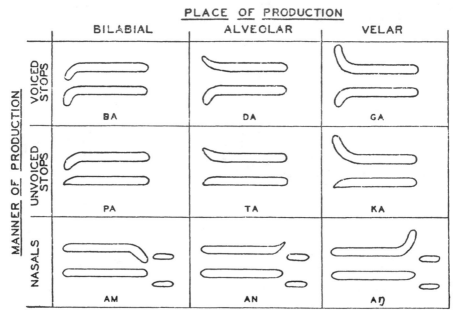

FIG. 31. NINE SYLLABLES WITH [a]
Reproduced with the permission of Haskins Laboratories.

54. Summary. One's natural a priori expectation, when beginning the study of acoustic phonetics, would probably be that each relatively small phonologic element—say each phoneme, or perhaps better each allophone—will appear on a spectrogram as a recognizable pattern, subject to minor variation from one occurrence to another but by and large clearly distinguishable from the pattern for any other phonologic element; and that the patterns for successive phonemes in a particular uttering of a particular utterance will be rather clearly set off from each other (at least as well as successive letters are in careless handwriting). One hardly expects an [f] to show up on a spectrogram in the visual configuration of the letter-shape "f" or "F," of course, but one assumes that there will be *some* sort of visual configuration which will regularly appear in response to [f], so that, in time, one could learn to read sequences of these configurations as though they were a phonetic alphabet with new shapes for the separate symbols.

We have seen that the results of actual experimentation are staggeringly at variance with any such expectations.

We might nevertheless insist on finding reasonably exact points of separation between successive "phones," so that by dividing a spectrogram into the right number of strips by cuts perpendicular to the time axis, we could assign one strip to each successive phone of the utterance. Such a strip then is (or represents) one *acoustic allophone* of the phoneme with which it correlates. If two strips (from two different utterances or from different parts of a single utterance) correlate with a single phoneme and look very much the same, we would say that they constitute occurrences of the same acoustic allophone. But we would soon find that, unlike anything encountered in the bulk of conventional phonologic study, acoustic allophones are *numerous, diverse,* and *intersecting.*

By "numerous" we mean that a single phoneme, instead of being represented by a small handful of allophones, is represented by dozens or even hundreds of clearly different ones.

By "diverse," we mean that the whole set of acoustic allophones which represent a single phoneme by no means necessarily appear as minor variations around some single measurable constant feature. In ordinary phonology we do not like to accept such a situation (save for junctures, §324). In acoustic phonetics we would have no choice.

By "intersecting," we mean that a given acoustic allophone of phoneme A may resemble some allophone of phoneme B much more closely than it does some other allophones of phoneme A. An [š] in one context looks virtually like an [s] in another. This is the sort of situation which we are prepared to tolerate in ordinary phonologic work providing that there is clear environmental difference between a given allophone as member of one phoneme and the "same" allophone as member of another phoneme; but in acoustic work the difference of environment is often very hard to pin down. Once again, however, we would have no choice.

Now it is quite possible to find, or invent, signalling systems in which logically this same sort of situation occurs. Suppose that two detectives are about to enter a house, where one of them, on the basis of what he observes, will have to signal instructions to the other. They cannot know in advance just what circumstances they will encounter, so they arrange for alternative signals for each instruction, to guarantee that at least one of the appropriate signals can be given. The first detective says "If I light a cigarette and have to use two matches, or if I sit down on the arm of a chair, or if I ask for a window to be opened, you make your excuses and get out and phone the boss. But if it takes me *three* matches to light a cigarette, or if I sit down on a table, or if I open a window myself, then grab him." Clearly, there is no physical feature shared by the three signals assigned to the first instruction, and excluded from the three for the second. Indeed, the two cigarette-lighting signals are more similar to each other than to any of the other signals, even though they have been assigned opposite meanings. We might even say that in each of the cigarette-lighting signals, one feature is (within the economy of the system) absolutely identical—actually lighting a cigarette; this feature carries one meaning or the other depending on the number of preceding vain attempts. This sort of multiple mapping is what we would face in seeking correlations between acoustic allophones and phonologic elements.

Now there is no reason to believe that any approach can be developed which will materially reduce the obvious complexity of phonologic-acoustic correlation. However, there is at least one readjustment which can be made in our definition of "acoustic allophone," which promises somewhat greater clarity, and also is seemingly more realistic. This is to relinquish the specification that we break the acoustic signal into acoustic allophones by cuts transverse to the time axis. By this change, we obtain allophones which are not only numerous, diverse, and intersecting, but also *overlapping*: that is, the allophones do not necessarily each end as the next one begins, but may have the latter part of one simultaneous with the beginning (at least) of the next. Thus in pruning *back*, as mentioned above, we get results such that we must say that the vowel-sound (defined as the segment during which there are clear formants) contains some of the /b/ allophone and some of the /k/ allophone. What a native listener does, therefore, to the signal which comes to his ear, is ultimately equivalent to redistributing the sound-qualities along the time-scale, putting some part of the vowel-quality into the preceding consonantal segment and some into the following one, so that each is perceived as being what it must be even if the consonantal phase (acoustically defined) is inaudible, and leaving the residue (after those subtractions) to be heard as the correct vowel phoneme.

Thus we must conceive of each phonologic unit in an utterance as an element the acoustic correlate of which is spread through a rather long time—an interval considerably longer than we take to be the average duration of single successive phonemes, as judged in the ordinary articulatory way. The Speech Transmitter of an individual receives a discrete series of impulses from his phoneme source, but the Speech Transmitter *slurs* this discrete series into a continuous muddy signal. Often enough, indeed—if we can judge from spectrograms of rapid normal speech —the speech transmitter slurs some of the successive impulses so badly that the speech signal contains no separately detectable trace of them.

The best analogy I have been able to think of for this is a very homely one. Imagine a row of Easter eggs carried along a moving belt; the eggs are of various sizes, and variously colored, but not boiled. At a certain point, the belt carries the row of eggs between the two rollers of a wringer, which quite effectively smash them and rub them more or less into each other. The flow of eggs before the wringer represents the series of impulses from the phoneme source; the mess that emerges from the wringer represents the output of the speech transmitter. At a subsequent point, we have an inspector whose task it is to examine the passing mess and decide, on the basis of the broken and unbroken yolks, the variously spread-out albumen, and the variously colored bits of shell, the nature of the flow of eggs which previously arrived at the wringer. Note that he does not have to try to put the eggs together again—a manifest physical impossibility—but only to identify.

The inspector represents the hearer. We have no reason to believe that the hearer is able to assemble scattered and thinned-out bits of evidence for a certain impulse (a certain egg, of certain size and color) any more efficiently than the acoustician can in his visual examination of spectrograms; rather, the hearer understands anyway (when, indeed, he does) because what reaches him is such as to necessitate, in terms of the whole economy of the language, the presence of the obscured impulse. Here are what looks like two large green eggs in succession. But on *this* belt (in *this* language) two large green eggs are never supplied in succession: there is always a small red egg between. Therefore I must interpret this situation as involving a small red egg, even though I see no direct evidence of it. We shall follow this clue further in §6.

In other words, the advantage of recognizing overlapping allophones is that, although it may be more difficult to extract and describe individual allophones of this type than of the non-overlapping building-block type, every success in extracting one results in a reduction of *intersection*—necessarily so, since the only criteria for correct separation of simultaneous allophones would be phonologic criteria, and in phonology we do not tolerate intersection. Only thus, by going as far as possible with splitting simultaneous allophones apart, would we have a chance of completing the job of finding the acoustic correlates of low-level phonologic units (components, phonemes). Whether the job actually can be completed is not known, but at present we believe that progress can still be made along this line, and as long as progress appears possible there will be no need to despair of ultimate success.

6. *Functional Load and Analytical Norms.* The positive correlations between phonologic structure and the speech signal, such as can be discovered via "spoon-fed" spectrograms and via psycho-acoustic experiments with the pattern play-back, are of challenging interest; but they are of minor importance as compared with the negative results obtained from spectrograms of natural flowing speech. From the latter, we discover that with surprising frequency a phonologic feature which *must* be present, as judged by the responses of native speakers and by the observations of the phonologist, is *not* represented by anything that we can locate in the speech signal. The receptive mechanisms of a native speaker, and those of the phonologist which he has trained to mimic those of a native speaker, must perform some sort of interpretive operation on the speech signal which hardware cannot match.

In a general way, we can understand how this is done. A spectrograph is unprejudiced. It reacts, at each moment, just to the gross acoustic input to its microphone. If there is energy at a given frequency, the spectrograph reacts to it; if there is none, it does not react. The previous history of the signal, and what comes later on, play virtually no role in this reaction. A native speaker of a language, on the other hand, is strongly prejudiced. We hear speech not merely in terms of the momentary quality of the speech signal, but in terms of our expectations and, often enough, in terms of what comes later. There seems to be no way, at the moment, in which such a complicated set of ever-changing prejudices can be built into a machine. But a linguist can build them into himself, by going through the ordinary procedures of linguistic analysis—which closely resemble, of course, the procedures by which one learns a language. For a linguist (or a student of any other phase of culture) to be "objective" means something rather different than for a physical scientist to be "objective." A linguist does not attain usable "objectivity", in analyzing a given language, merely by abandoning his own personal prejudices: in addition, he must acquire those of the native speaker of the language. It is for this reason that acoustic phonetics can hardly ever be regarded as supplying any evidence for phonologic analysis.

Yet acoustic phonetics plays the invaluable role of showing us not only how thoroughly prejudiced it is necessary for the hearing of a native speaker of a language to be, but also, at least in the long run, something of the *specific nature* of the prejudices. This is perhaps its greatest usefulness.

One factor which differentiates the hearing of a native speaker from that of a spectrograph is certainly the presence, in the former, of apparatus for the production and transmission of speech. A human hears a certain virtually identical burst of noise before [i], before [a], and before [u], but interprets it as [p] in the first and third cases, as [k] in the second. He makes this interpretation because, in his own articulation, he uses a bilabial articulation to achieve the acoustic effect of that burst when [i] or [u] follows, but a dorso-velar articulation to achieve the same burst before an [a]. As pointed out in §02, it may well be that the whole process by which the hearer's Speech Receiver decodes the speech signal involves a constant comparison of the signal with the articulatory motions which the hearer would himself use to produce a similar acoustic effect.

But there is more to it than this. The prejudices of a native speaker, as he listens to a specific utterance at a specific moment, can have been determined only by his whole past history as a speaker and hearer of the language. For this reason, a type of statistical analysis assumes an importance which has only recently been recognized. In this section we shall first discuss this aspect of phonologic statistics, and then take up several unsolved problems in point of view which are intimately related to it.

61. *Contrast: Existence versus Importance.* In analyzing the phonologic system of a language, we look for differences which distinguish otherwise similar or identical utterances. If we know that utterances A and B sound different to native speakers, then we know that some such phonologic difference is to be found, though it may be relatively easy or relatively difficult to pin down. By examining many pairs of utterances, we eventually manage to tabulate all the features, the differences between which can function to di.tinguish utterances. Such a complete tabulation constitutes half of the task of analysis: the other half is that of deciding just what features, in what arrangement, are present in any given utterance. This is sometimes quite difficult in a practical way: one can be convinced (and correctly so) that one has tabulated everything that counts, and still be uncertain whether, say, a certain word contains feature x or feature y at a given point.

In the process of tabulation, minimal pairs are the analyst's delight, and he seeks them whenever there is any hope of finding them. Before analysis is complete, one cannot be certain that a given pair is "minimal" in a strict phonologic sense—that there is but a single difference, at the level of ultimate phonologic constituents; for this reason, we prefer to mean something more vague but operationally more useful by the term. We mean simply a pair of utterances—usually quite short—that are obviously identical for the most part, though the difference may be somewhat greater than the strict interpretation would imply. English *blown* and *grown* would not count as a minimal pair for an investigator whose native language was any of those of the West, but it might well function as one for, say, a Polynesian-speaking analyst. A minimal pair, in this loose sense, proves that the detectable articulatory difference is phonologically distinctive: further steps are required before one can be sure whether the contrast is between one phoneme and another, or between one cluster and another, or between a phoneme and a cluster, or the like.

As useful as is the method of minimal pairs, it involves one important psychologic drawback. Quite properly, in analyzing a language we feel that the evidence of a single minimal pair (providing it is a genuine one, not the result of mishearing) is enough to prove a phonologic contrast. But this focusses all our attention on the fact of the *existence* of a contrast, and tends to conceal the equally relevant fact that contrasts may differ in *importance*. If some contrasts are more important than others, then that is part of the whole phonologic system, and we should not overlook it.

Two considerations show us immediately that contrasts do differ in relative importance: (1) the number of minimal pairs turning on a given pair of phonologic elements may be high or low; (2) most actual utterances, in real-life contexts, do not stand in anything like minimal contrast with other utterances which might conceivably be uttered in the same context.

Both points can be illustrated from English. Short ("one-word") utterances can be listed by the hundreds to show the phonological relevance of the contrast between [p] and [b]: *pet : bet, pit : bit, pat : bat, flappy : flabby, cop : cob, pride : bride*, and so on. (To constitute a valid minimal pair, of course, the two words of any such pair must be uttered with one and the same intonational pattern; but this is easy enough.) On the other hand, search as one will, no more than a small handful of minimal pairs can be found to attest the phonologic relevance of the contrast between [š] and [ž]. For at least some speakers of English, one or more of the following pairs are minimal, though there are others who make more distinction: *mesher : measure; Aleutian : allusion; Asher : azure; dilution : delusion*. In some cases an even more peculiar situation is encountered. I have in my speech, apparently, no word which is always pronounced with /ɨ/. Thus one pronunciation of the adverb *just*, /ǰɨst/, contrasts with a pronunciation /ǰəst/, which is the only pronunciation for the adjective *just* but also an alternative pronunciation of the adverb. The only minimal pair for /ɨ/ and /i/ is the adverb *just* (when so pronounced) versus *gist*. Unstressed /ɨ/ and /ə/ contrast often in *take 'im* /teykɨm/ versus *take 'em* /teykəm/; but the former is sometimes /teykɨm/ and the latter sometimes /teykɨm/.

The other point can be illustrated by taking any middle-length English utterance as a point of departure, and looking for closely similar utterances. Consider, for example,

$$\text{/}^{2}\eth\text{ɔ̀rz now sɨg}^{31}\text{nifɨkɨnsɨn ðisↆ /}$$

(which I have just pulled at random from a paper-backed detective story, transcribing it as I would naturally say it in its context). One can achieve a similar, though phonologically distinct, utterance by changing the intonation (say to /2 33↑/); but it is practically impossible to get another reasonable English utterance by deleting, or replacing, any one of the single consonants or vowels. Of course, long minimal pairs (apart from intonational ones) can be found, or coined: the point is not that they are impossible, but that they are devised only with relatively great difficulty, and that when one does succeed in devising a pair, it turns out to be highly unlikely that any single set of circumstances would be equally open to either member of the pair.

Most of the time, then, in the actual workings of language, what is actually said differs, from what might have been said but wasn't, not just in one phonologic feature, but in many. There is, so to speak, on the average a fair amount of phonologic "distance" between the whole set of utterances which are at all likely to occur in any given set of circumstances. In the technical jargon of information theory, we say that languages (in phonologic terms) have a certain degree of *redundancy*. And this redundancy implies that, most of the time, a certain amount of distortion, added to the message at one point or another along the route it follows, leaves the message still intelligible.

Suppose, for example, that someone says:

$$/\text{²děrs now sĭk}^{31}\text{nifĭkĭnsĭn disↆ/}$$

Under good hearing conditions, we would notice the peculiarities of pronunciation, but would have no difficulty in understanding what is said: the indicated arrangement of phonologic material can represent no arrangement of morphemes other than precisely that for which we normally expect the phonologic shape cited earlier. Under poorer hearing conditions, with a sufficiently strong reason to expect that something of this general nature is going to be said, we might well even fail to hear the phonologic peculiarities; our Speech Receivers, on the basis of expectations, would convert the sound waves into the stream of phonologic units first indicated. That is, we would in fact hear *wrongly* in terms of the speaker's *phonology*—but *correctly* in terms of his *grammar* (morphemes).

Suppose, for a second example, that someone says *There's no significance in this* in just the normal way first transcribed above, but that deterioration of the speech signal between his lips and our ears is such that, when it reaches the latter point, it has been worn down to something which could be schematically indicated as follows:

$$/\text{²-ŏr- -ow s-g}^{31}\text{nif- -ĭ-s-n -isↆ/}$$

Here we suppose that just over half of the successive vowels and consonants have "gotten through"; there is actually, in the speech signal as it reaches our ears, nothing whatsoever to specify the nature of the remaining vowels and consonants, though the spacing-out of the clear signal is such as to show that the gaps are located approximately as shown. *Normally we would be totally unaware of the deterioration.* Not only would we understand—in the sense of correctly decoding the signal into morphemes—but we would be unaware of the fact that we had "really" not heard all the phonemes. The redundancy of the system, all factors considered, is sufficiently great, and the efficiency with which our Speech

Receivers work (with any necessary help from any other component) is so high, that the gaps are filled in automatically and correctly at an entirely subconscious level. We say *normally*: of course there are times when we strain in vain to understand something heard poorly, and times when we have to go through a conscious trial-and-error process, lasting a measurable number of seconds, before we finally do get it. But in the situation as we have described it, the analyst would have to assert that, as received by the hearer, the *phonologic* structure of the utterance was entirely normal.

Any casual observation of language in action in everyday life shows that acoustically accurate hearing, accompanied by misunderstanding, occurs most often in the case of utterances with less-than-average differentiation (minimal pairs!), or in situations where the circumstances do not help to pin down what may reasonably be said. Consider the business of introducing people (in our culture). There are prescribed formulas for this. We know, when the circumstances arise, approximately the words which are going to be used by the introducer and by the two who are meeting. Consequently, no one has to speak very distinctly, and everyone catches on anyway. But there is one point in the operation at which our expectations are almost completely neutral, and thus of no help at all. This is the point at which a person's name is spoken. Most of us, having slurred the formulas, tend also to slur the person's name: our hearers, understanding the formulas because they know what to expect, often miss the name completely.

To summarize the above: Phonologic differences function to keep utterances apart, and differences of articulation are phonologic if they every perform this function. But most of the time a given phonologic difference works along with others, rather than alone; and some do more of the work of keeping utterances apart than do others.

62. *The Measurement of Functional Load.* It is the last clause of the last sentence above which concerns us in this subsection. The way in which some phonologic contrasts do more of the work of keeping utterances apart than others is the matter of *functional load*.

It is easy to get some rough notion of the relative functional loads carried by different contrasts within a phonologic system. Assuming that two phonemes, x and y, can contrast at all, then the functional load carried by the contrast will be greater if both x and y have relatively high text frequencies than if one has a high frequency and the other a low frequency, and greater under those second conditions than if both x and y have low frequencies. The large number of pairs of English words differing only in the presence of /p/ or of /b/ at a certain point obviously implies the potential existence of a larger number of long minimal pairs turning on /p/ and /b/ than on, say, /p/ versus the relatively low-frequency /š/; yet one will expect a larger number of the latter than of minimal pairs turning on /š/ versus the very low-frequency /ž/. Therefore we can be pretty safe in concluding that the /p/ : /b/ contrast carries a higher functional load than the /p/ : /š/ contrast, and the latter a higher load than the /š/ : /ž/ contrast—indeed, the functional load of the last contrast must be vanishingly small.

Functional load has been discussed in the past mainly in the context of diachronic linguistics. In the light of the fact that the sole function of phonologic differences is to keep utterances apart, it has been proposed that the probability that a given phonologic contrast will be extirpated through sound change stands in inverse ratio to the functional load carried by that contrast. The theory is at least negatively sound: it is true that sound change never leads to a complete obliterating of all phonologic contrasts—and hence to a destruction of the language. The notion is that certain very general factors, perhaps collectivizable under the label "laziness," lead to as much obliteration of distinctions as speakers can get away with, while certain other factors, chiefly the practical need for effective communication, stand in the way of obliteration, forcing speakers to speak more clearly whenever the point of unintelligibility is reached. But if a particular contrast carries a low enough functional load, then this correcting factor will not be apt to come into play, and the contrast may well be lost. Of course, it is recognized that other factors play a part too: low functional load in itself does not guarantee loss of contrast. Thus if in a given system the difference between /ž/ and /ŋ/ is of vanishingly small importance, there is nevertheless no great probability that they will fall together, since they are phonetically too diverse.

Whether this theory is sound in a positive sense is another matter. Granting that the functional loads of some contrasts are so low that loss of contrast would not impair communication, we must also find out whether any contrast carries so *high* a functional load that loss of contrast *would* impair communication. In order to test this, we must have (1) a consistent technique for quantifying functional load; (2) evidence showing what relative functional load is the critical maximum, which cannot be lost without intolerable impairment of communication. The procedures of modern information theory show us how to obtain (1); (2) is a matter for the future. We shall outline the mathematical technique for the measurement of functional load; unfortunately, the determination has not actually been made yet in any case (the amount of counting and computation necessary is formidable), so that we can give no example.

Let the phonemes of a language L be $\phi_1, \phi_2, \ldots, \phi_m$. Let the relative frequency of ϕ_i be p_i; then $\sum_{i=1}^{m} p_i = 1$.

The *first-order approximation* to the *entropy* of L *per phoneme-occurrence* is then

$$H_1 = \sum_{i=1}^{m} I(p_i)$$

where

$$I(p_i) = -p_i \log_2 p_i.$$

Next let $\{\phi_i \phi_j\}$ be the class of all two-phoneme sequences in L; the relative frequency of $\phi_i \phi_j = p_{ij}$. The *second-order* approximation to the entropy of L per phoneme-occurrence is

$$H_2 = \frac{1}{2} \sum_{i,j=1}^{m} I(p_{ij}).$$

Similarly, the nth-order approximation is

$$H_n = \frac{1}{n} \sum_{i_1, i_2, i_3, \cdots, i_n = 1}^{m} I[p(i_1 \, i_2 \, \ldots \, i_n)],$$

where $p(i_1 i_2 \ldots i_n)$ is the relative frequency of the n-phoneme sequence $\phi_{i_1} \phi_{i_2} \ldots \phi_{i_n}$.

The entropy H is defined as

$$H = \lim_{n \to \infty} H_n,$$

providing such a limit exists. To assume that the limit does exist is to assume that the phonologic pattern of any language is ergodic in the weak or Wienerian sense.

If in an imagined phonologic system L', with m phonemes, all the phonemes were constantly equiprobable, then the entropy would be

$$H' = H_1' = \sum_{i=1}^{m} I(p_i) = -\log_2 \frac{1}{m}.$$

In the actual system L the *relative entropy* is

$$E = \frac{H}{H'},$$

and the *redundancy* is

$$R = 1 - E.$$

Now suppose that in a system L we wish to measure the functional load carried by the contrast between phonemes ϕ_1 and ϕ_2. We construct a pseudo-system L^* in which all occurrences of phonemes ϕ_1 and ϕ_2 are replaced by occurrences of a single phoneme ϕ_1, but in which everything else remains as in L. This is tantamount to putting L through a single diachronic change, in which ϕ_1 and ϕ_2 fall together but everything else remains unchanged. The entropy of the pseudo-system L^* can be computed as we compute that of the system L; call this entropy H^*.

The *entropy-loss* as between L and L^* is then

$$H - H^*,$$

and the *functional load* carried by the contrast between ϕ_1 and ϕ_2 is

$$\frac{H - H^*}{H}.$$

That is: the functional load carried by a given contrast is the ratio of the entropy which would be lost if the contrast were abolished to the entropy of the unchanged system. This formulation has the advantage (as over against one in which entropy-loss is directly equated with functional load) that the sum of the functional loads carried by all contrasts is just the entropy of the whole system.

The key figure for functional load which cannot be sacrificed without intolerable impairment of communication is tied up, somehow, in the relationship between entropy-loss and redundancy. The best available estimates so far available suggest that all phonologic systems have a redundancy not far from .50, measured, however, not in terms of phoneme-occurrence but in terms of units of time (so that, everything else being equal, redundancy would decrease as rate of speech increased). If this figure is anywhere near correct, then presumably, if the redundancy mounts much higher, the system is inefficient and people become lazy enough to bring it down again, while if it falls much lower, speech becomes unintelligible and people speak with enough care to bring it up again. The problem, then, is to find the functional relationship between functional load and redundancy, so that one can predict how redundancy would be altered by the loss of a contrast bearing any given functional load; to determine how low the redundancy can go without serious impairment of communication; and, finally, to see whether any one contrast in any language ever carries a great enough proportion of the total functional load for its loss to have such disastrous consequences. Neither the mathematical nor the empiric aspect of this problem is clear to me at the moment.

It should hardly be necessary to dwell on the synchronic implications of functional load. A tabulation of all the phonologic contrasts in a system, showing the relative functional load carried by each, would constitute a valuable addition to any description of a phonologic system, and might help us considerably in deciding what to try to find on spectrograms of natural rapid speech. Although the amount of counting and figuring which would be necessary, even for an approximation, is enormous, there are various sorts of computing machines which could be used to reduce the labor, and we should not shy away from the task.

63. *Sporadic Intersection and Shimmering.* An utterance has a phonologic structure as it is produced by a speaker: this structure is dependent on the nature of the signals sent by the speaker's Phoneme Source to his Speech Transmitter (Figure 1) and on the concurrent functioning of the speaker's Speech Receiver, operating on feedback input. The speech signal has no phonologic structure in its own right. But the utterance once again has a phonologic structure as a hearer receives and interprets it. Although we can properly assume that *by and large* the phonologic structure of a given utterance is the same for speaker and for hearer, we certainly cannot assume that this is always true. Indeed, if a speaker is addressing several hearers, then there may be, all in all, as many differing phonologic structures for his utterance as there are participants. This raises a problem which is probably largely theoretic, and of no great practical importance: if the phonologic structure of an utterance differs for speaker and hearer(s), which is *the* phonologic structure of the utterance? Or (and this is still part of the question) is our first query meaningless? Must we simply recognize a multiplicity of simultaneous phonologic structures for a single event?

This is a large question, and only one facet of it will concern us here: the possible relationships between the speaker's actual articulatory motions and the phonologic structure of the utterance for a single hearer. Assuming that for the most part the relationship is just as we should normally expect it to be—on the basis of accurate hearing and interpretation—we must allow for two phenomena not normally recognized in phonologic analysis: *sporadic intersection* and *shimmering*.

Articulation is normally sloppy and careless. In especially careful speech, one may say *please pass the biscuits* with very clearly voiceless and aspirated /p/'s and a very clearly voiced /b/. In normal speech one or the other of the intended /p/'s may in fact be not only unaspirated but also even slightly voiced; or the /b/ may be entirely voiceless and even slightly aspirated. Regardless of the care or carelessness of articulation, the phonologic structure of the utterance for a given hearer depends not alone on the articulation, but also on how he interprets it. Suppose that on a given occasion a speaker says *please pass the biscuits* in such a way that the intended /b/ is completely voiceless and a bit aspirated. If the hearer "notices" this, then the phonologic structure of the utterance for him is *please pass the piscuits*. But often he will not "notice" it at all: the phonologic structure for him will be just that "intended" by the speaker, and thus in disagreement with the speaker's actual articulation. Under these conditions, we have an articulatory motion which would elsewhere be classed as a /p/ being received and treated, because of the whole context, as a /b/. This is an instance of what we mean by sporadic intersection. By definition, sporadic intersection cannot be observed by the hearer for whom it occurs—since if the deviation is observed, then there has been no sporadic intersection. But the phenomenon is observable, since the analyst can, so to speak, stand to one side of a speaker and a hearer and listen with care for things which the hearer misses.

It will be noticed that sporadic intersection, as defined, bears only a superficial resemblance to the old analytic mistake of "complete intersection." The doctrine of complete intersection holds that a given bit of articulation, *as heard and as intended,* may belong now to one phoneme, now to another, even in one and the same phonologic environment. This doctrine is the product of confusion of levels—phonologic and morphophonemic. Sporadic intersection is "complete" in the sense that not all intended-and-heard /b/'s, for example, are actually articulated in a way which is distinct from all intended-and-heard /p/'s, but apart from this it is entirely different from so-called "complete intersection."

Shimmering is closely related to sporadic intersection, but is morphophonemic rather than phonologic. Suppose that in the circumstances described above, where the speaker makes a completely /p/-like /b/ by accident, the hearer "notices" the error. Because he "notices" it, the utterance is phonologically *please pass the piscuits*. But this does not necessarily prevent understanding (compare the discussion in §61). The utterance, as phonologically understood, can still represent only one arrangement of one set of morphemes. There is no word *piscuit* in contrast to *biscuit*: *piscuit* is only a rare and sporadically occurring alternate morph representing the same morpheme usually represented by *biscuit*. Shimmering, then, is a kind of morphophonemic alternation—a kind in addition to all the sorts usually spoken about; a kind which is in a sense least relevant in the analysis of a language, yet which cannot be ignored. Although most morphemes are represented usually by just one, or by just a few, distinct morphs, every one of these clearly distinct morphs is surrounded by a family of closely similar ones which occasionally occur in its place. Shimmering is sporadic and quite unpredictable; all other types of morphophonemic alternation occur under describable conditions with a considerable degree of predictability.

64. *Analytic Norms.* We come, finally, to a question for which there is currently no clear answer: the choice between *frequency norms* and *clarity norms* in phonologic analysis.

The use of clarity norms in phonologic analysis is somewhat comparable to the use of spoon-feeding in acoustic phonetics. In most languages, if not in all, there is a prescribed pattern for extra-clear speech, to which one resorts when normal rapid speech is not understood, or when certain social factors prescribe it. In English, for example, there is a clarity-norm pronunciation of *matter* and *latter* which involves a fully voiceless and aspirated apical stop in the middle, and a clarity-norm pronunciation of *madder* and *ladder* which involves a slightly longer stressed vowel in the first syllable, followed by a fully voiced and somewhat prolonged apical stop. Some forms may not occur at all in clarity-norm speech: /didžə̆/, /wudžə̆/, and /wədɨyə̆/ (*Did-ya, would-ya, what do ya*) are not simply pronounced more slowly, but are replaced by /did yùw/, /wud yùw/, /hwət dùw yŭw/ or the like. Clarity-norm speech presumably has a higher redundancy (per unit of time—slower articulation is almost mandatory) than ordinary speech. In clarity-norm phonologic analysis, one deals exclusively with clarity-norm pronunciation in the first place, until one's picture is more or less complete; then one admits also any more rapid forms which fit easily into the picture as already drawn (except, perhaps, for speed of speech), but excludes others. Fast forms which do not easily fit the picture based on clarity-norm speech are regarded as mere deviants: their phonologic structure is taken to be the same as the clarity-norm alternants, and the fuzziness is regarded as a matter of personal or momentary idiosyncrasy.

Frequency-norm analysis insists, in theory, on accepting for analysis any utterance which is produced by a native speaker and understood, or understandable, by other native speakers. The choice of norm is involved in the gathering phase of analysis, rather than in the collation phase (§3); our description of gathering in §31 assumes frequency norm rather than clarity norm. The term "frequency" in our designation refers to the assumption that in interpreting the speech-signal, the hearer is governed by the relative frequencies with which he has previously heard various acoustic features as representations of various phonologic units; this, of course, is tied up intimately with the discussion of §61 and §62.

It will not do for us to sneer at either of these guiding principles in phonologic analysis. Most of us today would probably feel, offhand, that clarity-norm analysis is unjustified, and only frequency-norm analysis worth undertaking. A few may have the other preference: certainly earlier phonemic work was guided largely by the clarity norm, a fact which led Stetson to object strenuously to the whole phonemic theory. There is actually some doubt as to whether we ever succeed in following completely one norm or the other. We tend to prefer the frequency norm, but we perhaps do not accept all its consequences; where we refuse to accept its consequences, we are referring to the clarity norm instead. Clarity norm phonology has the merit (if it is a merit) of considerable simplification: one is faced by neither sporadic intersection nor shimmering; but one must suspect that the resulting phonologic picture is not "pure," having rather a certain intermixture of what belongs properly in morphophonemics. But if one insists on following the frequency norm, then before proceeding from phonology to grammar one usually undertakes some simplification of the phonologic picture which, in effect, is a deletion of phonologic complications which seem to be of no morphophonemic relevance, and which amounts to a partial reestablishment of the clarity norm.

Here is an example from Midwestern American English—at least my own speech. Clarity norm procedures show only two apical stops in contrast: /t/ and /d/. *Matter* and *latter* contain the first, *madder* and *ladder* the second. Frequency norm procedures force the recognition of a more complicated situation. Most of the time, my speech does not differentiate *matter* and *madder* at all, nor *latter* and *ladder*. The single common pronunciation of *matter* and *madder* has a relatively short stressed vowel followed by a voiced apical flap. But sometimes *madder* and *ladder* are pronounced with a lengthened voiced stop, and sometimes *matter* and *latter* are pronounced with a voiceless aspirated stop. We are forced to recognize not two but three (frequency-norm) phonemes: /t/, /ɹ/, and /d/. The clarity-norm morph for *matter* includes /t/, and the clarity-norm morph for *madder* includes /d/; but in each case shimmering can produce an alternate morph with /ɹ/. There is no valid procedure by which the flap can be assigned to the same phoneme as one or the other of the stops, and certainly we cannot assign it to both (since that would produce complete intersection). The functional load carried by the contrast between /t/ and /ɹ/, or by that between /ɹ/ and /d/, is certainly extremely small, but this does not justify any simpler treatment so long as we stick to frequency-norm phonology.

I do not think there is any simple answer to the methodologic questions presented by these two analytic norms. So long as phonologic analysis of a language is only partial—and the vast majority of the reports so far available are certainly not complete—the problems probably do not arise. In field work, we are by definition apt to discover first the contrasts of greatest functional importance, and only later those which carry less load: differences of an embarrassing nature between frequency-norm and clarity-norm analysis usually lie in the realm of contrasts with low functional load. But when analysis is carried far enough to discover discrepancies between the yield of the two norms, we have some sort of a choice to make, and the choice should be based on clearly formulated reasons. Probably, as in so many other choices of this sort, we shall in due time discover that certain contexts and purposes justify the option of one norm, other contexts and purposes the option of the other.

NOTES

Bibliographic references below refer to the Glossarial Index and Bibliography which follows the notes. Reference is made by author's name and year of publication, years in the twentieth century being represented by the last two digits only (e.g. "Bloomfield 33"); a lower-case letter is added when the bibliography lists more than one work by the given author for the given year. The digits "00" in place of a year indicate information received informally from the individual named. Page numbers are given, when necessary, after a decimal point: "K. Pike 43.16–24."

The notes are suggestive only, and the bibliography is in no sense intended as a complete list of publications bearing on phonology. Works which are not listed or referred to are not thereby implied to be unimportant in my estimation: in some cases, of course, they have not come to my attention, and in others their content impressed me as paralleling, more or less, that of works which are herein cited.

01. Typology: Trubetzkoy 29, 39; TCLP passim; Voegelin 51.

Hierarchical approach: Bloomfield 33 ch. 5–8; Hjelmslev 43; Kurylowicz 49; Pike and Pike 47. See now also Prieto 54.

The quotation is from Bloomfield 33.20. "Hocus-pocus" and "God's-truth": Householder 52. Bloch's postulates: Bloch 48.

020. On the controversy: K. Pike 47a; Hockett 49; K. Pike 52; also compare the Prague approach in general, perhaps as summarized in Martinet 49a, with Hockett 51.

021. The model presented here has been developing since 1936, when a very sketchy form of it was included in my M.A. Thesis (unpublished) at Ohio State University; the original impetus is no doubt Bloomfield's Jack and Jill diagram (33 ch. 2). Information theory (Shannon 49, Shannon and Weaver 49, Hockett 53a) affords an excellent frame of reference within which to work out the tenuous notions with which I had earlier been working. In Hockett 53a, under the heading *Phonology and Tactics*, the present model is hinted at; a fuller form in Hockett 52d. Also, now, compare the approach in certain sections of Osgood 54.

0210. Problems assigned to "biophysics" and to linguistics (or "sociobiology"); cf. Hockett 48a.

Neuron-to-wire linkage: that is, connecting a living neuron (or bundle thereof) to a wire in such a way that a nervous pulse traveling down the neuron will induce a voltage pulse in the wire, and vice versa. This problem is a crucial one in modern prosthetic theory, but, so far as I know, is nowhere near solution.

0212. Experiments on feedback: Joos 00. Role of Speech Transmitter in perception and understanding of speech: Joos 48.

0215. The term "meaning" is also used in some other ways: for example, one can say that the meaning of a morpheme is the transitions of G.H.Q.-state which its reception induces. This type of use of the word (though certainly cast in far different terminology) underlies the European tendency to think of meaning as "in" the linguistic system, in contrast to the Bloomfieldian slant. The conflict is purely one of terminology.

022. Hjelmslev's system: Hjelmslev 43.

023. On discreteness of contrast cf. Pike 46 ch. 7; on duality of pattern, Martinet 49c. Mazateco whistle speech: Cowan 48.

03. On code noise (or "semantic" noise): Hockett 52a.

04. Imitation-label: K. Pike 43.16–24. Böhtlingk 1851.

1. There have been dozens of treatments of articulatory phonetics. The most thorough and up to date, in many respects, is part II of K. Pike 43. Heffner 49 is more recent and covers the physiology of speech more completely; but one should consult also McQuown 51.

10. The list of the organs of speech: Bloch 48.

11. Stetson 45; Twaddell 53.

14. Term "velic": K. Pike 43.

150. Terms "vocoid" and "contoid": K. Pike 43. However, we do not quite follow his usage: ours is rather looser..

152. Our classification in general follows that of Bloch and Trager 42.

164. The hat diacritic for affrication is Jakobson's usage (00).

2. The languages discussed in this section are listed alphabetically in the Glossarial Index and Bibliography. There each language is identified and, if necessary, located; and references are given to the sources of information.

211. Following Trager and Smith 51, with modifications worked out by Joos, Agard, and myself. K. Pike (46) disagrees with the notion that the amount of terminal rise (subsumed indifferently by our /↑/) is nondistinctive. I feel no certainty on this point. I am by no means satisfied that the system as here reported subsumes everything that must be subsumed. The "metalinguistic" approach of Smith and Trager (Smith 52a,b) seems to turn up additional relevant phenomena, but the basis on which they exclude these from the ordinary phonologic system of the language seems very fragile.

212. Remarks on intonation in European languages are based on observations at Cornell and on informal reports of observations at the Foreign Service Institute. On Shawnee and Arapaho: observations made at the 1952 Linguistic Institute at Indiana University, in the company of H. L. Smith Jr., Carl F. Voegelin, and others. Mazahua: E. V. Pike 51.

22. "Syllables" have bothered phonologists for a long time. They have formed either the target of discussion, or an important secondary consideration, in such articles as Sommerfelt 31, 36, Stetson 36, Hjelmslev 36, 36–7, Kurylowicz 49, O'Connor and Trim 53. The most serious difficulty encountered in these discussions is an insufficiently wide coverage of languages of differing types. I made this point in Hockett 52b, specifically in criticism of Kurylowicz 49. In so doing, I missed the positive features of Kurylowicz's treatment which, with proper generalization, seem to afford a workable frame of reference, of the sort I try to present here.

230. The notion of isolability and its use as a criterion in IC-analysis is a transferral to phonology of the grammatical notions of freedom and bondage. On accentual systems: Trager 41.

2311. Recognition of zero is like Harris's notion of "zeroing out," but I have tried to make the criteria more realistic (Harris 51.337f).

242, 243. This elaborates the frame presented in Hockett 53b.

244. A comparison with Trubetzkoy s plan for the treatment of vowels (29, 39) will show that I "pare off" a great deal more material before calling the remainder a "vowel (phoneme)"; but for the rest I find it possible to follow Trubetzkoy's plan quite closely, and in this survey of vowel systems include languages discussed by him, on his testimony alone.

As pointed out at the end of §2440, our exclusion of the 3×2 pattern may be not only arbitrary, but wrong. Trager proposed the 2×3 interpretation for the oral vowels of Taos in Trager 46 (§2442), but has more recently suggested the 3×2 possibility (Trager 00):

$$\begin{array}{ccc} i & ə & u \\ e & a & o \end{array}.$$

These matters are not always determinate in a purely phonologic sense. When they are not— and perhaps even when they are—it is interesting to see what is suggested by morphophonemic considerations. Thus Dagor Mongol has a vowel-harmony system which pairs off high and low vowels to give

$$\begin{array}{ccc} i & ɨ & u \\ e & a & o \end{array},$$

although purely on their phonetic properties one might class them differently.

251. Cf. Fischer-Jørgensen 52, and her very excellent survey and bibliography of distributional studies.

2521. The procedure used in analyzing and classifying obstruent systems is in part reminiscent of Trubetzkoy's (39), though the terminology differs. Cf. also Catford 39, Jakobson 39.

262. Other interesting examples of componential analysis, showing various predilections:

Hockett 47b; Jakobson 49; Jakobson and Lotz 49; Bloch 50; Martin 51. The strictly phonetic componential descriptions of K. Pike 43 should also be compared.

273. Frequency figures for English spirants were obtained by converting those for all English consonants given in Bloomfield 33.137.

30. Boas on Kwakiutl: 11b, 47.

Boas (in 11a) is often thought to have presented one of the earliest formulations of the phonemic principle. His statement (p. 16) begins as follows: "One of the most important facts relating to the phonetics of human speech is, that every single language has a definite and limited group of sounds, and that the number of those used in any particular dialect is never excessively large." This is equivalent to about one-half of the Jonesian brand of phonemics. The assumption is clear, that one could in time make an exhaustive list of all the "speech sounds" to be found in any language at all, so that the stock of speech sounds used in any one language would appear as a larger or smaller selection from this stock. But the principle of contrast and complementation, which in effect forms the other half of Jonesian phonemics, is missing. Thus Boas's assumption would in no way lead one to regard certain pairs or triples of speech sounds as related with each other in a particularly close way (i.e., as allophones of a single phoneme), nor to simplify one's notation accordingly, even as a matter of convenience. And, both for Boas and for Jones, thinking is still in terms of *things* rather than *differences*.

In any case, throughout his linguistic career Boas never used what most of us would call a phonemic notation. However, it must be said in his defense that part of the reason may have been an unformulated, but instinctively sound, objection to the rather drastically oversimplified brand of "phonemics" which was current in this country during much of the third and fourth decades of the century.

Synchronic phonologic results sought via the philological method (interpretation of written records): Fry 41; Harris 41; Emeneau 46; Hall 46b; Moulton 48; Jensen 49; Stockwell and Barritt 51 (criticized by Kuhn and Quirk 53); Fairbanks 52; Lunt 53. Not all of these devote any discussion to the assumptions and methods involved. Bodman 54, dealing with Chinese, is forced to proceed quite differently because of the radically different nature of the writing-system. Similar in aim, but necessarily different in approach, are studies where reconstruction via comparison, rather than directly the interpretation of written records, is involved: Lehmann 52, Martin 53, Moulton 54.

31. The gathering aspect of phonologic work does not seem to have challenged the attention of European investigators (despite the extensive field work which some of them—for example, Trubetzkoy himself—have done). In England, similarly, there has been little tendency to theorize and generalize about gathering; it is interesting to note how many of Daniel Jones's studies in the phonetics of this or that language have been done in close collaboration with a native speaker to whom a fair amount of phonetic training has been given. The background for our discussion in this section is thus largely American: Bloch 48 (the earlier postulates); K. Pike 47a; Voegelin 49; Hockett 49; Harris 51; Hockett 52c.

321. Wells 47; Pittman 48; Hjelmslev 43.

3220. Swadesh 34a; Hockett 42; K. Pike 47b; Jones 50.

3222. Pike's aphorism: Pike 47b. Moulton 54.26.

3231. Our IC-analysis of Fox yields results somewhat different from those presented in §262.

3232. "Defective" phonemes: Swadesh 34a; in practice in such reports as Haas 41a, 41b, Swadesh 34b. The Prague approach: TCLP passim; Martinet 49; Hockett 51.

324. The approach to juncture in Bloch and Trager 42 is not logically valid. In his postulates (Bloch 48), Bloch removes the illogicality—and the possibility of recognizing juncture along with it. Harris's habit of calling juncture a "zero phoneme": Harris 51. According to Joos (00) there is some reason to believe that English juncture *does* involve a certain measurable and detectable feature in all occurrences: a slight lengthening of the "preceding" phoneme, be it vowel or consonant. Our approach does not render this unpleasing, if true; but does allow for the recognition of a juncture in some cases where perhaps no such constant phonetic feature is to be found.

325. Jakobson 49; Jakobson and Lotz 49; Harris 51.

Primary and secondary features: cf. the labelling of certain features as "redundant" in Jakobson, Fant, and Halle 52.

4. Our aim here is to show how an empiric approach can (and, indeed, must) in due time reach the type of abstract scheme proposed by Hjelmslev (43). It should be added that an abstract scheme *not* reached via an empiric approach remains pure mathematics, with no necessary relation to language.

Mutual convertibility: Bloch 48. Invariance under transformations between mutually convertible systematizations: Chao (00).

The relevance of articulation and acoustics despite the importance of abstraction: Haugen 54, criticizing certain points in the generally excellent book by Weinreich 53.

5. The special rôle of Martin Joos in the preparation of this section is described in the Preface. Joos 48 remains the standard fuller treatment, and contains references to the important earlier contributions to the field. Here we try to summarize the results of work done since the preparation of that book; newer items include Lisker 48, Delattre 48; Peterson 51, Delattre 51, Delattre and others 51, Liberman and others 52, Cooper and others 52, Delattre and others 52a,b, Jakobson and others 52, Schatz 54.

512. The spectrograph is more fully described in Joos 48. At the present writing, I know of only one pattern playback: it was built and is in use at the Haskins Laboratories in New York City. It is described somewhat more fully in Liberman 52.

520. Transducer study, as a phase of communication theory: Shannon and Weaver 49, Shannon 49.

5311. Delattre and others 51, 52a.

5312. Delattre 48, Delattre and others 52a.

5313. The point-vowel values were measured on spectrograms in Joos 48 and in Potter, Kopp, and Green 47 by H. A. Gleason Jr., for inclusion in a forthcoming book of his. The vowels shown by curves are from Joos 48, Fig. 25 and accompanying text.

5314. One-formant matching: Delattre and others 52a.

5315. We are forced to reject the tentative conclusion of Delattre 51. 870f.

5316. Joos 48; Delattre and others 52b.

532. Joos 48; on bursts, Liberman and others 52, Cooper and others 52.

533. [v] attained by shortening [f]: Delattre (00).

534. Pruning *back:* Joos (00). Psycho-acoustic tests with the pattern playback: Cooper 52, Delattre 52b.

54. The assumption that spectrograms might be read almost as "transcriptions" in a new phonetic alphabet apparently lies behind the "visible speech" notions in Potter, Kopp, and Green 47. Jakobson, Fant, and Halle 52 also show an oversimplified assumption of this sort. In both cases the factor of spoon-feeding is at least in part responsible.

61. Redundancy: as in information theory (Shannon and Weaver 49).

62. Functional load, in diachronic linguistics: Martinet 39, 49, 52, 53, and in various other articles. The mathematics for the measurement of functional load is a simple derivation from the information-theoretical formulations of Shannon (Shannon and Weaver 49).

64. Stetson 45.9–17.

GLOSSARIAL INDEX AND BIBLIOGRAPHY

Here we present, in a single alphabetization, everything that the reader might wish to find in alphabetical order. The entries are of three kinds:

(1) Language names, in italics. Each is followed by: (a) indication of its affiliation, and if necessary of its location; (b) reference to my sources of information; (3) reference to the subsection or subsections of §2 of this manual in which substantial information on the phonology of the language is given.

Language names are spelled in the generally accepted ways, omitting superfluous diacritics. Those spoken in the U.S.S.R. are spelled in English following W. K. Matthews 51. North American Indian languages are not located, since the location can be determined by referring to Voegelin and Voegelin 44. Nor do we locate languages such as English, French, German, Russian, Japanese.

Sources are referred to by name of author or authors, year of publication if necessary, and following "a," "b," etc. if necessary. Years in the twentieth century are represented by the last two digits: 43 = 1943. "00" means, however, information via personal communication or in unpublished notes. "H" means that I have heard the language; "Ha" that I have heard it and done a little analytical work on it; "HA" that I have worked fairly extensively on it.

(2) Technical and semitechnical terms, or names of topics, in Roman type. These are sometimes accompanied by a brief definition or comment, and always by a cross-reference to the sections of the manual where they are defined, used, or discussed.

(3) Bibliographical listings, by author or authors, then by year of publication. Any unobvious abbreviations are listed in proper alphabetical order, with explanation.

A

Aberle, D. F., and Wm. M. Austin, 51. A lexical approach to the comparison of two Mongol social systems, SIL 9.79–90.

Abkhaz. North Caucasian. Trubetzkoy 39. 2442.

abstraction, 4.

accent d'insistence (in French), 212.

accentual system, 23.

acoustic allophones, 54.

acoustic and articulatory, 04.

acoustic phonetics, 5. Defined, in terms of problems, 520.

acoustics: the branch of physics which studies sound, 51.

actualization, 3222.

Adyge. North Caucasian. Trubetzkoy 39. 2442.

affricates, 164.

Agard, Frederick B. 53. Noun morphology in Romanian. Lg. 29.134–42.

Alabama. Muskogean, eastern division. Haas 41. 2431, 252112, 2521321, 252213, 252225.

aleph = glottal catch, 12.

Algonquian, Central: comprises Cree, Fox, Menomini, Ojibwa, Potawatomi, Shawnee. 252213.

Algonquian, Proto-Central-. Bloomfield 46; A. 2441.

allophones, 31 end.

——, acoustic, 54.

——, logic of, 3222.

allophonically correct transcription, 31 end.

Amahuaca. Panoan; on Sepahua, Inuya, and Sheshea rivers in eastern Peru and into western Brazil. Osborn 48. 2441, 252112, 2521321, 252213, 252225, 2525.

amplitude, 511.

AmSp = American Speech.

Andrade, Manuel. 39. Quileute. HAIL 3.

Andrews, Henrietta. 49. Phonemes and morphophonemes of Temoayan Otomi. IJAL 15.213–22.

Apachean (southern branch of Athabascan): Chiricahua, Navaho. Hoijer 43. 2312, 2441, 2445.

Arapaho. Plains Algonquian. Voegelin 00; H. 212, 252112, 252212, 252221.

archiphoneme, 3232.

Armenian, East. Indo-Hittite (Indo-European?); Soviet Armenia. Stevick 00; H. 252112.

arrangement of ICs, 321.

arrangements, contrasting, 321.

articulation, point of, 1520.

——, position of, 1520.

articulator, 1520.

articulatory and acoustic, 04.

Arunta. North-Central Australia. Sommerfelt 39. 2441, 252112, 252131, 252213, 252225, 2525.

Aschman, Herman P. 46. Totonaco phonemes. IJAL 12.34–43.

aspirated stops, 162.

Athabaskan, Southern: see Apachean.

Athabaskan, West Coast and Northern. Li 30; Hoijer 43. 2212.

Austin, William N. 52. A brief outline of Dagor grammar. SIL 10.65–75.

Awar. North Caucasian. Trubetzkoy 29. 2442.

Aztec: see Nahuatl.

B

backness vs frontness of tongue, 1510.

Badaga. Dravidian; Nilgiri Hills in Southern India. Emeneau 39. 2431, 2442, 2445, 2446, 252112, 2521322, 252214, 252225, 25223, 2525.

balance, 271.

Bannock. Mono-Bannock, Plateau Shoshonean, Uto-Aztecan. Liljebled. 252113, 2521322, 252214, 252221, 2525.

Bariba. "West-Sudanic" (Afro-Asiatic); in Cercles of Parakou, Kondi, and Natitongou in Dahomey and in adjacent parts of Nigeria. Welmers 52a. 22112, 2322, 2442, 2443, 2445, 252114, 2521322, 252213, 252235, 2525.

Bella Coola. Coast Salishan. Newman 47. 2213, 252113, 2521332, 25220, 252213, 252225, 2524, 2525.

Bender, Ernest, and Z. S. Harris. 46. The phonemes of North Carolina Cherokee. IJAL 12.14–21.

bending of formants, 534.

bilateral symmetry, of speech tract and articulation, 10.

binit: the unit of measurement of informational capacity and entropy; the amount of information carried, on the average, by a system within which the source has only two signals and is equally likely to emit either. All other types of system can be handled in terms of this by proper mathematical conversion. [Usually called *bit* in the literature.]

Bisayan (of Cebu). HA. 2442.

Bloch, Bernard. 48. A set of postulates for phonemics. Lg. 24.3–46.

——, 50. Studies in colloquial Japanese IV: Phonemics. Lg. 26.86–125.

——, and George L. Trager. 42. Outline of Linguistic Analysis. Baltimore.

Bloomfield, Leonard. 17. Tagalog Texts, with Grammatical Analysis. University of Illinois Studies in Language and Literature 3: 2–4. Urbana.

——. 24a. The Menomini language. Proceedings of the Twenty-first International Congress of Americanists 336–43. The Hague.

——. 24b. Notes on the Fox language. IJAL 3.219–32.

——. 28. The Plains Cree language. Proceedings of the Twenty-second International Congress of Americanists 427–31. Rome.

——. 33. Language. New York.

Bloomfield, Leonard. 39. Menomini morphophonemics. TCLP 8.105–15.
——. 42. Outline of Ilocano syntax. Lg. 18.193–200.
——. 45–6. Spoken Dutch. New York.
——. 46. Algonquian. LSNA 85–129.
Boas, Franz. 11a. Introduction. HAIL I.1–83.
——. 11b. Kwakiutl. HAIL I.423–558.
——. 47. Kwakiutl grammar, with a glossary of the suffixes. Transactions of the American Philosophical Society 37:3. 199–377.
——, and Ella Deloria. 41. Dakota grammar. Memoirs of the National Academy of Sciences 23:2. Washington.
Bodman, Nicholas C. 54. A linguistic study of the *Shih Ming*. Harvard-Yenching Institute Studies 11. Cambridge.
Böhtlingk, O., 1851. Die sprache der Jakuten. St. Petersburg (= v. 3 of A. T. von Middendorf, Reise im äussersten Norden und Osten Sibiriens).
Bororo. Ge; south-central Matto Grosso, Brazil. Lounsbury 00. 252111.
boundaries, redrawing (between "successive" sounds), 3222.
brackets, use of, 10.
breathgroup, 11.
Breton (St. Pol-de-Léon). Celtic, Indo-European. Brittany, France. Smith 46. 252111, 2521332, 252214, 252222, 25223, 2525.
Bright, William. 52. Linguistic innovations in Karok. IJAL 18.53–62.
Bronx cheer, 153.
Bulgarian. Slavic, Indo-European. Trubetzkoy 29. 2442.
Bunzel, Ruth L. 39. Zuni. HAIL 3.389–515.
Burmese. Tibeto-Burman. Cornyn; McDavid; Ha. 2221, 252112, 2521322, 252214, 252225, 2525.
by-systems: communicative systems deriving very closely from language but not part of language in the narrow sense. 023.

C

Campa. Arawakan; east central Peru. Dirks. 2441, 252111, 2521331, 252214, 252225, 2525.
Cantonese. Chinese; Canton. Chao; Ha. 2221, 2322, 252214, 252222.
cardinal reference points (acoustic), 5311.
cardinal vowels, two-formant matching of, 5311.
——, one-formant matching of, 5314.
Carr, Denzel, 45. Notes on Marshallese consonant phonemes. Lg. 21.267–70.
Cashibo. Panoan; along Aguaitía River and its tributaries in Peru. Shell 50. 2424, 252113, 2521321, 252214, 252223, 2525.
Catford, J. C. 39. On the classification of stop consonants. Le Maître Phonétique III:65.2–5.
cavity friction, 12.
central (tongue-position), 1510.
channel noise (information-theoretical term), 03.
Chao, Y. R. 47. Cantonese Primer. Cambridge.
Chatino. Mixtecan?; district of Juquila in Oaxaca, Mexico. McKaughan. 2441, 2442, 2445, 2523, 2525.
Chavarria-Aguilar, O. L. 51. The phonemes of Costa Rican Spanish. Lg. 27.248–53.
Chawchila: dialect of Yokuts, q.v.
Cherokee (of North Carolina). Iroquian. Bender. 252112, 252131, 252225, 2525.
chest pulse, 163.
Cheyenne. Plains Algonquian. Smith 49; Ha. 252111, 2521321, 2525.
Chickasaw: see Choctaw.
Chinese: see Cantonese, Mandarin, Tangsic. 2221.
Chipewyan. Northern Athabascan. Li 46. 2442, 252113, 252135, 252213, 252222, 2524, 2525.
Chiricahua (Apache). Apachean. Hoijer 43, 46. 2221, 2312, 2433, 252112, 25212, 252135, 252213, 252221, 2524, 2525.

Chitimacha. Tunican. Swadesh 34b, 46a. 2431, 2442, 252112, 2521324, 252213, 252221, 2524, 2525.

Choctaw-Chickasaw. Muskogean. Haas 41. 2431, 252112, 2521321, 252213, 252225.

Chontal (Tequistlateco). Hokan? Waterhouse. 2431, 2442, 2525.

Choynimni: dialect of Yokuts, q.v.

Chukchansi: dialect of Yokuts, q.v.

Churchward, C. Maxwell. 41. A new Fijian grammar. (Sydney?)

clarity norm, in phonologic analysis, 64.

clear vs dark (laterals), 153.

clicks, 1521. [Greenberg (00) says that these, in languages of South Africa, are probably clusters.]

closure, 1520.

cluster: a sequence of two or more phonemes of the same general type: e.g., of two or more consonants, or of two or more vowels.

—— or single phoneme, 3231.

cluster, simultaneous: a simultaneous or effectively simultaneous combination of two sets of features, each of which sets occurs separately elsewhere as one phoneme, but incapable of being viewed structurally as an ordinary (sequential) cluster.

coarticulated stops, 1521.

coda, 220.

code noise (or "semantic" noise), 03.

Coeur d'Alene. Interior Salishan. Reichard; Swadesh 52. 2442, 252113, 2521332, 25220, 252213, 252223, 2524, 2525.

collation (phase of phonologic analysis), 30, 32. Definition and purpose, 320.

Comanche. Shoshone-Comanche, (Plateau) Shoshonean, Uto-Aztecan. Osborn and Smalley 49, Riggs. 252113, 252131, 2525.

common core (a slant in coverage of statements), 03.

complementary distribution = complementation, 3221.

complementation and contrast, 3221.

complementation, multiple, 3223, 3232.

complete intersection (or complete overlapping: a methodological error), 63.

complex (syllable peaks), 241.

componential analysis, heuristic value of, 262 end.

congruity, pattern, 3223.

consonant. Pretechnical 10; first strict definition 242; wider definition 250.

constituents, ultimate phonologic, 20.

constitute, 321.

constitutional classification (of consonants), 250, 252.

"content" (Hjelmslevian), 02 end.

continuant, nasal, 1521.

contoid, 150, 152, 153.

contrast, role of, 61.

—— and complementation, 3221.

Cooper, Franklin S., Pierre C. Delattre, Alvin M. Liberman, John M. Borst, and Louis J. Gerstman. 52. Some experiments on the perception of synthetic speech sounds. JASA 24.597–606.

coordinate (construction), 2212, 321.

Cornyn, William. 44. Outline of Burmese Grammar. Language Dissertation 38; Suppl. to Lg. 20:4.

covowel. 242.

Cowan, George M. 48. Mazateco whistle speech. Lg. 24.280–6.

Cree. Central Algonquian. Bloomfield 28, 46; Ha. 2431, 2441, 252112, 252131, 252221, 252225, 2525.

Creek-Seminole. Muskogean. Haas 41. 2431, 2441, 252112, 2521321, 252214, 252225.

Croft, Kenneth. 51. Practical orthography for Matlapa Nahuatl. IJAL 17.32–6.

Crow. (Missouri River) Siouan. Kaschube. 252112, 2521321, 252213, 252222, 2525.

Crowell, Edith E. 49. A preliminary report on Kiowa structure. IJAL 15.163–7.
Cuicateco. Mixtecan; northeastern Oaxaca, Mexico. Needham. 252113, 252131, 252213, 2525.
Cuitlateco. Guerrero, Mexico; affiliations unknown. McQuown 41b. 2442, 252113, 2521322, 252213, 252225, 2525.
Czech. Slavic, Indo-European. Goodison 00; H. 2442, 252112, 2521341, 252214, 252224, 25223, 2524, 2525.

D

Dakota. (Mississippi Valley) Siouan. Boas and Deloria 41. 252112, 252213, 252225, 2525.
Danish. North Germanic; Indo-European. Deardon; H. 2443.
Dargwa. North Caucasian. Trubetzkoy 29. 2442.
dark vs. clear (laterals), 153.
Deardon, Jeanette, and K. Stig-Nielson. 45–6. Spoken Danish. New York.
defective phoneme, 3232.
Delattre, Pierre. 48. Un triangle acoustique des voyelles orales du français. French Review 21, May.
——. 51. The physiological interpretation of sound spectrograms. PMLA 66.864–75.
——, Alvin M. Liberman, and Franklin S. Cooper. 51. Two-formant synthetic vowels and cardinal vowels. Le Maître Phonétique, July–December.
——, Alvin M. Liberman, Franklin S. Cooper, and Louis J. Gerstman. 52a. An experimental study of the acoustic determinants of vowel color; observations on one- and two-formant vowels synthesized from spectrographic patterns. Word 8.195–210. (The line drawings marked "Figure 2" and "Figure 7" in this article should be interchanged—but not the captions. Also, the IPA symbols for the low back unrounded and low back rounded vowels are reversed.]
——, Franklin S. Cooper, and Alvin M. Liberman. 52b. Some suggestions for teaching methods arising from research on the acoustic analysis and synthesis of speech. Report of the Third Annual Round Table Meeting on Linguistics and Language Teaching, The Institute of Languages and Linguistics, Georgetown University, 32–45.
Delaware. Eastern Algonquian. Voegelin 46; HA. 2431, 252112, 25212, 2521321, 252225, 2525.
demivowel, 242.
descriptive, 00, 03 end.
determined vs. determining, 325.
Dibabaon. Davao, Philippines. Forster 54. 2442, 252111, 2521322, 252214, 252225, 2525.
dimensionality of a vowel system, and acoustic correlates, 5315.
Dirks, Sylvester. 53. Campa (Arawak) phonemes. IJAL 19.302–4.
distribution, implications of wider, 3233.
——, limited, influence on interpretation, 25212.
distributional classification, 250, 251.
domain (of an accent or the like), 2221.
drum signals, African, 023.
duration, 511.
Dutch. West Germanic, Indo-European. Bloomfield 45–6; HA. 2442, 252111, 2521341, 252214, 252225, 2525.
Duwamish. Coast Salishan. Ransom. 252113, 2521332, 252211, 252225, 2524, 2525.
Dyen, I. 45–6. Spoken Malay. New York.
——. 49. On the history of the Trukese vowels. Lg. 25.420–36.

E

economy (criterion of), 3224.
Edel, May. 39. The Tillamook language. IJAL 10.1–57.
element, phonologic; defined 4.
Elson, Ben. 47. Sierra Popoluca syllable structure. IJAL 13.13–7.
——. 54. Sierra Popoluca intonation. MA thesis, Cornell University; unpublished.
Emeneau, Murray B. 39. The vowels of the Badaga language. Lg. 15.43–7.

——. 44. Kota texts, part I. University of California Publications in Linguistics 2:1.1–192.
——. 46. The nasal phonemes of Sanskrit. Lg. 22.86–93.
——. 51. Studies in Vietnamese (Annamese) grammar. University of California Publications in Linguistics 8:1.
empathy, 31.
emphatics (pharyngealized consonants), 13.
English. West Germanic, Indo-European. Trager and Smith 51; HA. 2222, 2311, 241, 2431, 2442, 2512, 252112, 2521341, 252214, 252225, 2524.
—— vowels, acoustics, 5313.
English, Middle (Chaucerian). Standard manuals; A. 2442, 2445.
English, Old. Standard manuals; Stockwell and Barritt; A. 2442.
Erzya. Dialect of Mordvin, Finno-Ugrian; northern and eastern part of Mordva Autonomous Republic, USSR. Trubetzkoy 29. 2442.
Eskimo, South Greenlandic. Eskimo-Aleut. Swadesh 46b. 2441, 252111, 2521321, 252215, 252224, 2525.
Eskimo, Unaaliq. Eskimo-Aleut. Swadesh 51. 252112.
Esthonian. Finno-Ugrian. Trubetzkoy 29. 2442.
"expression" (Hjelmslevian), 02 end.

F

Fairbanks, Gordon H. 52. The phonemic structure of Zographensis. Lg. 28.360–5.
feedback, role of, 0212.
field methods, 31. [Their logic, not practical procedures.]
Fijian. Malayo-Polynesian. Churchward; HA. 22114, 2442, 2511, 2513, 252111, 2523, 2525.
Finnish. Finno-Ugrian. Sebeok 47; H. 2222, 2311, 2442, 25212, 252131, 252214, 252225, 2525.
Fischer-Jørgensen, Eli. 52. On the definition of phoneme categories on a distributional basis. Acta Linguistica 7.8–39.
"form" (vs. "substance"), 02 end.
formants and vowels, 531.
formant line (on spectrogram), 512.
formants, bending of, 534.
Forster, Alice Jannette, 54. Dibabaon texts. University of Manila Journal of East Asiatic Studies 3:2.232–6.
——, and Howard P. McKaughan. 52. An adaptation of modern language teaching techniques to certain unusual situations. MA thesis, Cornell University; unpublished.
Fox. Central Algonquian. Bloomfield 24b; HA. 212, 22111, 2431, 2441, 2511, 2513, 252112, 2521321, 252221, 2525, 262.
Freeland, L. S. 47. Western Miwok texts with linguistic sketch. IJAL 13.31–46.
——. 51. Language of the Sierra Miwok. Indiana University Publications in Anthropology and Linguistics 6.
French. Romance, Italic, Indo-European. Hall 46, 48b; Trager 44; Martinet 49b; Jakobson and Lotz 49; HA. 212, 2442, 2443, 2445, 2446, 252111, 2521341, 252214, 252224, 252226, 2525.
—— vowels, acoustics, 5312.
frequency (in acoustics), 511.
frequency (statistical) norm, in phonologic analysis, 64.
fricative vs. frictionless, 153.
front (tongue position), 1510.
Fry, Allan H. 41. A phonemic interpretation of visarga. Lg. 17.194–200.
functional load, measuring, 62. Definition 61, 62.
fundamental (in sound), 511.

G

gap (in physical arrangement of ICs), 321.
Garvin, Paul L. 48. Kutenai I: phonemes. IJAL 14.37–42.

Garvin, Paul L. 50. Wichita I: phonemes. IJAL 16.179–84.
Gashowu: dialect of Yokuts, q.v.
gathering (phase in phonologic analysis), 30, 31.
geminate (cluster): a cluster of two occurrences of the same phoneme: /pp/, /aa/. 2221.
Georgian. South Caucasian. Vogt 36; HA. 2213, 2442, 25210, 252112, 2521333, 252135, 252213, 252222, 2525.
German. West Germanic; Indo-European. Moulton 47; Mueller; HA. 212, 2311, 2431, 2442, 252111, 2521332, 252214, 252224, 2524, 2525.
—— *dialect of Brienze,* Switzerland. Susman 51. 2521321, 252213, 252225, 2525.
Germanic: English Dutch, German, Scandinavian. 2222.
Germanic, Proto-. Standard manuals; Twaddell 48; A. 2441.
glide vs. peak vocoid, 165.
glottal catch (not a "stop" by our definition of the latter term), 12.
glottal spirant, voiced and voiceless, 12.
glottal stop = glottal catch; former term not used. 12.
glottal tone, 12.
glottalized stop, 1521.
glottis, 12.
Goodison, Ronald A. C. 51. The phonology of Czech. Ph. D. thesis, Cornell University; unpublished.
Gourma. West Africa. Welmers 00. 252114.
grammar, defined 02.
grammatical boundaries, 324 end.
Gray, Henry. 48. Anatomy of the human body. 25th edition, edited by Charles M. Goss. Philadelphia.
Greek (modern). Indo-European. Kahane; H. 212, 2442.
Greek, classical. Trubetzkoy 20; Sturtevant; A. 2442.
Greek, late classical and early medieval. Trubetzkoy 29. 2442.
Greenberg, Joseph H. 41. Some problems in Hausa phonology. Lg. 17.316–23.

H

[h] not necessarily a spirant, 12.
[h], "voiced," 12.
Haas, Mary R. 41a. The classification of the Muskogean languages. LCP.
——. 41b. Tunica. HAIL IV (extract only; New York).
——. 42. Types of reduplication in Thai. SIL 1:4.
——. 44. Men's and women's speech in Koasati. Lg. 20.142-9.
——. 46. A grammatical sketch of Tunica. LSNA 337–66.
——, and H. R. Subhanka. 45–6. Spoken Thai. New York.
HAIL = Handbook of American Indian Languages. HAIL I and II, Bureau of American Ethnology Bulletin 40, parts 1 and 2, Washington 1911, 1922. HAIL III: New York 1939. HAIL IV: only one "extract" printed, New York 1941.
Hall, Robert A. Jr., 43. The unit phonemes of Brazilian Portuguese. SIL 1:16. Occurrence and orthographical representation of phonemes in Brazilian Portuguese. SIL 2.6–13.
——. 44a. Hungarian grammar. Language Monograph 21; supplement to Lg. 20:4.
——. 44b. Italian phonemes and orthography. Italica 21.72–82.
——. 46a. Colloquial French phonology. SIL 4.70–90.
——. 46b. Old French phonemes and orthography. Studies in Philology 43.575–85.
——. 48a. Descriptive Italian grammar. Ithaca.
——. 48b. French. Language Monograph 24; supplement to Lg. 24:3.
——. 48c. The linguistic structure of Taki-Taki. Lg. 24.92–116.
——. 50. The reconstruction of Proto-Romance. Lg. 26.6–27.
Halpern, A. M. 46a. Yuma. LSNA 249–88.
——. 46b. Yuma I: Phonemics. IJAL 12.25–33.

Hooier, Harry, and Edward P. Dozier. 49. The phonemes of Tewa, Santa Clara dialect. IJAL 15.139–44.

Hopi. Shoshonean, Uto-Aztecan. Whorf 46a. 2431, 252113, 2521321, 252213, 252225, 2525.

Householder, F. 52. Review of Harris 51. IJAL 18.260–8.

Huasteco. Mayan; coast of Vera Cruz, and in Potosí, Mexico. Larsen. 2442, 252113, 2521323, 252213, 252223, 2524, 2525.

Huichol. Uto-Aztecan; states of Nayarit and Jalisco, Mexico. McIntosh. 2441, 252113, 252131, 252213, 252225, 2525.

Hungarian. Finno-Ugrian. Hall 44a; Sebeok 43; H. 2311, 2431, 2442, 25210, 252112, 2521322, 2521341, 252214, 252225, 2525.

I

IC = immediate constituent.

identification, criteria for, 322.

idiolect, 03.

IJAL = International Journal of American Linguistics.

Ilocano. Northern Luzon, Philippines. Bloomfield 42; Forster and McKaughan; H. 2442, 25111, 2521322, 252214, 252225, 2525.

imitation-label; definition and status, 04.

immediate constituent analysis, 241. Techniques of, 321.

injectives, 1521.

inspirated sounds (made during inhalation), 11.

intensity (acoustics), 511.

interlude, 220.

intersection, acoustic, 54.

——, complete (an analytical mistake, not a method), 63.

——, sporadic, 63.

intonation, 210, 260.

——, of English, 211.

——, of languages other than English, 212.

Iowa-Oto. (Mississippi Valley) Siouan. Whitman. 2441, 2442, 2445, 252112, 2525.

IPA (= International Phonetic Association/Alphabet), misuse of, 522 (3).

Iraqi (Arabic). Arabic, Semitic; Iraq. Van Wagoner; H. 2441, 2523, 2524, 2525.

Iroquoian: Seneca, Oneida, Cherokee. (Mohawk: Ha.) 252210, 252212.

Isleta. Tiwa, Tanoan. Trager 42. 252113, 2521342, 252225.

isolability, as a criterion, 230.

Isthmus Zapotec: see Zapotec.

Italian. Romance, Italic, Indo-European. Hall 44b, 48a; Ha. 2311, 2443, 252112, 2521322, 252214, 252222, 25223, 2525.

Ixcatepec: see Nahuatl.

J

Jakobson, Roman. 39. Observations sur la classement phonologique des consonnes. Proceedings of the Third International Congress of Phonetic Sciences 34–41.

——. 49. On the identification of phonemic entities. TCLC 5.205–13.

——, and J. Lotz. 49. Notes on the French phonemic pattern. Word 5.151–8.

——, C. Gunnar M. Fant, and Morris Halle. 52. Preliminaries to speech analysis. The distinctive features and their correlates. Cambridge.

JAOS = Journal of the American Oriental Society.

Japanese. Bloch 50; Ha. 2214, 2442, 252112, 2521322, 252214, 252225, 2525.

JASA = Journal of the Acoustical Society of America.

jaws, 1510.

Jensen, Ella. 49. The vowel system of the Flensborg by-laws. TCLC 5.244–55.

Jones, Daniel. 50. The phoneme: its nature and use. London.

Joos, Martin. 48. Acoustic phonetics. Language Monograph 23; supplement to Lg. 24:2.

length, in articulation, 161.
lengtheners (covowels), 2431.
——, scalar, 2431.
Lenormand, Maurice H. 52. The phonemes of Lifu (Loyalty Islands); the shaping of a pattern. Word 8.252–7.
Lesnin, I. M., Leonard Bloomfield, and Olga Petrova. 45–6. Spoken Russian. New York.
Lg. = Language, Journal of the Linguistic Society of America.
Li, Fang-kuei. 30. Mattole, an Athabaskan language. University of Chicago Publications in Anthropology.
——. 46. Chipewyan. LSNA 398–423.
——. 48. The distribution of initials and tones in the Sui language. Lg. 24.160–7.
Liberman, Alvin M., Pierre Delattre, and Franklin S. Cooper. 52. The rôle of selected stimulus-variables in the perception of the unvoiced stop consonants. The American Journal of Psychology 65.497–516.
Lifu. Loyalty Islands. Lenormand. 2442, 252112, 2521321, 252215, 252223, 2524, 2525.
Liljebled, Sven. 50. Bannack [sic] I: phonemes. IJAL 16.126–31.
linear (accentual system), 230, 231.
linguistics: alternative definitions, 02.
lips, in vocoid articulation, 1510.
Lisker, Leigh. 48. The distinction between [æ] and [ɛ]: a problem in acoustic analysis. Lg. 24.397–407.
Loma. West Africa, Sadler. 2312, 2443, 252114, 2521332, 252214, 252225, 2525.
Longacre, Robert E. 52. Five phonemic pitch levels in Trique. Acta Linguistica 7.62–82.
loudness, 511.
Lounsbury, Floyd G. 53. Oneida verb morphology. Yale University Publications in Anthropology 48. New Haven.
low (tongue position), 1510.
lowering lengthener (in complex syllable peaks), 2431.
Lowie, Robert H. 39. Hidatsa texts, with grammatical notes and phonograph transcriptions by Zellig Harris and C. F. Voegelin. Indiana Historical Society Prehistory Research Series 1:6.
LSNA = Harry Hoijer and others, Linguistic structures of native America. Viking Fund Publications in Anthropology 6, 1946.
Lukoff, Fred. 45–6. Spoken Korean. New York.
lungs, 11.
Lunt, Horace G. 53. Old Church Slavonic phonemes. Word 8.311–28.

M

macrosegment, 210. Redefinition (deleting intonation), 220.
Maidu. Penutian. Uldall. 2442, 252111, 2525.
Mak, Cornelia. 53. A comparison of two Mixtec tonemic systems. IJAL 19.85–100.
Malay. Malayo-Polynesian. Dyen 45–6. 2442, 2445.
Mandarin. Chinese. Hartmann; Hockett 47; HA. 212, 2222, 2321, 2442, 2513, 252112, 25212, 2521332, 252214, 252222, 2525.
Maninka. In and around Kankon, French Guinea. Welmers 49. 5231, 5232, 524.
manner (for consonants, esp. obstruents), 2521.
manner consonants, 2520, 2524.
Mano. West Africa. Welmers 00. 252114.
margin (of syllable; = onset, coda, or interlude), 242.
marked vs. unmarked, 3233.
markers, in IC analysis, 321.
Marshallese. Marshall Islands. Carr. 252111, 252131, 2523, 2524, 2525.
Martin, Samuel E. 51. Korean phonemics. Lg. 27.519–33.
——. 53. The phonemes of Ancient Chinese. JAOS supplement 16.

Martinet, André. 39. Équilibre et stabilité des systèmes phonologiques. Transactions of the Third International Congréss of Phonetic Sciences 30–4.
——. 49a. Phonology as Functional Phonetics. [First section in a pamphlet bearing the same title; Publications of the Philological Society, London.]
——. 49b. Les traits généraux de la phonologie du français. [Second section in the same pamphlet.]
——. 49c. La double articulation linguistique. TCLC 5.30–7.
——. 52. Function, structure, and sound change. Word 8.1–32.
——. 53. Concerning the preservation of useful sound features. Word 9.1–11.
Matlapa: dialect of Nahuatl, q.v.
Matthews, W. K. 51. Languages of the USSR. Cambridge.
Mazahua: dialect of Otomi, q.v.
Mazateco. Otomanguian; Oaxaca, Mexico. Pike and Pike 47. 2212, 2312, (2322), 2433, 2511, 2513, 252112, 2521321, 252214, 2525.
McDavid, Raven I., Jr. 44. Burmese phonemics. SIL 3.6–18.
McIntosh, John B. 45. Huichol phonemes. IJAL 11.31–5.
McKaughan, Howard. 54. Chatino formulas and phonemes. IJAL 20.23–7.
McQuown, Norman A. 41a. La fonémica de un dialecto Nahuatl de Guerrero. El México Antiguo 5.221–32.
——. 41b. La fonémica del Cuitlateco. El México Antiguo 5.239–54.
——. 42. La fonémica de un dialecto Olmeca-Mexicano de la Sierra Norte de Puebla. El México Antiguo 6.61–72.
——. 44–5. Spoken Turkish. New York.
——. 51. Review of Heffner 49. Lg. 27.344–62.
Mende. West Africa. Welmers 00. 252114.
Menomini. Central Algonquian. Bloomfield 00, 24a, 39; Ha. 2431, 2442, 252112, 252131, 252221, 2525.
Mesquital: dialect of Otomi, q.v.
Mexicano: see Nahuatl.
microjuncture (and syllable juncture), 2222.
microsegment, 2222.
mid (tongue position), 1510.
Mikasuki: see Hitchiti.
Milpa Alta: dialect of Nahuatl, q.v.
minimal pair, 61.
Miwok. Penutian. Freeland 47, 51. 2431, 2442, 252225. Western: 252112, 2521333, 252213, 2524, 2525. Sierra: 252112, 2521321, 252214, 2525.
Mixteco. Mixtecan; Guerrero and Oaxaca, Mexico. Mak. 2312, 2442, 252113, 2523, 2525.
modifications of vocoids (i.e., effects achieved other than by tongue height, tongue frontness or backness, and lip position). 1511.
Mongol. Altaic? Aberle and Austin. 244 note, 2444, 252112, 2521332.
monitoring (via feedback), 0212.
mora; unit of duration smaller than a syllable, when there is reason to distinguish the two structurally, 2221.
morph: the phonologic shape which represents a morpheme. Definition 02.
morpheme. Definition, 02. [A unit of content, not of expression.]
morphophonemics. Definition, 02.
Motilone. Cariban; Eroca valley, Andes Mts., Department of Magdalena, Colombia. Hanes. 252112, 2521321, 252213, 252221, 2525.
Moulton, William G. 47. Juncture in modern standard German. Lg. 23.212–26.
——. 48. The phonemes of Gothic. Lg. 24.76–86.
——. 54. The stops and spirants of early Germanic. Lg. 30.1–42.
Mueller, Hugo. 50. Stress phonemes in German. SIL 8.82–9.
multiple complementation, 3223, 3232.

murmur, 12.

murmur vowel: a slight voiced release for a consonant, either of indefinite color or of color which seems to be determined entirely by the surrounding consonantism.

musical distance between frequencies, 511.

musical note, 511.

Muskogean: Choctaw-Chickasaw, Alabama, Koasati, Hitchiti-Mikasuki, Creek-Seminole. Haas 41. 2441, 2525.

N

Nahuatl (Aztec, Mexicano). Uto-Aztecan. 2441, 252113, 2521321, 252213, 252225, 2525.

——, *Ixcatepec* dialect. McQuown 41a.

——, *Matlapa* dialect. Croft. 2431.

——, *Milpa Alta* dialect. Whorf 46b.

——, *Olmeca-Mexicano* dialect. McQuown 42.

——, *Sierra Nahuat* dialect. Key.

——, *Tetelcingo* dialect. Pittman 54. 252223.

nasal, nasality, nasal cavity, 14.

nasal continuant or sonorant, 1521, 25221.

nasalization, levels of appearance of, 2611. Acoustic correlates of, 5316.

Navaho. Apachean, Athabascan. Hoijer 45; Harris 45. 252113, 25212, 252135, 25220, 252213, 252221, 2524, 2525.

Navarro-Tomás, Tomás. 32. Manual de pronunciación española[4]. Madrid.

Needham, Doris, and M. Davis. 46. Cuicateco phonology. IJAL 12.139–46.

Neffgen, H. 18. Grammar and voçabulary of the Samoan language. London. (Tr., from earlier German edition, by Arnold B. Stock.)

Nellis, Jane G. 47. Sierra Zapotec forms of address. IJAL 13.231–2.

neutralization, 3232.

Newman, Stanley L. 44. The Yokuts language of California. Viking Fund Publications in Anthropology 4. New York.

——. 46. The Yawelmani dialect of Yokuts. LSNA 222–48.

——. 47. Bella Coola I: phonology. IJAL 13.129–34.

noise (everyday and acoustic sense), 511. Noise-bursts, in acoustics, 532.

noise (information-theoretical sense): 02, 6.

non-linear (accentual systems), 230, 232; 242.

Nootka. Wakashan. Sapir and Swadesh 39. 2213, 2321, 2431, 2442, 252113, 2521332, 25220, 252213, 2524, 2525, 262.

"north" and "south" (towards the mouth and nose, versus towards the lungs, in articulatory description), 10.

Norwegian. North Germanic, Indo-European. Haugen; Ha. 2321, 2443.

——, *Lyster* dialect. Lyster, Sogn, northwestern Norway. Oftedal. 2443.

nucleus, in IC analysis, 321. Nucleus and satellite 2212.

O

obstruent, definition 2520. Obstruent systems: 25210, 2521.

O'Connor, J. D., and J. L. M. Trim. 53. Vowel, consonant, and syllable—a phonological definition. Word 9.103–22.

octave, 511.

Oftedal, Magne. 49. A Norwegian dialect in Wisconsin. Lg. 25.261–7.

Ojibwa. Central Algonquian. Bloomfield 00; HA. (2221), 2441, 252112, 25212, 2521321, 252221, 2525.

Olmeca: dialect of Nahuatl, q.v.

Olmsted, David L. 50. The phonology of Polish. Ph.D. thesis, Cornell University; unpublished.

——. 51. The phonemes of Yoruba. Word 7.245–7.

omnipotent, definition 242.

Oneida. Iroquoian. Lounsbury. 2431, 2442, 252112, 252131, 252225, 2525.

onset (part of syllable), 220.

opposition: in strict Praguian theory "opposition" and "contrast" are distinguished; e.g., see Martinet 53, fn. 21, and compare Prieto 54. The distinction is of importance, but does not necessarily have to be made with just these two terms. Our use of "contrast" is general, and the word "opposition" is used only rarely, usually in the context of stating a Praguian position.

oral (vs. nasal), 14.

organs of speech (a metonymic expression), 10, 1.

Osage. Siouan. Wolff 52. 2441, 2442, 2445, 252112, 2525.

Osborn, Henry. 48. Amahuaca phonemes. IJAL 14.188–90.

——, and William H. Smalley. 49. Formulae for Comanche stem and word formation. IJAL 15.93–9.

oscillograph, oscillogram. 512.

Osgood, Charles E., Editor. 54. Psycholinguistics. Indiana University Publications in Anthropology and Linguistics, Memoir 10; supplement to IJAL 20:4.

Ossetic. Iranian, Indo-European; Caucasia, USSR. Vogt 44. 2520, 252112, 252135, 252213, 252225, 2525.

Oto: see Iowa.

Otomi. Otomanguian; central Mexico. 252214, 252225, 2525.

——, *Mazahua* dialect. E. V. Pike 51; Spotts. 212, 2442, 2445, 252113, 2521322.

——, *Mesquital* dialect. Sinclair. 252112, 2521332.

——, *Temoayan* dialect. Andrews. 2441, 2442, 252133, 2521322.

overall pattern (one slant in coverage of statements), 03.

P

parole and langue, 4.

parsimony, 3224.

Pashto. Iranian, Indo-European; Afghanistan. Penzl. 252112.

"pattern" (vs. "usage"), 02 end.

pattern and structure, 4.

pattern congruity, as criterion, 3223.

pattern playback (a device for reading spectrograms into sound), 512.

pause, 210.

peak (part of syllable), 220.

peaks, simple and complex, 241. Detailed analysis, 24.

peak vs. glide vocoid, 165.

Penzl, Herbert. 43. Aspect in the morphology of the Pashto (Afghan) verb. SIL 1:16.

perceptual distance between frequencies, 511.

Persian (modern colloquial). Iranian, Indo-European. Newman 00; H. 2442.

Peterson, Gordon E., The phonetic value of vowels. Lg. 27.541–53.

pharyngeal catch, 13.

pharyngeal spirant, 13.

pharyngealized sounds (= "emphatics"), 13.

pharynx, 13.

phase-relationship, 511; definition by example 512.

phoneme: rough definition 242. [No precise definition possible under the relativistic approach taken in this monograph.]

——, relativity of, 3224.

—— or cluster, 3231.

phonetic realism, phonetic similarity, as criterion, 3222.

phonetic system of a language; definition, 02.

phonetics, acoustic, 5.
phonetics, articulatory, 1.
phonology; definition, 02.
——, fundamental assumption of, 31.
Pickett, Velma. 51. Non-phonemic stress: a problem in stress placement in Isthmus Zapotec. Word 7.61–5.
——. 53. Isthmus Zapotec verb analysis. IJAL 19.292–6.
Picuris. Tiwa, Tanoan. Trager 42. 252113, 2521332, 252225.
Pike, Eunice V. 48. Problems in Zapotec tone analysis. IJAL 14.161–70.
——. 51. Tonemic-Intonemic Correlation in Mazahua (Otomi). IJAL 17.37–41.
Pike, Kenneth L. 43. Phonetics. Ann Arbor.
——. 46. The intonation of American English. Ann Arbor.
——. 47a. Grammatical prerequisites to phonemic analysis. Word 3.155–72.
——. 47b. Phonemics. Ann Arbor.
——. 52. More on grammatical prerequisites. Word 8.106–21.
——, and E. V. Pike. 47. Immediate constituents of Mazateco syllables. IJAL 13.78–91.
pitch, mechanism of production, 12; acoustics 511.
—— levels (intonational), 211.
Pittman, Richard S. 48. Nuclear structures in linguistics. Lg. 24.287–92.
——. 54. A grammar of Tetelcingo (Morelos) Nahuatl. Lg. Diss. 50, Suppl. to Lg. 30:1.
pivot (in IC structure), 321.
PL = pitch level (unit in an intonational system).
point of articulation, 1520.
Polish. Slavic, Indo-European. Trager 39; Olmsted 50; (local dialects) Trubetzkoy 29; H. 2442, 2443, 2512, 252112, 2521341, 252213, 2525.
Politzer, Robert L., 51. On the phonemic interpretation of Late Latin orthography. Lg. 27.151–3.
Polynesian: Samoan, Hawaiian, and many others. 2442, 252131.
Popoluca, Sierra. Popolucan; Vera Cruz, Mexico. Elson 47, 54. 212, 2431, 2442, 25210, 252112, 2521322, 2521342, 252224, 2525.
Portuguese. Romance, Italic, Indo-European. Hall 53; Agard 00; Ha. 2443, 2445, 2512, 252111, 2521341, 252214, 252222, 25223, 2525.
position, in classifying obstruents, 2521.
position of articulation, 1520.
Potawatomi. Central Algonquian. Hockett 48b; HA. 2442, 252112, 2 ɹ12, 2521321, 252221, 2525.
Potter, R. K., G. A. Kopp, and H. C. Green. 47. Visible Speech. New York.
pressure from lungs, importance of variations in, 150.
Preston, W. D., and C. F. Voegelin. 49. Seneca I. IJAL 15.23–44.
Prieto, Luis J. 54. Traits oppositionnels et traits contrastifs. Word 10.43–59.
primary vs. secondary feature, 325.
psycho-acoustic experiments (in acoustic phonetics), 521 (2).
pure tone, 511.

Q

Quechua: see Kechua.
Quileute. Chimakuan. Andrade. 252211.

R

[r], 153.
r-color, 5316.
raising lengthener (in complex syllable peaks), 2431.
Ransom, Jay E. 45. Notes on Duwamish phonology and morphology. IJAL 11.204–10.
redundancy, phonologic, 61.

Reichard, Gladys A. 38. Coeur d'Alene. HAIL 3.

release, of consonants, 162.

remainder (macrosegment, in original sense, minus intonation): 210. [After 21, "macro-segment" is redefined to exclude intonation and the term "remainder" is not used.]

resonance chamber, 14, 1510.

retroflexion, 1511.

rhythm, 166.

Riggs, Venda. 49. Alternate phonemic analyses of Comanche. IJAL 15.229–31.

rill (spirant), 1522.

Romance. 212. (Otherwise see separate languages.)

Romanian. Romance, Italic, Indo-European. Agard 53; H. 2442, 252112, 2521341, 252213, 252225, 2525.

rounding, 1510.

Russian. Slavic, Indo-European. Lesnin; Trager 34; Fairbanks 00; Ha. 2222, 241, 2441, 2442, 2445, 2446, 2512, 252112, 2521341, 252213, 252224, 2523, 2524.

Rutul. North Caucasian. Trubetzkoy 29. 2441.

S

Sadler, Wesley. 51. Untangled Loma. United Lutheran Board [no place given].

Saho. West Africa. Welmers 52b. 2442, 2521342, 252213, 252225, 2525.

Salishan: Bella Coola, Coeur d'Alene, Tillamook, Kalispel, Duwamish. Swadesh 52; Vogt 50b. 2213, 2441, 25220, 252211.

Samoan. Polynesian; Malayo-Polynesian. Neffgen. 252111, 2521321, 252210, 252214, 252222, 2525.

Sandia. Tiwa, Tanoan. Trager 42. 252113, 2521342, 252225.

Sanskrit. Indic, Indo-European. Whitney; Emeneau 46; Fry; A. 252112, 25212, 2521322, 2525.

Santa Clara. Tewa, Tanoan. Hoijer and Dozier 49; H. 252113, 2521342, 252214, 252225, 2524, 2525.

Sapir, Edward. 22. Takelma. HAIL II.

——. 2?. A Chinookan phonetic law. IJAL 4.105–10.

——, and Morris Swadesh. 39. Nootka texts. Philadelphia.

satellite (in IC structure), 321. Satellite and nucleus 2212. [We speak of satellite and nucleus only in an attributive or subordinate construction; in a coordinate construction the constituents cannot be so labelled.]

scalar lengthener (in complex syllable peaks), 2431.

Scandinavian: Norwegian, Swedish, Danish. 2321.

Schatz, Carol D. 54. The role of context in the perception of stops. Lg. 30.47–56.

scrape [r], 153.

Sebeok, Thomas A. 43. The phoneme /h/ in Hungarian. SIL 1:13.

——. 47. Spoken Finnish. New York.

secondary versus primary feature, 325.

segmental phoneme = our term "phoneme" in this manual, 242.

semantics: definition, 02.

semiconsonant. General definition, 242; not necessarily used in that precise sense in earlier sections.

Seminole: see Creek.

semivowel. General definition 242; not necessarily used in that precise sense in earlier sections.

Senadi. Senufo group; Korhogo, Ivory Coast. Welmers 50a. 22111, 2312, 2442, 2443, 2445, 252114, 2521341, 252212, 252215, 2525.

Seneca. Iroquoian. Preston and Voegelin. 2431, 252112, 2521321, 252221, 2525.

Serbo-Croatian. Slavic, Indo-European. Hodge 46; Jakobson 49. 2442, 252112, 2521341, 252214, 252224, 25223, 2525.

shannon: a unit of informational entropy or capacity, equal to one binit per second.
Shannon, Claude. 49. Information theory of secrecy systems. Bell System Technical Journal 28.656–715.
——, and Warren Weaver. 49. The mathematical theory of communication. Urbana.
shared constituent, 321.
Shawnee. Central Algonquian. Voegelin 35; Ha. 212, 2431, 2441, 252112, 2521321, 252225, 2525.
Shell, Olive A. 50. Cashibo I: phonemes. IJAL 16.198–202.
—— (after Buell Quain). 52. Grammatical outline of Kraho (Ge family). IJAL 18.115–29.
shimmering (kind of morphophonemic alternation), 63.
Shipibo. Panoan; around Ucuyali river in Peru. Lauriault. 252112, 2525.
Sierra Miwok: see Miwok.
Sierra Nahuat: see Nahuatl.
Sierra Popoluca: see Popoluca.
Sierra Zapotec: see Zapotec.
SIL = Studies in Linguistics.
simple (peak), 241.
Sinclair, Donald E., and K. L. Pike. 48. The tonemes of Mesquital Otomi. IJAL 14.91–8.
singing, 023.
slant lines, use of, 20.
Slavic: Russian, Polish, Czech, Bulgarian, Serbo-Croatian, Ukrainian, Zographensis. 212, 2222.
slit (spirant), 1522.
Slocum, Marianna C. 48. Tzeltal (Mayan) noun and verb morphology. IJAL 14.77–86.
slurring, in articulation, 54.
Smith, Henry Lee Jr. 52a. An outline of metalinguistic analysis. Report of the Third Annual Round Table Conference on Linguistics and Language Teaching, Georgetown University Institute of Languages and Linguistics. Washington.
——. 52b. An outline of metalinguistic analysis. Washington. [Expansion of 52a.]
Smith, William B. S. 46. The Breton segmental phonemes. SIL 4.52–69.
——. 49. Some Cheyenne forms. SIL 7.77–85.
Snoqualmie. Swadesh 52. 252113, 2521332, 252211, 252225, 2524, 2525.
Sobotta, Johannes. 33. Atlas of human anatomy. Edited from the eighth German edition by J. P. McMurrich; Third Revised English Edition. New York.
Sommerfelt, A. 31. Sur l'importance générale de la syllabe. TCLP 4.156–9.
——. 36. Can syllable divisions have phonological importance? Proceedings of the second international congress of phonetic sciences 30–3.
——. 39. Le système phonologique d'une langue Australienne. TCLP 8.209–12.
sonorant; definition, 2520. 2522.
"south" and "north" (in articulatory description), 10.
Spanish. Romance, Italic, Indo-European. Navarro-Tomás 32, Trager 39, King 52, Chavarria-Aguilar 51; HA. 22113, 2311, 2432, 252112, 2521332, 252214, 252222, 252223, 25223, 2525.
spectrograph, spectrogram, 512.
speech signal; definition, 510.
speech sound: term a figure of speech, 511.
Spencer, Robert F. 46. The phonemes of Keresan. IJAL 12.229–36.
spirantization, 1520.
sporadic intersection, 63.
Spotts, Hazel. 53. Vowel harmony and consonant sequences in Mazahua (Otomi). IJAL 19.253–8.
spread (of lips), 1510.
Stetson, R. H. 36. The relation of the phoneme and the syllable. Proceedings of the Second International Congress of Phonetic Sciences 245–52.
——. 45. Bases of phonology. Oberlin.

Stevens, S. S., and J. Volkmann. 40. The relation of pitch to frequency: a revised scale. American Journal of Psychology 53.329–53.

Stockwell, R. P., and C. W. Barritt. 51. Some Old English graphemic-phonemic correspondences: *ae*, *ea* and *a*. SIL Occasional Papers 4. Washington.

stop, 1520, 1521.

stops, coarticulated, 1521.

——, glottalized, 1521.

stress-timed rhythm, 166.

strong insolability (of a term in an accentual system), 230.

structure and pattern, 4.

Sturtevant, Edgar H. 40. The pronunciation of Latin and Greek[2]. Special Publications, Linguistic Society of America. Philadelphia.

subordinate (in IC structure), 321.

"substance" (vs. "form", Hjelmslevian), 02 end.

Sui. Tai; southeastern Kueichow, China. Li 48. 252112, 25212, 2521321, 252215, 252222, 2525.

Supide. Senufo group; Sikasso, French Sudan. Welmers 50b. 2442, 2443, 2445, 25210, 252112, 2521322, 2521341, 252214, 252225, 2525.

Supple, Julia, and Celia M. Douglass. 49. Tojolabal (Mayan): phonemes and verb morphology. IJAL 15.168–74.

suprasegmental, 242.

surface (spirant), 1522.

Susman, Amelia. 43. The accentual system of Winnebago. New York.

—— [Schultz], Amelia. 51. Segmental phonemes of Brienzerdeutsch. SIL 9.34–65.

Swadesh, Morris. 34a. The phonemic principle. Lg. 10.117–29.

——. 34b. The phonetics of Chitimacha. Lg. 10.345–62.

——. 37. The phonemic interpretation of long consonants. Lg. 13.1–10.

——. 46a. Chitimacha. LSNA 312–36.

——. 46b. South Greenlandic (Eskimo). LSNA 30–54.

——. 51. Kleinschmidt Centennial III: Unaaliq and Proto-Eskimo. IJAL 17.66–70.

——. 52. Salish phonologic geography. Lg. 28.232–48.

——. 53. Mosan I: A problem of remote common origin. IJAL 19.26–44.

Swedish. Scandinavian, Germanic, Indo-European. 2321.

syllable, 220, 22.

syllable juncture (and microjuncture), 2220.

syllable-timed rhythm, 166.

syllable-types, languages classified as to, 22.

symmetrical set (of obstruents); definition 25210.

symmetry, 272.

synchronic (vs. descriptive), 00, 03 end.

T

Tabassaran. North Caucasian. Trubetzkoy 29. 2441.

"tactics" (term eliminated) 02 end.

Tagalog. North-Central Luzon, Philippines. Bloomfield 17; H. 2442, 252111, 2521322, 252214, 252225, 2525.

Takelma. Penutian? Sapir 22. 25210, 252111, 25212, 2521322, 2521332, 252213, 252225, 2525.

Taki-Taki. Creolized English; Paramaribo and environs, Dutch Guiana. Hall 48c. 2442, 252111, 2521332, 252214, 252225, 2525.

Tangsic. Village of Tangsi; one of the Wu group of dialects, Chinese. Kennedy 52; Ha. 2322, 2525.

Taos. Tiwa, Tanoan. Trager 42, 46, 48. 2212, 2321, 2433, 2442, 2445, 2446, 252113, 2521332, 252225. [Trager 48 reanalyzes as clusters many of the obstruents which we have treated as units.]

tap [r], 153.

Tarascan. Michoacan, Mexico. Swadesh 00; Ha. 252112, 2521324, 252214, 252222, 2525.

TC = terminal contour (an element in an intonational system).

TCLC = Travaux du Cercle Linguistique de Copenhague.

TCLP = Travaux du Cercle Linguistique. de Prague.

Temoayan: dialect of Otomi, q.v.

tense (vs. lax), 1510.

Tequistlateco: see Chontal.

Terena. Arawakan; near towns of Aquiduana, Taunay, and Miranda, in Mato Grosso, Brazil. Harden. 2442, 2445, 252111, 252131, 252213, 252223, 2525.

terminal contour (intonational), 211.

terminal feature (intonational), 212.

Tetelcingo: dialect of Nahuatl, q.v.

Tewa: (Tanoan), see Santa Clara.

Thai. Haas 45–6; Ha. 2221, 2442, 252112, 2521333, 252214, 252225, 2524, 2525.

Tillamook. Coast Salishan. Edel; Swadesh 52. 252112, 2521332, 252212, 252225, 2524, 2525.

timing differences, 166.

Tiwa (Tanoan): Taos, Picuris, Sandia, Isleta. 252213, 2524, 2525.

Tlingit. Na-Dene? Velten. 252113.

Tojolabal. Mayan; southeastern Chiapas, Mexico. Supple. 2431, 2442, 252112, 2521323, 252213, 252225, 2524, 2525.

tone, levels of appearance of, 2612.

"tone languages" (meaninglessness of term), 2612 end.

tone quality, 511.

tongue, in vocoid articulation, 1510.

Tonkawa. Hoijer 46. 2431, 2442, 252113, 25212, 2521321, 252213, 252225, 2525.

Totonac. Hidalgo, Puebla, and Vera Cruz (coast), Mexico. Aschman; McQuown 00; H. 2431, 2441, 252112, 2521321, 252213, 252225, 2525.

Trager, George L. 34. The phonemes of Russian. Lg. 10.334–44.

——. 39a. La systématique des phonèmes du Polonais. Acta Linguistica 1.179–88.

——. 39b. The phonemes of Castillian Spanish. TCLP 8.217–22.

——. 41. The theory of accentual systems. LCP 131–45. Menasha.

——. 42. The historical phonology of the Tiwa languages. SIL 1:5.

——. 44. The verb morphology of Spoken French. Lg. 20.131–41.

——. 46. An outline of Taos grammar. LSNA 184–221.

——. 48. Taos I: A language revisited. IJAL 14.155–60.

——, and Henry Lee Smith Jr. 51. An outline of English structure. SIL Occasonal Papers 3. Washington.

transition (between successive consonants), 162.

trilling, 153.

Trique. In triangle between Tlaxiaco, Putla, and Juxtlahuaca in Oaxaca, Mexico. Longacre. 2312.

Trubetzkoy, N. 29. Zur allgemeinen theorie der phonologischen vokalsysteme. TCLP 1.39–67.

——. 39. Grundzüge der phonologie. TCLP 7.

Trukese. Malayo-Polynesian; Truk and nearby islands. Dyen 49. 2442, 252113, 2521321, 252215, 252225, 2525.

Tsotsil. Mayan; Chiapas, Mexico. Weathers. 252112, 2521323, 252213, 252225, 2524, 2525.

Tubatulabal. Shoshonean, Uto-Aztecan. Voegelin 35b. 2431, 2521322, 252214, 252225, 2525.

Tunica. Tunican. Haas 41, 46. 2441, 2443, 2445, 252112, 2521321, 252213, 252225, 2525.

Turkish. Turkic. Voegelin 43; McQuown 45–6; Ha. 212, 2441, 252112, 2521341, 252213, 252224, 2525.

Twaddell, W. Freeman. 48. The prehistoric Germanic short syllabics. Lg. 24.139–51.

——. 53. Stetson's model and the 'supra-segmental phonemes'. Lg. 29.415–53.

two-formant theory. 5310. Rejected 5315.

Tzeltal. Mayan; Chiapas, Mexico. Slocum. 252112, 2521323, 252213, 252225, 2524, 2525.

U

Ubykh. North Caucasian. Trubetzkoy 39. 2442.
Ukrainian. Slavic, Indo-European. Trubetzkoy 29; Fairbanks 00; H. 2422.
Uldall, H. J. 54. Maidu phonetics. IJAL 20.8–16.
ultimate phonologic constituents (or features or components), 26.
unmarked and marked, 3233.
"usage" (vs. "pattern", Hjelmslevian), 02 end.
uvular trill, 153.

V

Van Wagoner, Merrill Y. 49. Spoken Iraqi Arabic. New York.
variation, non-distinctive; implications of amount of, 3233.
velic, 14.
Velten, H. V. 44. Three Tlingit stories. IJAL 10.168–80.
Vietnamese. Emeneau 51; Jackson 00; H. 2221, 2322.
Viking Fund (Publications. . .) = (now) Wenner-Gren.
Villa Alta Zapotec: see Zapotec.
vocal cords, 12.
vocoid, 150, 151; 153.
Voegelin, Carl F. 35a. Shawnee phonemes. Lg. 11.23–37.
——. 35b. Tübatulabal grammar. University of California Publications in American Archeology and Ethnography 34:2.55–190.
——. 46. Delaware, an eastern Algonquian language. LSNA 130–57.
——. 49. Review of K. Pike 47a. IJAL 15.75–84.
——. 51. Inductively arrived-at models for cross-genetic comparisons of American Indian languages. Papers from the symposium on American Indian linguistics held at Berkeley July 7, 1951. [University of California Publications in Linguistics 10.1–68 (1954), 27–45.]
——, and M. E. Ellinghausen. 43. Turkish structure. JAOS 63.34–65.
——, and E. W. Voegelin. 44. Map of North American Indian Languages. American Ethnological Society and Indiana University; New York.
Vogt, Hans. 36. Esquisse d'une grammaire de géorgien moderne. Oslo. (Extrait de NTS.)
——. 40a. The Kalispel language. Oslo.
——. 40b. Salishan studies. Skrifter utgitt av det Norske Videnskaps-Akademi, Oslo, II Hist.-Filos. Klasse No. 2.
——. 44. Le système des cas en Ossète. Acta Linguistica 4.17–41.
voice bar (on spectrogram), 533.
voiced and voiceless, 12.
voiceless consonants, acoustics, 532.
voicing, acoustic correlates of, 533, 534.
——, bilabial, 153.
volume, mechanism of production, 12.
Votyak. Finno-Ugrian; Kama River, USSR. Trubetzkoy 29. 2442.
vowel (pretechnical) 10; first structural definition, 242; more inclusive structural definition, 2440.
vowel systems, 2440, 244.

W

Waterhouse, Viola, and May Morrison. 50. Chontal phonemes. IJAL 16.35–9.
Weathers, Nadine. 47. Tsotsil phonemes with special reference to allophones of b. IJAL 13.108–11.
Weinreich, Uriel. 53. Languages in contact: findings and problems. Publ. of the Linguistic Circle of New York 1.
Wells, Rulon S. 47. Immediate constituents. Lg. 23.81–117.

Welmers, William E. 47. Hints from morphology for phonemic analysis. SIL 5.91–100.
——. 49. Tonemes and tone writing in Maninka. SIL 7.1–17.
——. 50a. Notes on two languages of the Senufo group I. Senadi. Lg. 26.126–46.
——. 50b. Notes on two languages of the Senufo group II. Sup'ide. Lg. 26. 494–531.
——. 52a. Notes on the structure of Bariba. Lg. 28.82–103.
——. 52b. Notes on the structure of Saho. Word 8.145–62, 236–51.
Western Miwok: see Miwok.
whispering, 023, 12.
white noise, 511.
Whitman, William. 47. Descriptive grammar of Ioway-Oto. IJAL 13.233–48.
Whitney, William Dwight. 1879 (subsequent printings through 1924). A Sanskrit grammar.
    Leipzig.
Whorf, Benjamin L. 46a. The Hopi language, Toreva dialect. LSNA 158–83.
——. 46b. The Milpa Alta dialect of Aztec. LSNA 367–97.
Wichita. Caddoan. Garvin 50. 2431, 2441, 252113, 252131, 25224, 2525.
Wikchamni: dialect of Yokuts, q.v.
Winnebago. (Mississippi Valley) Siouan. Susman 43; H. 2432, 2441, 2445, 2446, 252112,
    25212, 2521321, 252212, 252221, 2525.
Wise, C. M., and Wesley Hervey. 52. The evolution of Hawaiian orthography. Quarterly
    Journal of Speech 38.311–25.
Wishram. Chinookan. Sapir 2?. 2441.
Wolff, Hans. 48. Yuchi phonemes and morphemes, with special reference to person markers.
    IJAL 14.240–3.
——. 52. Osage I: phonemes and historical phonology. IJAL 18.63–8.
Wonderly, William L. 46. Phonemic acculturation in Zoque. IJAL 12.92–5.
——. 51. Zoque II: phonemes and morphophonemes. IJAL 17.105–23.
written sources (synchronic analysis via philologic technique), 30.

Y

Yawelmani: dialect of Yokuts, q.v.
Yokoyama, Masako. 51. Outline of Kechua structure I: morphology. Lg. 27.38–67.
Yokuts. Penutian. Newman 44, 46. 2431, 2442, 2511, 25220, 252213, 252225, 2524, 2525.
——, *Chawchila-Choynimni-Gashowu* dialects. 252112, 2521333.
——, *Chukchansi* dialect. 252112, 2521333.
——, *Wikchamni* dialect. 252112, 2521333, 252214, 252221.
——, *Yawelmani* dialect. 2212, 252112, 25212, 2521333.
Yoruba. West Africa. Olmsted 51. 252114.
Yuchi. Wolff 48. 2431, 2442, 2445, 2446, 252112.
Yuma. Yuman, Hokan. Halpern 46a,b. 2431, 2442, 2445, 2446, 252112, 2521321, 252214, 252225,
    25223, 2525.

Z

Zapotec. Oaxaca, Mexico.
——, *Isthmus* dialect. Pickett 51, 53. 252111, 2523, 2525.
——, *Sierra* dialect. Nellis. 252113, 252213, 252223, 2525.
——, *Villa Alta* dialect. E. V. Pike 48. 252113, 2525.
zero, accentual systems with or without. 230, 23.
Zographensis [the Slavic language of the manuscript called this]. Fairbanks 52. 2443.
Zoque. Mixe-Zoque-Huave, Penutian?; the dialect of Copainalá, Chiapas, Mexico. Wonderly
    46, 51. 2442, 252112, 2521322, 252215, 252225, 2525.
Zuni. Azteco-Tanoan? Bunzel; Newman 00. 2431, 2442, 252113, 2521323, 252213, 252225,
    2524, 2525.
Zyryan. Uralian; northern Russia. Trubetzkoy 29. 2442.